the Yogurt Bible

the Yogurt Bible

Pat Crocker

Robert ROSE

For complete cataloguing information, see page 307.

Disclaimer
The Yogurt Bible is intended to provide information about the preparation and use of yogurt. It is not intended as a substitute for professional medical care. The publisher and author do not represent or warrant that the use of recipes or other information contained in this book will necessarily aid in the prevention or treatment of any disease, and specifically disclaim any liability, loss or risk, personal or otherwise, incurred as a consequence, directly or indirectly, of the use and application of any of the contents of this book. Readers must assume sole responsibility for any diet, lifestyle and/or treatment program that they choose to follow. If you have questions regarding the impact of diet and health, speak to a healthcare professional.

   The recipes in this book have been carefully tested by our kitchen and our tasters. To the best of our knowledge, they are safe and nutritious for ordinary use and users. For those people with food or other allergies, or who have special food requirements or health issues, please read the suggested contents of each recipe carefully and determine whether or not they may create a problem for you. All recipes are used at the risk of the consumer.

   We cannot be responsible for any hazards, loss or damage that may occur as a result of any recipe use.

   For those with special needs, allergies, requirements or health problems, in the event of any doubt, please contact your medical adviser prior to the use of any recipe.

Design and Production: Kevin Cockburn/PageWave Graphics Inc.
Editor: Carol Sherman
Recipe Editor: Jennifer MacKenzie
Copy Editor: Jo Calvert
Indexer: Gillian Watts
Food Photographer: Colin Erricson
Associate Photographer: Matt Johannsson
Food Styling: Kathryn Robertson
Prop Styling: Charlene Erricson
Illustrations: Kveta/Three in a Box
Chapter opener photograph: © iStockphoto.com/Artem Efimov

Cover image: French Vanilla Yogurt (page 24) with Fresh Berry Topping (page 46)

We acknowledge the financial support of the Government of Canada through the Book Publishing Industry Development Program (BPIDP) for our publishing activities.

Published by Robert Rose Inc.
120 Eglinton Avenue East, Suite 800, Toronto, Ontario, Canada M4P 1E2
Tel: (416) 322-6552 Fax: (416) 322-6936

Printed and bound in Canada

1 2 3 4 5 6 7 8 9 SP 18 17 16 15 14 13 12 11 10

Contents

To those seeking to add a bit of culture to their lives

Acknowledgments

When I begin a book, there is always a short period of time in which I drift along, immersed in the research, just getting acquainted with the subject and getting to know people who are experts in the field. At this stage, I generally cast a very wide net and communicate with a varied and interesting group of people. Thanks to all my friends (the original yogurt experts), who recounted their own yogurt-making experiences during the 1970s and 1980s, and especially to Tom Weber for sharing his extensive farmer network.

My thanks to Browne & Co. for providing the efficient Donvier Yogurt Maker Electronic. This easy-to-use device transformed gallons of milk and other liquids into the creamy yogurt that went into my new recipes. I came to rely on it almost every other day. KitchenAid made testing easy with its fabulous food processor and ice cream maker attachment for its stand mixer. I used both the KitchenAid attachment and the Donvier nonelectric ice cream mixer for testing the frozen yogurt recipes, and I am happy to report that both produce a fine frozen product.

Carol Sherman, as always, lent her editing expertise to the project. Thanks also go out to Jennifer MacKenzie for recipe testing and development of some of the homemade flavored yogurt recipes, and Jo Calvert for copy editing. Thanks to Kevin Cockburn at PageWave Graphics for designing the book. Thanks to photographer Colin Erricson, associate photographer Matt Johannsson, food stylist Kathryn Robertson and food prop stylist Charlene Erricson for creating such beautiful photographs.

Introduction

It's been at least a decade since there's been a comprehensive book detailing how to make yogurt and how to use yogurt in cooking. There are a few generations of cooks out there who may not even know that it is not only possible, but it is satisfying and easy, to make your own delicious yogurt. This book picks up where most of the how-to or recipe books left off, and it takes you where no other book has gone when it comes to making your own yogurt.

Just as commercial yogurt has evolved into a dizzying array of styles and flavors, this book offers a dairy case full of homemade yogurts — including four recipes for making basic homemade yogurt and — most exciting of all — 19 temptingly delicious recipes for making homemade flavored yogurts. For the first time, to the best of my knowledge, here is a book that offers directions for making your own French Vanilla, luscious Lemon and even Mocha Yogurt, in addition to all-time favorites such as Chocolate, Strawberry, Coconut and Fruit-Bottom. You will love making and tasting these rich and pure flavors in yogurts that contain nothing except the fresh milk and other whole ingredients you combined to make them.

For a long time now we have known about the health benefits of aligning our eating patterns with those of Mediterranean populations. We have discovered that people living particularly in Greece and southern Italy have long life expectancies due to diet and other lifestyle factors. Their secret: Eat very little red meat and fill up on a wide variety of fresh fruit and vegetables, nuts, seeds, whole grains and legumes, olive oil, fish, seafood and — yogurt.

For years and in several books, I have been encouraging you to eat a whole-food diet, namely one that matches the typical Mediterranean diet. Now with this book, *The Yogurt Bible*, I am zeroing in on a particular ingredient but still pairing it with the whole foods that we so desperately need. My message has not changed, if anything, it is simply getting clearer: Eat well to be well.

So, as you thumb through the recipes, you will find dishes high in fiber, vitamins, minerals and antioxidants from vegetables, legumes and nuts that are low in saturated fats. You shouldn't be surprised to find that relatively few red-meat recipes are provided, because red meat is consumed only about once or twice per month throughout the Mediterranean region. Even poultry, cheese, fish and eggs appear only once or twice a week, and the rest of the meals consist of plant-based whole foods with perhaps a nip of red wine now and then.

Recipes with a distinct Italian, Greek, Turkish or Baltic flair are abundant in this book, because these cultures use yogurt in ways that make the most of its unique attributes. We have so much to learn about the healthy eating customs of other cultures, and one of the most delicious traditions is that of eating fresh, tangy yogurt as a snack and including it as an ingredient in mealtime dishes.

Yogurt History

Because milk spoils so quickly, people in many countries have, for uncounted centuries, clabbered (soured) and fermented milk — mare's milk, ewe's milk, goat's milk and camel's milk (which contains no butterfat), as well as cow's milk — to make various kinds of yogurt, which lasts much longer than plain milk.

When the right conditions are present, namely temperature and friendly bacteria, milk coagulates and then ferments, causing it to become thick and dense in texture and tangy in taste. This custard-like fermented milk has come to be known as *yogurt*, the word being a direct derivative of the Turkish word. We call fermented-milk products — such as yogurt, sour cream, buttermilk, kefir and crème fraîche — "cultured" milk products.

One form or another of cultured milk product has been in use for more than 4,500 years, or perhaps as far back as the Neolithic era.[1] With references to it in the Bible and in medieval Turkish records dating

1 Tannahil, Reay. *Food in History*. Crown Publishing Group, 1995.

to the 11th century, and mentions by Homer in the *Illiad*, yogurt has been a staple of Asian, Balkan, and Central and Southeastern Europe from antiquity onward.

It was the 1908 Nobel Prize–winning Russian biologist, Ilya Ilyich (Elie) Mechnikov (Metchnikoff), working at the dawn of the 20th century to find ways to impede the ravages of age, who discovered that Bulgarians lived longer, on average, than any other people. While a director at the Institut Pasteur in Paris, Mechnikov worked tirelessly to prove that the long life span of Bulgarian peoples was a direct result of their consumption of yogurt. Although that proof evaded him, Mechnikov furthered the whole field of microbiology with his research on yogurt, and, by 1907, the two benign bacteria cultures responsible for the fermentation of milk into true yogurt had been isolated. They are *Lactobacillus delbrueckii* (subspecies *bulgaricus*) and *Streptococcus lactis*.

Modern production of yogurt was advanced by Isaac Carasso, who founded the Danone Company (named after his son Daniel) in 1919. Today, the Danone Company, located on the outskirts of Paris, France, is one of the leading producers of yogurt in Western Europe. Its sister company in New York State, Dannon Co. Inc., popularized yogurt in the United States in the 1950s. Dannon has remained that nation's leading producer of yogurt, due

to the development of a fruit-flavored yogurt that is more pleasing than plain yogurt to the American palate.

By the last half of the first decade in the 21st century, DanActive, a probiotic dairy drink intended to strengthen the body's natural defenses, was being made in Dannon's plant in Fort Worth, Texas. According to *The New York Times* (01-22-07), "In the year since the Dannon Company introduced Activia, a line of yogurt with special live bacteria that are marketed as aiding regularity, sales in United States stores have soared well past the $100 million mark, a milestone that only a small percentage of new foods reaches each year." Yoplait brand (the 19th largest dairy producer in the United States) and Dannon both announced in 2009 that they will no longer purchase milk from milk producers that inject their cows with the controversial genetically engineered synthetic hormone, recombinant Bovine Growth Hormone (rBGH also known as BST or rBST). BST is illegal in Canada, the European Union, Australia and New Zealand.

It would seem that a 4,500-year-old tradition has met with modern technology and marketing acumen to distribute a "new" old product that, essentially unchanged in all that time, has been quietly helping humans stay healthy for eons.

Health Benefits of Yogurt

Like many "discovery" sagas, the story of the "shepherd carrying milk in a goatskin through the desert" who discovered how to make yogurt may be a bit simplified, but there is nothing simple about the flavor and health benefits that yogurt provides.

Due to ongoing research, there is now general consensus among health professionals that probiotics, such as those found in live-culture yogurt, may help improve health by aiding digestion, improving nutrient and mineral (especially calcium) absorption, boosting the body's natural defenses and fighting off harmful bacteria. In addition, there is a growing body of research linking yogurt's beneficial bacteria to relief of irritable bowel syndrome and yeast infections, as well as diarrhea that results from certain illnesses. Many pediatricians recommend yogurt for children suffering from diarrhea and indigestion or intestinal infection.

In a study by E. Fabian published in *Annals of Nutrition & Metabolism*, women consuming probiotic yogurt not only had a substantial lowering of LDL (bad) cholesterol, but their HDL (good) cholesterol significantly increased. Studies are also linking calcium-rich

NUTRIENT	FUNCTION	% RECOMMENDED DIETARY DAILY ALLOWANCE
Iodine	necessary for hormone production	58%
Calcium	critical to healthy bones and teeth as well as cells, including those in the heart, lungs and nerves, which rely on calcium for their proper functioning; calcium in yogurt is more easily absorbed and "bioavailable" than that found in other calcium-rich foods	45%
Phosphorus	helps the body metabolize (use) protein, calcium and glucose, and is needed for bone and tooth formation, cell growth and to keep organs functioning	35%
Vitamin B_2 (riboflavin)	helps repair and maintain healthy skin, hair and eyes; helps prevent degenerative diseases such as cancer, heart disease, Alzheimer's disease; helps the body convert food into energy	32%
Protein	builds and repairs muscle and tissue; yogurt also has an iron-binding protein, lactoferrin, which boosts the growth and activity of the cells that build bone (osteoblasts)	25%
Vitamin B_{12}	protects the nerve endings; lowers risk of stroke, cancer, heart disease and other degenerative diseases; regulates growth plus maintenance of cells; helps produce hemoglobin	25%
Potassium	works with sodium (salt) to maintain the body's water balance and may lower blood pressure	20%
Zinc	supports a healthy nervous system; promotes mental and emotional health; strengthens the immune system; helps control blood-sugar level and protects against free radicals	15%
Vitamin B_5	supports the adrenal gland, which assists metabolism; fights allergies and maintains skin, muscles and nerves	15%

Nutrients in 1 cup (250 mL) Low-Fat Yogurt

foods, especially low-fat milk, yogurt and kefir, to lower body weight. In fact, research data points to as much as a 70% reduced risk of overweight when calcium intake is increased by two servings over the recommended servings for each age and gender group.

Early animal studies indicate that *Lactobacillus* found in yogurt may offer preventive and curative effects on arthritis. The ulcer-promoting bacterium *Helicobacter pylori* has also been proven to be effectively suppressed by yogurt containing probiotic bacteria.

For people with a protein allergy or those who are lactose intolerant, yogurt may be accepted by the body because it is easier to digest than milk. The live-active cultures partially digest the milk protein, making it easier to absorb and less allergenic. The *Lacto* bacteria in yogurt promote the growth of healthy bacteria in the colon, and also reduce the conversion of bile into carcinogenic bile acids. These *Lacto* bacteria, along with the high amount of calcium in yogurt, may help to prevent colon cancer.

Yogurt can help to control yeast infections. Research shows that the consumption of 8 oz (250 g) of live-culture yogurt daily, causes yeast colonies in the vagina to decrease and lowers the incidence of vaginal yeast infections. For more information about yogurt and health, see page 60.

Whole Foods and Yogurt

There is no doubt about it. What you eat affects not only who you are and what you can accomplish, but also how you look and feel, including your overall health and vitality. Eating a variety of whole, fresh foods — including fruit and vegetables — is essential. As more people in the developed countries consume more and more refined and processed foods — such as sugarcoated breakfast cereals, fat- and chemical-laden, frozen and convenience foods, and empty-calorie snack foods — there is also an increase in "modern" diseases.

Whole foods — those foods that are as close to their natural state as possible when they are consumed — are our first line of defense against those diseases. Whole foods are full of the essential vitamins, minerals, proteins, enzymes, complex carbohydrates and phytonutrients that combine to keep us active, alert and resistant to disease.

When is Yogurt not a Whole Food?

Check the labels on commercial yogurt for nutrients and ingredients. When sugar (fructose, corn syrup, sucrose, dextrose), fillers and colorings are added to yogurt, it begins to take on the problems associated with refined foods. A key to spotting not-so-healthy yogurt is to check the calories, carbohydrate and protein levels. As a general guideline, calories in an 8 oz (250 g) container of low-fat yogurt should not peak above 100. Healthy carbohydrate levels are 10 grams or less, and protein should be 20 grams or more.

The very best yogurt contains only live and active cultures plus milk, as does the yogurt you make at home from low-fat milk and live-culture yogurt. If a manufacturer treats the finished yogurt with heat or pasteurizes it, all active bacteria will be killed and there will be added sugar, stabilizers and perhaps chemical preservatives.

Salad dressings and sauces that contain yogurt, sweetened yogurt-covered raisins, chocolate, candy or pretzels do not contain live and active beneficial cultures of bacteria. If possible, check that the frozen yogurt you purchase has been labeled as containing at least 10 million live and active cultures per gram, and check the amount of sugar and other additives it contains, to determine how close to a whole food and healthy it is.

What is the Best Yogurt to Make and Buy?

Plain low-fat yogurt with live and active cultures is by far the very best yogurt you can make and buy to use in preparing the recipes in this book. Plain yogurt has about half the calories found in the same amount of fruit-added yogurt. In addition, plain yogurt contains almost twice the amount of protein and more calcium.

Making Homemade Yogurt

Why Make Your Own Yogurt?

This is one commercial food product that we can all take back with very little effort. Once we do, we decide what goes into this delicious and healthy food. We control the type of liquid (cow's, sheep's or goat's milk), and fat and sugar levels. In addition, homemade yogurt contains no chemical preservatives, artificial colors or flavorings. Now that I am making my own yogurt and have a constant fresh supply, I find that I use it to replace other commercial and higher-fat products such as sour cream, mayonnaise and cream cheese. Making homemade yogurt is just so darn easy.

What Do You Need to Get Started?

There are only three aspects to homemade or commercial yogurt that are critical: fresh milk, live bacterial culture and temperature. Once you understand these key elements, you can enjoy as much of the lemony-fresh and creamy elixir as you wish. Use it on its own, with the flavorings and toppings starting on page 45, or cook with it using the recipes in the chapters that follow.

You will need a stainless-steel saucepan, food thermometer and a constant heat source or an electric yogurt maker.

Milk

Most commercial yogurt is made from pasteurized low-fat cow's milk, with instant skim milk powder added as a thickener. Since the same low-fat milk is widely available to consumers that is the milk most people use to make their yogurt at home. For a growing number of people, though, making yogurt from organic milk is important due to health concerns surrounding the growth hormones and antibiotics fed to the animals on nonorganic farms, and genetically modified organisms (GMOs) and pesticides in their grains.

Homogenization is a mechanical process of breaking up the fat globules in milk (or other liquids) and evenly distributing them throughout so they do not float to the top. It is not necessary to use homogenized milk to make yogurt. In fact many artisanal yogurt makers use pasteurized, but non-homogenized, whole goat's milk for their yogurt products.

Pasteurization is the actual sterilization of milk (or other liquids) by heating it to 145°F (63°C) and holding it there for at least 30 minutes. Another pasteurization method is "flash," which pasteurizes milk at 161°F (72°C) for a minimum of 16 seconds. Both methods kill harmful bacteria. Almost all milk sold in North America is pasteurized.

Types of Milk for Yogurt Making

Essential: Use the freshest milk available.

Cow's milk has the highest percentage of water than other animals' milk. Fat in cow's milk ranges from 0% to more than 18%. Cow's milk is available in the following types:

- whole milk — 1 cup (250 mL) has approximately 165 calories and produces dense, creamy yogurt without the addition of instant skim milk powder.
- 2% — 1 cup (250 mL) has approximately 115 calories and produces a thinner yogurt; with the addition of 1/3 cup (75 mL) instant skim milk powder, the result is dense, creamy yogurt with an enhanced protein content.
- 1% — 1 cup (250 mL) has approximately 100 calories and produces a thinner yogurt; with the addition of 1/3 cup (75 mL) instant skim milk powder, the result is dense, creamy yogurt with an enhanced protein content.
- skim milk — 1 cup (250 mL) has approximately 82 calories and produces a thinner yogurt; with the addition of 1/3 cup (75 mL) instant skim milk powder, the result is dense, creamy yogurt with an enhanced protein content.
- evaporated milk — This is whole milk with 50% of the water removed (2% partly skimmed and fat-free skim-milk versions are also available). It is canned and must be reconstituted with water; 1 cup (250 mL) has approximately 173 calories and produces thick and creamy yogurt. See Basic Evaporated Milk Yogurt (page 22), which calls for evaporated milk to make yogurt.

- sweetened condensed milk — This is whole milk with 60% of the water removed and sugar added. Yogurt made from sweetened condensed milk is sweeter and high in calories. It is used in this book only for dessert yogurts (pages 265 to 274).

Goat's milk is higher in calcium, potassium, magnesium and vitamin A than cow's milk. Some people who cannot tolerate cow's milk are able to drink goat's milk without any problems. It is more easily digestible because the fat globules are smaller and remain suspended without homogenization. Yogurt made from goat's milk is whiter (because all of the beta-carotene in the milk is converted into vitamin A) and thinner than cow's milk yogurt, so instant skim milk powder is added to help thicken it.

Sheep's milk is higher in vitamins A, B, C and E than cow's milk, and has twice the calcium and more protein. In addition to absorbing cholesterol from the foods we eat, our body naturally produces it. It is thought that sheep's milk may help the body in burning or using cholesterol. Sheep's milk is higher in solids than either cow's or goat's milk, and therefore yields a thicker, creamier yogurt without the need to add instant skim milk powder.

Mare's milk has twice the vitamin C of human milk and four times that of cow's milk.

Reindeer's milk has the highest percentage of nutrients of all of the animal milks consumed by humans.

Water buffalo's milk makes a very thick, brilliant white yogurt without any added thickeners, because it contains less water than cow's milk and is low in beta-carotene, so the milk is whiter. Water buffalo's milk yogurt contains more fat, lactose, protein and calcium than cow's milk and also produces a stronger tasting yogurt.

Other Liquids

You may find recipes (on the Internet in particular) using other liquids, such as soy milk, rice milk, fruit milk or nut milk to make what may be called "cultured" or "soy yogurt."

Any liquid other than edible animal milk (as listed left) will not be transformed into yogurt because it is the action of the *Lacto* bacteria on the milk sugars that allow the bacteria to grow and ferment or thicken the milk. If you add *Lacto* bacteria to nondairy liquids, the bacteria will die and the resulting product will be watery and will not have the characteristic taste of yogurt. If you add nondairy bacteria to nondairy liquids, you may get a fermented product, but it will not be yogurt and it may not have the probiotic advantages of the *Lacto* bacteria. Homemade nondairy fermented products will require natural thickeners, stabilizers and flavorings in order to imitate the texture and flavor of yogurt. In my opinion, these are poor substitutes for the real thing and, since they are not usable in cooking, not worth the effort.

Be aware that simply adding bacteria to warm liquids (such as juice, bean or nut milk) and holding them at a constant temperature of 115°F (46°C) for up to 14 hours could pose potential safety issues. This is especially dangerous if rogue bacteria should find their way into the other containers.

For these reasons, I have not included recipes using any other liquid except animal milk (and a recipe that uses coconut milk along with 2% milk and instant skim milk powder) for making yogurt at home.

Live Bacterial Culture

Critical to yogurt making is the fermentation process, which involves the partial conversion of the sugar in milk (called lactose) to lactic acid. This fermentation process is made possible by lactic-acid producing bacteria. By the end of the 19th century, these "*Lacto*" bacteria had been isolated and named *Streptococcus delbrueckii* and *Lactobacillus bulgaricus*.

In the United States, the Food and Drug Administration (FDA) requires that two specific strains of bacteria — *Streptococcus thermophilus* (a subspecies of *S. delbrueckii*) and *Lactobacillus bulgaricus* — be used in all yogurt products sold in the United States, as a yogurt standard of identity. Canada does not have this regulation, although most yogurt manufacturers use these strains.

Bulgarian yogurt (also known as Balkan-style yogurt) is generally accepted as the best yogurt there is today. This may be due, in part, because the original "starters" were *L. bulgaricus* bacteria and another that may have been introduced by shepherds who added juice from the roots of indigenous plants which contained the bacteria. The habit of using the best-tasting, thickest yogurt as a starter for each subsequent batch made it possible for a unique and "true" Bulgarian yogurt to evolve.

When you make your own yogurt, you can use freeze-dried, powdered *L. bulgaricus* and *S. thermophilus*, or you can simply use a few spoonfuls of your own homemade yogurt or your favorite commercial yogurt as the starter for your next batch. As long as the yogurt starter you use is live-culture and fresh, the bacteria will work their magic if introduced to warm milk and held at roughly 110°F (43°C) for several hours. Live-culture yogurt is widely available (just check labels to be sure the brand you buy is live-culture). Freeze-dried powdered bacteria are available in some supermarkets, online, and in whole food or specialty food stores that sell yogurt-making equipment.

What is Probiotic Yogurt?

In addition to the *L. bulgaricus* and *S. thermophilus* bacteria, many commercial yogurts contain other probiotic ("pro" meaning promoting, "bio" meaning life) cultures, such as *Lactobacillus acidophilus*, *Bifidobacterium longum*, and *Bifidobacterium infantis*, which are bacteria normally found in your intestines. Some of these bacteria live in your intestines and help with digestion and the synthesis of vitamins. Although there is conflicting evidence pointing to the fact that the standard "yogurt" bacteria, *L. bulgaricus* and *S. thermophilus*, may not survive in your intestines, the probiotic yogurts are now considered important for replacing beneficial flora and helping to prevent digestive ailments.

If you have been taking antibiotics ("anti" meaning against), which tend to kill all beneficial intestinal flora as well as whatever bacteria are making you ill, you should eat plenty of probiotic yogurt to help replace the benign bacteria in your digestive system. Using a starter from a probiotic yogurt that contains these digestive bacteria will ensure that your homemade yogurt has them as well.

What are Cultured Products?

When benign-bacteria cultures are used to produce foods or products with different characteristics than the original dairy products they were made from, we call these products "cultured." Crème fraîche, sour cream, buttermilk, blue cheese (and other cheeses that rely on bacteria to change their nature) and yogurt are all cultured foods.

Temperature

The benign *Lacto* bacteria multiply and are happiest at temperatures ranging from 90°F (32°C), which is just below body temperature, to about 120°F (49°C). As these bacteria change the milk sugar (lactose), the milk ferments and forms acids. These acids curdle (or denature) the proteins in the milk, causing them to swell and clump together. This fermenting and curdling happens in all cultured products.

The easiest and most foolproof method to keep cultured milk at the perfect yogurt-making temperature is to use an electric yogurt maker. There are several brands on the market, with different prices, but they all are easy to use and reliable. The yogurt maker that I have used for all of the testing and recipes in this book is the Donvier Yogurt Maker Electronic. It comes with a thermometer that is marked for easy use in determining exactly the point at which the milk is at the correct temperature for adding the culture. No guesswork and no fuss. You simply fill the cups, cap them and set the timer for the number of hours you want the milk to sit.

I have heard of all kinds of inventive ways to hold milk within the ideal range of temperatures, without an electric yogurt maker, for the 6 to 10 hours it takes for the bacteria to multiply enough to form a creamy yogurt. Some of them are more reliable than others. Since I have not tried any of them, I cannot vouch for these methods, but offer some of them, below. Follow the basic directions for making yogurt (pages 20 to 43), then experiment with the following ways to hold the milk at about 115°F (46°C) for 6 to 10 hours.

Towel-wrapped thermos — Pour the cooled milk and bacteria into a thermos and wrap it with clean towels or a blanket, or place the thermos in an insulated cooler on top of the refrigerator. The latter method is a throwback from years ago, when refrigerators gave off heat and the top was a good place to set a container of milk and bacteria to ferment. With today's energy-efficient refrigerators, there is no heat rising from the top and this is not a viable way to hold the temperature.

Cooler with two hot water bottles — An insulated cooler will keep the heat of a couple of hot water bottles and, if a covered container of cooled milk and bacteria is placed inside, the temperature will likely remain stable long enough for the bacteria to turn the milk into yogurt. You can use two jugs of hot water (from the tap) in place of the hot water bottles, to keep the cooler warm, but keep replacing the hot water in the jugs at regular intervals (every couple of hours or so), so the temperature in the cooler doesn't drop below 115°F (46°C).

Slow cooker — Try placing the cooled milk and bacteria in a slow cooker turned to low. The heat may still be too high; if the yogurt does not set because the bacteria is killed, try leaving the lid off.

Heating pad — If you have a reliable heating pad with a low-heat setting, you can try placing a shallow, covered container of cooled milk and bacteria on top, being careful to check on the pad from time to time.

Electric blanket — Place the cooled milk and bacteria in a covered dish and wrap it in an electric blanket set on the lowest heat setting, being careful to check on the blanket from time to time.

Low-temperature oven — Set the covered container of milk and bacteria on a baking pan in a 115°F (46°C) oven or in a gas oven with a pilot light, or turn the oven on and off at regular intervals. An oven thermometer will help you to determine if the oven is at the correct temperature, and regular checking should tell you if the temperature is getting too high or too low.

Electric Yogurt Makers

There are advantages to using a machine specifically designed to make yogurt. It will be safe and easy to use, and can be relied upon to keep the milk and bacteria constantly at the optimum temperature for promoting the growth of the bacteria. When you use a yogurt machine there is no need to constantly monitor and check the safety or the temperature, and the milk is kept still so the bacteria are undisturbed.

Most electric yogurt makers are similar in that they have a plastic exterior and lid, although their design varies from square to round to oblong, tall or squat. The most significant difference between the yogurt makers on the market today is in the size and materials used for the yogurt cups or containers.

The "cups," "jars" or containers are reusable, easy to clean and most have lids. Most yogurt makers have from six to eight 8-oz (250 g) containers, which each hold $\frac{1}{2}$ cup (125 mL) of yogurt. These are called "small" containers, and they match the individual-serving sizes of the commercial yogurt most widely available in stores. Small containers appeal to families with children or individuals who wish to consume a serving with every meal or a serving a day. In addition, if you have a yogurt maker with the smaller containers, it is possible to make half a batch of plain yogurt and flavor the other half.

Most manufacturers today are making the individual containers from plastic. My preference is glass but if plastic has been used, be sure it is Bisphenol A (BPA) free. Some makers come with extra lids and a thermometer, which are beneficial.

You may find a yogurt maker that holds one larger quantity of yogurt. This is handy for people who wish to cook with yogurt, because it is easier to measure larger quantities from one container than several small ones.

Preparing Yogurt-Making Equipment

Starting with clean equipment ensures that harmful bacteria, which interfere with the fermenting *Lacto* bacteria — or worse, which cause illness — are eliminated before you begin.

You need to decide how you will keep your milk at the optimum temperature for the bacteria to ferment it. If you prefer one of the low-tech methods mentioned on page 17, be sure that the heating apparatus and towels are spotlessly clean each time you make yogurt. If using an electric yogurt maker, check that the jars and lids are clean and that the maker itself is clean before you begin.

Boiling water should be used to scald the utensils (such as a wire whisk, spoon, mixing bowl and thermometer) you will use in the process. Pouring boiling water from a kettle over the utensils set in a dish or pan, then letting them sit in the hot water until you're ready to use them, does this. Or you can set the utensils in a large saucepan and cover them with hot water and bring the water to a boil over high heat. Boil for 1 minute, turn off the heat and let the pan sit on the burner until you're ready to use the utensils.

Should I Sweeten my Homemade Yogurt?

One of the reasons for making your own yogurt is to control the ingredients. Most people start by making unflavored unsweetened yogurt, and continue to make this most often since it is the most versatile. You can use it in all of the recipes in this book, and you can top it with fresh fruit or any of the toppings (pages 45 to 58) or sauces (pages 249 to 264), when a sweeter treat is desired.

If you and your family prefer a sweetened yogurt, of course that is the type you should make. You can still make a healthier sweetened yogurt than commercial types, because you will be using less sugar.

Any of the following sweeteners may be used to sweeten homemade yogurt:
Agave nectar
Brown rice syrup
Corn syrup
Liquid honey
Maple syrup

Homemade Yogurt Recipes

Basic Yogurt- Making Recipes

Use this method for full-fat (whole) cow's milk and milk from either water buffalo or reindeer. Because of their high solids content, it is not necessary to fortify these milks with skim milk powder.

Tips

- Use the freshest milk you can get and be sure that if you are using a commercial yogurt for a starter it is fresh and contains live bacteria (it should be stated on the label).

- The recipe may be doubled.

- Always store yogurt in the refrigerator. Homemade yogurt will keep for up to 1 week and after that, the value of its beneficial bacteria will be diminished. Commercial yogurt has a "best before" date clearly marked on the package.

Basic Whole and High-Solid Milk Yogurt

- *Food thermometer*
- *Electric yogurt maker*

4 cups	fresh whole milk (see Tips, left)	1 L
⅓ cup	instant skim milk powder	75 mL
¼ cup	organic live-culture yogurt or 5 g freeze-dried yogurt culture (see Tips, page 21)	60 mL

1. In a stainless-steel saucepan, heat milk to the scalding point (see Tips, page 22) over medium-low heat, stirring frequently. Add skim milk powder and stir until incorporated. Remove from heat and let cool to 110° to 120°F (43° to 49°C), stirring often. Cooling could take up to 1 hour.

2. In a bowl, combine starter yogurt or freeze-dried yogurt culture with about ½ cup (125 mL) of the cooled milk. Add to remaining cooled milk and stir well to distribute yogurt culture.

3. Pour into clean cups, secure lids if suggested by manufacturer, and place in yogurt maker. Set the time for 8 to 12 hours or minimum time recommended in manufacturer's instructions. The longer yogurt ferments, the firmer and more tart it will be.

4. Do not disturb the milk as it is fermenting. Check one container after 8 hours and, if yogurt has reached desired consistency, remove cups from yogurt maker, secure lids, if necessary, and refrigerate immediately. If it is not set to your liking, replace test cup and ferment for another 1 to 2 hours, or until desired consistency is reached. Refrigeration stops the fermentation process. Let yogurt chill completely before serving or using in recipes.

Basic Lower-Fat Milk Yogurt

Many people choose to make a lower-fat yogurt from nonfat (skim), 1% or 2% milk. When lower-fat milk is used, skim milk powder is added to boost the solids and produce a thicker yogurt.

Tips

- Powdered milk adds more protein to the milk and creates thicker yogurt that takes less time to ferment. Some nonfat (skim) and 1% milk may have added milk proteins, which make yogurt less watery and as thick as yogurt with added powdered milk. Check the ingredients labels for these fortified milks.

- Purchase live-culture yogurt at supermarkets, whole food stores and corner stores (check the label to be sure the bacteria is "live").

- Freeze-dried yogurt culture may be purchased at some supermarkets, online and at whole food stores.

- For storage info see Tips, page 20.

- *Food thermometer*
- *Electric yogurt maker*

4 cups	fresh nonfat (skim), 1% or 2% milk	1 L
1/4 cup	instant skim milk powder (see Tips, left)	60 mL
3 tbsp	organic live-culture yogurt or 5 g freeze-dried yogurt culture (see Tips, left)	45 mL

1. In a stainless-steel saucepan, heat milk to the scalding point (see Tips, page 22) over medium-low heat, stirring frequently. Add skim milk powder and stir until incorporated. Remove from heat and let cool to 110° to 120°F (43° to 49°C), stirring often. Cooling could take up to 1 hour.

2. In a bowl, combine starter yogurt or freeze-dried yogurt culture with about 1/2 cup (125 mL) of the cooled milk. Add to remaining cooled milk and stir well to distribute yogurt culture.

3. Pour into clean cups, secure lids if suggested by manufacturer, and place in yogurt maker. Set the time for 8 to 12 hours or minimum time recommended in manufacturer's instructions. The longer yogurt ferments, the firmer and more tart it will be.

4. Do not disturb the milk as it is fermenting. Check one container after 8 hours and, if yogurt has reached the desired consistency, remove cups from yogurt maker, secure lids, if necessary, and refrigerate immediately. If it is not set to your liking, replace test cup and ferment for another 1 to 2 hours, or until desired consistency is reached. Refrigeration stops the fermentation process. Let yogurt chill completely before serving or using in recipes.

Basic Evaporated Milk Yogurt

Canned evaporated milk is convenient and makes a very nice yogurt. You can use whole or partly skimmed (2%) evaporated milk in this recipe.

Tips

- *To scald milk:* Heat milk in a saucepan over medium-low heat, stirring frequently, until bubbles form around outside of pan and steam starts to rise from it. The temperature should reach 170°F (77°C).

- Always store yogurt in the refrigerator. Homemade yogurt will keep for up to 1 week; after that, the value of its beneficial bacteria will be diminished. Commercial yogurt has a "best before" date clearly marked on the package.

- *Food thermometer*
- *Electric yogurt maker*

1	can (12 oz/370 mL) evaporated milk	1
2½ cups	water	625 mL
1½ cups	instant skim milk powder	375 mL
¼ cup	organic live-culture yogurt or 5 g freeze-dried yogurt culture	60 mL

1. In a stainless-steel saucepan, combine milk and water. Heat to the scalding point (see Tips, left) over medium-low heat, stirring frequently. Add skim milk powder and stir until incorporated. Remove from heat and let cool to 110° to 120°F (43° to 49°C), stirring often. Cooling could take up to 1 hour.

2. In a bowl, combine starter yogurt or freeze-dried yogurt culture with about ½ cup (125 mL) of the cooled milk. Add to remaining cooled milk and stir well to distribute yogurt culture.

3. Pour into clean cups, secure lids if suggested by manufacturer, and place in yogurt maker. Set the time for 8 to 12 hours or minimum time recommended in manufacturer's instructions. The longer yogurt ferments, the firmer and more tart it will be.

4. Do not disturb the milk as it is fermenting. Check one container after 8 hours or minimum time stated in instructions and, if yogurt has reached the desired consistency, remove cups from yogurt maker, secure lids, if necessary, and refrigerate immediately. If it is not set to your liking, replace test cup and ferment for another 1 to 2 hours, or until desired consistency is reached. Refrigeration stops the fermentation process. Let yogurt chill completely before serving or using in recipes.

Cultured Coconut Milk "Yogurt"

Look for cans of natural coconut milk with no preservatives, thickeners, sweeteners or other additives. Since most of the flavor and nutrients from the coconut are in the fat, it makes sense to use regular, full-fat coconut milk.

Fine pieces of shredded coconut are suspended in this deliciously coconut-flavored and lightly tangy yogurt. You may strain off the coconut before adding the other ingredients in Step 1 if you prefer a smooth texture.

Tip

- *To scald milk:* Heat milk in a stainless-steel saucepan over medium-low heat, stirring frequently, until bubbles form around outside of pan and steam starts to rise from it. The temperature should reach 170°F (77°C).

- *Food thermometer*
- *Electric yogurt maker*

2	cans (each 14 oz/400 mL) coconut milk	2
⅓ cup	unsweetened desiccated coconut	75 mL
⅓ cup	instant skim milk powder	75 mL
3 tbsp	pure maple syrup	45 mL
¼ cup	organic live-culture yogurt or 5 g freeze-dried yogurt culture	60 mL

1. In a stainless-steel saucepan, combine coconut milk and coconut. Heat to the scalding point (see Tip, left) over medium-low heat, stirring frequently. Add skim milk powder and maple syrup and stir until incorporated. Remove from heat and let cool to 110° to 120°F (43° to 49°C), stirring often. Cooling could take up to 1 hour.

2. In a bowl, combine starter yogurt or freeze-dried yogurt culture with about ½ cup (125 mL) of the cooled coconut milk. Add to remaining cooled coconut milk and stir well to distribute yogurt culture.

3. Pour into clean cups, secure lids if suggested by manufacturer, and place in yogurt maker. Set the time for 8 to 12 hours or minimum time recommended in manufacturer's instructions. The longer yogurt ferments, the firmer and more tart it will be.

4. Do not disturb the liquid as it is fermenting. Check one container after 8 hours and, if yogurt has reached the desired consistency, remove cups from yogurt maker, secure lids, if necessary, and refrigerate immediately. If it is not set to your liking, replace test cup and ferment for another 1 to 2 hours, or until desired consistency is reached. Refrigeration stops the fermentation process. Let yogurt chill completely before serving or using in recipes.

Flavored Homemade Yogurts

French Vanilla Yogurt

For a fragrant vanilla yogurt, use one fresh vanilla bean. This will yield a slightly sweeter and truly vanilla-flecked yogurt that is perfect for topping fresh fruit and fruit desserts or to eat on its own. Reduce the amount of maple syrup to ¼ cup (60 mL) for a tangier yogurt. You may also use vanilla extract instead (see Tips, below).

Tips

• You may substitute 1 tbsp (15 mL) pure vanilla extract in place of the vanilla bean but some people find that alcohol-based vanilla interferes with the texture of the yogurt and does not lend a natural vanilla taste. Never use artificial vanilla flavoring.

• *To scald milk:* Heat milk in a stainless-steel saucepan over medium-low heat, stirring frequently, until bubbles form around outside of pan and steam starts to rise from it. The temperature should reach 170°F (77°C).

• *Food thermometer*
• *Electric yogurt maker*

4 cups	1% or 2% milk	1 L
1	vanilla bean, split in half lengthwise (see Tips, left)	1
⅓ cup	instant skim milk powder	75 mL
⅓ cup	pure maple syrup, or to taste	75 mL
3 tbsp	organic live-culture yogurt or 5 g freeze-dried yogurt culture	45 mL

1. In a stainless-steel saucepan, heat milk to the scalding point (see Tips, left) over medium-low heat, stirring frequently. Add vanilla bean and skim milk powder and stir well. Remove from heat and let cool to 110° to 120°F (43° to 49°C), stirring often. Cooling could take up to 1 hour.

2. Using tongs, lift out vanilla pod halves and scrape the tiny seeds from the insides. Add seeds back to the cooled milk and discard or reserve the pod halves for another use. Stir in maple syrup.

3. In a bowl, combine starter yogurt or freeze-dried yogurt culture with about ½ cup (125 mL) of the cooled milk. Add to remaining cooled milk and stir well to distribute yogurt culture.

4. Pour into clean cups, secure lids if suggested by manufacturer, and place in yogurt maker. Set the time for 8 to 12 hours or minimum time recommended in manufacturer's instructions. The longer yogurt ferments, the firmer and the more tart it will be.

5. Do not disturb the liquid as it is fermenting. Check one container after 8 hours and, if yogurt has reached the desired consistency, remove cups from yogurt maker, secure lids, if necessary, and refrigerate immediately. If it is not set to your liking, replace test cup and continue to ferment for another 1 to 2 hours, or until desired consistency is reached. Refrigeration stops the fermentation process. Let yogurt chill completely before serving or using in recipes.

Fruit-Bottom Yogurt

Makes 4 cups (1 L)

Using homemade fruit preserves with homemade yogurt makes good sense but, if you don't have homemade preserves, use commercial jams, jellies or preserves. The results are almost as good. If the preserves have been stored in the refrigerator, be sure to let them come to room temperature before use. If the preserves are cold when the warm milk is added, it will take longer for the bacteria to do their work.

Tips

* Use strawberry, raspberry, cherry, blueberry, peach, apricot or other fruit preserves in this recipe.

* For diabetics, use artificially sweetened fruit preserves and omit the honey.

* Food thermometer
* Electric yogurt maker

4 cups	1% or 2% milk	1 L
1/3 cup	instant skim milk powder	75 mL
2 to 4 tbsp	honey (see Tips, left)	30 to 60 mL
1 tbsp	pure vanilla extract	15 mL
1/2 cup	fruit preserves (see Tips, left)	125 mL
3 tbsp	organic live-culture yogurt or 5 g freeze-dried yogurt culture	45 mL

1. In a stainless-steel saucepan, heat milk to the scalding point (see Tips, page 24) over medium-low heat, stirring frequently. Add skim milk powder and stir well. Remove from heat and let cool to 110° to 120°F (43° to 49°C), stirring often. Stir in honey and vanilla. Cooling could take up to 1 hour.

2. Meanwhile, divide fruit preserves evenly and spoon into bottom of each yogurt cup. Set aside until milk is ready.

3. In a bowl, combine starter yogurt or freeze-dried yogurt culture with about 1/2 cup (125 mL) of the cooled milk. Add to remaining cooled milk and stir well to distribute yogurt culture.

4. Pour into prepared cups, secure lids if suggested by manufacturer, and place in yogurt maker. Set the time for 8 to 12 hours or minimum time recommended in manufacturer's instructions. The longer yogurt ferments, the firmer and more tart it will be.

5. Do not disturb the liquid as it is fermenting. Check one container after 8 hours and, if yogurt has reached the desired consistency, remove cups from yogurt maker, secure lids, if necessary, and refrigerate immediately. If it is not set to your liking, replace test cup and continue to ferment for another 1 to 2 hours, or until desired consistency is reached. Refrigeration stops the fermentation process. Let yogurt chill completely before serving or using in recipes.

Strawberry Yogurt

Using a homemade jam in this yogurt makes it all your own but if you have a favorite commercial jam (one with lots of fruit in it), use it here.

Tips

* Add fruit jam, cooked, frozen or canned fruit (not fresh fruit) to the milk mixture as the enzymes and acid in fresh fruit may cause curdling.

* *To scald milk:* Heat milk in a stainless-steel saucepan over medium-low heat, stirring frequently, until bubbles form around outside of pan and steam starts to rise from it. The temperature should reach 170°F (77°C).

Variation

* Use ²⁄₃ cup (150 mL) cherry, blueberry or raspberry jam in place of the strawberry in this recipe.

* *Food thermometer*
* *Electric yogurt maker*

4 cups	1% or 2% milk	1 L
²⁄₃ cup	strawberry jam (see Tips, left)	150 mL
¹⁄₃ cup	instant skim milk powder	75 mL
¹⁄₄ cup	organic live-culture yogurt or 5 g freeze-dried yogurt culture	60 mL

1. In a stainless-steel saucepan, combine milk and jam and heat milk to the scalding point (see Tips, left) over medium-low heat, stirring frequently. Add skim milk powder and stir well. Remove from heat and let cool to 110° to 120°F (43° to 49°C), stirring often. Cooling could take up to 1 hour.

2. In a bowl, combine starter yogurt or freeze-dried yogurt culture with about ¹⁄₂ cup (125 mL) of the cooled milk. Add to remaining cooled milk and stir well to distribute yogurt culture.

3. Pour into clean cups, secure lids if suggested by manufacturer, and place in yogurt maker. Set the time for 8 to 12 hours or minimum time recommended in manufacturer's instructions. The longer yogurt ferments, the firmer and more tart it will be.

4. Do not disturb the liquid as it is fermenting. Check one container after 8 hours and, if yogurt has reached the desired consistency, remove cups from yogurt maker, secure lids, if necessary, and refrigerate immediately. If it is not set to your liking, replace test cup and continue to ferment for another 1 to 2 hours, or until desired consistency is reached. Refrigeration stops the fermentation process. Let yogurt chill completely before serving or using in recipes.

Chocolate Yogurt

If you have chocolate-flavored whey protein, use it in place of the skim milk powder to help thicken this yogurt. Use a good-quality cocoa powder or replace the honey and cocoa with 1/3 cup (75 mL) sweetened chocolate syrup.

Variation

• You can substitute chocolate-flavored milk for the 1% or 2% milk in this recipe. However, if you use chocolate milk or dairy beverage (see below) in this or the Mocha Yogurt (page 28), reduce the chocolate flavoring to 2 tbsp (30 mL) honey and 2 tbsp (30 mL) cocoa powder or 3 tbsp (45 mL) chocolate syrup.

Chocolate Dairy Beverage

• I have found that yogurt made from chocolate dairy beverage is soft and watery. In fact, the yogurt seems to weep a clear liquid, which may be drained off or stirred back in.

• Be sure to check the label. Ingredients may vary with each brand, but most will include additives.

• *Food thermometer*
• *Electric yogurt maker*

4 cups	1% or 2% milk	1 L
1/3 cup	instant skim milk powder	75 mL
1/3 cup	liquid honey	75 mL
3 tbsp	unsweetened cocoa powder	45 mL
3 tbsp	organic live-culture yogurt or 5 g freeze-dried yogurt culture	45 mL

1. In a stainless-steel saucepan, heat milk to the scalding point (see Tip, page 26) over medium-low heat, stirring frequently. Add skim milk powder and stir well.

2. Meanwhile, in a bowl, combine honey and cocoa powder and using a fork mash to form a smooth paste. Add to hot milk and stir well. Remove from heat and let cool to 110° to 120°F (43° to 49°C), stirring often. Cooling could take up to 1 hour.

3. In a separate bowl, combine starter yogurt or freeze-dried yogurt culture with about 1/2 cup (125 mL) of the cooled milk. Add to remaining cooled milk and stir well to distribute yogurt culture.

4. Pour into clean cups, secure lids if suggested by manufacturer, and place in yogurt maker. Set the time for 8 to 12 hours or minimum time recommended in manufacturer's instructions. The longer yogurt ferments, the firmer and more tart it will be.

5. Do not disturb the liquid as it is fermenting. Check one container after 8 hours and, if yogurt has reached the desired consistency, remove cups from yogurt maker, secure lids, if necessary, and refrigerate immediately. If it is not set to your liking, replace test cup and continue to ferment for another 1 to 2 hours, or until desired consistency is reached. Refrigeration stops the fermentation process. Let yogurt chill completely before serving or using in recipes.

Mocha Yogurt

If you happen to have a chocolate-flavored whey protein, use it in place of the skim milk powder to help thicken this yogurt. Use good-quality cocoa powder, or replace the honey and cocoa with ⅓ cup (75 mL) sweetened chocolate syrup.

Tips

- If using the full-flavor gourmet coffee powder available at specialty cafés, use 1 or 2 packets.

- *To scald milk:* Heat milk in a stainless-steel saucepan over medium-low heat, stirring frequently, until bubbles form around outside of pan and steam starts to rise from it. The temperature should reach 170°F (77°C).

- *Food thermometer*
- *Electric yogurt maker*

4 cups	1% or 2% milk	1 L
⅓ cup	instant skim milk powder	75 mL
3 tbsp	instant coffee granules (see Tips, left)	45 mL
⅓ cup	liquid honey	75 mL
¼ cup	unsweetened cocoa powder	60 mL
3 tbsp	organic live-culture yogurt or 5 g freeze-dried yogurt culture	45 mL

1. In a stainless-steel saucepan, heat milk to the scalding point (see Tips, left) over medium-low heat, stirring frequently. Add skim milk powder and coffee granules and stir well. Remove from heat and let cool to 110° to 120°F (43° to 49°C), stirring often. Cooling could take up to 1 hour.

2. Meanwhile, in a bowl, combine honey and cocoa powder and using a fork, mash to form a smooth paste. Add to cooling milk and stir well.

3. In a separate bowl, combine starter yogurt or freeze-dried yogurt culture with about ½ cup (125 mL) of the cooled milk. Add to remaining cooled milk and stir well to distribute yogurt culture.

4. Pour into clean cups, secure lids if suggested by manufacturer, and place in yogurt maker. Set the time for 8 to 12 hours or minimum time recommended in manufacturer's instructions. The longer yogurt ferments, the firmer and more tart it will be.

5. Do not disturb the liquid as it is fermenting. Check one container after 8 hours and, if yogurt has reached the desired consistency, remove cups from yogurt maker, secure lids, if necessary, and refrigerate immediately. If it is not set to your liking, replace test cup and continue to ferment for another 1 to 2 hours, or until desired consistency is reached. Refrigeration stops the fermentation process. Let yogurt chill completely before serving or using in recipes.

Lemon Yogurt

If you really like lemon yogurt, you probably have your favorite commercial brand and if you wish to match the taste and texture of it, you will have to tinker with this recipe until you get it just the way you like it. This recipe is rich and thick, and has a professional "set" or texture to it. Real lemon rind is used, along with lemon-flavored jelly powder that gives it the "gel." Jelly powder does contain some preservatives as well as gelatin.

Variation

• For even more lemon taste and a softer texture, make this recipe without the lemon-flavored jelly powder and add 1 tbsp (15 mL) Lemon Sauce (page 55) to the bottom of each cup before adding the cooled milk mixture.

• *Food thermometer*
• *Electric yogurt maker*

2 cups	1% or 2% milk	500 mL
1 ½ cups	table (18%) cream	375 mL
½ cup	heavy or whipping (35%) cream	125 mL
2 tbsp	grated lemon zest	30 mL
2 tbsp	instant skim milk powder	30 mL
⅓ cup	pure maple syrup	75 mL
3 tbsp	organic live-culture yogurt or 5 g freeze-dried yogurt culture	45 mL
2 tbsp	lemon-flavored jelly powder	30 mL

1. In a stainless-steel saucepan, combine milk, table cream, whipping cream and lemon zest and heat to the scalding point (see Tips, page 28) over medium-low heat, stirring frequently. Add skim milk powder and maple syrup and stir well. Remove from heat and let cool to 110° to 120°F (43° to 49°C), stirring often. Cooling could take up to 1 hour.

2. In a bowl, combine starter yogurt or freeze-dried yogurt culture with about ½ cup (125 mL) of the cooled milk. Stir in jelly powder and add to remaining cooled milk and stir well to distribute yogurt culture.

3. Pour into clean cups, secure lids if suggested by manufacturer, and place in yogurt maker. Set the time for 8 to 10 hours or minimum time recommended in manufacturer's instructions. The longer yogurt ferments, the firmer and more tart it will be.

4. Do not disturb the liquid as it is fermenting. Check one container after 8 hours and, if yogurt has reached the desired consistency, remove cups from yogurt maker, secure lids, if necessary, and refrigerate immediately. If it is not set to your liking, replace test cup and continue to ferment for another 1 to 2 hours, or until desired consistency is reached. Refrigeration stops the fermentation process. Let yogurt chill completely before serving or using in recipes.

Coconut Yogurt

This is a rich and creamy, full-fat yogurt treat. It tastes to me like a sinful tropical dessert, which of course it is. If you prefer a lower-fat coconut yogurt, see Cultured Coconut Milk "Yogurt" (page 23). The coconut bits from the fine (dessicated) and creamed coconut actually float to the top in this yogurt, so they need to be stirred into the yogurt before eating. I have found that 7 hours of incubation is optimum for this yogurt.

- *Food thermometer*
- *Electric yogurt maker*

1	can (14 oz/400 mL) coconut milk	1
2 cups	2% milk	500 mL
1 cup	heavy or whipping (35%) cream	250 mL
1/3 cup	unsweetened desiccated coconut	75 mL
3 tbsp	instant skim milk powder	45 mL
1/3 cup	pure maple syrup	75 mL
3 tbsp	crumbled pure creamed coconut (see page 31)	45 mL
3 tbsp	organic live-culture yogurt or 5 g freeze-dried yogurt culture	45 mL

1. In a stainless-steel saucepan, combine coconut milk, milk, cream and desiccated coconut and heat to the scalding point (see Tip, right) over medium-low heat, stirring frequently. Remove from heat and stir in skim milk powder.

2. In a small bowl, combine maple syrup and creamed coconut and using a fork, mash to make a lumpy paste. Stir into hot milk mixture. Let cool to 110° to 120°F (43° to 49°C), stirring often. Cooling could take up to 1 hour.

3. In a bowl, combine starter yogurt or freeze-dried yogurt culture with about 1/2 cup (125 mL) of the cooled milk mixture. Add to remaining cooled milk mixture and stir well to distribute yogurt culture.

4. Pour into clean cups, secure lids if suggested by manufacturer, and place in yogurt maker. Set the time for 8 to 12 hours or the minimum time recommended in manufacturer's instructions. The longer yogurt ferments, the firmer and more tart it will be.

5. Do not disturb the liquid as it is fermenting. Check one container after 8 hours and, if yogurt has reached the desired consistency, remove cups from yogurt maker, secure lids, if necessary, and refrigerate immediately. If it is not set to your liking, replace test cup and continue to ferment for another 1 to 2 hours, or until desired consistency is reached. Refrigeration stops the fermentation process. Let yogurt chill completely before serving or using in recipes.

Tip

* *To scald milk:* Heat milk in a stainless-steel saucepan over medium-low heat, stirring frequently, until bubbles form around outside of pan and steam starts to rise from it. The temperature should reach 170°F (77°C).

Pure Creamed Coconut

* Creamed coconut is a block of pressed, pure coconut flesh. Usually packaged in a double plastic bag within a cardboard box, and found on supermarket shelves, creamed coconut is widely used in Thai, Indian and Caribbean cooking. It adds a distinctive coconut flavor and rich, creamy texture to dishes. Chopped into chunks, it can be mixed with liquid sweeteners for yogurt or stirred directly into sauces to thicken them. It can also be reconstituted with hot water before use, following package or recipe instructions. Store unopened creamed coconut in a cool, dark place and in an airtight container in the refrigerator once opened.

Peach Maple Yogurt

Pure maple syrup is the perfect partner for the peaches in this delicately flavored yogurt.

Tips

- Add canned or frozen fruit (not fresh fruit) to the milk mixture as the enzymes and acid in fresh fruit may cause curdling.

- *To scald milk:* Heat milk in a stainless-steel saucepan over medium-low heat, stirring frequently, until bubbles form around side of pan and steam starts to rise from it. The temperature should reach 170°F (77°C).

- Food thermometer
- Electric yogurt maker

4 cups	1% or 2% milk	1 L
½ cup	instant skim milk powder	125 mL
⅔ cup	puréed drained canned or thawed frozen peaches (see Tips, left)	150 mL
¼ cup	pure maple syrup, or to taste	60 mL
¼ cup	organic live-culture yogurt or 5 g freeze-dried yogurt culture	60 mL

1. In a stainless-steel saucepan, heat milk to the scalding point (see Tips, left) over medium-low heat, stirring frequently. Add skim milk powder, peaches and maple syrup and stir well. Remove from heat and let cool to 110° to 120°F (43° to 49°C), stirring often. Cooling could take up to 1 hour.

2. In a bowl, combine starter yogurt or freeze-dried yogurt culture with about ½ cup (125 mL) of the cooled milk. Add to remaining cooled milk and stir well to distribute the yogurt culture.

3. Pour into clean cups, secure lids if suggested by manufacturer, and place in electric yogurt maker. Set the time for 8 to 12 hours or minimum time recommended in manufacturer's instructions. The longer yogurt ferments, the firmer and more tart it will be.

4. Do not disturb the liquid as it is fermenting. Check one container after 8 hours and, if yogurt has reached the desired consistency, remove cups from yogurt maker, secure lids, if necessary, and refrigerate immediately. If it is not set to your liking, replace test cup and continue to ferment for another 1 to 2 hours, or until desired consistency is reached. Refrigeration stops the fermentation process. Let yogurt chill completely before serving or using in recipes.

Basic Whole and High-Solid Milk Yogurt (page 20)
with Spiced Pear Salsa (page 50)

Basic Lower-Fat Milk Yogurt (page 21)
with Oatmeal Cinnamon Topping (page 56)

French Vanilla Yogurt (page 24)
with Fresh Berry Topping (page 46)

Fruit-Bottom Yogurt (page 25)

Strawberry Yogurt (page 26)
with Granola Topping (page 58)

Chocolate Yogurt (page 27)

Lemon Yogurt (page 29)
with Tropical Topping (page 48)

Coconut Yogurt (page 30)
with Pomegranate-Orange Topping (page 46)

Pear Cardamom Yogurt

Use the freshest ground cardamom you can get or grind your own from fresh whole seeds. The lemony and flowery flavor of the cardamom with its hint of camphor adds a warm and slightly smoky note to the floral pear in this yogurt.

Tips

• Choose canned pears packed in fruit juice, rather than syrup, for the freshest pear flavor. If your pears are packed in syrup, you may not need to add any honey. Taste the milk mixture after adding pears and only add honey to taste, if necessary. Keep in mind that the yogurt will be more tangy once fermented and less sweet once chilled.

Variation

• *Pear Ginger Yogurt:* Replace the cardamom with ½ tsp (2 mL) ground ginger or 1 tbsp (15 mL) very finely chopped crystallized ginger.

* *Food thermometer*
* *Electric yogurt maker*

4 cups	1% or 2% milk	1 L
½ cup	instant skim milk powder	125 mL
¼ tsp	ground cardamom	1 mL
⅔ cup	puréed drained canned pears (see Tips, left)	150 mL
1 to 2 tbsp	liquid honey	15 to 30 mL
¼ cup	organic live-culture yogurt or 5 g freeze-dried yogurt culture	60 mL

1. In a stainless-steel saucepan, heat milk to the scalding point (see Tips, page 32) over medium-low heat, stirring frequently. Add skim milk powder, cardamom, pears and honey and stir well. Remove from heat and let cool to 110° to 120°F (43° to 49°C), stirring often. Cooling could take up to 1 hour.

2. In a bowl, combine starter yogurt or freeze-dried yogurt culture with about ½ cup (125 mL) of the cooled milk. Add to remaining cooled milk and stir well to distribute the yogurt culture.

3. Pour into clean cups, secure lids if suggested by manufacturer, and place in electric yogurt maker. Set the time for 8 to 12 hours or minimum time recommended in manufacturer's instructions. The longer yogurt ferments, the firmer and more tart it will be.

4. Do not disturb the liquid as it is fermenting. Check one container after 8 hours and, if yogurt has reached the desired consistency, remove cups from yogurt maker, secure lids, if necessary, and refrigerate immediately. If it is not set to your liking, replace test cup and continue to ferment for another 1 to 2 hours, or until desired consistency is reached. Refrigeration stops the fermentation process. Let yogurt chill completely before serving. Gently stir yogurt before serving or using in recipes.

Cappuccino Yogurt

If coffee is your thing, this yogurt might possibly be your favorite flavor. Be sure to start with espresso granules for the extra-bold and authentic cappuccino taste.

Tip

• Look for instant espresso coffee granules in supermarkets where the instant coffee is stocked. The flavor is more intense and worth seeking out for the best results in this yogurt. If you find the very concentrated instant espresso powder, use the amount suggested for 8 cups of espresso.

Variation

• *Cinnamon Yogurt*: Reduce sugar to 2 to 3 tbsp (30 to 45 mL), reduce skim milk powder to ½ cup (125 mL), omit espresso and increase cinnamon to 1 tsp (5 mL).

• *Food thermometer*
• *Electric yogurt maker*

4 cups	1% or 2% milk	1 L
⅔ cup	instant skim milk powder	150 mL
⅓ cup	organic cane sugar crystals or granulated sugar	75 mL
¼ cup	instant espresso coffee granules (see Tips, left)	60 mL
½ tsp	ground cinnamon	2 mL
¼ cup	organic live-culture yogurt or 5 g freeze-dried yogurt culture	60 mL

1. In a stainless-steel saucepan, heat milk to the scalding point (see Tips, page 32) over medium-low heat, stirring frequently. Add skim milk powder, sugar, espresso and cinnamon and stir well until sugar has dissolved. Remove from heat and let cool to 110° to 120°F (43° to 49°C), stirring often. Cooling could take up to 1 hour.

2. In a bowl, combine starter yogurt or freeze-dried yogurt culture with about ½ cup (125 mL) of the cooled milk. Add to remaining cooled milk and stir well to distribute the yogurt culture.

3. Pour into clean cups, secure lids if suggested by manufacturer, and place in electric yogurt maker. Set the time for 8 to 12 hours or minimum time recommended in manufacturer's instructions. The longer yogurt ferments, the firmer and more tart it will be.

4. Do not disturb the liquid as it is fermenting. Check one container after 8 hours and, if yogurt has reached the desired consistency, remove cups from yogurt maker, secure lids, if necessary, and refrigerate immediately. If it is not set to your liking, replace test cup and continue to ferment for another 1 to 2 hours, or until desired consistency is reached. Refrigeration stops the fermentation process. Let yogurt chill completely before serving. Gently stir yogurt before serving or using in recipes.

Ginger Yogurt

Honey and ginger are a classic flavor duo in this homemade yogurt. Crystallized ginger or stem ginger in syrup are the best forms to use for both flavor and texture in homemade yogurt.

Tips

• Do not add fresh gingerroot to the milk mixture because it will cause curdling.

• Crystallized ginger and stem ginger in syrup are available in the baking sections of supermarkets, and at bulk food or natural food stores.

• *To scald milk:* Heat milk in a stainless-steel saucepan over medium-low heat, stirring frequently, until bubbles form around side of pan and steam starts to rise from it. The temperature should reach 170°F (77°C).

• *Food thermometer*
• *Electric yogurt maker*

4 cups	1% or 2% milk	1 L
1/2 cup	instant skim milk powder	125 mL
2 tbsp	very finely chopped crystallized ginger (see Tips, left)	30 mL
2 to 4 tbsp	liquid honey	30 to 60 mL
1/4 cup	organic live-culture yogurt or 5 g freeze-dried yogurt culture	60 mL

1. In a stainless-steel saucepan, heat milk to the scalding point (see Tips, left) over medium-low heat, stirring frequently. Add skim milk powder, ginger and honey and stir well. Remove from heat and let cool to 110° to 120°F (43° to 49°C), stirring often. Cooling could take up to 1 hour.

2. In a bowl, combine starter yogurt or freeze-dried yogurt culture with about 1/2 cup (125 mL) of the cooled milk. Add to remaining cooled milk and stir well to distribute the yogurt culture.

3. Pour into clean cups, secure lids if suggested by manufacturer, and place in electric yogurt maker. Set the time for 8 to 12 hours or minimum time recommended in manufacturer's instructions. The longer yogurt ferments, the firmer and more tart it will be.

4. Do not disturb the liquid as it is fermenting. Check one container after 8 hours and, if yogurt has reached the desired consistency, remove cups from yogurt maker, secure lids, if necessary, and refrigerate immediately. If it is not set to your liking, replace test cup and continue to ferment for another 1 to 2 hours, or until desired consistency is reached. Refrigeration stops the fermentation process. Let yogurt chill completely before serving. Gently stir yogurt before serving or using in recipes.

Chai Tea Yogurt

The spicy flavor of this yogurt is reminiscent of exotic Asian tearooms. This yogurt may not set up as firm as other homemade yogurts, but the flavor is exceptional.

Tips

- If you don't have loose black tea, use 4 tea bags and just remove and discard bags from cooled milk, without squeezing, instead of straining the milk mixture.

- *To scald milk:* Heat milk in a stainless-steel saucepan over medium-low heat, stirring frequently, until bubbles form around side of pan and steam starts to rise from it. The temperature should reach 170°F (77°C).

- *Food thermometer*
- *Electric yogurt maker*

4 cups	1% or 2% milk	1 L
⅔ cup	instant skim milk powder	150 mL
2 tbsp	loose green or black tea leaves	30 mL
¾ tsp	ground cinnamon	3 mL
½ tsp	ground ginger	2 mL
¼ tsp	ground cardamom	1 mL
Pinch	ground cloves	Pinch
⅓ cup	liquid honey	75 mL
½ tsp	vanilla extract	2 mL
¼ cup	organic live-culture yogurt or 5 g freeze-dried yogurt culture	60 mL

1. In a stainless-steel saucepan, heat milk to the scalding point (see Tips, left) over medium-low heat, stirring frequently. Add skim milk powder, tea, cinnamon, ginger, cardamom, cloves, honey and vanilla and stir well. Remove from heat and let cool to 110° to 120°F (43° to 49°C), stirring often. Cooling could take up to 1 hour. Strain through a fine sieve into a large measuring cup or a bowl and discard tea leaves.

2. In a bowl, combine starter yogurt or freeze-dried yogurt culture with about ½ cup (125 mL) of the cooled milk. Add to remaining cooled milk and stir well to distribute the yogurt culture.

3. Pour into clean cups, secure lids if suggested by manufacturer, and place in electric yogurt maker. Set the time for 8 to 12 hours or minimum time recommended in manufacturer's instructions. The longer yogurt ferments, the firmer and more tart it will be.

4. Do not disturb the liquid as it is fermenting. Check one container after 8 hours and, if yogurt has reached the desired consistency, remove cups from yogurt maker, secure lids, if necessary, and refrigerate immediately. If it is not set to your liking, replace test cup and ferment for another 1 to 2 hours, or until desired consistency is reached. Refrigeration stops the fermentation process. Let yogurt chill completely before serving. Gently stir yogurt before serving or using in recipes.

Blueberry Mango Yogurt

Cooking the blueberries and mango before adding them to the milk for fermentation eliminates the problems caused by adding fresh fruit to milk (see Tips, below). The combination of blueberries and mango gives this yogurt a fresh and rather exotic taste.

Tips

- Add cooked, frozen or canned fruit (not fresh fruit) to the milk mixture, as the enzymes and acid in fresh fruit may cause curdling.

- *To scald milk:* Heat milk in a stainless-steel saucepan over medium-low heat, stirring frequently, until bubbles form around side of pan and steam starts to rise from it. The temperature should reach 170°F (77°C).

- Food thermometer
- Electric yogurt maker

½ cup	frozen or fresh blueberries	125 mL
½ cup	finely diced fresh or thawed frozen mango	125 mL
3 tbsp	agave syrup, liquid honey or pure maple syrup, divided	45 mL
4 cups	1% or 2% milk	1 L
½ cup	instant skim milk powder	125 mL
¼ cup	organic live-culture yogurt or 5 g freeze-dried yogurt culture	60 mL

1. In a small saucepan, combine blueberries, mango and 2 tbsp (30 mL) of the agave syrup. Bring to a boil over medium heat, stirring often. Reduce heat and boil gently, stirring often and mashing fruit slightly, for about 5 minutes or until fruit is tender and mixture is slightly jam-like. Remove from heat and let cool.

2. Meanwhile, in a stainless-steel saucepan, heat milk to the scalding point (see Tips, left) over medium-low heat, stirring frequently. Add skim milk powder, blueberry mixture and remaining agave syrup and stir well. Remove from heat and let cool to 110° to 120°F (43° to 49°C), stirring often. Cooling could take up to 1 hour.

3. In a bowl, combine starter yogurt or freeze-dried yogurt culture with about ½ cup (125 mL) of the cooled milk. Add to remaining cooled milk and stir well to distribute the yogurt culture.

4. Pour into clean cups, secure lids if suggested by manufacturer, and place in electric yogurt maker. Set the time for 8 to 12 hours or minimum time recommended in manufacturer's instructions. The longer yogurt ferments, the firmer and more tart it will be.

5. Do not disturb the liquid as it is fermenting. Check one container after 8 hours and, if yogurt has reached the desired consistency, remove cups from yogurt maker, secure lids, if necessary, and refrigerate immediately. If it is not set to your liking, replace test cup and ferment for another 1 to 2 hours, or until desired consistency is reached. Refrigeration stops the fermentation process. Let yogurt chill completely before serving or using in recipes.

Cherry Pomegranate Yogurt

Cherries are mixed into the yogurt and pomegranate molasses is drizzled over! This is a festive and very attractive homemade yogurt and one that is not found in the dairy case.

Tips

- Look for jars of sour (tart) cherries where the canned fruit is stocked at the supermarket, or at European specialty stores. Extra cherries and juice can be frozen in smaller portions for later use.

- Do not add Pomegranate Molasses until after the yogurt is fermented or the milk will curdle.

- *Pomegranate Molasses:* In a saucepan, combine 2 cups (500 mL) unsweetened pomegranate juice and ¼ cup (60 mL) granulated sugar. Bring to a boil over medium-high heat, stirring until sugar has dissolved. Reduce heat and simmer for 45 minutes or until syrupy and reduced to ½ cup (125 mL). Let cool. Store in a clean jar in the refrigerator for up to 2 months. Makes ½ cup (125 mL).

- *Food thermometer*
- *Electric yogurt maker*

4 cups	1% or 2% milk	1 L
½ cup	instant skim milk powder	125 mL
1 tbsp	organic cane sugar crystals or agave syrup	15 mL
⅔ cup	puréed drained jarred or thawed frozen sour (tart) cherries (see Tips, left)	150 mL
¼ cup	organic live-culture yogurt or 5 g freeze-dried yogurt culture	60 mL
¼ cup	Pomegranate Molasses (see recipe left)	60 mL

1. In a stainless-steel saucepan, heat milk to the scalding point (see Tips, right) over medium-low heat, stirring frequently. Add skim milk powder and sugar and stir well until sugar has dissolved. Remove from heat and let cool to 110° to 120°F (43° to 49°C), stirring often. Cooling could take up to 1 hour. Stir in cherries.

2. In a bowl, combine starter yogurt or freeze-dried yogurt culture with about ½ cup (125 mL) of the cooled milk. Add to remaining cooled milk and stir well to distribute the yogurt culture.

3. Pour into clean cups, secure lids if suggested by manufacturer, and place in electric yogurt maker. Set the time for 8 to 12 hours or minimum time recommended in manufacturer's instructions. The longer yogurt ferments, the firmer and more tart it will be.

4. Do not disturb the liquid as it is fermenting. Check one container after 8 hours and, if yogurt has reached the desired consistency, remove cups from yogurt maker. If it is not set to your liking, replace test cup and ferment for another 1 to 2 hours, or until desired consistency is reached. Refrigeration stops the fermentation process.

5. Spoon pomegranate molasses evenly on top of each cup of yogurt and gently swirl through yogurt with a spoon or narrow spatula. Cover with lids and refrigerate immediately. Let yogurt chill completely before serving or using in recipes.

Raspberry Lemon Yogurt

Raspberry and lemon, two of my favorite flavors, team up in this outstanding yogurt. I think the lemon intensifies the raspberry essence, but you can omit it if you prefer an all-raspberry version.

Tips

* Add cooked, frozen or canned fruit (not fresh fruit) to the milk mixture, as the enzymes and acid in fresh fruit may cause curdling.

* *To scald milk:* Heat milk in a stainless-steel saucepan over medium-low heat, stirring frequently, until bubbles form around side of pan and steam starts to rise from it. The temperature should reach 170°F (77°C).

* *Food thermometer*
* *Electric yogurt maker*

4 cups	1% or 2% milk	1 L
2 tbsp	freshly grated lemon zest	30 mL
⅔ cup	instant skim milk powder	150 mL
½ cup	mashed thawed frozen raspberries (see Tips, left)	125 mL
⅓ cup	pure maple syrup	75 mL
¼ cup	organic live-culture yogurt or 5 g freeze-dried yogurt culture	60 mL

1. In a stainless-steel saucepan, combine milk and lemon zest and heat to the scalding point (see Tips, left) over medium-low heat, stirring frequently. Add skim milk powder, raspberries and maple syrup and stir well. Remove from heat and let cool to 110° to 120°F (43° to 49°C), stirring often. Cooling could take up to 1 hour.

2. In a bowl, combine starter yogurt or freeze-dried yogurt culture with about ½ cup (125 mL) of the cooled milk. Add to remaining cooled milk and stir well to distribute the yogurt culture.

3. Pour into clean cups, secure lids if suggested by manufacturer, and place in electric yogurt maker. Set the time for 8 to 12 hours or minimum time recommended in manufacturer's instructions. The longer yogurt ferments, the firmer and more tart it will be.

4. Do not disturb the liquid as it is fermenting. Check one container after 8 hours and, if yogurt has reached the desired consistency, remove cups from yogurt maker, secure lids, if necessary, and refrigerate immediately. If it is not set to your liking, replace test cup and ferment for another 1 to 2 hours, or until desired consistency is reached. Refrigeration stops the fermentation process. Let yogurt chill completely before serving or using in recipes.

Caramel Yogurt

If you like caramel, you will love this yogurt. It has all of the classic caramel ingredients: cream, vanilla and sugar, but without the butter!

Tips

* When making the caramel, you may need to swirl the pan gently when the sugar starts to color, to avoid hot spots, but don't stir with a spoon otherwise the sugar may seize. Be careful when adding the cream — the mixture will bubble up and is extremely hot.

* *To scald milk:* Heat milk in a stainless-steel saucepan over medium-low heat, stirring frequently, until bubbles form around side of pan and steam starts to rise from it. The temperature should reach 170°F (77°C).

* *Food thermometer*
* *Electric yogurt maker*

⅓ cup	granulated sugar	75 mL
⅓ cup	heavy or whipping (35%) cream, at room temperature	75 mL
½ tsp	vanilla extract	2 mL
4 cups	1% or 2% milk	1 L
½ cup	instant skim milk powder	125 mL
¼ cup	organic live-culture yogurt or 5 g freeze-dried yogurt culture	60 mL

1. In a small saucepan, combine sugar and 2 tbsp (30 mL) water. Bring to a boil over medium heat, stirring just until sugar has dissolved. Boil, without stirring, until sugar turns a deep caramel color (see Tips, left). Carefully pour in cream, whisking until blended. Remove from heat and whisk until bubbles subside, then whisk in vanilla. Let caramel cool.

2. While caramel cools, in a stainless-steel saucepan, heat milk to the scalding point (see Tips, left) over medium-low heat, stirring frequently. Add caramel and skim milk powder and stir well. Remove from heat and let cool to 110° to 120°F (43° to 49°C), stirring often. Cooling could take up to 1 hour.

3. In a bowl, combine starter yogurt or freeze-dried yogurt culture with about ½ cup (125 mL) of the cooled milk. Add to remaining cooled milk and stir well to distribute the yogurt culture.

4. Pour into clean cups, secure lids if suggested by manufacturer, and place in electric yogurt maker. Set the time for 8 to 12 hours or minimum time recommended in manufacturer's instructions. The longer yogurt ferments, the firmer and more tart it will be.

5. Do not disturb the liquid as it is fermenting. Check one container after 8 hours and, if yogurt has reached the desired consistency, remove cups from yogurt maker, secure lids, if necessary, and refrigerate immediately. If it is not set to your liking, replace test cup and ferment for another 1 to 2 hours, or until desired consistency is reached. Refrigeration stops the fermentation process. Let yogurt chill completely before serving. Gently stir yogurt before serving or using in recipes.

Honey Lavender Yogurt

If you can find a flowery honey like clover, bergamot or even dandelion, use it in this floral yogurt. Lavender has a penetrating, sweetly floral and spicy essence, so measure accurately and don't overdo it.

Tips

- Be sure to use food-grade lavender that hasn't been treated with preservatives. It is available at specialty food stores and some bulk or natural food stores.

- *To scald milk:* Heat milk in a stainless-steel saucepan over medium-low heat, stirring frequently, until bubbles form around side of pan and steam starts to rise from it. The temperature should reach 170°F (77°C).

- *Food thermometer*
- *Electric yogurt maker*

4 cups	1% or 2% milk	1 L
2 tsp	dried lavender flowers (see Tips, left)	10 mL
½ cup	instant skim milk powder	125 mL
¼ cup	liquid honey	60 mL
¼ cup	organic live-culture yogurt or 5 g freeze-dried yogurt culture	60 mL

1. In a stainless-steel saucepan, combine milk and lavender and heat to the scalding point (see Tips, left) over medium-low heat, stirring frequently. Add skim milk powder and honey and stir well. Remove from heat and let cool to 110° to 120°F (43° to 49°C), stirring often. Cooling could take up to 1 hour. Strain through a fine sieve into a large measuring cup or a bowl and discard lavender.

2. In a bowl, combine starter yogurt or freeze-dried yogurt culture with about ½ cup (125 mL) of the cooled milk. Add to remaining cooled milk and stir well to distribute the yogurt culture.

3. Pour into clean cups, secure lids if suggested by manufacturer, and place in electric yogurt maker. Set the time for 8 to 12 hours or minimum time recommended in manufacturer's instructions. The longer yogurt ferments, the firmer and more tart it will be.

4. Do not disturb the liquid as it is fermenting. Check one container after 8 hours and, if yogurt has reached the desired consistency, remove cups from yogurt maker, secure lids, if necessary, and refrigerate immediately. If it is not set to your liking, replace test cup and ferment for another 1 to 2 hours, or until desired consistency is reached. Refrigeration stops the fermentation process. Let yogurt chill completely before serving or using in recipes.

Cranberry Orange Yogurt

This flavor opens up so many possibilities for holiday desserts and savory sauces. The combination of citrusy orange and tart cranberry is modified by the addition of honey, which of course may be increased or decreased depending on your own taste.

Tips

* It's necessary to add the cooked cranberry mixture to fermented yogurt to avoid curdling.

* *To scald milk:* Heat milk in a stainless-steel saucepan over medium-low heat, stirring frequently, until bubbles form around side of pan and steam starts to rise from it. The temperature should reach 170°F (77°C).

* *Food thermometer*
* *Electric yogurt maker*

4 cups	1% or 2% milk	1 L
2 tbsp	freshly grated orange zest	30 mL
½ cup	instant skim milk powder	125 mL
⅓ cup	liquid honey, divided	75 mL
¼ cup	organic live-culture yogurt or 5 g freeze-dried yogurt culture	60 mL
¾ cup	fresh or frozen cranberries	175 mL

1. In a stainless-steel saucepan, combine milk and orange zest and heat to scalding point over medium-low heat, stirring frequently. Add skim milk powder and 2 tbsp (30 mL) honey and stir well. Remove from heat and let cool to 110° to 120°F (43° to 49°C), stirring often. Cooling could take up to 1 hour.

2. In a bowl, combine yogurt culture with about ½ cup (125 mL) of the cooled milk. Add to remaining cooled milk and stir well to distribute the yogurt culture.

3. Pour into clean cups, secure lids if suggested by manufacturer, and place in electric yogurt maker. Set the time for 8 to 12 hours or minimum time recommended in manufacturer's instructions. The longer yogurt ferments, the firmer and more tart it will be.

4. Do not disturb the liquid as it is fermenting. Check one container after 8 hours and, if yogurt has reached the desired consistency, remove cups from yogurt maker, secure lids, if necessary, and refrigerate immediately. If it is not set to your liking, replace test cup and ferment for another 1 to 2 hours, or until desired consistency is reached. Refrigeration stops the fermentation process.

5. Meanwhile, in a small saucepan, combine cranberries and remaining honey. Bring to a boil over medium heat, stirring often. Reduce heat and boil gently, stirring often and mashing berries, for about 3 minutes or until mixture is thick and sauce-like. Transfer to a bowl and let cool. Cover and refrigerate until yogurt is ready.

6. Divide cranberry sauce evenly and spoon on top of each cup of yogurt and gently swirl through yogurt with a spoon or narrow spatula. Cover with lids and refrigerate immediately. Let yogurt chill completely before serving or using in recipes.

Tasting almost like an orange cream soda, this yogurt will delight fans of that old-fashioned drink.

Tips

* Use the fine side of a box grater or a Microplane-style zester to remove only the fragrant orange zest, avoiding any of the bitter white pith.

* *To scald milk:* Heat milk in a stainless-steel saucepan over medium-low heat, stirring frequently, until bubbles form around side of pan and steam starts to rise from it. The temperature should reach 170°F (77°C).

Orange Cream Yogurt

* *Food thermometer*
* *Electric yogurt maker*

3 cups	1% or 2% milk	750 mL
1 cup	heavy or whipping (35%) cream	250 mL
2 tbsp	freshly grated orange zest (see Tips, left)	30 mL
½ cup	instant skim milk powder	125 mL
¼ cup	liquid honey	60 mL
¼ cup	organic live-culture yogurt or 5 g freeze-dried yogurt culture	60 mL

1. In a stainless-steel saucepan, combine milk, cream and orange zest and heat to the scalding point (see Tips, left) over medium-low heat, stirring frequently. Add skim milk powder and honey and stir well. Remove from heat and let cool to 110° to 120°F (43° to 49°C), stirring often. Cooling could take up to 1 hour.

2. In a bowl, combine starter yogurt or freeze-dried yogurt culture with about ½ cup (125 mL) of the cooled milk. Add to remaining cooled milk and stir well to distribute the yogurt culture.

3. Pour into clean cups, secure lids if suggested by manufacturer, and place in electric yogurt maker. Set the time for 8 to 12 hours or minimum time recommended in manufacturer's instructions. The longer yogurt ferments, the firmer and more tart it will be.

4. Do not disturb the liquid as it is fermenting. Check one container after 8 hours and, if yogurt has reached the desired consistency, remove cups from yogurt maker, secure lids, if necessary, and refrigerate immediately. If it is not set to your liking, replace test cup and ferment for another 1 to 2 hours, or until desired consistency is reached. Refrigeration stops the fermentation process. Let yogurt chill completely before serving or using in recipes.

Your yogurt didn't set. What went wrong?

- Because you are using living organisms to thicken (ferment) milk, it is important that you give them optimal conditions in which to thrive. Batches of yogurt will vary depending on how you administer the three variables of milk, temperature and bacteria.

Here are some guidelines to ensure your yogurt is perfect every time:

- Use fresh milk at the right temperature. Starting with fresh milk is essential. If the milk is too warm when the bacterial culture is added the culture can be killed. Be sure to use a thermometer and do not add the culture until the temperature has cooled (or warmed) to 110° to 120°F (43° to 49°C).

- Keep the milk warm during fermentation. If the milk drops below 110°F (43°C), the culture will not thrive and thicken the milk. If this has happened, you may save the batch by warming the milk to 110°F (43°C) and keeping it at that temperature for 6 to 8 hours. Similarly, if the temperature rises above 120°F (49°C), the culture is threatened. In this case, however, lowering the temperature will not save the yogurt or bring back the bacteria if they have been killed.

- Use fresh "starter." Use fresh, live-culture starter from fresh, unflavored commercial or homemade yogurt. Be sure to check the label to be absolutely certain that any yogurt you buy contains live cultures of bacteria. Some people use fresh commercial yogurt as a starter for every second or third batch, in the belief that new bacteria will perform better than bacteria that have worked to create several homemade batches. If you use freeze-dried culture, be sure it is fresh, and store it in a cool place (the door of the refrigerator is perfect) as directed on the package.

- Follow the recipes. If you add too much starter, the culture may be crowded and may not have enough food to grow and produce a thick yogurt from the amount of milk available. The result will be sour, watery yogurt.

- Be scrupulously clean. If there are rogue bacteria (from the air or other contaminants) on your equipment or utensils, they can interfere with the yogurt culture or, worse, can cause serious health issues if the product is eaten.

Note: Any liquid other than animal milk (see page 15) does not ferment into true yogurt, and will require some stabilizer and thickener in order to give the appearance of yogurt.

Sweet and Savory Yogurt Toppings

Fruit Toppings

The antioxidant power of pomegranate is teamed with fresh orange segments in this unusual yogurt flavoring.

Pomegranate-Orange

I cup	unsweetened pomegranate juice	250 mL
¼ cup	granulated sugar	60 mL
I tbsp	freshly squeezed lemon juice	15 mL
I	orange, cut into segments	I

I. In a heavy-bottomed saucepan, combine pomegranate juice, sugar and lemon juice. Bring to a gentle boil over medium-high heat, stirring, until sugar has dissolved. Reduce heat and simmer gently for about 30 minutes or until a light syrup is attained. Let cool and gently fold in the orange segments. Use immediately and/or transfer remaining topping to a jar with a lid and store in the refrigerator for up to 1 month.

Use fresh or frozen strawberries, raspberries, cherries or blueberries for this colorful and delicious real fruit topping.

Fresh Berry Topping

I cup	fresh or frozen berries (see Intro, left)	250 mL
¼ cup	unsweetened orange or apple juice	60 mL
I tbsp	freshly squeezed lemon juice	15 mL
¼ cup	granulated sugar	60 mL
I tbsp	cornstarch	15 mL

I. In a heavy-bottomed saucepan, combine berries, orange juice and lemon juice. Bring to a gentle boil over medium-high heat, stirring occasionally.

2. In a bowl, combine sugar and cornstarch. Stir into berry mixture. Reduce heat and simmer, stirring constantly, for about 5 minutes or until mixture has thickened to syrup consistency. Use immediately and/or cover remaining berries tightly and store in the refrigerator for up to 1 week.

Apricot Topping

1 cup	coarsely chopped dried apricots	250 mL
½ cup	unsweetened orange or apple juice	125 mL
⅓ cup	granulated sugar	75 mL
1 tbsp	freshly squeezed lemon juice	15 mL

This is an easy and unusual topping for fresh or frozen yogurt, which can be made year-round with dried apricots. If you wish to use fresh apricots, reduce the juice and the sugar and simmer longer until thickened.

1. In a heavy-bottomed saucepan, combine apricots, orange juice, sugar and lemon juice. Bring to a gentle boil over medium-high heat, stirring constantly. Reduce heat and simmer gently, stirring occasionally, for about 15 minutes or until mixture has thickened to syrup consistency. Use immediately and/or cover remaining topping tightly and store in the refrigerator for up to 1 week.

Banana Purée

1 cup	water	250 mL
½ cup	granulated sugar	125 mL
1	very ripe banana	1
2 tbsp	freshly squeezed lemon juice	30 mL
¼ tsp	ground nutmeg	1 mL

Make this with very ripe bananas. Use it as you would a fruit preserve in the bottom of the cups (page 25) or spoon over fresh or frozen yogurt. Either way, if you like bananas, you will like this topping.

1. In a heavy-bottomed saucepan, combine water and sugar. Bring to a gentle boil over medium-high heat, stirring, until sugar has dissolved. Reduce heat and simmer gently, stirring occasionally, for about 25 minutes or until mixture has thickened. Let cool.

2. In a bowl, using a fork, mash banana with lemon juice. Add to syrup and mix well. Stir in nutmeg. Use immediately.

Kiwi Topping

With its unusual green color, this topping is bright as well as flavorful.

1 cup	water	250 mL
½ cup	granulated sugar	125 mL
2 tbsp	freshly squeezed lemon juice	30 mL
2	kiwifruits, coarsely chopped	2

1. In a heavy-bottomed saucepan, combine water, sugar and lemon juice. Bring to a gentle boil over medium-high heat, stirring, until sugar has dissolved. Reduce heat and simmer gently, stirring occasionally, for about 25 minutes or until mixture has thickened. Let cool. Stir in kiwis. Use immediately and/or cover remaining topping tightly and store in the refrigerator for up to 1 week.

Tropical Topping

This is an exotic and delicately flavored topping.

Tip

- Use drained canned, fresh, or thawed frozen mango, peach, melon, papaya or pineapple in any combination.

1 cup	water	250 mL
½ cup	granulated sugar	125 mL
1 cup	coarsely chopped tropical fruit (see Tip, left)	250 mL
2 tbsp	freshly squeezed lemon juice	30 mL

1. In a heavy-bottomed saucepan, combine water and sugar. Bring to a gentle boil over medium-high heat, stirring, until sugar has dissolved. Reduce heat and simmer gently, stirring occasionally, for about 25 minutes or until mixture has thickened. Let cool.

2. In a bowl, combine fruit with lemon juice. Stir into cooled syrup. Use immediately and/or cover remaining topping and store in the refrigerator for up to 1 week.

Apple-Cinnamon

For extra zip, add a
pinch of chile powder
to the applesauce.
This pure applesauce
works in homemade
Fruit-Bottom Yogurt
(page 25).

½ cup	water	125 mL
⅓ cup	lightly packed brown sugar, or to taste	75 mL
2	apples, coarsely chopped	2
1 tbsp	freshly squeezed lemon juice	15 mL
½ tsp	ground cinnamon	2 mL

Variation

• Try pears or a
combination of apple
and pear in this fruity
topping.

1. In a heavy-bottomed saucepan, combine water and brown sugar. Bring to a gentle boil over medium-high heat, stirring, until sugar has dissolved. Add apples, lemon juice and cinnamon. Simmer gently, stirring occasionally, for about 15 minutes or until apples are soft. Use immediately and/or cover remaining topping tightly and store in the refrigerator for up to 1 week.

Chutneys and Salsas

Makes 1½ cups (375 mL)

Fresh pears and spices combine with raisins in this sweet yogurt. Try adding chopped almonds or walnuts.

Tip

• Garam masala is a common term for a basic blend of ground spices widely used in India. It is available in specialty food or South-Asian markets.

Spiced Pear Salsa

2	pears, diced	2
I	apple, diced	I
2 tbsp	freshly squeezed lemon juice	30 mL
3 tbsp	liquid honey or agave nectar	45 mL
2 tbsp	golden raisins	30 mL
¼ tsp	ground cinnamon	I mL
¼ tsp	curry powder or garam masala spice blend, optional (see Tip, left)	I mL

I. In a large bowl, toss pears and apple with lemon juice to coat fruit. Add honey, raisins, cinnamon and curry, if using. Toss to mix. Use immediately and/or cover remaining salsa tightly and store in the refrigerator for up to 1 week.

Makes 1 cup (250 mL)

Almost savory, this exotic fruit topping blends with the tang of fresh homemade yogurt.

Mango Chutney

I	mango, diced	I
2 tbsp	freshly squeezed lime juice or lemon juice	30 mL
I tsp	toasted sesame oil	5 mL
3 tbsp	chopped fresh parsley	45 mL
½ tsp	ground cumin	2 mL

I. In a bowl, toss mango with lime juice to coat fruit. Add sesame oil, parsley and cumin. Toss to mix. Use immediately and/or cover remaining chutney tightly and store in the refrigerator for up to 1 week.

Whether you blend
this salsa with fresh
yogurt or spoon over
puddings and other
desserts or simply use it
as a topping for yogurt,
the combination is
very pleasant.

Walnut-Fig Salsa

• *Food processor or blender*

½ cup	coarsely chopped walnuts	125 mL
½ cup	coarsely chopped fresh or dried figs	125 mL
3 tbsp	agave nectar or liquid honey	45 mL
1 tbsp	freshly squeezed lemon juice	15 mL
	Unsweetened apple juice, optional	

1. In a food processor or blender, combine walnuts, figs, agave nectar and lemon juice. Pulse mixture until finely chopped but not a paste. If the consistency is too thick, add apple juice 1 tbsp (15 mL) at a time, pulsing after each addition. Use immediately and/or cover remaining salsa tightly and store in the refrigerator for up to 1 week.

The tart taste of
rhubarb is enlivened
by the lemony tang of
freshly made yogurt. I
like to serve the French
Vanilla Yogurt (page 24)
with this compote.

Rhubarb Compote

1 cup	coarsely chopped fresh or frozen rhubarb (thawed if frozen)	250 mL
¼ cup	water	60 mL
¼ cup	lightly packed brown sugar or honey, or to taste	60 mL

1. In a saucepan, combine rhubarb and water. Bring to a boil over medium-high heat, stirring frequently. Add brown sugar and simmer, stirring frequently, until compote has thickened, for 4 to 8 minutes, depending on if fresh or frozen. Use immediately and/or cover remaining compote tightly and store in the refrigerator for up to 1 week.

Tomato Relish

Sometimes we want a savory hit for topping vegetables or a yogurt snack, or to complement other side dishes. This relish is the perfect accompaniment for rounding out the tang of fresh yogurt. You can double the batch and process it in a hot-water bath (check the canning directions from the jar manufacturer) in order to preserve it, but I just like to make small batches and use it up quickly.

• *Two 1-cup (250 mL) preserving jars with lids*

2 lbs	tomatoes, seeded and coarsely chopped	1 kg
1	small red onion, coarsely chopped	1
½ cup	white or red wine vinegar	125 mL
1 tbsp	finely chopped candied ginger	15 mL
½ tsp	freshly ground sea salt	2 mL
¼ tsp	ground allspice	1 mL
1 cup	granulated sugar	250 mL

1. In a large stainless-steel saucepan or canning kettle (if doubling the recipe), combine tomatoes, red onion, vinegar, ginger, salt and allspice. Bring to a boil over high heat, stirring frequently. Stir in sugar and bring to a boil. Reduce heat and simmer, uncovered, stirring occasionally, for 45 minutes or until thickened.

2. Meanwhile, in a large pot, cover preserving jars with hot water. Bring to a simmer and keep hot over medium-low heat until ready to fill with relish. Ladle hot relish into hot jars, cap and let cool. Use immediately and/or cover remaining relish and store in the refrigerator for up to 2 weeks.

Sauces and Syrups

Makes 1 cup (250 mL)

You can use dried dates instead of figs in this syrup and the flavor will be sweeter.

Maple-Fig Syrup

- *1-cup (250 mL) jar with lid, optional*

1 cup	chopped dried figs	250 mL
½ cup	pure maple syrup	125 mL
¼ cup	water	60 mL
1 tbsp	freshly squeezed lemon juice	15 mL

1. In a heavy-bottomed saucepan, combine figs, maple syrup, water and lemon juice. Bring to a boil over medium-high heat, stirring constantly. Reduce heat and simmer gently, stirring frequently, for 15 minutes or until syrup has slightly thickened. Let cool and use as is or strain through a sieve to remove seeds. Use immediately and/or store remaining syrup in a capped jar in the refrigerator for up to 2 weeks.

Makes about 4 cups (1 L)

This is an easy way to add some sweet and fruity flavor to fresh yogurt. Use it with fresh yogurt, cooked oatmeal, pancakes and puddings, and to drizzle over fresh fruit salads. If you sterilize the jar, the syrup will keep longer.

Tip

- Use fresh or frozen (thawed and drained) blueberries, strawberries, blackberries, raspberries or other berries. Crush them with a potato masher in single layers, then measure 3 cups (750 mL).

Berries in Syrup

- *1-quart (1 L) jar with lid, optional*

3 cups	crushed berries (see Tip, left)	750 mL
¾ cup	granulated sugar	175 mL
⅓ cup	water	75 mL
2 tbsp	freshly squeezed lemon juice	30 mL

1. In a heavy-bottomed saucepan, combine berries, sugar, water and lemon juice. Bring to a boil over medium-high heat, stirring constantly. Reduce heat and simmer gently, stirring frequently, for 15 minutes or until syrup has thickened. Let cool and use as is or strain through a sieve to remove seeds. Use immediately and/or store remaining chutney in a capped jar in the refrigerator for up to 3 weeks.

Use pure or naturally flavored green tea for this sauce.

Green Tea Sauce

- *1-cup (250 mL) jar with lid, optional*

2	green tea bags	2
I cup	boiling water	250 mL
½ cup	granulated sugar	125 mL
I tsp	rice vinegar	5 mL

I. In a heavy-bottomed saucepan, combine tea bags and boiling water. Cover and gently simmer over medium-low heat for 4 minutes. Remove tea bags and discard. Add sugar and vinegar and simmer, uncovered and stirring occasionally, for about 10 minutes or until sauce has thickened. Let cool. Use immediately and/or store remaining sauce in a capped jar in the refrigerator for up to 3 weeks.

For a sweet treat, drizzle this rich sauce over fresh yogurt or, when making homemade yogurt, add some caramel sauce to the bottom of each cup before adding the cooled milk mixture. A deep-sided, heavy-bottomed saucepan is essential to prevent the sugar from burning and the sauce from foaming up over the top of the pan.

Tip

- Use heavy or whipping cream that is 25% butterfat or higher and do not substitute any other fat for the butter.

Caramel Sauce

- *2-cup (500 mL) jar with lid*

I cup	granulated sugar	250 mL
6 tbsp	butter	90 mL
½ cup	heavy or whipping (35%) cream	125 mL

I. In a deep, heavy-bottomed saucepan, heat sugar over medium-high heat, stirring vigorously with a wooden spoon. Bring sugar to a boil and keep boiling without stirring. Swirl pan from time to time, to melt sugar crystals on sides, but let sugar caramelize without stirring.

2. When all of the sugar crystals have melted and liquid sugar is dark amber (not burned), immediately stir in butter and beat until butter has melted. Remove pan from heat and let mixture stand for a few seconds. Slowly whisk cream into mixture (see Tips, page 40). It will foam up considerably. Keep whisking until sauce is smooth and creamy.

3. Let cool in pan for 10 minutes and pour into jar. Let cool completely. Use immediately and/or store remaining sauce in a capped jar in the refrigerator for up to 1 week.

Thick and lemony, this sweet-tart sauce mellows and enhances the lemony acidic bite of fresh yogurt.

Lemon Sauce

• *2-cup (500 mL) jar with lid, optional*

1 cup	granulated sugar	250 mL
2 tbsp	cornstarch	30 mL
¼ tsp	salt	1 mL
1½ cups	water	375 mL
2	egg yolks, beaten	2
2 tbsp	butter	30 mL
	Grated zest and juice of 1 lemon	

1. In a bowl, combine sugar, cornstarch and salt. In a heavy-bottomed saucepan, bring water to a boil over high heat. Using a wooden spoon, slowly stir in sugar mixture. Bring to a boil, stirring constantly. Reduce heat and simmer, stirring constantly, until mixture turns clear and has thickened.

2. Drop 2 spoonfuls of the hot mixture into egg yolks and stir to warm them. Add more hot mixture, stirring to combine well. Scrape warm egg mixture into saucepan and cook over medium-low heat, stirring constantly, for 3 to 5 minutes or until thickened.

3. Remove from heat and stir in butter. Stir vigorously until melted. Stir in lemon zest and juice until sauce is smooth. Let cool. Use immediately and/or store remaining sauce in a capped jar in the refrigerator for up to 1 week.

Dry Toppings

Use walnuts, almonds, Brazil nuts, pecans, peanuts, cashews or any of your favorite nuts. A combination works nicely, as well.

Dried Fruit Nut Topping

¼ cup	chopped nuts (see Intro, left)	60 mL
¼ cup	chopped raisins	60 mL
¼ cup	chopped dried apricots	60 mL
¼ cup	sunflower seeds	60 mL
2 tbsp	finely chopped candied ginger	30 mL
2 tbsp	sesame seeds	30 mL
3 to 4 tbsp	liquid honey	45 to 60 mL
1 to 2 tbsp	hemp or other polyunsaturated oil	15 to 30 mL

I. In a large bowl, combine nuts, raisins, apricots, sunflower seeds, ginger and sesame seeds. Drizzle with honey to taste, 1 tbsp (15 mL) at a time, stirring with a fork to incorporate. Mixture will be sticky and hard to stir, but should hold together. Drizzle with oil and, using 2 forks, toss to coat, then separate into smaller clumps. Store in an airtight container in a cool place for 2 to 3 weeks.

Easy to make and great for sprinkling over fresh yogurt, this topping adds fiber. For a healthy alternative to butter, try coconut oil, which is solid at room temperature. The fat should be room temperature (soft but not liquid).

Variation

• Try adding ¼ cup (60 mL) raisins, chopped nuts or seeds, or a combination of these.

Oatmeal Cinnamon Topping

2 tbsp	coconut oil or butter, at room temperature	30 mL
2 tbsp	lightly packed brown sugar	30 mL
1 cup	large-flake (old-fashioned) rolled oats or spelt flakes	250 mL
½ tsp	ground cinnamon	2 mL

I. In a bowl, beat together coconut oil and brown sugar until smooth. Add rolled oats and cinnamon and stir to incorporate. The mixture will be crumbly. Store in an airtight container in the refrigerator for up to 1 month.

Date and Nut Topping

The cooked dates are divine in this date and nut square adaptation. The smooth dates, combined with the small amount of butter, make the mixture very buttery without all the fat of a regular crumb topping.

1 cup	chopped dried dates	250 mL
½ cup	water or unsweetened fruit juice	125 mL
2 tbsp	butter	30 mL
1 tbsp	freshly squeezed lemon juice	15 mL
1 tbsp	lightly packed brown sugar	15 mL
½ cup	chopped walnuts	125 mL
1 to 1½ cups	large-flake (old-fashioned) rolled oats or spelt flakes	250 to 375 mL

1. In a saucepan, combine dates and water. Bring to a boil over high heat. Cook, stirring constantly, for 5 to 8 minutes or until smooth. Remove from heat and beat in butter, beating until melted and combined with dates. Transfer to a large bowl and add lemon juice and brown sugar, beating well to incorporate.

2. Add walnuts and stir well to incorporate. Sprinkle about ½ cup (125 mL) of the rolled oats over date mixture in bowl. Stir well and keep adding remaining rolled oats until mixture is dry and crumbly. Store in an airtight container in the refrigerator for up to 1 month.

Cherry Almond Topping

You can use blanched almonds but I prefer raw, natural almonds in their skins for most almond recipes. If you like, add a few drops of pure almond extract for a very intense almond flavor.

• *Food processor or blender*

1 cup	dried cherries or cranberries	250 mL
1 cup	natural almonds	250 mL

1. In a food processor or blender, combine cherries and almonds. Process until finely chopped and crumbly. Store in an airtight container in the refrigerator for up to 1 month.

Granola Topping

Just as with homemade yogurt, it's worth making homemade granola topping because you control the ingredients. Of course, if you have a favorite commercial granola that is additive-free, use that to sprinkle over fresh yogurt.

Variation

• Use spelt flakes in place of, or in combination with, the rolled oats and add 1 tbsp (30 mL) amaranth or chia seeds or teff grain, if you have them available.

• *Preheat oven to 375°F (190°C)*
• *Rimmed baking sheet, lightly oiled*

1 cup	large-flake (old-fashioned) rolled oats	250 mL
½ cup	natural bran or bran flakes cereal	125 mL
⅓ cup	chopped almonds	75 mL
⅓ cup	chopped walnuts or pecans	75 mL
3 tbsp	sesame seeds	45 mL
¼ cup	liquid honey	60 mL
1 tbsp	chopped candied ginger	15 mL
½ tsp	ground cinnamon	2 mL
¼ tsp	ground allspice	1 mL
¼ cup	chopped dried apricots	60 mL
¼ cup	raisins	60 mL
¼ cup	dried cranberries or cherries	60 mL

1. In a bowl, combine rolled oats, bran, almonds, walnuts and sesame seeds. Spread evenly on prepared baking sheet and bake in preheated oven, stirring once, for 6 to 8 minutes or until grains and nuts are lightly browned.

2. Meanwhile, in a small saucepan over medium heat, combine honey, ginger, cinnamon and allspice and cook, stirring constantly, just until simmering lightly. Turn off heat and keep pan on element to keep mixture warm.

3. Transfer toasted oat mixture to a bowl. Drizzle with warm honey mixture. Add apricots, raisins and cranberries and stir lightly to mix. Let cool. Store in an airtight container in the refrigerator for up to 2 months.

Healthy Body Systems

Healthy Living

Today, the big killers in Western societies are the cancers, cardiovascular disease, diabetes and hypertension, most of which are preventable by diet. Immunity and obesity play a role in either reducing or elevating disease, and they in turn are both affected by the foods we eat.

Doctors, scientists, naturopaths, nutritionists and medical herbalists all agree: to be healthy and prevent disease, a healthy lifestyle is essential. Following these guidelines will maintain and help restore good health.

Guidelines for Including Yogurt in Your Diet

Yogurt is so healthy and nutritious that many dietitians and health practitioners recommend eating at least one serving per day and when taking antibiotics, three servings daily. One cup (250 mL) a day is a delicious way to achieve almost 60% of your recommended daily allowance (RDA) of iodine and almost 50% of your RDA of calcium, along with significant amounts (25% of your RDA or higher) of phosphorus, vitamin B_2, protein and vitamin B_{12}. Canada's Food Guide and the USDA Food Pyramid include yogurt as part of the Milk Group of essential, everyday foods. For more on the health benefits of yogurt see page 12.

Yogurt and a Healthy Diet
The fact remains that being healthy begins with a healthy diet. Whole foods that fall into either Canada's Food Guide or the USDA's Food Pyramid and daily servings of yogurt are essential to being and staying well. In addition to helping to maintain a healthy digestive system and to contributing to the health of both the immune and the musculoskeletal systems, some of the other benefits from eating yogurt on a daily basis are listed here.

Will yogurt improve your cholesterol profile?
A study published in the *Annals of Nutrition & Metabolism* showed that daily consumption of two servings (1 cup/250 mL or two 4-oz/125 g containers) of live-culture yogurt reduces LDL (bad) cholesterol and increases HDL (good cholesterol).

Will yogurt help with weight management?
Studies have shown that calcium and polyunsaturated fats are consistently linked to lower body fat in both children and adults. When lower-fat yogurt is regularly used to replace saturated fat foods, such as butter, sour cream, mayonnaise and cream, the result is a healthy diet that is lower overall in fat and higher in a key weight-controlling nutrient: calcium. Additional studies have shown that a reduced calorie diet that is high in low-fat dairy foods — yogurt and milk — promotes fat loss faster than the same low-calorie diet without those calcium-rich foods. Simply taking calcium supplements while consuming the same low calorie diet was proven to be not as effective as the combination of calcium-rich foods and a low-calorie diet.

What else is yogurt thought to relieve?
The effect of yogurt to help prevent and relieve arthritis is now being studied. Yogurt's ability to destroy the ulcer-causing bacterium, *Helicobacter pylori*, is also being tested.

Guidelines to Good Health

- Limit alcohol consumption — post-menopausal women who drink less than one drink per day can decrease the risk of dying of breast cancer by up to 30%

- Exercise — moderate daily physical activity can lower cancer risk, boost the immune system, help prevent obesity, decrease estrogen and insulin growth factor (IGF), improve overall health and emotional well-being
- Do not smoke — smoking is related to one-third of all cancers and 80% of all lung cancer
- Eat well — a healthy diet is the best defense against disease

Guidelines to Eating Well

- Eat a minimum of five servings of fruit and vegetables every day
- Focus on the most colorful fruit and vegetables, such as red peppers, dark greens, oranges, carrots, apricots, blueberries
- Choose whole grains over processed grains and white flours
- Limit refined carbohydrates, such as pastries, sweetened cereals, soft drinks, candy, salty snacks
- Cook with olive or organic canola oil
- Avoid trans-fats found in many margarines, baked and convenience products
- Limit intake of saturated fats and cholesterol found in meats and dairy products
- Add avocados, natural nuts, seeds, cold water fish (cod, sardines, salmon) to the diet
- Control portion sizes

Healthy Bodies

The body may be characterized by seven major systems: Cardiovascular (the heart and its components); Digestive (stomach, pancreas, bowels); Endocrine (glands and hormones); Immune (protective cells); Musculoskeletal (muscles, bones, joints, connective tissue); Nervous (the brain, spinal cord and nerves); and Respiratory (nose, trachea, bronchial tubes, lungs). Each system has a role to play in keeping the body disease-free. And each system responds positively to specific whole foods.

In the following pages, you will find information on each system, including its importance to our health, what kinds of problems we develop when the systems break down, and the diet and lifestyle changes we need to make to keep each system working at top capacity.

As always, check with a health-care specialist if you are experiencing health problems.

Cardiovascular System

Healthy Cardiovascular System

The cardiovascular system consists of the heart, the blood, the arteries and veins. The heart is a muscular organ responsible for pumping oxygenated blood that has just come from the lungs, and for delivering it via the arteries to all body tissues and organs. The body's tissues and organs depend on this oxygen and other nutrients to function. The heart is also responsible for bringing de-oxygenated blood back from the body via the veins to the heart so this blood can be sent to the lungs to get more oxygen.

Cardiovascular Disease

Atherosclerosis, high cholesterol, high blood pressure

Cardiovascular disease — or heart disease, as it is most commonly called — is an illness that pertains to the heart and the blood vessels. Atherosclerosis is the most common precursor to heart disease.

Atherosclerosis occurs when fatty deposits build up on the inside of the arteries, restricting blood flow to the organs supplied by the arteries. If this narrowing and decreased blood flow happens in the coronary arteries, the arteries that supply the heart muscle itself, coronary heart disease occurs. Coronary heart disease has few signs or symptoms, until the arteries become severely occluded, resulting in tissue death and a heart attack.

With repeated heart attacks, the heart becomes weakened and the few areas that are still functioning are left to do most of the work. This inefficiency creates a backup of blood in the heart, lungs and other tissues. This is called congestive heart failure, and can result in difficult breathing even at rest and eventually heart failure and death.

Atherosclerosis also affects other organs and tissues, such as the brain and the legs and feet. If the occlusion happens in the brain, an area of the brain tissue dies and a stroke results. If the legs and feet are restricted of blood and oxygen, we get diminished peripheral circulation, pain with walking and even swelling and ulcerations of the legs.

For years, high cholesterol has been named as the culprit for the presence of fatty deposits inside of the arteries. But in fact, it is the presence of oxidized cholesterol in the bloodstream that can turn the fatty deposits in the arteries into harder plaques and eventually occlusion. This is why antioxidants in our foods are so important. It is also important to note that there are different types of cholesterol. LDL or low-density lipoprotein, is the "bad" cholesterol, the one that gets oxidized and causes the damage. On the other hand, HDL or high-density lipoprotein, is the "good" cholesterol and protects against heart disease.

Another important risk factor for heart disease is a high level of homocysteine. Homocysteine seems to reduce the integrity of the artery walls, as well as cause direct damage to the arteries. Vitamins B_6 (pyridoxine), B_{12} and folic acid help break down homocysteine in the body and keep levels low.

High blood pressure can damage the inside of the artery walls, starting the plaque build-up process and leading to heart disease. It is also much harder work for the heart to pump blood through a system with higher pressure, leading to heart disease and stroke.

Many risk factors contribute to high blood pressure, high levels of oxidized LDL cholesterol and atherosclerosis. The good news is that most of these risk factors can be controlled with diet, exercise and lifestyle modifications.

Optimizing Cardiovascular Function

To protect the cardiovascular system from disease, we need to maintain a healthy body weight, eat an antioxidant-plentiful diet, educate ourselves on the types of fats we should and should not consume, exercise regularly and learn how to cope with stress.

Increase antioxidant-rich foods

Antioxidants are responsible for preventing oxidation of LDL cholesterol inside the arterial walls. This makes it essential for preventing heart disease as it stalls the blockage of the arteries and allows oxygenated blood to be delivered to the organs. Vitamin C is especially important because it prevents the formation of free radicals, which damage the arterial walls, but it also helps heal the damaged areas before the plaque formation process begins. Numerous studies have shown antioxidants such as vitamin E, selenium and coenzyme Q10 to be efficient in both the prevention and treatment of heart disease.

Best foods
- Polyphenols: extra virgin olive oil
- Bioflavonoids (quercetin): strawberries, onions, apples, green and black tea
- Vitamin C: oranges, strawberries, kiwifruit, red bell peppers, sweet potatoes, broccoli, kale
- Vitamin E: wheat germ, almonds, sunflower seeds, cooked organic soybeans
- Selenium: Brazil nuts, garlic, cooked barley, brown rice, oatmeal, tofu
- Coenzyme Q10: soy oil, mackerel, sardines, peanuts

Increase intake of whole foods that are high in soluble and insoluble fibers

Fruits and legumes are high in soluble fiber, vegetables and whole grains are high in insoluble fiber, and most foods have a combination of both. Soluble fiber, which forms a gel-like compound when dissolved in water, helps eliminate excess cholesterol by binding the cholesterol in the bowels and getting it ready for elimination. Oats in particular contain beta-glucans, which bind cholesterol, and have a significant impact on preventing heart disease. Insoluble fiber, which does not dissolve in water, aids in lowering cholesterol by forming bulk in the stool, and helping to move the bowels.

Best foods
- Legumes (beans, such as black, kidney, lima, pinto, navy, white) and lentils, chickpeas, split peas
- Rolled oats (large flake whole oats/not quick-cooking or instant varieties) and oat bran
- Fruits (apples, oranges, pears), fruit pectin
- Ground flaxseeds

Increase unsaturated fats in your diet

Foods high in unsaturated fatty acids are an important part of a heart healthy diet. Research studies have shown that gamma-linolenic acid (GLA), an omega-6 fatty acid found in evening primrose oil, can decrease LDL levels and increase HDL levels, reducing the risk for atherosclerosis. GLA has also proven to decrease blood pressure levels.

Please note that along with increasing unsaturated fats in your diet, you should also avoid saturated fats (found in animal products such as meats and dairy products) and trans fats (which occur from the hydrogenation process of oils for some margarines and fast foods to make them more stable and increase shelf life). Research shows that trans fats elevate LDL cholesterol and reduce HDL cholesterol.

Best foods
- Extra virgin olive oil, evening primrose oil, nuts and seeds, flaxseed oil, fresh fish

Learn stress management techniques and keep stress levels low

When people are under stress, they form more free radicals, which cause more LDL cholesterol oxidation. Stress also stimulates the release of adrenaline, which can create more clots and increase the thickness of the blood. Clots are the start of plaque formation and increase the risk of atherosclerosis. They can also get lodged and lead to a heart attack or stroke. Daily relaxation techniques and learning some stress coping mechanisms can protect against heart disease.

It has also been found that with deep breathing, the body eliminates more sodium than with shallow breathing. This means that deep-breathing techniques can help reduce blood pressure levels by having an effect on water retention.

Best techniques
- Daily relaxation techniques, deep-breathing, rest, hobbies

Exercise regularly and maintain a healthy weight

Exercising regularly helps maintain a healthy body weight, lowers stress and anxiety, and lowers blood pressure levels — all essential components of a heart disease prevention program. Exercise also helps decrease LDL levels and elevate HDL cholesterol levels in the blood, protecting against heart disease. Aim for at least 20 minutes, three times a week. Before starting on a new exercise routine, consult your physician.

Best exercises
- Yoga, brisk walking, swimming, bicycling, dancing

Top 10 Best Bets for Heart Health

1 Broiled or baked fish: Fish oils contain omega-3 fatty acids that help prevent heart disease and stroke. Studies have shown that there is a difference in health benefits between different types of cooking methods for fish. For example, broiled or oven-baked fish lower the risk of stroke, while fried fish or fish burgers increase the risk of stroke.

2 Garlic: Garlic contains thioallyls, including allicin, which help platelet aggregation and blood pressure, decreasing the risk for heart disease and stroke.

3 Soy foods and other beans: Soy isoflavones, the active constituents in soy foods, help protect the cardiovascular system. Soy foods can significantly lower LDL cholesterol levels by decreasing cholesterol and absorption of bile acid from the gastrointestinal tract, but they also decrease the oxidative damage to LDL with their strong free-radical scavenging potential. Look for organic, non-genetically modified soy.

4 Pomegranate: This delicious and fun-to-eat fruit is important due to its benefits on the cardiovascular system. Pomegranate juice has been shown to reduce the oxidation of LDL cholesterol, protect the arteries from becoming thicker and reduce the development of atherosclerosis. Even though the mechanism of the pomegranate's action is not completely understood, the strong antioxidant potential from its polyphenol compounds may be partly responsible for the benefits.

5 Extra virgin olive oil: Olive oil is an essential part of the Mediterranean diet, which has been shown to reduce blood pressure and improve lipid profiles, even compared to a lower-fat diet. Olive oil is also a source of antioxidant and anti-inflammatory polyphenols and is high in monounsaturated fats.

6 Whole oats and oat bran: Whole oats and oat bran are an easy and inexpensive way to achieve a healthy heart. Oats contain beta-glucan, a soluble fiber that binds cholesterol in the bowels and prevents it from being reabsorbed into the bloodstream.

7 Celery: Celery contains a compound called 3-n-butyl phthalide, which benefits the cardiovascular system. Four ribs of celery per day can help to reduce blood pressure levels.

8 Apples: Apples are rich in pectin, a soluble fiber that is effective in lowering cholesterol levels, as well as an antioxidant against the oxidation of LDL.

Apples are also rich in the bioflavonoid quercetin, a multipurpose nutrient that contributes to heart health. Quercetin acts as an antioxidant by scavenging free radicals to inhibit LDL damage inside the arteries, and also by regenerating the levels of vitamin E. Quercetin has anti-inflammatory and antihistaminic properties that help control inflammation and allergic reactions anywhere in the body.

9 Asparagus and leafy greens: Asparagus and leafy green vegetables are high in folate, essential for the lowering of homocysteine levels. High homocysteine levels are an independent risk factor for cardiovascular disease and stroke. Keep in mind that vitamins B_6 and B_{12} are also important factors for controlling the levels of homocysteine in the blood, and that vitamin B_{12}, which is found mostly in animal products, is hard to find in a vegetarian diet.

10 Tea and cocoa: Tea and cocoa are good providers of bioflavonoids. Studies show that drinking an average of 3 cups (750 mL) of brewed black tea per day can have a long-term positive effect on the cardiovascular system. Similarly, when consumed in moderation, flavonoid-rich chocolate or cocoa can be a component of a heart-healthy diet.

Foods that Protect the Heart

Best Foods that Protect the Heart	Cardiovascular System Benefits	Comments
FRUITS		
Citrus: • Oranges • Mandarins • Lemons • Grapefruits • Kiwifruit • Strawberries • Pomegranate	Rich in vitamin C and bioflavonoids, which are antioxidants. Contain pectins. Kiwifruit also contains vitamin E, a powerful antioxidant. Strawberries contain quercetin, a bioflavonoid.	Kiwifruit has proven to be one of the most nutrient-dense fruits. Caution: Grapefruit juice can interfere with some medication
• Apples	Pectin in apples clean up and bind cholesterol in the intestines, preventing it from being absorbed into the bloodstream. Also high in quercetin.	Studies show that pectin, the soluble fiber found in apple peel, is comparable in results to cholesterol-lowering drug
Orange/Yellow: • Apricots • Mangoes	Contain carotenoids and vitamin C, which are antioxidants. Apricots and mangoes are rich in potassium, which helps control blood pressure.	Choose firm and bright orange-colored apricots.
• Bananas	High in potassium, which helps keep blood pressure in check.	
Blue/Purple: • Blueberries and other berries • Purple grapes • Plums	Contain anthocyanins, which destroy free radicals. Also high in pectin and vitamin C.	Frozen berries carry all the heart-health benefits that fresh berries do.
VEGETABLES		
Red Nightshades: • Tomatoes • Red bell peppers	Rich in lycopene, a potent antioxidant. High in Vitamin C and beta-carotene.	Lycopene is fat-soluble and must be eaten with a fat in order to be absorbed. Lycopene is also found in processed tomato products, such as tomato juice, ketchup and pizza sauce.
Orange/Yellow: • Carrots • Yams • Sweet potatoes • Pumpkin and other winter squashes	Contain carotenoids, which make LDL cholesterol less susceptible to oxidation.	
Green: • Spinach • Swiss chard • Asparagus • Dandelion greens • Other dark leafy greens	Contain folic acid, essential for lowering homocysteine levels. Contain magnesium, calcium and potassium, which help control blood pressure. Asparagus is high in folate, which helps reduce homocysteine levels.	1 cup (250 mL) of leafy vegetables is equal to one serving.
Cruciferous Family: • Broccoli • Cabbage • Cauliflower	Broccoli contains large amounts of vitamin C and beta-carotene, both powerful antioxidants. All contain folic acid and potassium.	

Foods that Protect the Heart

Best Foods that Protect the Heart	Cardiovascular System Benefits	Comments
VEGETABLES (cont.)		
• Celery	Contains 3-n-butyl phthalide and high amounts of potassium to help with lowering blood pressure.	4 ribs of celery per day can help reduce blood pressure level's.
Allium Family: • Garlic • Onions • Chives	Allicin in garlic lowers blood pressure and reduces blood clotting. Yellow or red onions are high in quercetin.	Released during crushing, allicin gives garlic its characteristic smell. Eat garlic raw and cooked.
LEGUMES		
• Beans • Organic soybeans • Lentils • Peas • Chickpeas	Legumes are a source of soluble fiber that can help eliminate excess cholesterol through the bowels. Rich in flavonoids, which prevent LDL oxidation and damage to the artery lining.	For soy foods, see page 103. 1 cup (250 mL) of cooked soybeans contains 25% of recommended daily fiber and 1 oz (30 g) of protein. Soy products contain phytoestrogens, which may act like weak estrogens in the body. Consult with your naturopathic doctor or nutritionist before consuming large amounts of soy.
WHOLE GRAINS		
• Whole oats and oat bran • Brown rice • Pot barley • Whole ancient grains: spelt, kamut, amaranths.	Beta-glucans in oats bind cholesterol molecules in the bowel for elimination. They can lower LDL levels without lowering HDL levels.	Whole grains, such as whole oats and brown rice, contain more fiber than processed flours, pasta, crackers and bread.
NUTS AND SEEDS		
Nuts: • Almonds • Brazil nuts • Walnuts	Nuts contain monounsaturated fats, vitamin E and fiber. They help decrease LDL while leaving HDL unchanged. Brazil nuts, high in selenium, are antioxidant.	Buy raw or dry-roasted nuts and seeds. Choose an unsalted variety; salt can increase blood pressure.
Seeds: • Flaxseeds • Sesame seeds • Sunflower seeds • Pumpkin seeds	Flaxseeds are high in omega-3 oils, fiber and calcium, and help decrease LDL cholesterol, platelet stickiness and blood pressure. Sesame seeds are an excellent source of vitamin E.	Flaxseeds must be ground to maximize absorption and digestion. Once ground, they go rancid quickly, especially if not refrigerated. Best to purchase small quantities of whole flaxseeds, store in the refrigerator and grind fresh just before using.
FATS AND OILS		
• Cold-pressed oils: • Extra virgin olive oil • Grapeseed oil • Flaxseed oil • Avocados	Olive oil, grapeseed oil and avocados contain heart-healthy monounsaturated fats. Grapeseed oil contains significant amounts of vitamin E and, unlike many fats, increases HDL levels.	Look for cold-pressed, less refined oils that are packaged in dark glass containers. Keep oils in the refrigerator to keep them from going rancid.

Foods that Protect the Heart

Best Foods that Protect the Heart	Cardiovascular System Benefits	Comments
HERBS AND SPICES		
• Cayenne • Ginger • Garlic	Cayenne stimulates blood flow and strengthens the heart beat and metabolic rate. Ginger can lower cholesterol and decrease stickiness of platelets.	
OTHER		
• Beer • Chocolate • Coffee • Black tea • Wine	Black tea and red wine contain quercetin. Beer is rich in bioflavonoids from the fermented grains. Phenols in dark chocolate and red wine are antioxidant.	Caution: Caffeine and alcohol consumption can increase blood pressure levels. Consume in moderation. Not recommended during pregnancy and lactation.

Digestive System

Healthy Digestive System

The digestive system is responsible for mixing the food we eat and breaking it down into smaller molecules that our body can absorb and use. Digestion starts at the mouth with chewing and breaking carbohydrate molecules down with the aid of enzymes found in saliva. Food then travels down the esophagus into the stomach, where hydrochloric acid, also known as HCl, and digestive enzymes break down proteins and allow for the absorption of some substances. Most digestion and absorption of nutrients take place in the small intestine, with the help of the liver and gall bladder, which provide bile, and the pancreas, which provides digestive enzymes. Food molecules, such as monosaccharides (carbohydrate units), amino acids (protein units) and fatty acids, as well as vitamins, minerals and water are absorbed into the bloodstream and lymphatic system, while indigestible foods (mostly fiber) continue down to the large intestine and eventually get eliminated.

The entire digestive system is lined with mucous membranes. Mucous membranes act as a barrier and are responsible for mucous secretions that aid in the digestive process. A smooth muscle layer also exists in the entire digestive tract and is responsible for mixing and breaking food down, as well as propelling food downwards through the digestive tract.

How does yogurt help with digestion?

In addition to supplying the body with essential nutrients, yogurt has been scientifically shown to maintain good intestinal health. Daily consumption of as little as one serving (½ cup/125 mL or a 4-oz/125 g container) of live-culture (probiotic) yogurt tips the balance of helpful bacteria over harmful bacteria, and helps prevent intestinal conditions such as constipation, diarrhea, indigestion, gas and bloating, if they are due to a lack of beneficial bacteria. It is the beneficial bacteria or flora in the gut, which are always present or can be replaced by eating probiotic yogurt, that assist in the process of breaking food down and helping to eliminate the waste.

The elderly, in particular, benefit from the regular consumption of yogurt because, as people age, their hydrochloric stomach acid may decrease. Live-culture bacteria in yogurt steps in and replaces this necessary acid.

Yogurt is also a digestive aid because it is already partially broken down (or digested) before it is even consumed. This makes it a good food for most post-surgery and good for people with sensitive digestive tracts.

For babies and children suffering from diarrhea, yogurt has been shown to be effective at reducing their symptoms. Some people who have an intolerance to cow's milk may tolerate yogurt because the milk sugar (lactose) has been partially digested by the bacteria.

Digestive Problems

Heartburn, constipation, inflammatory bowel disease, colon cancer

Heartburn is one of the most common digestive complaints. It can be a symptom of gastric reflux, a hiatal hernia or a gastric or duodenal ulcer. Determining the cause of heartburn is important, as these conditions can be easily treated but can become serious if not attended to.

Another common indicator of suboptimal digestive function is constipation. Constipation occurs when bowel movements are infrequent or difficult, causing bloating, headaches or hemorrhoids, to name a few symptoms. Constipation can be caused by a lack of fiber or water in the diet, stress, or perhaps disease.

Constipation can be an indicator of other digestive system diseases. For example, constipation alternating with diarrhea can be one of the symptoms of irritable bowel syndrome (IBS). Other symptoms of IBS include abdominal pain and cramps, excess gas and bloating. IBS can be caused by sensitivity to foods and is often associated with emotional stress — and it can be extremely disabling.

Inflammatory bowel disease (IBD) includes two conditions with chronic inflammation of the bowels: Crohn's disease and ulcerative colitis. In these conditions, inflammation of the bowel can result in such symptoms as diarrhea, bleeding, cramping and a feeling of urgency. The cause of these conditions is not known. Consult a physician if you are suffering from any of the above symptoms.

The digestive system is also susceptible to cancer. Colon cancer is the second most common form of cancer, and one that can be easily prevented with a healthy lifestyle and regular bowel movements. Colon cancer is treatable, but early detection and treatment are crucial. If you experience a change in bowel habits, blood in the stool, unexplained weight loss or fatigue, consult your physician.

Optimizing Digestive Function

To protect the digestive system from disease and allow for optimal digestive function, we need to maintain healthy mucous membranes, and to heal them when necessary; create and maintain a healthy intestinal flora; eat a diet rich in fiber and antioxidants; drink plenty of water; eat fresh foods, which are rich in digestive enzymes, instead of frozen or prepared foods; and eliminate foods that irritate the bowel or cause inflammation. As the digestive system is closely linked with the nervous system, daily routines and stress-management techniques are also beneficial for digestive function.

Eat foods that create and maintain a healthy lining of the digestive tract

The lining of the digestive tract is responsible for choosing what is absorbed into the body and what gets eliminated, so it must be intact. The digestive process breaks food down into smaller molecules that are checked by the immune system as they are absorbed. If digestion is poor and food is not broken down properly, or the mucous membranes become increasingly permeable ("leaky gut"), molecules pass through the barrier in a larger form, and the immune system recognizes them as foreign invaders. This hypersensitivity of the immune system can create a number of symptoms that can manifest in any part of the body.

You can maintain the health of the digestive tract's lining by promoting repair of intestinal cells, reestablishing a healthy bacterial flora and decreasing inflammation. Foods such as cabbage are high in glutamine, an amino acid that helps regenerate and repair the cells of the digestive tract. Probiotics — the healthy bacteria that populate the intestines — and fiber help maintain a healthy intestinal environment and crowd out toxic bacteria. Fish oils and quercetin from apples and onions help decrease the inflammatory response, minimize damage to the digestive lining and dampen food sensitivity reactions.

Best foods
- Fish oils, whole grains (brown rice, rye, spelt, quinoa, millet)
- Fruits (apples, blueberries, blackberries, grapes)
- Vegetables (cabbage, onions, red bell peppers)
- Legumes (beans, peas, lentils)

Eat foods that create and maintain a healthy bacterial environment in the intestines

Friendly bacteria in our intestines are an important part of a healthy digestive system. They are responsible for crowding out pathogens and maintaining a beneficial acid-base balance (a balanced pH in the digestive tract is created by many factors, one being the production of lactic acid by "friendly bacteria,") that helps prevent infection from bacteria, viruses, yeast and parasites. Friendly bacteria optimize digestion by producing digestive enzymes. They also make B vitamins and vitamin K and protect against food allergies by maintaining a healthy immune system in the digestive tract.

When we eat a diet that is rich in processed foods and chemicals or take antibiotics to treat infection, the population of healthy bacteria is reduced. We can increase this by supplementing with probiotics and by eating foods that contain prebiotics. Prebiotics are vegetable fibers or complex sugars, which the healthy bacteria depend on for survival. These carbohydrate compounds, including fructooligosaccharides (FOS) are found in foods such as fruits, vegetables, whole grains and legumes.

Best foods
- Garlic, onions, asparagus, leeks, artichokes, probiotic yogurt

Why eat yogurt when taking antibiotics?

Yogurt has been shown to reverse the negative effects of antibiotics on the body. When drugs such as penicillin and tetracycline (and all other antibiotic drugs) are used to fight infection, they are proven to kill the beneficial flora (or bacteria) in the intestines, along with the harmful bacteria they are targeting. It is essential that the beneficial bacteria be reintroduced to the intestines, first because they are critical in helping the body digest and eliminate food, and second, and perhaps more importantly, fungus and mold will move into the void (and spread to other organs) if intestinal flora are not present in the intestines.

It is recommended that individuals who are taking antibiotics eat $1/2$ cup (125 mL) or a 4-oz (125 g) container of yogurt with every meal, in order to restore the intestinal flora that has been destroyed. Once the antibiotics are finished, eating one serving ($1/2$ cup/125 mL or a 4-oz/125 g container) of live-culture yogurt per day may be resumed as a healthy maintenance strategy.

Eat a diet rich in fiber and increase water intake

Fiber is the part of plant food that goes through the digestive tract undigested. It is necessary to clean the digestive tract by collecting dead cells and debris, and also helps prevent cholesterol and excess hormones from being reabsorbed back into the bloodstream. In general, both soluble and insoluble fibers help with these functions. Insoluble fiber is necessary to form bulk and stimulate the muscles of the digestive tract to move the bowels. Soluble fiber acts as a food source for friendly bacteria in the intestinal tract. Together with proper intake of water, all these factors help maintain a healthy digestive tract and protect against digestive system diseases, such as constipation, hemorrhoids and colon cancer. In fact, insufficient fiber contributes to a large percentage of digestive disorders. Fiber can come from many foods, such as whole grains, fruits and vegetables, nuts and seeds, and beans and other legumes. Most processed foods and animal products are devoid of fiber.

Best foods
- Whole grains (brown rice, rye, oats, millet, buckwheat, quinoa, spelt, whole wheat)
- Fruits (apples, pears, oranges, berries, peaches, dates, fresh or dried figs, prunes)
- Vegetables (carrots, celery, leafy greens and cruciferous vegetables, such as cabbage, broccoli, cauliflower)
- Seeds (sesame seeds, sunflower seeds, pumpkin seeds, flaxseeds)
- Nuts (almonds, hazelnuts, walnuts)
- Legumes (beans, lentils, peas, chickpeas, organic soybeans)

Eat foods that promote digestion

Digestion depends on different substances to break foods down, prepare them for absorption and help the body to utilize them. For example, starting at the mouth, salivary glands produce saliva, which can initiate the digestion of carbohydrates. Then hydrochloric acid (HCl) in the stomach helps dissolve food particles and activates other enzymes. Similarly, in the small intestine, digestive enzymes produced by the pancreas and bile from the liver and gall bladder help emulsify fats, break down carbohydrates, proteins and fats, and get them ready for absorption. See Top 10 Best Bets for foods that stimulate the release of saliva and enhance the production of HCl and the release of digestive enzymes and bile into the digestive tract. Foods high in enzymes (bananas, papaya, mangoes, pineapple) along with a nutritionally dense diet, can ensure healthy body functions.

Best foods
- Cider vinegar, bitter foods (dandelion greens and other bitter greens), lemon juice, "live" (sprouted) foods, bananas, pineapple, papaya, unpasteurized honey, sauerkraut, probiotic yogurt

Practice stress-management techniques and regular bowel habits

Conditions such as heartburn and irritable bowel syndrome (IBS) are closely linked with the nervous system. It is also helpful to establish a daily routine that includes a regular time for bowel elimination. This encourages daily bowel movements and decreases the incidence of constipation. Managing stress and following a daily routine can help maintain a healthy digestive system, increase the frequency of bowel movements and reduce the risk for colon cancer.

Best techniques
- Yoga, breathing exercises, daily bowel routine (in this case, an overall daily routine is helpful for stress management), regular bowel habits, counseling for emotional stress

Top 10 Best Bets for Digestive Health

1. **Cabbage:** Cabbage is rich in glutamine, an amino acid used by the intestinal cells as their principal fuel source. Glutamine helps the cells repair and regenerate themselves and prevents undigested foods from passing through the intestinal lining. Cabbage is also used to make sauerkraut through the process of fermentation. Sauerkraut helps populate the intestinal micro flora and contains digestive enzymes.

2. **Onions and garlic:** Onions are a source of quercetin, which helps decrease hypersensitivity in the intestines, and, in turn, helps to protect the lining of the digestive system from irritation and protect the body from food sensitivities. Because they contain a complex sugar (fructooligosaccharide), onions and garlic feed the healthy bacteria in our digestive systems. Garlic is a powerful antimicrobial that protects against harmful parasites, yeast infections, viruses and bacteria.

3. **Apples and apple cider vinegar:** Apples are high in pectin, a soluble fiber that absorbs 100 times its weight in water. Pectin from apples helps calm the intestinal tract during diarrhea and prevents constipation. Quercetin, a flavonoid found in apples, helps stabilize immune reactions and decrease inflammation and irritation of the digestive system.

   Apple cider vinegar helps increase production of hydrochloric acid (HCl) in the stomach. HCl helps break food particles down and activates other enzymes to digest proteins. As part of the immune system, HCl helps kill food pathogens before they reach the rest of the digestive system.

4. **Probiotic yogurt:** Yogurt that contains beneficial, probiotic bacteria — friendly bacteria in addition to *Lactobacillus delbrueckii* (subspecies *bulgaricus) and Streptococcus lactis* — is proven to bolster and replace naturally-occurring friendly

bacteria in the gut. Since these bacteria help in the process of digestion, they are essential for healthy digestive processes. Daily consumption of one to three servings of probiotic yogurt can greatly improve digestion, if the problem stems from a diminishing number or lack of these beneficial flora in the gut.

⑤ Fennel and caraway seeds: Fennel and caraway seeds help stimulate digestion and appetite. In Asian countries, they are also commonly chewed after a meal to relieve bloating, flatulence and colic, and even to freshen the breath.

⑥ Peppermint: Peppermint is one of the most effective digestive herbs. It helps relax the stomach and intestines when they suffer from cramping and spasms, and it helps relieve nausea. This also means that peppermint can relax the esophageal sphincter. When relaxed, the sphincter can open and food and stomach acids from the stomach can travel upward to the esophagus and cause symptoms of heartburn. If you suffer from gastric reflux, avoid peppermint.

⑦ Dandelion greens and other bitter greens: Dandelion greens and other bitter greens are indispensable to optimize digestion. These bitter foods help stimulate the release of bile from the gall bladder and digestive enzymes from the pancreas, enhancing digestive function. The greens can be eaten in a salad to increase appetite before the main course of a meal.

⑧ Pineapple and papaya: Pineapple and papaya contain bromelain and papain, digestive enzymes that can complement the enzymes already produced by the body. These enzymes help break foods down in the digestive tract and can decrease symptoms of food sensitivities, as well as reduce bloating and flatulence after a meal.

⑨ Brown rice: Brown rice and other whole grains are a source of insoluble fiber. Insoluble fiber increases bulk in the stool and helps prevent constipation and protect against colon cancer. Brown rice is an ideal food for people who suffer from IBS, IBD or constipation, in part because, unlike wheat, rye and spelt, brown rice is a gluten-free grain that does not seem to cause intestinal irritation or allergic reactions in patients with gluten sensitivity. In addition, brown rice contains phytic acid, which seems to protect against colon cancer.

⑩ Beans and other legumes: Beans and other legumes are an excellent source of soluble fiber. Soluble fiber is a food source for friendly bacteria in the intestines, which then produce short chain fatty acids. These fatty acids create an optimal pH balance in the digestive tract and protect the lining of the digestive tract against colon cancer.

Foods that Protect the Digestive System

Best Foods for Protecting the Digestive System	Digestive System Benefits	Comments
FRUITS		
Citrus: • Oranges • Mandarins • Lemons • Grapefruit • Kiwifruit • Strawberries	Contain pectin and other soluble fiber, which provide food for healthy intestinal bacteria and protect against constipation and other digestive diseases.	Lemon juice can increase the release of HCl, helping with protection against pathogens, break down of proteins and absorption of nutrients.
• Apricots • Peaches • Pears • Apples	Contain pectin and other soluble fiber that prevent constipation and colon cancer. Apples contain quercetin, which helps decrease irritability in the digestive tract.	Most fruits and vegetables contain a mixture of soluble and insoluble fibers.
• Fresh or dried figs • Prunes	Help increase bowel frequency and prevent bowel toxicity and colon cancer.	Prunes are high in fiber; prune juice is not. (Prune juice is a natural laxative, but it does not contain fiber and does not have all the other benefits of a high-fiber food like prunes.)
Tropical fruits: • Bananas • Pineapple • Papaya	These tropical fruits are loaded with natural digestive enzymes that enhance the break down of foods in the digestive tract.	Take digestive tropical fruit drinks one hour before a meal.
Berries: • Blueberries • Blackberries • Grapes	Berries contain flavonoids, which help maintain the health of the lining in the digestive tract.	
VEGETABLES		
Green: • Spinach • Swiss chard • Asparagus • Dandelion greens • Endive • Other dark leafy greens	Dandelion greens and other bitter greens help improve digestion by stimulating the release of bile and digestive enzymes.	Raw foods are more difficult to digest. Steaming, covered, or sautéing briskly can make foods easier to digest without much loss of nutritive value.
Cruciferous Family: • Broccoli • Cabbage • Sauerkraut • Cauliflower	Sauerkraut contains healthy intestinal bacteria and digestive enzymes. Cabbage contains glutamine - an energy source for intestinal cells - and helps prevent a "leaky gut."	Sauerkraut is made of finely sliced cabbage that is fermented by various lactic acid bacteria, including Lactobacillus.
Allium Family: • Garlic • Onions	Garlic, onions and asparagus contain fructooligosaccharides (FOS) or prebiotics. Onions contain quercetin, which helps decrease intestinal irritability and immune system hypersensitivity.	Garlic is an important antimicrobial for all the systems and fights against bacteria, viruses, yeast and parasites.

Foods that Protect the Digestive System

Best Foods for Protecting the Digestive System	Digestive System Benefits	Comments
YOGURT		
• Plain, low-fat yogurt	Eating probiotic yogurt with every meal every day will help in the digestion of other foods.	See page 69 for using yogurt to treat digestive problems.
LEGUMES		
• Beans • Organic soybeans • Lentils • Peas • Chickpeas	Legumes are a source of soluble fiber, which feeds healthy intestinal bacteria.	Soaking beans for 8 hours before cooking makes them easier to digest.
WHOLE GRAINS		
• Oats (soluble fiber) • Brown rice • Pot Barley • Buckwheat • Quinoa • Whole wheat • Spelt • Rye	Whole grains are a source of insoluble fiber; they increase bulk and help prevent constipation. Contain phytic acid, which protects against colon cancer.	Whole grains containing gluten can be irritating to people with IBS, and cannot be tolerated by people with Crohn's disease.
NUTS AND SEEDS		
Nuts: • Almonds • Brazil nuts • Walnuts • Hazelnuts • Pine nuts	Nuts contain fiber. Brazil nuts are high in selenium, an antioxidant that helps protect against colon cancer.	
Seeds: • Flaxseeds • Sesame seeds • Sunflower seeds • Pumpkin seeds	Flaxseeds are high in omega-3 fatty acids, which help decrease inflammation, and lignins, an insoluble fiber that creates bulk for the stool and prevents constipation.	Lignins in flaxseeds also help maintain optimal levels of estrogen in the body. Flaxseeds must be freshly ground to avoid rancidity and maximize absorption and digestion.
FATS AND OILS		
Cold-pressed oils: • Extra virgin olive oil • Grapeseed oil • Flaxseed oil • Avocados	Oils are necessary for the absorption of fat-soluble vitamins A, E, D and K.	Adding a capsule of vitamin E into your oil container helps prevent oxidation and rancidity.
HERBS AND SPICES		
• Cayenne • Turmeric • Coriander • Fennel • Peppermint	These herbs and spices enhance digestion, help flush toxins out of the body and help improve absorption and assimilation of nutrients. Ginger can stimulate digestion.	Eat or make tea with ginger. Take a slice of fresh ginger 30 to 60 minutes before a meal for optimal digestion.

A Note about Food Combining

One short-term method of relieving indigestion, flatulence, fatigue, food allergies and, in some cases, inflammatory bowel and peptic ulcer, is to follow a discipline of eating certain foods in a set order. This order is as follows:

Fruits Alone

Fruits require the least time and energy for the body to digest and because of this it is recommended that fruit be eaten before a meal or at least two hours after a meal. Fruits are best taken alone at breakfast or as small, between-meal snacks.

Proteins with Non-starchy Vegetables

Protein foods (fish, eggs, nuts, seeds, dairy products, soy products) take the longest and use up the most of the body's effort to digest. When fruit or starchy vegetables are eaten before or with proteins, they break down and ferment long before the proteins are digested. This causes the digestive problems listed earlier. It is best to eat protein foods with non-starchy vegetables (leafy greens, asparagus, broccoli, cabbage, celery, cucumber, onion, sweet bell peppers, sea vegetables, tomatoes, zucchini).

Whole Grains with Non-starchy Vegetables

Whole grains and non-starchy vegetables are complex carbohydrates that break down at about the same rate, providing the body with a slow and steady supply of starches and sugars for fuel. If eaten together, they are best without fruit or protein.

Starchy Vegetables, Legumes and Refined Grains in Small Amounts, Alone

Squash, legumes, pasta, refined grains, beets, parsnips, carrots, sweet potatoes and pumpkin are starchy carbohydrate foods that break down faster than protein foods and other carbohydrates but not as quickly as fruits. It is recommended that starchy carbohydrates be eaten in small amounts, away from other foods.

Endocrine System

Healthy Endocrine System

The endocrine system consists of endocrine glands and the hormones produced by these glands, which work together to serve as one of the body's main control systems. Hormones are chemicals that carry messages through the blood. To do this, hormones travel from the endocrine glands in which they are produced to the target cells where they will perform their function. For example, the thyroid gland produces and secretes thyroid hormones (thyroxine or T4, and triiodothyronine or T3), which control the body's metabolic rate. The adrenal glands, located on top of the kidneys, secrete a number of hormones, including cortisol, which is released in response to stress and can help balance the immune system. Epinephrine, also known as adrenaline, and norepinephrine are also released in response to stress and can have an effect similar to that of sympathetic nerves (the "fight or flight" response).

Some organs have a function in more than one body system. For example, the pancreas, which secretes digestive enzymes as part of the digestive system, also performs an endocrine function by releasing the insulin and glucagon responsible for balancing blood sugar.

The reproductive organs are also part of the endocrine system. In females, the ovaries manage the functioning, growth and development of the female reproductive system, including the breasts, via hormones such as estrogen and progesterone. In males, the testes produce testosterone, which is responsible for the functioning, growth and development of the male reproductive system.

The hypothalamus in the brain and the pituitary gland just below it control many of these glands through hormones they secrete. Hormonal feedback can signal to these glands to produce more or less hormones that help keep the body's functions in balance.

Many other glands and organs are part of the endocrine system and no doubt many others remain to be discovered.

Endocrine Disorders

Hormone imbalance, hyperthyroidism, hypothyroidism, diabetes

Most endocrine disorders occur when too much or too little of a hormone is produced by an endocrine gland, when the target cell exerts a reduced response, or in some cases, when our body cannot properly eliminate excess hormones.

Hyperthyroidism is a condition where the thyroid gland secretes too much of the thyroid hormone, creating symptoms of an increased metabolic rate. On the other hand, in hypothyroidism, there is too little of the active thyroid hormone, giving rise to such symptoms as fatigue, weight gain, cold intolerance and other signs of low metabolic function. Hypothyroidism can be caused by mineral deficiencies, as minerals are essential to produce and activate the thyroid hormone, or by a destruction of thyroid cells due to inflammatory disease.

Adrenal glands produce cortisol, which has potent anti-inflammatory and immunosuppressive properties important for normal immune responses. However, under constant stress, cortisol is overproduced and the body's immune system can be suppressed, leading to an increased risk of infections. Also, as part of the blood glucose-regulating system, increased cortisol and epinephrine production due to chronic stress can lead to higher blood glucose and insulin levels and subsequent weight gain.

In Type 1 diabetes, the pancreas does not produce enough insulin, whereas in Type 2 diabetes, the target cells resist insulin. In both cases, glucose cannot enter the cells and there is an elevation of blood sugar levels that can lead to serious complications. For people with diabetes, diet is critically important to help restore insulin sensitivity, control blood sugar levels and prevent complications.

In the reproductive system, an excess of estrogen that is unbalanced by progesterone can be linked with many female disorders, such as menstrual difficulties, endometriosis, fibrocystic breasts, infertility and breast cancer. Estrogen and progesterone balance is affected by many factors, including the use of oral contraceptives and hormone replacement therapy, diet and chemicals in food and the environment. In males, testosterone is released from the testes and converted into the hormone dihydrotestosterone (DHT), which stimulates the synthesis and growth of prostate cells. High levels of DHT can cause benign prostatic hyperplasia or prostate cancer.

What makes the endocrine system so complex is that most times hormones act in concert with one another to produce their physiologic effects, and the improper function of one can deeply affect the function of others.

Optimizing Endocrine Function

Eat a diet rich in complex carbohydrates

The glycemic index (GI) is a dietary guide that ranks foods based on how they affect blood sugar levels. It is often used by people with diabetes to help them choose foods that do not increase blood sugar levels rapidly. Foods with a high GI rating increase blood sugar levels at a fast rate, which an individual with too little insulin (Type 1 diabetes) or insulin-resistant cells (Type 2 diabetes) may not be able to tolerate. In general, simple carbohydrates, found in foods such as pasta, breads and crackers made with refined flours, as well as in soft drinks and candy, have a high GI. Foods that contain complex carbohydrates, fat and proteins have a low GI and will slow the absorption of sugar into the bloodstream. The GI should be utilized

with other tools, as it does not take into consideration the fat content or the type of fat a food contains.

In particular, the fiber contained in complex carbohydrates is capable of slowing down the digestion and absorption of blood sugar and increasing insulin sensitivity, therefore giving it a low score on the GI scale. Water-soluble fiber is the most beneficial type for blood sugar control. Fruits and legumes are the best sources of water-soluble fiber. Soluble and insoluble fibers also encourage regular bowel movements, which helps eliminate excess estrogen from the body and prevent an estrogen/progesterone imbalance and breast cancer.

Best foods
- Whole grains (oats, brown rice, barley, quinoa, spelt, kamut, whole wheat)
- Legumes (beans, soybeans, chickpeas, lentils)
- Fruits (pears, apples, oranges, plums)
- All vegetables except white potatoes and parsnips
- Nuts and seeds (almonds, cashews, walnuts, sesame seeds, sunflower seeds, pumpkin seeds, ground flaxseeds)

Eat a diet rich in essential fatty acids
Essential fatty acids are precursors to all hormones and therefore constitute an indispensable part of a diet that promotes a healthy endocrine system.

Omega-3 fatty acids are part of cell membranes, where insulin receptors are located. Insulin receptors become more responsive to insulin when there are more omega-3 fatty acids in the cell membrane. Therefore, omega-3 fatty acids can help prevent insulin resistance and diabetes.

Best foods
- Fish oils (wild salmon, mackerel, albacore tuna, sardines, herring), flaxseed oil, soy oil, hempseed oil, canola oil, walnuts

Eat foods rich in minerals

Minerals are important in every aspect of endocrine function. For example, iodine is a component of thyroid hormones T4 and T3, and it must be obtained from the diet. T4 and some T3 are produced and released by the thyroid gland and travel to tissues where these hormones act in the body. Within the cell, T4 is converted to T3, the most active form. This conversion depends on the minerals zinc, copper and selenium.

Chromium, vanadium, manganese and zinc are essential for regulating blood sugar, either by increasing the production of insulin, by increasing the target cell's sensitivity to insulin or by acting on enzyme systems of glucose metabolism. That is why these minerals are important in the prevention of diabetes.

Minerals such as selenium and manganese are antioxidants, prevent damage to the cell's DNA and decrease the risk of cancer.

Best foods
- Zinc: black-eyed peas, pumpkin seeds, tofu, wheat germ
- Copper: nuts, legumes, potatoes, vegetables, cereal grains (oats and wheat)
- Selenium: Brazil nuts, yeast, whole grains
- Chromium: brewer's yeast, grains, some beers
- Vanadium: cereal grains, parsley, mushrooms, corn, soy foods
- Manganese: nuts, wheat germ, wheat bran, leafy green vegetables, beet tops, pineapple, seeds
- Iodine: iodized salt, sea vegetables (kelp), vegetables grown in iodine-rich soil

Learn ways of coping with stress

When a person suffers from stress, cortisol and adrenaline are released from the adrenal glands. These adrenal hormones can then trigger the pancreas to release glucagon, which is responsible for increasing blood sugar levels when the body demands more sugar to be available as an energy source. This usually happens when a person has not eaten in a while or in stress situations ("fight or flight" response) by a process called glycolysis, where stored glycogen is broken down into glucose molecules and released into the blood stream. This response is ideal during a state of crisis, but can be detrimental to the endocrine system over a long period. It is important to keep in mind that sugar and caffeine tend to stimulate the adrenal glands and it is best to consume these products in moderation, especially at times of high stress.

Techniques that induce a relaxation response and prevent the release of excess stress hormones from the adrenal glands can be beneficial.

Best methods
- Daily routine, meditation, prayer, breathing exercises, physical exercise, counseling

Exercise

The benefits of exercise for the endocrine system cannot be overstated. Exercise can decrease insulin resistance, and it increases the concentration of chromium in the tissues, helping the body maintain normal blood sugar levels. Exercise can help increase metabolic rate, energy and endurance, and for many people it helps achieve a proper body weight. Maintaining an ideal body weight is an important factor for prevention of diabetes. Exercise can help stimulate blood and lymphatic circulation, essential for the transport of hormones and elimination of excess hormones. Exercise also reduces secretions of stress hormones from the adrenal glands in response to psychological stress.

Best exercises
- Weight lifting, brisk walking, jogging, bicycling, swimming, dancing, yoga, racquet sports (such as tennis), team sports

Top 10 Best Bets for Endocrine Health

1 **Cruciferous vegetables:** Cruciferous vegetables, such as broccoli, cauliflower, kale, Brussels sprouts and bok choy contain a phytochemical called indole-3-carbinol, which induces the break down of estrogen into its harmless metabolites, decreasing the risk for breast cancer.

2 **Sea vegetables:** Sea vegetables, such as nori, arame, kelp, dulse and kombu, contain iodine, an essential mineral that is needed for the production of thyroid hormones. As part of thyroid hormones, iodine helps increase metabolism and reduce the risk of symptoms of hypothyroidism.

3 **Pumpkin seeds:** Pumpkin seeds are high in zinc, a mineral essential for the normal function of the male reproductive system. Zinc is associated with proper testosterone levels, sperm production and sperm motility. Maintaining adequate levels of zinc may help prevent male infertility. Eat a handful of raw pumpkin seeds daily.

4 **Stevia:** Stevia is an extract from the plant *Stevia rebaudiana*. The extract has 200 times the sweetness of sugar and contains no calories. It is a safe alternative for people with diabetes as it does not raise blood sugar levels and has glucose-lowering properties. Stevia extract can be used to sweeten foods and drinks. (See also Herbs, page 159)

5 **Soy foods:** Soybeans contain phytoestrogens, chemicals that are plant-based and similar in structure to estrogen. Although the research is conflicting and inconclusive, the phytoestrogens found in soy (genistein and daidzein), act like weak estrogens and may help block estrogen's cancer promoting effect. Soybeans and soy foods should only be consumed if they are organic and non genetically modified.

6 **Onions and garlic:** Onions and garlic have blood sugar-regulating properties. They contain sulfur, which aids in liver detoxification and elimination of excess hormones. Garlic is also high in selenium, a potent antioxidant that can help prevent cancer.

7 **Ground flaxseeds:** Ground flaxseeds are a source of omega-3 fatty acids and phytoestrogens. Lignins, the phytoestrogens found in flaxseeds, stand out in their ability to regulate the menstrual cycle in women. They have been shown to be mildly estrogenic or anti-estrogenic, depending on the body's need to balance hormones.

8 **Brewer's yeast:** Brewer's yeast is the dried, powdered form of the Saccharomyces cerevisiae fungus used in the brewing process. It is the highest source of chromium, a mineral that works in conjunction with insulin to promote the uptake of glucose by the target cells. For this reason, chromium is essential for blood sugar regulation and diabetes prevention.

9 **Citrus fruits:** Citrus fruits are a rich source of vitamin C. Vitamin C is stored in high concentration in the adrenal glands and helps in the production of adrenal hormones. In addition, vitamin C increases insulin's response to sugar, thus helping lower blood sugar levels. Vitamin C is also an antioxidant that can help prevent breast and prostate cancer.

10 **Spinach:** Spinach is one of the best sources of alpha-lipoic acid, a vitamin-like nutrient that is very important for glucose metabolism and prevention of diabetes. Alpha-lipoic acid is also an antioxidant that helps prevent free-radical damage and decreases the risk of cancer. Spinach is also a source of many minerals that can be beneficial for endocrine function.

Foods that Protect the Endocrine System

Best Foods for Protecting the Endocrine System	Endocrine System Benefits	Comments
FRUITS		
Citrus: • Oranges • Mandarins • Lemons • Grapefruit • Kiwifruit • Strawberries	Contain soluble fiber, which helps control blood sugar levels. Contain vitamin C and bioflavonoids, antioxidants that can help reduce the risk of cancer. Vitamin C in particular is essential for the production of stress hormones by the adrenal glands.	Fructose, the natural sugar found in fruits, is first absorbed in the digestive tract and then has to be converted into glucose, so it does not increase blood sugar levels as rapidly as other simple sugars obtained from the diet.
• Apricots • Peaches • Pears • Apples	Contain pectin and other soluble fiber, the most beneficial type of fiber for the control of blood sugar levels.	Most fruits and vegetables contain a mixture of soluble and insoluble fibers and can slow down the absorption of sugar.
Berries and grapes: • Blueberries • Blackberries • Raspberries • Grapes	Berries and grapes are a rich source of bioflavonoids. These are antioxidants and help prevent breast and prostate cancer.	Bioflavonoids help the body use vitamin C. They are found in highest concentration in the skin or peel of fruits and vegetables.
VEGETABLES		
Green: • Spinach • Swiss chard • Dandelion greens	Rich in many minerals needed for optimal endocrine function, including iodine, selenium and manganese. Spinach is a source of alpha-lipoic acid, an important nutrient for glucose metabolism.	
Red Nightshades: • Bell peppers • Tomatoes	Tomatoes are the best source of lycopene, a strong antioxidant that helps protect cells against damage and plays an important role in cancer prevention.	Lycopene is a carotene that gives tomatoes their deep red color.
Cruciferous Family: • Broccoli • Cabbage • Sauerkraut • Cauliflower • Kale • Bok choy	Cruciferous vegetables contain indole-3-carbinol, a chemical that helps break down estrogen into its harmless metabolites.	Cooking destroys indoles, so eat these foods raw or lightly steamed.
Sea Vegetables: • Nori • Arame • Kelp • Dulse • Kombu	Contain minerals, including iodine, calcium and iron. Iodine is needed for the production of thyroid hormones.	Caution: Do not consume sea vegetables if you have a hyperthyroid condition. Also, hijiki may contain high levels of inorganic arsenic, a carcinogen, and food safety agencies in many countries, including Canada and Britain, have cautioned against its consumption.
Allium Family: • Garlic • Onions	Garlic and onions can help regulate blood sugar levels.	

Foods that Protect the Endocrine System

Best Foods for Protecting the Endocrine System	Endocrine System Benefits	Comments
LEGUMES		
• Beans (kidney, adzuki, mung) • Lentils • Peas (black-eyed) • Chickpeas	Legumes are a source of soluble fiber, which helps eliminate excess estrogen through the bowels. Black-eyed peas and tofu are rich sources of zinc, essential for endocrine system function.	Consult with your naturopathic doctor or nutritionist before consuming large amounts of soy.
WHOLE GRAINS		
• Whole oats • Brown rice • Pot Barley • Buckwheat • Quinoa • Whole wheat • Spelt • Rye	Barley is the grain with the lowest glycemic index (GI) rating, which means it is highly efficient at slowing the rate at which sugar is absorbed into the blood stream.	Whole grains score lower in the GI scale in comparison to refined carbohydrates.
NUTS AND SEEDS		
Nuts: • Almonds • Brazil nuts • Walnuts • Hazelnuts • Pine nuts	Nuts contain fiber, which helps control blood sugar levels. Nuts are high in minerals, such as zinc and manganese, essential for the functioning of the endocrine system.	Try natural nut butters without added hydrogenated oils, sugar or salt.
Seeds: • Flaxseeds • Sesame seeds • Sunflower seeds • Pumpkin seeds	Seeds are high in fiber and unsaturated fats, which help control blood sugar levels. Sesame seeds are a source of iodine, a component of thyroid hormones. Pumpkin seeds are high in zinc, needed for all aspects of insulin metabolism and male reproductive system.	Try natural seed butters without added hydrogenated oils, sugar or salt.
FATS AND OILS		
Cold-pressed oils: • Flaxseed oil • Soybean oil • Hempseed oil • Canola oil • Avocados	Flaxseed and hempseed oils are rich sources of omega-3 fatty acids, necessary for the production of all hormones.	Do not cook with flaxseed oil (or any of the oils listed at the left), but use them unheated, in small amounts with foods such as cooked vegetables, salads, beans, grains or smoothies.
HERBS AND SPICES		
• Turmeric • Sage	Turmeric has antioxidant and antitumor activity, helping prevent against cancer. Sage balances endocrine glands.	Add turmeric to stir-fries, soups or curry dishes. Caution: Sage should not be consumed during pregnancy. Sage contains steroid-like factors and can encourage miscarriage.
• Brewer's yeast	Best source of chromium, a mineral that works closely with insulin and helps increase insulin sensitivity, reducing the risk of diabetes.	Do not confuse brewer's yeast with baking yeast or nutritional yeast.

Immune System

Healthy Immune System

The immune system consists of a complex collection of cells found throughout the body. These cells are responsible for protecting the body against infection, as well as for constant surveillance and destruction of the cancer cells.

The skin and mucous membranes, along with chemical substances like mucous, tears and stomach acid, are also an important part of the immune system, acting as front-line barriers that prevent foreign materials and pathogenic organisms from entering and harming the body.

When the immune system does not work optimally, we see an increased risk for infections and cancers, as well as the development of allergies and inflammatory disease.

Support and enhancement of the immune system through consumption of whole foods, proper intake of water, regular moderate exercise and mental relaxation can increase the body's resistance to colds, flus and cancers, and keep allergies and inflammation in check.

Will yogurt boost your immune response?

Studies on both laboratory animals and humans confirm that a daily serving of live-culture yogurt boosts the body's immune response to viruses, yeasts infections and parasites.

Immune System Disorders

Frequent and chronic infections, cancer, inflammation, allergies

Frequent and chronic infections may include anything from a common cold, flu, ear infections and urinary tract infections to more serious illnesses, such as herpes virus infections, bronchitis and pneumonia. Viruses, bacteria, fungi and parasites can all cause infections, especially when they do not meet adequate resistance from a weakened immune system.

Similarly, cancer risk increases when there is damage to a cell's DNA and the immune system's DNA repair or cancer surveillance systems are not functioning at an optimal level. DNA can be damaged by free radicals produced inside the body or by elements from the external environment, such as chemicals, radiation or viruses.

Another way the body defends itself is through inflammation. Inflammation is a normal immune system response responsible for destroying invaders or setting the stage for tissue repair. When the immune system is out of control, inflammation can become chronic and cause pain and damage body tissues.

Allergies are the body's exaggerated response to foreign invaders. This reaction is usually a manifestation of a leaky gut (an increase in permeability of the lining of the digestive tract, which allows undigested food particles to enter the bloodstream and be recognized as foreign invaders or antigens — see Digestive System, page 69), and/or excessive allergens overtaxing the immune system. Maintaining a whole foods diet can have a profound effect on the management of allergies.

Optimizing the Immune System

To optimize the functioning of the immune system, we need to choose foods that increase antioxidant levels, boost cellular immunity and enhance mucous membrane integrity, maintain proper levels of stomach acid and other body secretions, and stabilize immune reactions.

Eat five to nine servings of fruit and vegetables daily

Antioxidants in fruit and vegetables, nuts, seeds and whole grains act as a defense mechanism against free radicals by collecting the free electron that floats outside some oxygen-containing molecules. This action makes the molecule more stable and prevents it from damaging the cell's DNA. Beta-carotene, lycopene and other carotenoids, vitamin E, vitamin C, selenium and glutathione are some of the best antioxidants we can find in our foods. Many of these substances have antihistamine properties (vitamin C) and tumor destruction abilities (selenium). Studies also show that carotenoids can boost immune cells. Green tea is also an excellent antioxidant with antimicrobial properties.

Best foods
- Beta-carotene, lycopene and other carotenoids: carrots, tomatoes, red and orange bell peppers, sweet potatoes, pumpkin and other winter squashes, kale, spinach, apricots, mango
- Vitamin E: wheat germ, almonds, sunflower seeds, cooked organic soybeans
- Vitamin C: oranges, strawberries, kiwifruit, red bell peppers, sweet potatoes, broccoli, kale
- Selenium: Brazil nuts, garlic, barley, brown rice, oatmeal, tofu
- Glutathione: watermelon, avocados, cruciferous vegetables

Increase foods that are high in lean protein

The body uses amino acids, the building blocks of protein, to assemble immune cells and immunoglobulins responsible for fighting infections. These building blocks are also essential for skin and mucous membrane integrity and as biological enzymes. Enzymes are needed for chemical reactions in the body, including antioxidant and detoxification systems.

Best foods
- Legumes (beans, peas, lentils, organic soybeans)
- Nuts and seeds (ground flaxseed, sesame seeds, sunflower seeds, almonds, cashews)
- Fresh fish

In particular, soy foods, which are rich in protein, are also high in phytoestrogens, plant derived estrogens that may protect against some cancers by blocking estrogen's cancer-promoting effect. (See Caution, page 88.)

Best foods
- Organically, non-genetically modified soybeans, tofu, soy milk

Increase unsaturated fats in your diet

Reducing trans-fats and saturated fats can boost immune function because these fats appear to impair the immune system. Omega-3 and omega-6 polyunsaturated fatty acids are anti-inflammatory (omega-3) and help protect against cancer. They also help with the absorption of fat-soluble vitamins, such as vitamins A and E. Phytosterols, or plant-based oils, also help reduce inflammation. Of particular benefit are sterols and sterolins, which can be found in abundance in nuts and seeds.

Best foods
- Avocados, olives and extra virgin olive oil, nuts and seeds (especially flaxseeds and flaxseed oil), fresh fatty fish (salmon, halibut, sardines)

Learn stress-management techniques and keep stress levels low

When our body is exposed to constant high levels of stress, our adrenal glands produce higher levels of the hormone cortisol. Cortisol is the body's natural corticosteroid, which in normal amounts helps keep allergies and inflammation under control. At high levels, however, cortisol is an immune suppressant, causing the body to have a reduced ability to fight infections.

Best techniques
- Regular moderate exercise, daily relaxation techniques, deep breathing, daily routine, rest

Top 10 Best Bets for Immune Health

1 Soy foods: High in protein, complex carbohydrates and phytonutrients, organic, non-genetically modified soy products are a favorite food for disease prevention. Although the research is conflicting and inconclusive, the soy phytoestrogens, genistein and daidzein may protect women against some forms of cancer by blocking estrogen receptors. Some studies show that a diet rich in phytoestrogens may also reduce the risk of prostate cancer in men. Look for organic, non-genetically modified soybeans and soy foods. (See Caution, page 88)

2 Cruciferous vegetables: Broccoli, cauliflower, cabbage, Brussels sprouts, kale and collard greens are part of the cruciferous, or Brassica, family. These are a favorite because they provide a wide range of nutrients, including indoles. Indole-3-carbinol has the ability to convert a harmful estrogen molecule into its non-harmful metabolites, thereby protecting against some forms of cancer.

3 Flaxseed oil: Flaxseed oil is an excellent choice because it is one of the few sources rich in omega-3 polyunsaturated fatty acids. Polyunsaturated fatty acids from flaxseed oil are converted to EPA (eicosapentaenoic acid), the active molecule also found in fish oils, which acts to inhibit the inflammatory cascade. Studies show that using flaxseed oil in foods reduces the substances that contribute to inflammation. So, add

flaxseed oil to salads and soups or blend a small amount in smoothies in the morning. Remember not to heat flaxseed oil, and keep it refrigerated in a dark bottle to prevent rancidity.

4 Shiitake mushrooms: Time and time again, shiitake mushrooms have been reported to have cancer-preventing properties. Mycochemicals, the active constituents in shiitake mushrooms, may stop the growth of tumors by suggesting a programmed death to the individual cancer cells.

5 Tomatoes: Lycopene, found abundantly in tomatoes, plays a crucial role as an antioxidant in our bodies, providing protection against some forms of cancer (including lung and prostate) and boosting the immune system. Lycopene is also found in tomato juice and pizza sauce. In fact, processed and cooked tomato products contain a more bioavailable form of lycopene than do raw tomatoes.

6 Avocados: This simply delicious fruit — among the most studied and documented foods — proves to be one of the best in providing symptom relief for patients with osteoarthritis. Avocados are high in the antioxidant glutathione and rich in monounsaturated fats.

7 Brown rice: Rice is a staple of the diet in Asia, where the incidence of breast and colon cancer is below that of the Western world. Rice can offer protection against cancer, including breast and colon cancers, when eaten unprocessed instead of in its white form. Brown rice is also extraordinary in that it has low allergenic potential when compared to other grains. This makes it less of a burden for our immune system, which is overtaxed by many other allergens and pollutants.

8 Blueberries: Blueberries are a rich source of anthocyanins, which destroy free radicals in the body. In fact, studies put blueberries at the top of the list of best antioxidant foods, especially on the basis of typical serving sizes.

9 Green tea: Polyphenols in green tea have significant antioxidant, anti-inflammatory and antimicrobial properties. Even with moderate consumption (2 cups/500 mL per day), green tea has the ability to protect against oxidative damage of the DNA in the cells, lowering the risk of cancer.

10 Pumpkin seeds: Pumpkin seeds are high in zinc, a mineral that boosts immunity, protects against free radicals and is needed for wound repair. Zinc helps prevent recurrent infections, and reduce the duration of cold symptoms. Pumpkin seed oil can also be used to destroy parasites in the intestinal tract.

Foods that Enhance the Immune System

Best Foods for Enhancing Immune System	Immune System Benefits	Comments
FRUITS		
Citrus: • Oranges • Mandarin • Lemons • Grapefruit	Rich in vitamin C and bioflavonoids, which are antioxidants and protect against cancer.	Whole fruit is best; otherwise, use freshly squeezed juices. Caution: Grapefruit juice can interfere with some medications.
Orange/Yellow: • Mangoes • Apricots • Peaches	Contain carotenoids and vitamin C, which are antioxidants. Enhance immune system function.	Choose locally grown fruits when possible.
Blue/Purple: • Blueberries and other berries • Purple grapes • Plums	Contain anthocyanins, which destroy free radicals.	Blueberry season runs from May though September; otherwise, choose frozen ones to use in your cooking.
VEGETABLES		
Red Nightshades: • Tomatoes • Red bell peppers	Rich in the antioxidant lycopene. High in beta-carotene, which has immune cell-boosting properties.	Lycopene is fat-soluble and must be eaten with a fat in order to be absorbed.
Orange/Yellow: • Carrots • Yams • Sweet potatoes • Pumpkin and other winter squashes	Contain carotenoids rich in antioxidants and support the immune system.	Eat carrots lightly steamed for better nutrient absorption.
Green: • Spinach • Swiss chard • Asparagus • Dandelion greens • Other dark leafy greens	Contain folic acid, essential for healthy cell reproduction and genetic material (DNA) replication.	1 cup (250 mL) of leafy vegetables is 1 serving.

Foods that Enhance the Immune System

Best Foods for Enhancing Immune System	Immune System Benefits	Comments
VEGETABLES (CONTINUED)		
Cruciferous Family: • Broccoli • Cauliflower • Brussels sprouts • Cabbage • Kale • Collard greens	Contain glutathione, a powerful antioxidant. Contain indoles, which eliminate excess estrogens and carcinogens, helping in cancer prevention.	Eat raw or lightly steamed.
Allium Family: • Garlic • Onions and chives	Contain allyl sulfides, which destroy cancer cells and support immune function. Contain antimicrobial properties.	Use garlic and onions daily in your cooking, raw or cooked.
Mushrooms: • Shiitake • Maitake • Enoki	Powerful immune-boosting and antiviral properties.	Enjoy them in soups and salads. Can be found dried. Rehydrate them in boiling water and keep the soaking liquid for a rich and nutritious soup.
LEGUMES		
• Beans • Organic soybeans • Lentils • Peas • Chickpeas	Beans are high in protein, soluble fiber and complex carbohydrates. Soybeans contain phytoestrogens, plant-derived estrogens that may protect against some cancers.	Soy products include tofu, tempeh, organic soybeans and soy milk. Use dried peas and beans in soups, salads and dips. Must be soaked before cooking.
WHOLE GRAINS		
• Brown rice • Whole oats • Barley	Whole grains are important for their B vitamin content. Many contain high amounts of the antioxidant selenium. Brown rice seems to be less allergenic than other grains.	Choose whole grains rather than refined products and flours. The hull, removed during processing, contains most of the nutrients.
NUTS AND SEEDS		
Nuts and nut butters: • Brazil nuts • Almonds • Walnuts	High in protein, fiber and unsaturated fats needed for healthy immune function.	Nut and nut butters add protein to salads, snacks and soups. Nuts are an incomplete source of protein; complete the protein by eating with a grain.
Seeds and seed butters: • Sunflower seeds • Pumpkin seeds • Sesame seeds • Flaxseeds	Contain essential fatty acids (EFAs), needed for healthy immune function. Flaxseeds contain omega-3 fats, which have anti-inflammatory properties. Pumpkin seeds are high in zinc, essential for boosting cellular immunity and thymus gland development.	Eat the seeds whole or freshly ground daily. Try seed butters. Flaxseeds must be ground.
FATS AND OILS		
Cold-pressed oils: • Extra virgin olive oil • Flaxseed oil	Flaxseed oil contains omega-3 essential fatty acids (EFAs), which have anti-inflammatory properties.	Look for cold-pressed, less refined oils that are packaged in dark glass containers. Keep oils in the refrigerator to keep them from going rancid.

Foods that Enhance the Immune System

Best Foods for Enhancing Immune System	Immune System Benefits	Comments
HERBS AND SPICES		
• Fennel • Ginger • Turmeric • Rosemary • Thyme • Sage	Most herbs are antioxidant. Turmeric has anti-inflammatory properties. Thyme has 75 identified antioxidants.	Use fresh or dried in cooking on a regular basis.
OTHER		
• Beer • Coffee • Tea • Wine	Rich in bioflavonoids. Green tea is a rich source of the catechin epigallocatechin gallate (EGCG) that seems to offer antigen-fighting abilities.	Consume in moderation. Not recommended during pregnancy and lactation. Limit coffee to one cup per day and substitute green tea for the other times when coffee might be consumed.

Caution

A large percentage of soybeans grown today are genetically modified and are produced using high amounts of pesticides. Fresh soybeans contain enzyme inhibitors that block protein digestion and may cause serious gastric distress and organ damage. The inhibitors are not present in such high amounts in the fermented bean products of tofu, tempeh or soy sauce. The high amounts of phytic acid in soybeans and soy foods may block the uptake of essential minerals and cause deficiencies. Isoflavones, once thought to minimize cell damage from free radicals, block the damaging effects of hormonal or synthetic estrogens, and inhibit tumor cell growth, may in fact, be toxic.

Soybeans and soy foods contain goitrogens, naturally occurring substances in certain foods that can interfere with the functioning of the thyroid gland. Individuals with already existing and untreated thyroid problems may want to avoid soy foods.

Textured vegetable protein (TVP) made from soybeans is produced using chemicals and harmful techniques and is not considered a whole food.

Excessive soy intake should be avoided during pregnancy and soy-based baby formulas should not be used.

Musculoskeletal System

Healthy Musculoskeletal System

Muscles, bones, joints and connective tissue make up the musculoskeletal system, responsible for the movement of the human body and its individual parts. The musculoskeletal system also gives structure to the body and physically protects the internal organs.

Nutrition is very important in the management of this system. For example, muscle contraction and relaxation depend on minerals like calcium and magnesium to perform movements and maintain an upright posture and balance. Bones also need minerals to maintain their density and withstand the pulling forces created by the muscles and the impact of accidents and falls.

Another important part of the musculoskeletal system is the joints, such as the hip, knees and elbows. Within the joints, the ends of the bones are covered with cartilage and are surrounded by synovial fluid, a lubricating fluid, which allows smooth and frictionless motion where two bones meet.

Will yogurt help prevent osteoporosis?

Yogurt contains an iron-binding protein called lactoferrin. Lactoferrin, along with calcium, helps build more bone cells. It also helps reduce the rate at which bone cells die. Daily consumption of yogurt will help to prevent or reverse osteoporosis.

Musculoskeletal Disorders

Arthritis, osteoporosis, low back pain, muscle spasms and cramps, sprains and strains

Muscle cramping and spasms can occur with dehydration and if minerals such as calcium, sodium, potassium and magnesium are not in the proper balance. This can cause simple cramping of the calf muscle or can aggravate existing conditions, such as low back pain. Low back pain can also be due to misalignment of the spine or other parts of the skeleton, nerve impingement, injury and chronic inflammation.

Inflammation also occurs during arthritis. There are many types of arthritis, some with more inflammation than others. For example, osteoarthritis, the most common type, is characterized by wear and tear at the joints, wearing down of the joint cartilage, and causing changes in the bone. Although minimal, osteoarthritis consists of some inflammation at the joint and in surrounding tissues. Symptoms can be stiffness and pain at the joint and eventually restricted joint function. On the other hand, rheumatoid arthritis is an autoimmune condition characterized by chronic inflammation that can affect the joints as well as other areas of the body. Rheumatoid arthritis can give symptoms of inflammation at the joint, such as pain, redness, swelling and eventually deformity, but also generalized symptoms of fatigue, weakness and low-grade fever. Regardless of the cause and the differing symptoms and location, nutrition is essential to repair and build cartilage and decrease inflammation.

Unlike arthritis, osteoporosis is mostly symptom-free, which is why people at increased risk must get regular bone-density checks. In osteoporosis, the bone density is diminished and the bones become brittle and susceptible to fractures. The density of the bone depends on many nutrients, such as calcium, magnesium and zinc, for the strength to withstand trauma, perform movement and provide support.

Optimizing Musculoskeletal Function

To maintain the musculoskeletal system in top shape, we need to eat foods that are high in vitamins and minerals, foods that help us maintain a balanced acid-base environment, and foods that deal with inflammation. Of course, regular exercise is just as important as eating well.

Eat foods that are high in minerals

Foods such as leafy green vegetables, nuts and seeds, legumes and grains are loaded with minerals that are essential for the functioning of the muscles, the building of bones and the maintenance of healthy joints. For example, calcium and magnesium are essential for muscle contraction and relaxation. Calcium, magnesium, zinc and many trace minerals, such as boron, manganese and copper, are needed to build strong bones and prevent the risk of fractures with osteoporosis.

Best foods
- Calcium: leafy green vegetables, broccoli, almonds, canned fish bones (sardines, salmon), tofu, soy milk, corn tortillas
- Magnesium: nuts and seeds, grains, beans, dark green vegetables
- Zinc: pumpkin seeds, black-eyed peas, tofu, wheat germ
- Boron: raisins, prunes, almonds
- Manganese: nuts and seeds, wheat, leafy green vegetables, beet tops, pineapple
- Copper: nuts, legumes, cereals, potatoes

Eat foods that are high in vitamins

Many vitamins essential for lowering the risk of osteoporosis can be found in foods such as leafy green vegetables, cruciferous vegetables and fish. For example, vitamin D, which is converted to its active form by the ultraviolet rays of the sun, helps increase the absorption of the calcium that is important for keeping bones strong.

Vitamin K helps mineralize bone during bone formation. Increasing the levels of vitamin K can decrease the risk of osteoporosis. This is easily achieved by increasing the consumption of leafy green vegetables.

B vitamins, especially vitamins B_6 (pyridoxine), B_{12} and folate, are needed to decrease homocysteine levels in the blood. High levels of homocysteine are detrimental in cardiovascular disease, as well as increasing the risk of osteoporosis by interfering with bone formation.

Best foods
- Vitamin D: sunlight, cod liver oil
- Vitamin K: leafy green vegetables (kale, collard greens, beet greens, parsley, broccoli, spinach)
- B vitamins: B_6: chickpeas, halibut
- B_{12}: fish, leafy green vegetables, grains

Eat foods that alkalinize the diet

When we eat a diet rich in fruits and vegetables, especially leafy greens, the body's acid-base (or pH) balance is at normal levels and calcium remains in the bones. On the other hand, when we eat a diet high in protein, refined sugars and soft drinks, as is common in our society, the pH of the body decreases and becomes too acidic. To buffer this high acidity, calcium from the bones is leached into the bloodstream, decreasing the density of the bone and increasing risk of osteoporosis and bone fractures.

Refined sugars, a high-protein diet and soft drinks (high in phosphates) can also increase the excretion of calcium in the urine.

Best foods
- String green beans, bananas, dandelion greens, grapes, fresh or dried figs, prunes, raisins, Swiss chard
- Also almonds, asparagus, avocados, beets, carrots, cranberries, kale, pomegranate, raspberries, spinach

Eat foods that decrease inflammation

Whole foods are especially important for the musculoskeletal system, which deals with trauma such as sprains and strains; and cases of chronic inflammation, such as arthritis. Fish oils are high in omega-3 fatty acids, which redirect the inflammation cascade and ease such symptoms as pain, swelling and stiffness.

Best foods
- Fish (salmon, mackerel, albacore tuna, sardines, herring), ground flaxseed and flaxseed oil, hemp seeds and hemp seed oil

Participate in a regular exercise routine

When a bone is exposed to repetitive physical stresses, its mass will increase over time. An increase in bone mass makes the bone stronger and less susceptible to fracture. Weight-bearing exercises, such as when the bones make contact with the ground while supporting body weight or when the muscles pull on the bone to make a movement, are an excellent way to place physical stress on bones. For example, walking is considered a weight-bearing exercise as compared to swimming. Swimming is still a good form of cardiovascular exercise, but it does not entail supporting the body's weight against the forces of gravity and contact with the ground. Lifting light weights is another safe way to increase bone density and decrease the risk of osteoporosis.

Exercise is also excellent for maintaining a healthy body weight. And it helps reduce pain and stiffness, increase circulation, and keep muscles toned to support the joints and prevent injuries.

Best exercises
- Brisk walking, weight training, yoga, jogging, swimming

Top 10 Best Bets for Musculoskeletal Health

1. **Almonds:** Almonds are high in calcium and, like other nuts, high in magnesium. These minerals are important for contraction and relaxation of muscle and mineralization of bone. Almonds are a great all-round nutritious snack that is high in protein and monounsaturated fats.

2. **Tofu:** Tofu has been the staple food of Asian cultures. It is made from curdled soy milk, the milky liquid extracted from cooked and ground soybeans. Tofu is an excellent source of high-quality protein, calcium (check the label first to see if calcium was added as a coagulant), iron and zinc. With its high mineral content, tofu is a great food to prevent against loss of bone mass and risk of fractures with osteoporosis.

   Tofu, like all other soybean products, contains phytoestrogens (isoflavones), plant-based estrogens that may help to prevent osteoporosis, especially in post-menopausal women. Whenever possible, choose calcium sulfate (over magnesium sulfate) as the coagulating additive in tofu.

3. **Cruciferous vegetables:** Broccoli, cabbage, cauliflower, Brussels sprouts and especially kale are very high in an easily absorbed form of calcium. Calcium, along with other minerals, is essential for maintaining high-bone density, helping decrease the risk of osteoporosis. Calcium is also essential for muscle contraction and nerve conduction.

   Cruciferous vegetables are also high in vitamin C, which protects the joints against free-radical damage created during inflammation and helps stop the progression of arthritis by repairing and building new cartilage in the joints.

4 **Leafy greens:** Vitamin K, found in leafy green vegetables, such as collard greens, Swiss chard, dandelion greens and beet greens, helps bind calcium to the bone matrix and reduce the excretion of calcium in the urine. Leafy green vegetables are also high in calcium and folic acid. Leafy greens are also beneficial because they create an alkaline environment in the body and prevent calcium extraction from the bones, thus protecting the body from osteoporosis.

5 **Fish oils:** There is growing evidence that omega-3 fats are beneficial in the prevention and treatment of arthritis. Omega-3 fatty acids, found in fish and flaxseed oil, have anti-inflammatory properties. Fish oils in particular contain the fatty acids in their final form and help control inflammation, while fatty acids from flaxseed oil must be converted in the body before they can perform their anti-inflammatory function.

6 **Turmeric:** Turmeric can halt the enzyme that produces inflammation and inhibits the break down of cortisone in the body, which makes turmeric a great anti-inflammatory. Cortisone, the body's own anti-inflammatory steroid, helps reduce inflammation. Through these means, turmeric can help decrease the symptoms of arthritis and prevent further damage to the cartilage in the joints.

7 **Ginger:** Ginger is anti-inflammatory in two ways. One way it decreases inflammation is by inhibiting the enzymes that promote inflammation. This helps terminate the inflammation cascade and prevent swelling and pain. Ginger also

helps make white blood cells more stable so they release fewer inflammation mediators. This means that ginger can help diminish the destruction of cartilage and reduce symptoms of arthritis.

8 **Citrus fruit:** Citrus fruits, such as oranges, grapefruit, lemons, limes and mandarins, are alkalinizing to the body. Foods that alkalinize are beneficial in preventing osteoporosis because the body no longer needs to take calcium from the bones to buffer acidity. Vitamin C from citrus fruits is also essential for building cartilage in the joints and other connective tissue. This can help with the progression of osteoarthritis and the repair of muscles, tendons and ligaments after surgery or injury. Vitamin C has anti-inflammatory, antihistaminic and antioxidant properties.

9 **Sunlight:** Ultraviolet light from the sun converts 7-dehydrocholesterol in the skin into vitamin D_3. Vitamin D_3, which is converted to its more active forms in the liver and kidneys, stimulates the absorption of calcium through the digestive tract and the kidneys. This process is essential in the prevention of osteoporosis. People who live farther away from the equator, have darker skin or use a sunscreen with SPF 8 or higher may need longer exposure to the sun to get the same benefits.

10 **Nuts and seeds:** Nuts and seeds are an excellent source of magnesium, a mineral that is just as important for bone formation as is calcium, making it an essential nutrient for the prevention and treatment of osteoporosis. Magnesium from nuts and seeds is also essential for muscle relaxation, and can prevent muscle spasms and pain in such conditions as chronic low back pain.

Foods that Enhance the Musculoskeletal System

Best Foods for Enhancing Musculoskeletal System	Musculoskeletal System Benefits	Comments
FRUITS		
Citrus: • Oranges • Lemons • Limes • Grapefruit • Kiwifruit • Strawberries	Rich in antioxidants essential to prevent damage to inflamed joints. Citrus fruits alkalinize the body and inhibit the calcium loss from bones. Rich in vitamin C, which helps build and repair cartilage and connective tissue.	Choose oranges that do not look perfect and are not spongy in texture. Perfect-looking oranges likely have been treated with preservatives, pesticides and colorings. Spongy texture may indicate that the fruit is soft inside and either damaged or not fresh.
• Pineapple • Papaya • Mangoes • Apricots • Melons (cantaloupe, honeydew, watermelon)	Contain vitamin C, which helps build and repair cartilage in joints.	
Blue/Purple: • Blueberries and other berries • Purple grapes • Plums	Contain anthocyanins, which destroy free radicals and prevent further damage to the joints.	Choose blueberries that are dark blue, plump, firm, dry and free from stems and leaves.
VEGETABLES		
Nightshades: • Tomatoes • Potatoes • Peppers (bell peppers, hot peppers) • Eggplant	Contain vitamin C and carotenoids.	Avoiding nightshade vegetables, which contain solanine, may bring relief to some arthritis patients.
Leafy green vegetables: • Spinach • Swiss chard • Dandelion greens • Beet greens	Contain folate, which helps decrease homocysteine levels, a risk factor for osteoporosis. Leafy green vegetables help alkalinize the diet and keep calcium in the bones. Source of vitamin K for mineralization of bone.	Vitamin K is not available as a supplement. High doses can interfere with the effect of some pharmaceutical drugs.
Cruciferous Family: • Broccoli • Cauliflower • Brussels sprouts • Cabbage • Kale • Collard greens	Collard greens have leaves that are relatively tough in texture. Cook for 8 to 10 minutes on medium heat. Use as a substitute for cabbage. Great for juicing.	High in calcium needed for muscle contraction and bone formation.

Foods that Enhance the Musculoskeletal System

Best Foods for Enhancing Musculoskeletal System	Musculoskeletal System Benefits	Comments
LEGUMES		
Beans Organic soybeans Lentils Peas Chickpeas	Beans are high in magnesium for muscle relaxation and bone building. Soybeans contain phytoestrogens, which may help protect women against osteoporosis. Tofu is a great source of calcium, as this mineral is often added to help set the tofu.	Generally, soy milk is fortified with calcium and other minerals. Soft tofu is ideal for blending into smoothies, creamy soups and dressings. Consult with your naturopathic doctor or nutritionist before consuming large amounts of soy.
WHOLE GRAINS		
Brown rice Whole oats Barley	Whole grains are important for their B vitamin content, which helps keep homocysteine levels low and decrease the risk of osteoporosis.	Choose whole grains rather than refined products and flours. The hull, removed during processing, contains most of the nutrients.
NUTS AND SEEDS		
Nuts and nut butters: Brazil nuts Almonds Walnuts	Contain magnesium, essential for muscle relaxation; and preventing some forms of low back pain. Magnesium is also needed for making energy in the body.	Eat 10 raw almonds per day. Try almond butter.
Seeds and seed butters: Sunflower seeds Pumpkin seeds Sesame seeds Flaxseeds	Seeds are high in magnesium and zinc (pumpkin seeds), which are necessary for bone mineralization.	Eat the seeds whole or freshly ground daily. Try seed butters.
FATS AND OILS		
Cold-pressed oils: Extra virgin olive oil Flaxseed oil Hemp seed oil Canola oil	Flaxseed oil and hemp seed oil contain omega-3 essential fatty acids (EFAs), which have anti-inflammatory properties. Canola oil is a source of vitamin K, needed for bone formation.	Vitamin K is a fat-soluble vitamin that must be eaten with a source of fat in order to be absorbed. Vitamin K is also produced by the healthy bacteria in the intestines.
HERBS AND SPICES		
Ginger Turmeric	Ginger is highly effective at decreasing pain and inflammation. Turmeric has anti-inflammatory properties.	One teaspoon (5 mL) of ground turmeric blended in a smoothie will help prevent post-exercise cramping.

Nervous System

Healthy Nervous System

The nervous system is a highly complex system made up of two main parts, the central and the peripheral nervous systems, which together allow us to respond to our internal and external environments. The central nervous system consists of the brain and the spinal cord, while the peripheral nervous system is made up of nerves (sensory and motor) and connects the central nervous system with other parts of the body.

The peripheral nervous system is responsible for receiving information, such as taste, sound or hormone levels, from the internal and external environments and for relaying that information to the central nervous system via peripheral sensory nerves. The spinal cord and brain integrate this information in the central nervous system and generate a response, which is then sent to other parts of the body via the peripheral motor nerves. For example, the peripheral sensory nerves might relay information about a song on the radio to the spinal cord and the brain. A response would then be sent through the peripheral motor nerves to make a movement to turn up the radio.

Of course, not all responses are conscious. The peripheral nervous system also consists of the autonomic nervous system, which controls internal organs and glands, such as the heart, or the thyroid gland, which is responsible for the body's metabolism. Through this system, consisting of sympathetic and parasympathetic responses, the body can maintain an internal balance and react to different stimuli based on the needed responses. For example, a sympathetic or "fight or flight" response is created when you are frightened or stressed. This response causes your heart rate to increase. In contrast, a parasympathetic response allows you to perform such functions as relaxing and digesting your food after a meal. These two parts of the autonomic nervous system act on the same organs and glands, but have opposing effects, helping maintain balance in the body.

Individual nerve cells (neurons) use neurotransmitters, chemicals that allow them to communicate with each other and with other cells in the body. For example, the neurotransmitter seratonin is involved in memory, emotions, wakefulness, sleep and temperature regulation. Acetylcholine allows for communication between the nervous system and the muscles to create a movement. An imbalance of neurotrasmitters can result in dysfunction in the nervous system, which is why neurotransmitters are often the target of pharmaceutical and recreational drugs.

Nervous System Disorders

Depression and seasonal affective disorder (SAD), memory loss and decreased cognitive function

Depression is a condition that occurs when there is an imbalance of neurotransmitters in the brain. It can be characterized by a loss of interest or pleasure in usual activities and a lack of energy. It can also affect appetite, with either a decrease or increase, and subsequent changes in body weight. Depression can be quite debilitating and can trigger feelings of worthlessness or even thoughts of death or suicide.

Seasonal affective disorder (SAD) is a form of depression that occurs with diminished exposure to sunlight in the winter months. This disorder may result in the general symptoms of depression, and also an increase in sleep, appetite and perhaps body weight.

Anxiety is a devastating psychiatric disorder that can consist of feelings of agitation, nervousness, fearfulness, irritability or shyness. Other symptoms may include heart palpitations, flushing of the face, sweating, shallow breathing or even fainting. Both anxiety and depression can be caused by psychological factors; a physical cause, such as trauma or illness; nutrient deficiencies; or the side effects of medications.

As a result of normal living and aging, the nervous system suffers from oxidation of its cells, improper nutrient status and a decrease in blood circulation. These and other factors can lead to a decline in neurotransmitter levels, a decrease in the number of connections between neurons and an actual decrease in brain size, leading to a decrease in cognitive function and memory loss.

Optimizing the Nervous System

To help maintain optimal nervous system functioning, you must eat whole foods that are rich in vitamins and minerals and that help maintain constant blood sugar levels. It's also important to engage in regular physical exercise, go outside to catch some sunlight and practice relaxation techniques.

Eat a diet rich in complex carbohydrates

The brain relies on a constant supply of glucose as its primary source of energy. Glucose is one of the building blocks of carbohydrates. However, there are a few other things to take into consideration. Carbohydrates can come in two forms — simple and complex. Simple carbohydrates, when broken down in the digestive tract, are absorbed rapidly into the bloodstream and can cause a quick rise in blood sugar. This rapid increase in blood sugar can lead to symptoms of hyperactivity or anxiety and is followed by a rapid decline or sugar "crash," which can give symptoms of fatigue, irritability or depression. Pasta, breads, crackers and cereals made of refined products, candy and soft drinks are examples of simple carbohydrates. These foods are also devoid of nutrients, such as vitamins and minerals.

On the other hand, complex carbohydrates contain fiber, which slows down the rate at

which sugar is absorbed into the body, allowing for a more constant level of blood sugar that can help stabilize mood patterns. Complex carbohydrates are found in whole grains, beans and other legumes, fruits and vegetables, and nuts and seeds. Proteins and fats can also help slow down the absorption of sugar into the bloodstream.

It is also important to note that caffeine can affect blood sugar levels in a negative manner and can cause symptoms of hyperactivity, depression, fatigue, irritability, insomnia or anxiety.

Best foods
- Whole grains, legumes (beans, soybeans, chickpeas, lentils)
- All fruits and vegetables
- Nuts and seeds (almonds, cashews, walnuts, sesame seeds, sunflower seeds, pumpkin seeds)

Eat a diet rich in omega-3 fatty acids

The nervous system, including the brain, contains a high concentration of omega-3 fatty acids, which cannot be made in the body and must be obtained from the diet. Omega-3 fatty acids, such as those obtained from flaxseed oil and fish oils, are not only components of all cell membranes, including nerve cells (neurons), but they also help regulate nerve cell function and signal transmission. The brain and neurons are highly dependent on the quality of the fats from the diet, and this factor can impact behavior, mood and mental function.

Omega-3 fatty acids have also been proven to have some effect through their anti-inflammatory function, preventing the production of inflammatory mediators that might be linked with mood disorders.

Best foods
- Fish oils (salmon, mackerel, albacore tuna, sardines, herring), flaxseed oil, organic soy oil, hempseed oil, canola oil, walnuts

Eat a diet rich in B vitamins

B vitamins are essential for the functioning of the nervous system. For example, the brain needs vitamin B_1 (thiamin) to be able to use glucose as fuel. Without vitamin B_1, the brain cannot function properly and can lead to symptoms of anxiety, irritability, fatigue and depression. B_1 also inhibits an enzyme that breaks down neurotransmitters, thereby boosting their levels in the brain. Vitamins B_6 (pyridoxine), B_{12} and folic acid are absolutely essential for the manufacturing of mood-regulating neurotransmitters, such as melatonin, seratonin and dopamine, which may be why these vitamins seem to have antidepressant effects. Vitamin B_{12} is also involved in the production of the myelin sheath, the fatty covering of the neurons that helps protect them and speed up the conduction of nerve impulses.

Foods such as whole grains, legumes and fish are good sources of B vitamins. It is also interesting that refined carbohydrates and some prescription medications, including oral contraceptives and antidepressants, can deplete the body's levels of B vitamins. If you are taking prescription medications, check with your health professional to see what foods you should be eating to prevent deficiencies.

Best foods

- Vitamin B_1: whole wheat, sweet potatoes, peas, beans, fish, peanuts
- Vitamin B_6: potatoes, bananas, legumes (lentils, chickpeas) fish (halibut), whole grains (rice)
- Vitamin B_{12}: fish (and other animal products), spirulina (blue-green algae), seaweed
- Folate: lentils, pinto beans, rice, leafy green vegetables

Learn ways of coping with stress

The stress of everyday life or stress caused by a major life event can produce a sympathetic response known as a "fight or flight" response. The nervous system here works in conjunction with the endocrine system by signaling to the adrenal glands to release adrenalin and other stress-related hormones. These hormones can alter blood sugar levels and change moods accordingly. In fact, excess or ongoing stress, can create feelings of irritability, fatigue, insomnia, depression or anxiety.

Techniques that induce a relaxation response and switch the nervous system from sympathetic to parasympathetic mode help optimize your nervous system.

Best techniques

- Meditation, prayer, breathing exercise, physical exercises, counseling

Get plenty of exercise

Exercise is one the most powerful antidepressants available and has repeatedly proven to decrease feelings of anxiety, depression and fatigue. Exercise increases endorphins, neurotransmitters that give a sense of well-being and elevate mood. It can also help increase self-image, self-confidence, mental performance and happiness.

Physical activity can benefit the nervous system in many different ways. For example, group exercises or sports can help elevate mood by creating a feeling of belonging. Other exercises give you a chance to "play" and can also be an excellent channel to let out frustrations and anger. Exercise can make you feel productive if lawn mowing, vacuuming or other types of yard or housework make up part of your work-out routine. Similarly, activities such as hiking or cross-country skiing can take you outdoors, breathing fresh air and enjoying different scenes. Any of these forms of physical activity are a step toward achieving a balanced nervous system.

Best exercises

- Weight lifting, brisk walking, jogging, bicycling, swimming, dancing, yoga, lawn mowing, vacuuming, racquet sports (such as tennis), team sports

Top 10 Best Bets for Nervous System Health

1 **Fish:** The human brain is more than 60% fat, the majority being omega 3-fatty acids, which cannot be made in the body and must be obtained from the diet. Fish oils are the best source of omega-3 fatty acids. These fatty acids are essential for regulating mood and emotions and preventing depression. Fish oils are also beneficial for attention and memory.

Fish oils are also an excellent source of B vitamins, including vitamin B_{12}, which can be hard to find in a vegetarian diet. B vitamins are necessary for neurotransmitter and myelin sheath production, nerve conduction and utilization of fuel by the brain.

2 **Whole grains:** Among the most important nutrients for the proper functioning of the nervous system is the group of B vitamins. B vitamins can be found in whole grains, such as whole wheat, whole oats, barley and brown rice. B vitamins are responsible for the manufacture of neurotransmitters and the proper use of fuel by the brain.

Whole grains also help maintain stable moods and energy levels throughout the day by helping to control blood sugar levels.

3 **Spirulina or blue-green algae:** Spirulina, or blue-green algae, is a microscopic plant that is found in some lakes. Spirulina is a rich source of protein, as it contains amino acids essential for neurotransmitter production. It also contains vitamins, minerals and essential fatty acids. Spirulina can provide small amounts of vitamin B_{12}, which helps produce red blood cells and myelin, helping to increase oxygen to the brain and the speed of nerve impulses.

4 **Oats:** Oats are one of the best foods for nourishing the nervous system. They can be used specifically to prevent debility and exhaustion caused by anxiety and depression. Oats can help relax the nervous system in conditions, such as insomnia, anxiety and stress. Oats can also help with the symptoms of drug withdrawal, especially nicotine withdrawal in smoking cessation. Oats are a rich source of B vitamins and contain fiber, which can help control blood sugar levels.

5 **Brewer's yeast:** Brewer's yeast is the dried, powdered Saccharomyces cerevisiae fungus used in the brewing process. Brewer's yeast is an extraordinary source of B vitamins, which help maintain a healthy nervous system. It is also the best source of chromium, a mineral that is essential for blood sugar regulation.

6 **Blackstrap molasses:** Molasses is a by-product of the manufacture of sugar. Blackstrap molasses is mostly sugar, but unlike refined sugars, it contains significant amounts of vitamins and minerals. In particular, blackstrap molasses is a source of B vitamins, calcium, magnesium and iron. These nutrients help with the production of brain neurotransmitters and general nervous system functioning.

7 **Chocolate:** Chocolate consumption has been linked with the release of seratonin in the brain, a neurotransmitter that is thought to produce feelings of pleasure. Caution: Chocolate contains small amounts of caffeine and most likely contains sugar, substances that can lead to blood sugar fluctuations and mood changes. Consume dark chocolate in moderation.

8 **Exercise:** Exercise is a very important component of a healthy nervous system. Exercise helps increase the circulation of blood, oxygen and glucose to the brain, which can help sharpen your cognitive skills such as memory. It also helps increase self-confidence and self-image, and by stimulating the release of endorphins, it can elevate mood.

9 **Barley:** The glycemic index (GI) is an index that ranks foods on how they affect blood sugar levels. Barley is exceptional because it has the lowest GI rating of any grain. This means that when eating barley, blood sugar levels remain relatively constant and so does the supply of glucose to the brain. The low GI of this food means it can help prevent mood fluctuations that may occur with anxiety, depression, hyperactivity or premenstrual syndrome in women.

⑩ Nuts and seeds: Nuts and seeds are a source of protein that when broken down provide amino acids, the building blocks for neurotransmitters. B vitamins, also found in these foods, help with the production of these neurotransmitters and make glucose available to the brain for fuel. Nuts and seeds also contain fiber, which helps keep blood sugar levels constant. Magnesium, calcium, zinc and selenium, found in a variety of nuts and seeds, may help prevent neurological disorders.

Foods that Protect the Nervous System

Best Foods for Protecting the Nervous System	Nervous System Benefits	Comments
FRUITS		
Citrus: • Oranges • Mandarins • Lemons • Grapefruit • Kiwifruit • Strawberries	Fruit juice contains large amounts of fructose, a natural sugar, and it does not contain fiber. Fruit juice can raise blood sugar levels rapidly.	Contain fiber, which helps control blood sugar levels. Contain vitamin C and bioflavonoids, required to synthesize neurotransmitters and as antioxidants for the nervous system.
• Apricots • Peaches • Pears • Apples	Contain pectin and other soluble fiber that can help control blood sugar levels. Pears contain B vitamins, and can help optimize nervous system function.	Most fruits and vegetables contain a mixture of soluble and insoluble fibers and have the ability to slow down the absorption of sugar.
Berries and grapes: • Blueberries • Blackberries • Raspberries • Red grapes	Red grapes are a great source of B vitamins, and like berries are rich sources of bioflavonoids. These protect brain cells against oxidation, and some nervous system disorders.	
VEGETABLES		
Green: • Spinach • Swiss chard • Dandelion greens • Endive • Other dark leafy greens	Leafy green vegetables contain folate, essential for the manufacture of neurotrasmitters and optimal function of the nervous system.	Lightly steam these vegetables to reduce nutrient loss and increase nutrient absorption.
Cruciferous Family: • Broccoli • Cabbage • Sauerkraut • Cauliflower • Kale • Bok choy	Cruciferous vegetables contain large amounts of vitamin C, a powerful antioxidant that helps protect the nervous system and restore normal levels of neurotransmitters.	Note that oral contraceptives, antibiotics, stress, pregnancy, infection and surgery can increase the need for vitamin C.

Foods that Protect the Nervous System

Best Foods for Protecting the Nervous System	Nervous System Benefits	Comments
LEGUMES		
• Beans (lima, navy, organic soybeans) • Lentils • Peas • Chickpeas	Legumes are a source of soluble fiber. Soybeans are a good source of vitamins B_1, B_3, B_5 and B_6, which help prevent anxiety and depression. Lima and navy beans contain folate.	Soaking beans for 8 hours and rinsing well before and after cooking makes them easier to digest.
WHOLE GRAINS		
• Whole oats • Brown rice • Pot Barley • Buckwheat • Quinoa • Whole wheat • Spelt • Rye	Barley is one of the best whole grains for controlling the rate at which glucose is absorbed into the bloodstream.	All whole grains are a good source of B vitamins.
NUTS AND SEEDS		
Nuts: • Almonds • Brazil nuts • Walnuts • Hazelnuts • Pine nuts	Nuts contain fiber, which helps control blood sugar levels and contain B vitamins. They also contain amino acids, the building blocks for mood-regulating neurotransmitters. Brazil nuts are high in selenium, which can elevate mood and decrease anxiety.	Magnesium, which is found in abundance in nuts, may help prevent depression and other neurological disorders.
Seeds: • Sesame seeds • Sunflower seeds • Pumpkin seeds	Seeds are high in fiber, and fats, which help control blood sugar levels. Contain amino acids, the building blocks for mood-regulating neurotransmitters.	Zinc found in pumpkin seeds may help prevent depression.
FATS AND OILS		
Cold-pressed oils: • Flaxseed oil • Soy oil • Hempseed oil • Canola oil • Avocados	These oils are a source of omega-3 fatty acids, which are an essential component of the nervous system and necessary for its function. Avocados are a good source of B vitamins.	Other vegetable oils, such as sunflower and safflower oils, are higher in omega-6 fatty acids, another type of essential fatty acid that must be obtained from the diet. These vegetable oils contain little omega-3 fatty acids.

Foods that Protect the Nervous System

Best Foods for Protecting the Nervous System	Nervous System Benefits	Comments
OTHER		
• Blackstrap molasses	Contains B vitamins, essential for nervous system function. Also a source of magnesium, required for neurotransmitter production.	1 cup (250 ml) molasses can be used as a substitute for 1 cup (250 mL) liquid honey, $\frac{1}{2}$ cup (125 mL) brown sugar or 1 cup (250 mL) dark corn syrup or 1 cup (250 mL) pure maple syrup.
• Brewer's yeast	A good source of B vitamins, including B_1, B_3, B_5, B_6 and folate.	Do not confuse brewer's yeast with baking yeast or nutritional yeast.
• Spirulina (blue-green algae) Seaweed	A source of vitamin B_{12}, otherwise hard to find in a vegetarian diet. Essential for the manufacture of neurotransmitters and myelin sheath and for nerve conduction.	Hydrochloric acid (stomach acid) and intrinsic factor (a protein that binds vitamin B_{12}) are both produced by the stomach cells and aid its absorption in the large intestine.

Respiratory System

Healthy Respiratory System

The respiratory system is responsible for the exchange of oxygen and carbon dioxide between the external environment and the blood. The air that we breathe travels in through the nose, past the pharynx and larynx, down the trachea, into the bronchi and bronchioles and eventually reaches its destination, the lungs. In the lungs, the exchange of gases occurs in tiny air sacs called alveoli, where oxygen from the air enters the bloodstream and carbon dioxide from the bloodstream enters the air to be expelled. Through the actions of inspiration and expiration, the air flows in and out of the lungs providing all body cells with the fresh supply of oxygen essential to them for survival.

The respiratory system is also responsible for protecting the body against microbes, toxic chemicals and foreign matter. This is achieved with the help of cilia, tiny hair-like structures that sweep mucous and foreign materials out of the system. The cilia also work with the immune system to produce mucous and perform phagocytosis (engulfing pathogens and debris).

Respiratory System Disorders

Asthma and allergies, respiratory tract infections, lung cancer
Asthma is the most common illness associated with the respiratory system. It is an inflammatory condition of the lungs and airways in which swelling, smooth muscle contraction and excess mucous production create acute breathing difficulties. Someone who suffers from asthma might experience a feeling of tightness and constriction of the chest, with shortness of breath, wheezing and coughing. It is believed that asthma, like allergies, is a hypersensitivity disorder and therefore greatly linked to the immune system.

The respiratory system is the most susceptible to infection because it is directly exposed to the external environment. Therefore, respiratory infections, such as colds, sinusitis, bronchitis and pneumonia, also greatly depend on the immune system. Here, the immune system is responsible for protecting the respiratory system by producing mucous, attacking foreign invaders and developing a proper response to fight pathogens once they enter the body.

The respiratory system is also susceptible to cancer. Lung cancer is the most prevalent form of cancer today and can affect one or both lungs. Smoking is the biggest risk factor for lung cancer, so quitting smoking is a valuable method in its prevention. Other methods include eating a vitamin-rich diet, which can help reduce the risk of cancer, but there is also the chance that cancer will come back once treated.

Optimizing the Respiratory System

To protect the respiratory system from disease, we need to heal and moisten the mucous membranes, keep the cilia healthy and functioning well, strengthen and restore the balance of the immune system (see Immune System, page 83), and eliminate possible environmental triggers and foods that produce mucous and irritate the respiratory tract.

Eat foods that moisten the respiratory tract and thin excess mucus
Proper water intake helps keep the mucus membranes in the respiratory tract moist and capable of resisting infection. Water also helps thin mucous that builds up in your respiratory passageways and causes congestion. Vegetable broths and hot herbal teas can also be beneficial for maintaining hydration and clearing congestion. Warm drinks also help

the cilia move to clear pathogens and foreign materials from the system.

Spices and flavoring agents, such as garlic, cayenne and horseradish, can also help get things moving by thinning mucus and stimulating the respiratory tract.

Humidifiers that moisten the air can help the respiratory system by preventing the mucous membranes from becoming dry and prone to infection, especially in the winter months.

On the same note, avoid foods and beverages that stimulate production of excess mucus (dairy products, sugar), dehydrate the body or irritate the respiratory passageways (alcohol, coffee).

Best foods
- Plenty of filtered water, hot herbal teas (peppermint, fennel, thyme), homemade vegetable broths

Eat a diet rich in antioxidants

In general antioxidants help prevent damage of the respiratory system by protecting against free radicals and boosting immune function. Antioxidants are also important in the prevention of cancer.

Vitamin A helps maintain healthy mucous membranes in the mouth, nose, sinuses and lungs, as well as the cilia in the respiratory passageways. This helps protect the passageways from virus and bacteria. Vitamin A also helps boost the immune system.

Vitamin C has an antihistaminic effect that can benefit asthma and allergy sufferers. It also protects against infection, helps heal wounds and strengthens the adrenal glands, essential glands for fighting allergic reactions and inflammation.

Vitamin E helps maintain healthy mucous membranes and is a powerful antioxidant.

Quercetin, a bioflavonoid, has anti-inflammatory and antihistaminic properties. Histamine is the substance that is released during an allergic reaction causing symptoms of itching and swelling. Quercetin can help with allergies, asthma and respiratory infections.

Best foods
- Beta-carotene (converted in the body into vitamin A): apricots, carrots, cantaloupe, pumpkin and other winter squashes
- Vitamin C: bell peppers, broccoli, cantaloupe, cauliflower, kale, kiwi, oranges, strawberries, sweet potatoes, tomatoes
- Vitamin E: almonds, hazelnuts, walnuts, sunflower seeds, vegetable oils
- Quercetin: apples, red and yellow onions, black tea, tomatoes

Eat foods that contain essential fatty acids

Asthma, allergies and respiratory infections are associated with inflammation of the respiratory tract. Foods that are high in omega-3 fatty acids, such as fish oils and flaxseed oil, have anti-inflammatory properties that can keep allergies and asthma in check. Essential fatty acids along with other unsaturated fats help keep mucous membranes healthy and resistant to infection.

Best foods
- Fresh fish (salmon, mackerel, albacore tuna, sardines, herring)
- Flaxseeds and flaxseed oil, borage oil, evening primrose oil

Breathe good-quality air and do breathing exercises

The quality of the air we breathe is directly related to the condition of the lining of the respiratory tract. If the air we breathe is polluted with pollens, dust, dander, mold, smoke, bacteria and viruses, it can cause chronic irritation and inflammation of our airways and lungs. If you live or work in a polluted environment, use air filters to purify the air.

Breathing exercises increase the amount of oxygen that enters our system and the amount of carbon dioxide that is eliminated via the lungs.

Best techniques
• Use air filters, vacuum and clean carpets frequently, check homes and basements for mold, dust frequently, practice abdominal breathing

Top 10 Best Bets for Respiratory Health

1 **Sprouted seeds and grains:** According to traditional Chinese medicine, sprouted seeds and grains are alive and full of chi (life energy). These foods help strengthen the lungs and respiratory system.

2 **Fish oils:** Omega-3 fatty acids in fish oils have anti-inflammatory properties that may help relieve asthmatic patients. Studies have shown that when asthma patients consume more fish oils, they breathe more easily and use less medication.

3 **Garlic:** The antibacterial properties of garlic have been proven to be effective against the bacteria that cause pneumonia. Garlic fights viruses and fungal infections that target the respiratory system.

4 **Pumpkin seeds:** Studies have found that people who suffer from allergic asthma and other allergies have a deficiency of zinc. Pumpkin seeds are an excellent source of zinc, which may help reduce the incidence of allergies and asthma as well as boosting the immune system to protect against infection. Have a handful per day as a snack.

5 **Yellow and red onions:** Yellow and red onions contain quercetin, a bioflavonoid that has antioxidant, anti-inflammatory and antihistaminic properties. Quercetin seems to protect the lungs against viral infections, such as those caused by the flu virus.

6 **Ginger:** Ginger extracts have been shown to have antimicrobial activity against bacteria and viruses that cause respiratory infection. Ginger is also an antioxidant and has anti-inflammatory properties. Make a ginger tea by slicing and slightly bruising fresh gingerroot and adding the slices to boiling water. Continue to boil the water until it looks darker in color. Let it steep.

7 **Almonds:** Like all other nuts, almonds are a great source of calcium and magnesium, which are essential for muscle contraction and relaxation, even for the smooth muscle in the respiratory airways. Almonds also contain monounsaturated fats and are a good source of protein.

8 **Berries:** Berries contain anthocyanins, which destroy free radicals, and are high in vitamin C. Vitamin C is a natural antioxidant and anti-inflammatory. Vitamin C is also antihistaminic, as it makes mast cells (the cells that contain histamine) more stable during allergic reactions. Vitamin C in berries is essential in the prevention of allergies, asthma and inflammation and helps boost the immune system.

9 **Cruciferous vegetables:** Broccoli, cauliflower, cabbage, Brussels sprouts and bok choy contain cancer-fighting chemicals and other minerals important for health. Cabbage, with its high glutamine content, is beneficial for the building and repair of mucous membranes, including the mucous membranes in the respiratory tract. This helps keep allergens, and pathogens from attacking the body.

10 **Thyme and Oregano:** Thyme has a high content of volatile oils that are powerful agents for fighting infections. Thyme can be used to soothe sore throats and calm irritating coughs by helping reduce spasm reactions. It is also used for bronchitis, whooping cough and asthma. It can be taken as a delicious and refreshing tea.

Oregano is a powerful antioxidant with potent antibacterial, antifungal and antiparasitic properties, which make it useful for treating swollen glands, asthma, cough, earache and viral infections. Take oregano oil diluted in herbal tea or water.

Foods that Protect the Respiratory System

Best Foods for Protecting the Respiratory System	Respiratory System Benefits	Comments
FRUITS		
Citrus: • Oranges • Mandarins • Lemons • Grapefruit • Kiwifruit • Strawberries	Rich in vitamin C and bioflavonoids, which are antioxidants. Vitamin C containing foods are anti-inflammatory and antihistaminic, helping reduce allergic-type reactions including asthma and allergies.	Caution: Grapefruit juice can interfere with some medications. Strawberries are heavily sprayed; choose organic when possible.
Orange/Yellow: • Apricots • Mangoes • Cantaloupe	Contain carotenoids and vitamin C, which are antioxidants. Beta-carotene helps maintain healthy mucous membranes of the respiratory tract.	When buying cantaloupe, choose fruit that is thick, with a coarse surface and veins standing out. Avoid fruit with mold.
Blue/Purple: • Blueberries and other berries • Purple grapes • Plums	Choose well-colored, plump grapes that are firmly attached to their stems.	Contain anthocyanins, which destroy free radicals. Also high in pectin and vitamin C.
VEGETABLES		
Red Nightshades: • Tomatoes • Red bell peppers	Rich in the antioxidant lycopene. High in vitamin C and beta-carotene, which help keep mucous membranes intact and control allergic reactions.	Lycopene is fat-soluble and must be eaten with a fat in order to be absorbed.
Orange/Yellow: • Carrots • Yams • Sweet potatoes • Pumpkin and other winter squashes	Contain carotenoids, which maintain resistance in mucous membranes and cilia to protect against infections and foreign materials.	
Green: • Spinach • Swiss chard • Asparagus • Dandelion greens • Other dark leafy greens	Contain magnesium, which helps decrease bronchial reactivity and constriction in asthma sufferers.	1 cup (250 mL) of these leafy vegetables is equal to one serving.
Cruciferous Family: • Bok choy • Broccoli • Brussels sprouts • Cabbage • Cauliflower • Kale	Broccoli contains large amounts of vitamin C, beta-carotene and calcium. Calcium is a mineral needed for smooth muscle relaxation of the respiratory tract.	Broccoli sprouts have high amounts of cancer fighting nutrients.
Allium Family: • Chives • Garlic • Onions	Yellow or red onions are high in quercetin, an antihistaminic compound that helps reduce allergy symptoms. Garlic has antimicrobial properties that help the body fight infections.	Allicin, which is released during crushing, gives garlic its characteristic smell. Research indicates that for optimum benefit, garlic should be crushed and allowed to sit for a few minutes before using. Eat garlic raw or cooked.

Foods that Protect the Respiratory System

Best Foods for Protecting the Respiratory System	Respiratory System Benefits	Comments
LEGUMES		
• Beans (lima, pinto, organic soy) • Lentils • Peas (black-eyed peas) • Chickpeas	A source of protein essential for building and repairing tissues and immune cells to fight infection. A source of zinc, essential for resisting infection and tissue repair.	
WHOLE GRAINS		
• Whole wheat • Whole oats • Brown rice • Barley • Quinoa • Millet	Grains are a source of selenium, a strong antioxidant that works along with vitamin E. High in B vitamins, including B_6, which nourishes the adrenal glands.	Brown rice, quinoa and millet are less allergenic, so choose these grains, especially when the body is fighting an infection to prevent excess mucous formation.
NUTS AND SEEDS		
Nuts: • Almonds • Walnuts • Brazil nuts • Hazelnuts • Pecans	Nuts contain monounsaturated fats, vitamin E and magnesium. Almonds are a good source of calcium. Magnesium and calcium help relax the smooth muscle of the respiratory airways.	Buy raw or dry-roasted nuts and seeds. Choose an unsalted variety.
Seeds: • Flaxseeds • Sesame seeds • Pumpkin seeds • Sunflower seeds	Flaxseeds are high in omega-3 oils, which are anti-inflammatory. Sesame and sunflower seeds are an excellent source of vitamin E, a fat- soluble antioxidant. Pumpkin seeds are high in zinc, essential for immune function.	Sunflower seeds, pumpkin seeds and sesame seeds are excellent mixed together and eaten as a snack. Make your own trail mix.
FATS AND OILS		
Cold-pressed oils: • Extra virgin olive oil • Flaxseed oil • Borage oil • Evening primrose oil • Avocados	Flaxseed, borage and evening primrose oil have been known to offset inflammation.	Do not use flaxseed oil for cooking. Use in salads, smoothies or over vegetables.
HERBS AND SPICES		
• Thyme • Sage • Ginger • Parsley • Oregano • Cumin • Mustard • Basil • Peppermint	Ginger is antiviral, antioxidant and anti-inflammatory. Peppermint stops coughs and releases congestion. Thyme helps clear the respiratory passageways and fight infection.	Caution: Peppermint can relax the stomach sphincter and stimulate acid reflux.
OTHER		
• Beer • Chocolate • Coffee • Tea • Wine	Tea and red wine contain quercetin. Beer is rich in bioflavonoids from the fermented grains. Phenols in dark chocolate and red wine are antioxidant.	Caution: Caffeine and alcohol can dehydrate and irritate the respiratory tract. Not recommended during pregnancy and lactation.

Whole Foods

Whole Foods for Health

There is no doubt about it. What you eat affects not only who you are and what you can accomplish, but also how you look and feel, including your overall health and vitality. Eating a variety of whole, fresh foods including fruit and vegetables is essential. As developed countries produce more and more refined and processed foods — foods like sugar-coated breakfast cereals, fat and chemical-laden, frozen and convenience foods and empty-calorie snack foods — there is also an increase in "modern" diseases. According to the 1988 U.S. Surgeon General's Report on Nutrition and Health, dietary choices are a factor in two-thirds of all deaths from coronary heart disease, stroke, atherosclerosis, diabetes and some cancers.

Whole foods are our first line of defense against those diseases. Whole foods are those foods that are as close to their natural state as possible. They are full of the essential vitamins, minerals, proteins, enzymes, complex carbohydrates and phytonutrients that combine to keep us active, alert and free from disease. What follows is a comprehensive outline of whole foods — foods that contain the optimum healing compounds so vital for human health.

For many reasons, locally grown, organic whole foods are the best possible foods we can choose for our family. Most notably, children are most vulnerable to pesticides, fertilizers, ionizing radiation and growth hormones, but everyone deserves to enjoy food that is produced without these human and environmental hazards. Farmers who use renewable resources, along with soil and water conservation practices, produce organic food in order to preserve a healthy environment for future generations. Most organic farms sell food locally. Their consumers are their friends and neighbors. Organic living provides a practical and painless first step that everyone can take towards a healthier lifestyle and planet.

Fruits

Açai

Euterpe oleracea

A small, round, dark purple berry from an Amazon palm tree, available in frozen form from whole and natural foods stores in North America. The flavor of the berries is an unusual blend of chocolate and blueberry.

Actions: Antioxidant, anticancer.

Uses: Due to an exceptionally high concentration of phenolic pigments and anthocyanins with antioxidant properties, açai is being researched for its role in the prevention of numerous human disease conditions. The berry is high in omega-6 and omega-9 fatty acids, fiber, calcium, copper, iron, magnesium, phosphorus, potassium and zinc.

Buying and Storing: Açai is available in several forms: dried pulp purée; bottled liquid pulp purée; frozen whole or puréed berries; and freeze-dried capsules. Look for whole pulp pure organic açai berries for juicing or pulping.

Apples

Malus pumila

Actions: Tonic, digestive, diuretic, detoxifying, laxative, antiseptic, lower blood cholesterol, antirheumatic, liver stimulant.

Uses: Fresh apples help cleanse the system, lower blood cholesterol levels, keep blood sugar levels up, and aid digestion. The French use the peels in preparations for rheumatism and gout as well as in urinary tract remedies. Apples are useful components in cleansing fasts because their fiber helps eliminate toxins. Apples are good sources of vitamin A and also contain vitamins C, B$_2$ (riboflavin) and K. Apples are high in the phytonutrients pectin and boron and are a good source of proanthocyanidins, which may contribute to maintenance of urinary tract and heart health.

Buying and Storing: Look for blemish-free apples with firm, crisp flesh and smooth, tight skin. Because of the widespread use of pesticides on apples, choose organic whenever possible or peel before using. Apple orchards produce seasonal gluts and since apples have excellent keeping qualities, local varieties may be available out of season. Keep in a cool dry and dark place (or the produce drawer of your refrigerator) for 1 month or more.

Culinary Use: Apples can be blended with most fruits and many vegetables. They add natural sweetness and lots of fiber and texture to both sweet and savory dishes. Not all sweet, crisp and delicious eating apple varieties are as good when cooked. Cox's Orange Pippin, Jonathan, Gravenstein or Baldwin apples are varieties that can be eaten raw and used as an ingredient in cooked dishes.

One apple, peeled and cored yields approximately 1 cup (250 mL) roughly chopped fruit. Homemade or commercially canned, unsweetened applesauce may be used in recipes as a natural sweetener.

Apricots

Prunus armeniaca

Actions: Antioxidant, anticancer.

Uses: Apricots are very high in beta-carotene, a precursor of vitamin A. Vitamin A may prevent the formation of plaque deposits in the arteries, thus preventing heart disease. Three small fresh apricots deliver 2,770 IU and $\frac{1}{2}$ cup (125 mL) dried contains 8,175 IU of vitamin A. Also high in B$_2$ (riboflavin), potassium, boron, iron, magnesium and fiber, apricots have virtually no sodium or fat. Fresh or dried apricots are especially recommended for women because they are a good source of calcium and an excellent source of vitamin A. Apricots help normalize blood pressure, heart function and maintain normal body fluids.

Buying and Storing: Choose firm, fresh apricots that range from dark yellow to orange. Keep in a dry cool place for up to 1 week. Dried apricots have the highest protein content of all dried fruit. Buy naturally sun-dried, sulphur-free dried fruit whenever possible, and without exception, if given regularly to children. The sulphur dioxide gas used to fumigate dried fruit (to keep the bright colors) is poisonous and if taken in excess can cause severe alimentary problems and possibly genetic mutations.

Culinary Use: Leave the peel on fresh apricots if organic but do not use the seeds. Peel in the same way as peaches, by pouring boiling water over and allowing them to cool enough to slip the skins off. Lemon juice will prevent browning.

Dried apricots are an excellent source of natural sugar and are generally sweeter than fresh fruit so use them to reduce refined sugar in sauces and cooked fruit recipes. Substitute 2 dried apricot halves for each fresh apricot. Canned apricots in unsweetened juice may also be used in dessert recipes and smoothies.

Bananas

Musa cavendishii, syn. *M. chinensis*

Actions: Boost immunity, lower cholesterol, prevent ulcers, antibacterial.

Uses: Due to their ability to strengthen the surface cells of the stomach lining and protect against acids, bananas are recommended when ulcers (or the risk of ulcers) are present. High in potassium and vitamin B_6 (pyridoxine) bananas help prevent heart attack, stroke and other cardiovascular problems.

Buying and Storing: Look for ripe bananas that are soft to the touch, yellow from neck to bottom and that are only very slightly speckled. Store in a cool dry and dark place.

Culinary Use: Bananas are peeled and added to salads and desserts just before serving whenever possible. Brushing bananas with lemon juice will prevent browning. Over-ripe bananas (very darkly speckled, almost solid brown) may be used in quick breads, puddings and sauces. Plantains are larger and green, usually used for cooking baked goods or in Caribbean and African dishes.

To Freeze Bananas: For freezing, choose fully yellow bananas with no bruises or brown spots. Peel and cut each into four chunks and arrange on a baking sheet. Freeze in coldest part of the freezer for 30 minutes. Transfer to one large or several individual resealable freezer bags. Seal and store in freezer for up to 6 months. Four frozen chunks are equal to one whole fresh banana. Use frozen bananas in baked goods and smoothies.

Blackberries

Rubus species

Actions: Antioxidant.

Uses: Blackberries are an excellent source of vitamin C and fiber. They have high levels of potassium, iron, calcium and manganese.

Buying and Storing: Choose plump berries with dark, glossy color and firm flesh. Fresh blackberries are best used immediately (if necessary, store for 1 day only in the refrigerator). Wash just before using.

Culinary Use: Use blackberries in all recipes that call for blueberries, raspberries or strawberries. Blackberries combine well with other berries, apples and peaches in pies, jams, puddings and soufflés.

Black Currants

Ribes nigrum

Actions: Antioxidant, antibacterial, boost immunity, promote healing, antidiarrheal, anticancer.

Uses: Black currant flesh is extremely high in vitamin C. Three ounces (90 grams) contain 200 mg of vitamin C. Black currant skins and the outer layers of their flesh contain anthocyanins, a flavonoid, proven to prevent the development of bacteria such as E. coli. Black currants (especially the seeds) are high in gamma linolenic acid (GLA), important for heart health and a number of body functions. Although red currants are not as common as black, they have similar properties.

Buying and Storing: Black (or red) currants are not widely available but are sometimes found in midsummer at farmers' markets. While not as fragile as blackberries or raspberries, fresh currants must be stored in the refrigerator and will keep up to 1 week. Wash just before using.

Culinary Use: Remove the tiny stems before cooking fresh black currants. Fresh currants are usually simmered in water until tender before being used in recipes. Dried currants are not generally the dried version of fresh currants, but tiny raisins from the small seedless grapes of Corinth. Soak dried currants in water before using in baked goods or compotes.

Blueberries

Vaccinium species

Actions: Antidiarrheal, antioxidant, antibacterial, antiviral.

Uses: High concentrations of tannins are found in blueberries. Tannins kill bacteria and viruses and help prevent (or relieve) bladder infections. Anthocyanosides in blueberries protect blood vessels against cholesterol buildup. Anthocyanidins bolster cellular antioxidant defenses and may contribute to maintenance of brain function. Blueberries are high in pectin, vitamin C, potassium and natural aspirin and add extra fiber to the diet.

To Prevent Bladder Infections: Add at least ½ cup (125 mL) fresh or frozen blueberries to smoothies, cereals or salads and take daily for a minimum of 3 weeks.

Buying and Storing: A silvery bloom on blueberries indicates freshness. Choose plump, firm, dark blue berries with smooth skin. Pick over and discard split or soft berries. Blueberries are best used immediately but can be stored in the refrigerator for up to 3 days. Wash just before using.

Culinary Use: The flavor of blueberries can be tart, especially in wild varieties, so combine with sweeter fruits (apples, apricots, bananas, pineapple) in order to avoid adding sugar to recipes. Frozen, canned or dried blueberries can be used when fresh are not available without sacrificing their medicinal qualities.

Cantaloupe

See Melons

Cherries

Prunus species

Actions: Antibacterial, antioxidant, anticancer.

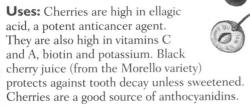

Uses: Cherries are high in ellagic acid, a potent anticancer agent. They are also high in vitamins C and A, biotin and potassium. Black cherry juice (from the Morello variety) protects against tooth decay unless sweetened. Cherries are a good source of anthocyanidins.

Buying and Storing: Choose sweet varieties and look for dark red, firm, plump, tight-skinned, glossy fruit with the stems attached. Whole ripe cherries are best used immediately but will keep in the refrigerator for up to 2 days.

Culinary Use: Wash, cut in half and remove stones. Sweet cherries such as the Bing variety range from pale yellow to deep purple-red and are juicy-sweet. The bitter, dark-skinned cherries are used mainly for jam that will be sweetened. When fresh cherries are not available, use pitted frozen, dried, or canned in recipes.

Citrus Fruits

Citrus species
oranges, lemons, limes, grapefruit, tangerines

Actions: Antioxidant, anticancer.

Uses: All citrus fruits are high in vitamin C and limonene, which is thought to inhibit breast cancer. Red grapefruit is high in cancer-fighting lycopene. Oranges are a good source of choline, which improves mental functioning. The combination of carotenoids, flavonoids, terpenes, limonoids and coumarins make citrus fruits a total cancer-fighting package.

Buying and Storing: Plump, juicy citrus fruits that are heavy for their size and yield slightly to pressure are best. Although citrus fruits will keep for at least a couple of weeks if kept moist in the refrigerator, they are best if used within a week. Look for organic citrus fruits because they are not injected with gas for transportation.

Culinary Use: Make fresh citrus juice with a citrus press or juicing machine. Lemon or lime juice adds a fresh, sharp-tasting edge that complements many vegetable dishes and tones down the cloying sweet taste of other fruits. One half of a lemon or lime yields about 3 tbsp (45 mL) of juice. Sauces and dressings use various citrus juices. Whole or sliced citrus fruit is used in salads, desserts and some main dish recipes.

Buy organic citrus fruit and wash the peel with food-safe soap if using the rind. Candied citrus peel is used in cakes, cookies and fruit compotes. Canned oranges or grapefruit and their juice may be used in most dishes, such as sauces and compotes, that call for those fruits.

Caution: Grapefruit juice can interfere with some medications.

Cranberries

Vaccinium macrocarpon

Actions: Antibacterial, antiviral, antioxidant, anticancer.

Uses: The proanthocyanidins in cranberries make them extremely useful in urinary and bladder infections. Whole cranberries or juice work in the same way as elderberries to prevent the barbs on the bacteria from attaching to the cells of the bladder or urinary tract, rendering them ineffective in causing infection. Best used as a first step in preventing urinary tract and bladder infection, cranberry juice does not take the place of antibiotic drugs, which are more effective in eliminating bacteria once an infection has taken hold. High in vitamins C and A, iodine and calcium, cranberries also prevent kidney stones and deodorize the urine.

To Prevent Bladder Infections: Add at least $\frac{1}{2}$ cup (125 mL) cranberries to smoothie recipes or fruit salads and take every day for a minimum of 3 weeks.

Buying and Storing: Choose bright red, plump cranberries that bounce. Keep fresh cranberries in a cold, dark place or produce drawer of the refrigerator for 2 to 3 weeks. Cranberries may be frozen whole in a freezer bag. Wash just before using.

Culinary Use: Unless used in small quantities or combined with very sweet fruits, their tartness makes it appropriate to use fresh cranberries with honey, stevia or other sweeteners. Cook fresh cranberries in a small amount of water or juice before combining with other ingredients in recipes. Canned whole cranberries or cranberry sauce are high in sugar so dried, fresh or frozen cranberries are preferred.

Crenshaw Melon

See Melons

Dates

Phoenix dactylifera

Actions: Boost estrogen levels, laxative.

Uses: Dates are good sources of boron, which prevents calcium loss, so important in the fight against osteoporosis and weakening of bones. Dates contain vitamins A, B_1 (thiamin), B_2 (riboflavin), C and D and valuable mineral salts as well as fiber.

Buying and Storing: Dried dates are widely available and keep in a cool dark place for a couple of months. Fresh dates may be found in Middle Eastern markets when in season. Buy firm, plump, fresh dates with dark shiny skins. Fresh dates will keep for several days in the refrigerator.

Culinary Use: High in sugar (60% in fresh and 70% in dry), dates sweeten and add fiber to stews, tagines, salads, baked goods, puddings, grain dishes and desserts. Golden or dark brown in color, fresh dates are very different from dried and are becoming more and more common in upscale supermarkets. Use fresh dates in appetizer and salad recipes to show off their superior flavor and texture.

Elderberries

Sambucus nigra

Actions: Increase perspiration, diuretic, laxative.

Uses: Elderberries support detoxification by promoting bowel movements, urination, sweating and mucus secretion. They are effective in combating viruses, such as those that cause colds and flu. Elderberries work in the same way as cranberries, by providing protection from the barbs that puncture the body's cell walls. Viruses slide off and are eliminated before they can enter the cells and cause damage.

Buying and Storing: Elderberries are still mainly harvested from the wild (although some are now grown commercially in the United States and Canada). They are usually available at farmers' markets from mid- to late summer. Look for plump, deep, purple-black berries with tight, shiny skin and firm flesh. Use immediately or if necessary, store for 1 day in the refrigerator. Wash just before using.

Culinary Use: Elderberries add a dark blue color to foods. Their taste can be sweet or slightly tart. Use fresh or frozen elderberries, or small amounts of elderberry syrup, or elderberry jam in puddings, sauces, dressings, salads, beverages and vegetable dishes. Elderberries may be used in place of blueberries or raspberries in recipes.

Figs

Ficus carica

Actions: Antibacterial, anticancer, antiulcer, digestive, demulcent, laxative.

Uses: Figs contain benzaldehyde, a cancer-fighting agent. They are also high in potassium, B vitamins, calcium and magnesium, and are naturally sweet.

Buying and Storing: Dried figs are readily available in supermarkets throughout the year. In summer and early fall, some supermarkets and most Middle Eastern food markets carry fresh figs. There are over 700 varieties of figs and they range in color from green to purple or dark brown. Choose soft, plump fresh figs with thin skins that yield to a gentle touch. Fresh figs are delicate but keep in a cool dark place for several days.

Culinary Use: Fresh figs contain 12% sugar and are best eaten whole, with cheese or fruit. Cook with dried figs, which contain about 50% sugar. Dried figs are used to sweeten and thicken dressings, puddings and sauces. Figs can be substituted for apricots and dates in most recipes.

Gooseberries

Ribes grossularia

Actions: Protect skin and gums, laxative.

Uses: High in vitamin C, potassium and pectin, gooseberries are often added to jams to make them set.

Buying and Storing: Once found in many home gardens, gooseberries are now sometimes found at farmers' markets in early summer. Be sure to use dessert varieties (early ripening amber and yellow varieties) and look for plump, bright, almost transparent berries with tight, shiny skin and firm flesh. Use immediately or if necessary, store for 1 day in the refrigerator. Wash just before using.

Culinary Use: Refreshingly tart-sweet, gooseberries add depth to the sweet taste of seasonal berries and bananas. Red-skinned and green gooseberries are too tart to use raw and require sweetening when cooked.

Grapefruit

See Citrus Fruits

Grapes

Vitis vinifera

Actions: Antioxidant, antiviral, anticancer.

Uses: Grapes contain large amounts of ellagic and caffeic acids, which deactivate carcinogens. Grapes are a good source of potassium. The flavonoids in grape juice protect the heart, and the resveratrol found in red wine and red grape juice has a protective effect on the cardiovascular system. Grapes are also high in boron, a substance that helps maintain estrogen levels and may be instrumental in preventing osteoporosis.

Buying and Storing: Organic grapes are preferred due to the high amounts of pesticides used on commercial crops. Look for bright color, firm flesh and unwrinkled skin. Wash grapes in food grade hydrogen peroxide or vinegar because they are heavily sprayed. Store in the produce drawer of refrigerator for 3 or 4 days.

Culinary Use: Grapes are sweet and their mild taste blends with most fruit in salads and desserts. Grapes are generally used raw but may be added to tagines and other cooked dishes that will not overpower their delicate flavor.

Raisins are dried grapes and are a good source of fiber, boron, calcium, phosphorus, iron, potassium and vitamin A. They add natural sweetness to recipes. Add ¼ cup (60 mL) to salads, baked goods and grain recipes. Golden sultanas are a very good cooking variety because they are light in color and plump. Use only sulphur-free raisins that have not been sprayed with mineral oils.

Honeydew Melon

See Melons

Kiwifruits

Actinidia chinensis

Actions: Antioxidant, anticancer, aid digestion.

Uses: Kiwifruits are often used as part of a cleansing regimen or to aid digestion. They are high in vitamins C and E (one of few fruits that contain vitamin E) that both act as antioxidants, protecting cells from damage. Kiwifruits are also high in potassium and contain some calcium.

Buying and Storing: Choose ripe kiwifruit that yield to gentle pressure. Kiwifruit will ripen at room temperature in a brown paper bag after 2 or 3 days. Ripe kiwifruit keep for at least 1 week in the produce drawer of the refrigerator.

Culinary Use: Use fresh in salads, jams, cakes and desserts. They make an attractive garnish for cooked sweet or savory dishes.

Lemons

See Citrus Fruits

Limes

See Citrus Fruits

Mangoes

Mangifera indica

Actions: Antioxidant, anticancer.

Uses: High in vitamins A (there are 8,000 IU of beta-carotene in one mango) and C, potassium, B$_3$ (niacin) and fiber, mangoes help protect against cancer and atherosclerosis. They help the body fight infection and maintain bowel regularity.

Buying and Storing: Choose large, firm, yellow to yellow-red, unblemished fruit with flesh that gives slightly when gently squeezed. Store ripe fresh mangoes in the produce drawer of refrigerator for 3 or 4 days.

Culinary Use: Mangoes are fibrous with a sweet, banana-pineapple flavor. They combine well with peaches, apricots, nectarines and plums. Use fresh mangoes in salads, grain dishes, desserts and beverages.

Handle mangoes carefully because the peel contains a skin irritating sap. To separate the flesh from the fibrous seed, cut the fruit lengthwise on one side, close to the seed. Repeat on the other side of the seed. With the tip of a paring knife, separate the two halves from the seed. Using a large spoon, scoop the flesh out of the skin. Dried mangoes are available, but use them sparingly due to their extra sweetness and look for ones that are dried naturally (and not treated with sulphur).

Melons

Cucumis melo
cantaloupe, honeydew, crenshaw, Spanish, musk

Actions: Antioxidant, anticancer, anticoagulant (cantaloupe and honeydew).

Uses: Melons are a good source of vitamin A and contain vitamin C and calcium. Adenosine, the anticoagulant chemical found in cantaloupes and honeydews lessens the risk of heart attacks and strokes due to its ability to thin the blood.

Buying and Storing: Ripe melons are heavy and have a full, sweet perfume. Blemished, soft fruit should be avoided.

Culinary Use: The low caloric value along with their high water content and delicate sweet flavor make melons a good choice for desserts, smoothies and sweet or savory salads. Melons are often paired with savory spreads or fillings and served as appetizers.

Musk Melon

See Melons

Nectarines

Prunus persica var. *nectarina*

Actions: Antioxidant, anticancer.

Uses: Nectarines are a good source of vitamins A and C, and potassium. They are an original ancient fruit and not, as many people think, a cross between a peach and a plum.

Buying and Storing: Choose fruit that have some bright red areas and are smooth and tight without soft patches. Nectarines should be heavy (full of juice) and firm when pressed, giving way gently, but not hard.

Culinary Use: Nectarines are usually sweeter than peaches and can be used in place of peaches, plums and apricots in recipes. Peel in the same way as peaches, by pouring boiling water over and allowing them to cool enough to slip the skins off. Lemon juice will prevent browning.

Oranges

See Citrus Fruits

Papayas

Carica papaya

Actions: Antioxidant, anticancer, aid digestion.

Uses: High in vitamins A, E and C, folate and potassium.

Buying and Storing: Choose large, firm, yellow, unblemished fruit with flesh that gives slightly when gently squeezed. Store in the produce drawer of refrigerator for 3 or 4 days.

Culinary Use: Papayas sweeten and blend well with other fruits in dressings, sauces and desserts. Use fresh papayas with breakfast grain dishes and in smoothies where they add a creamy texture. Dried papaya is usually treated with sulphur and is very sweet, so use sparingly.

Peaches

Prunus persica

Actions: Antioxidant, anticancer.

Uses: Rich in vitamin A and potassium, peaches also contain boron, B$_3$ (niacin) and some iron and vitamin C. Peaches help protect against cancer, osteoporosis and heart disease. Their sugar content is low (about 9%).

Buying and Storing: Fruit that is full and heavy with fuzzy down and flesh that gives when lightly pressed is preferable. Store peaches in the produce drawer of the refrigerator for up to 4 days. Freestone varieties (such as Loring and Redhaven) are easier to pit than clingstone varieties.

Culinary Use: Use frozen or canned peaches packed in unsweetened juice when the fresh fruit is not in season. Peaches can replace nectarines, plums and apricots in recipes. They complement blackberries, blueberries and raspberries in salads and fruit desserts. Peel by pouring boiling water over and allowing them to cool enough to slip the skins off. Lemon juice will prevent browning. Dried peaches are added to compotes, chutneys and other long-simmering dessert dishes.

Pears

Pyrus communis

Actions: Protect the colon.

Uses: Pears are a good source of fiber, which helps prevent constipation and ensures regularity and protects the colon. Pears' insoluble fiber binds to cancer-causing chemicals in the colon, preventing them from damaging the colon cells.

Perhaps one of the oldest cultivated fruit, pears are a good source of vitamin C, boron and potassium. Healthcare professionals often recommend pears because they are less likely to cause an adverse response. For this reason, they are one of the first fruits introduced to infants.

Buying and Storing: Shop for pears that are lightly firm, unblemished and sweetly "pear smelling." Often available before fully ripe, pears may be ripened in a brown paper bag for 1 to 3 days. Eat pears as soon as they ripen or store in the produce drawer of the refrigerator for up to 3 days.

Culinary Use: Use fresh, frozen or canned pears in sweet and savory dishes. Juicy varieties such as Bartlett, Comice, Seckel and Bosc are great for poached pear desserts. Pears soften in cooking faster than apples so add to stewed fruit compotes 5 to 10 minutes after the apples. Pears team nicely with plums and grapes in recipes.

Pineapples

Ananas comosus

Actions: Aid digestion.

Uses: A 1-cup (250 mL) serving of pineapple delivers 128% of the body's daily requirement of manganese and is a good source of potassium and vitamin C. Pineapples also contain vitamin B_1 (thiamin), copper, iron and vitamin B_6 (pyridoxine).

Buying and Storing: Choose large, firm fruits (heaviness in the ripe fruit indicates juiciness), with overall yellow color.

Culinary Use: Pineapples add a fresh sweet taste to smoothies, salads and dessert dishes. The sweetness of pineapples helps soften the tartness of cranberries, blueberries and gooseberries. Pineapple juice is very sweet. Frozen or canned pineapple packed in unsweetened juice may be used in recipes.

To Use Fresh Pineapple: Trim off the base and top leaves. Cut in half and use one half at a time. Slice one half into four wedges. Slice away and discard the skin from each wedge and remove and discard the woody core. One whole, fresh wedge yields about 1 cup (250 mL) chopped fresh pineapple.

Plums

Prunus species

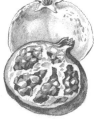

Actions: Antibacterial, antioxidant.

Uses: Plums contain vitamins A and C, a small amount of vitamin B_2 (riboflavin) and potassium. They have an exceptionally high content of unique phytonutrients called neochlorogenic and chlorogenic acids. These substances, found in both plums and prunes, are classified as phenols, and their function as antioxidants has been well documented.

Buying and Storing: Ripe plums are firm with no soft spots or splits. Look for bright, (yellow, black or red sweet plums), tight skin and heavy, sweet smelling fruit. Keep in the produce drawer of the refrigerator for up to 4 days.

Culinary Use: Wash and peel (if not organic) and remove pit. Dessert plums can be eaten fresh or added to fruit salads. Cooking plums may be stewed in a little water for 10 to 15 minutes or until soft. Canned and frozen plums may be substituted for fresh in some recipes.

Prunes are dried plums and are high in colon cancer-fighting pectin (and other insoluble fiber), low in sugar, and act as a natural laxative.
To treat constipation: Take 4 to 6 dried or stewed prunes up to three times a day for 1 or 2 days.

Pomegranates

Punica granatum

Actions: Antidiarrheal, antifever, astringent.

Uses: Used in gargles and thought to reduce fevers, pomegranates are widely used in Indian medicines.

Buying and Storing: Choose firm, even-colored and heavy fruit. Keep in the produce drawer of the refrigerator for up to 4 days.

Culinary Use: The bright red, juicy seeds are eaten fresh and for Middle Eastern recipes are dried and pounded to a powder. Fresh pomegranate seeds are used in salads and as a garnish for dips and desserts and can be pressed for drinks. Crushed dried seeds are sprinkled on hummus and used in Middle Eastern sweet dishes. Pomegranate molasses is available in specialty stores and may be used in place of honey in beverages, dressings, sauces, puddings and other desserts.

Raspberries

Rubus idaeus

Actions: Support the immune system.

Uses: Raspberries are rich in manganese and vitamin C (supplying over 50% of the daily recommended amounts of each). They contain folate, vitamin B_2 (riboflavin), magnesium, vitamin B_3 (niacin), potassium and copper. See also Red Raspberry leaf (page 157).

Buying and Storing: Buy or pick fresh raspberries in peak season and choose whole, plump berries with bright color. Sort and discard soft or broken berries. Use immediately or store in the produce drawer of refrigerator for 1 day. Wash just before using.

Culinary Use: Raspberries blend with other berries in desserts and salads and the taste is enhanced with a small amount of citrus juice. Substitute frozen, dried or canned raspberries for fresh. Up to ¼ cup (60 mL) raspberry jam may also be used in sauces and dressings.

Rhubarb

Rheum species

Actions: Laxative.

Uses: Actually a vegetable that is almost always used as a fruit, rhubarb is high in potassium and contains a fair amount of iron. The amount of calcium in 1 cup (250 mL) cooked rhubarb is twice that of milk.

Caution: Never use the leaves of rhubarb, which are toxic and inedible due to the high concentration of oxalic acid in them.

Buying and Storing: If a rhubarb patch is not available, farmers' markets may be the only source in spring. Choose thin, firm stalks with all or 90% red color. Rhubarb should snap when bent. Store in a cool dry place or the produce drawer of refrigerator for 1 or 2 days only.

Culinary Use: Cooking mellows the tart taste and softens the laxative effect. To cook fresh rhubarb: Place 1 cup (250 mL) chopped fresh rhubarb in a saucepan. Add 1 cup (250 mL) chopped apple and ¼ cup (60 mL) sugar or honey or 2 tsp (10 mL) stevia to sweeten. Cover with water or apple juice and simmer until soft. Frozen or canned rhubarb may also be used in recipes.

Spanish Melon

See Melons

Starfruits

Averrhoa carambola

A tropical fruit that grows in the shape of a star.

Actions: Antioxidant

Uses: High in vitamin C, potassium, proanthocyanidins, epicatechins and carotene, starfruit is traditionally used to treat arthritis, coughs, diarrhea, hangovers, hemorrhoids, bladder stones, kidney stones and toothache.

Caution: People who suffer from gout or with kidney or other renal problems and/or diabetes should avoid starfruit due to its oxalic acid.

Strawberries

Fragaria species

Actions: Antioxidant, antiviral, anticancer.

Uses: Effective against kidney stones, gout, rheumatism and arthritis, strawberries are also used in cleansing juices and as a mild tonic for the liver. Strawberries are high in the cancer fighting ellagic acid and vitamin C. They are also a good source of vitamin A and potassium and contain iron. Both the leaves and the fruit have been used medicinally. A tea from strawberry leaves is used for diarrhea and dysentery.

Buying and Storing: Pick your own or choose brightly colored, firm berries with hulls attached. They are best used immediately but may be stored for no more than a couple of days in the refrigerator. Wash just before using.

Caution: Strawberries are heavily sprayed; choose organic when possible.

Culinary Use: Strawberries add a sweet and powerful flavor to salads, desserts, sauces, dressings and drinks. They blend well with bananas and other berries and the taste is enhanced with a small amount of lemon or lime juice.

Tangerines

See Citrus Fruits

Watermelon

Citrullus vulgaris

Actions: Antibacterial, anticancer.

Uses: Watermelons contain vitamins C and A, iron and potassium. Their high water content makes them a refreshing summer ingredient.

Buying and Storing: A watermelon should be bright green with firm flesh (no blemishes or soft spots) and feel heavy for its size.

Culinary Use: Watermelon is a refreshing summer fruit that combines well with other fruits as a sweet thirst quencher. To use in salads and smoothies, cut in half lengthwise and use half at a time. Use a slice whole as a garnish or remove and discard rind and seeds, and chop the flesh. One slice (from half a watermelon) yields approximately 1 cup (250 mL) chopped fruit. Wrap tightly and keep cut watermelon in the refrigerator.

Vegetables

Artichokes (Globe)

Cynara scolymus

Actions: Antioxidant, anticancer, heart protective.

Uses: Artichokes are high in flavanones, phytochemicals that offer protection against heart disease. They also contain phosphorus, iron, zinc and calcium.

Buying and Storing: Artichokes are the flower of a thistle plant and as such, have tough outer leaves and hairy, inedible centers or chokes. Choose bright green-purple artichokes with no signs of browning and tightly closed leaves.

Culinary Use: Fresh artichokes have a delicate flavor. Trim the thick stems and remove the tough outer leaves. Simmer in a saucepan half filled with boiling water for 30 to 40 minutes or until the outer leaves pull away easily. Cut in half and remove the hairy, inedible center. Serve fresh artichokes with any of the mayonnaise recipes (pages 178 and 179) for a starter dish. Canned artichoke hearts are usually marinated and are more flavorful than fresh. Artichoke hearts are used in salads, pasta and in baked legume and grain dishes.

Asparagus

Asparagus officinalis

Actions: Antioxidant, anticancer, promotes healing, prevent cataracts, diuretic.

Uses: Asparagus is an excellent source of vitamin K (supplying over 100% of the Recommended Daily Amount) and folate, needed for the production of red blood cells and the release of energy from food. It is also a good source of vitamins C and A. It contains B vitamins, tryptophan, manganese, copper, protein, potassium, iron, zinc and some calcium.

Buying and Storing: Look for tight buds at the tips and smooth green stalks with some white at the very end. Fresh asparagus will snap at the point where the tender stalk meets the tougher end. Store stalks upright in $\frac{1}{2}$ inch (1 cm) of water in the refrigerator for up to 2 days.

Culinary Use: Wash grit from flower ends by soaking and swishing in cool water. Snap off and discard the tough stem bottoms. Roasting caramelizes the sugars and brings out the nutty, slightly smoky flavor of asparagus. Steam tender tips by standing whole stalks upright in a tall, narrow pot so that only the lower two-thirds of the stems are immersed in boiling water. Cover and gently simmer for 3 to 5 minutes. Frozen or canned asparagus may be substituted in recipes when fresh is not available.

Avocados

Persea americana

Actions: Antioxidant, anticancer, heart protective.

Uses: Avocados contain more potassium than many other fruits and vegetables (banana is just slightly higher). While high in essential fatty acids, they contain 17 vitamins and minerals including vitamins K, C, A, E and B_6 (pyridoxine), iron, calcium, copper, phosphorus, zinc, B_3 (niacin), magnesium, selenium, folate as well as the highest amount of protein of any fruit. Not only are avocados a rich source of monounsaturated fatty acids including oleic acid, they are also a concentrated dietary source of the carotenoid lutein.

Buying and Storing: Look for ripe, heavy avocados with dull dark green skin. When held in the hand, ripe avocados give gently. Don't press the flesh and avoid avocados with dents in the skin. Ripen in a paper bag and store in the refrigerator for just over 1 week once ripe.

Culinary Use: One avocado added to salads adds a creamy texture and exceptional nutrients. Brush with lemon juice to keep avocado flesh from turning brown once peeled. Avocados thicken uncooked sauces, dips and smoothies (in much the same way as bananas) due to their lower water content. Up to 30% of the fruit's weight may be oil and for this reason, avocados should be used sparingly.

Beans and Peas

Phaseolus vulgaris
Pisum sativum
fresh green runner, yellow
wax runner, broad, flat,
Italian, snap, string; also
green peas, snow peas

For Legumes (dried peas
and beans), see page 131.

Actions: Help memory, antioxidant.

Uses: Green beans and peas are leguminous plants — the same botanically as dried beans and peas because they all produce their seeds in pods. However, fresh beans and peas have a lower nutrient level than dried legumes. A good source of choline, which improves mental functioning beans, beans and peas contain vitamin A and potassium along with some protein, iron, calcium and vitamins B and C. The amino acids in beans and peas make them a valuable food for vegetarians.

Buying and Storing: Buy fresh peas and beans with firm pods showing no signs of wilting. The bigger the size of the pea or bean inside the pod the older the vegetable. Fresh yellow or green beans are pliant but still snap when bent. Store unwashed fresh peas (in their pods) and beans in a vented plastic bag in the refrigerator for 2 or 3 days. Parboiled fresh beans and peas freeze well.

Culinary Use: Fresh, frozen, canned or cooked dried peas and beans (legumes) can all be used in recipes. Fresh summer beans are exceptional as a dish on their own or in salads or baked vegetable dishes and they complement grains.

Beets

Beta vulgaris

Actions: Antibacterial, antioxidant, tonic, cleansing, laxative, fight colon cancer.

Uses: Beets (the roots of the beet plant) are high in folate, manganese, potassium and the enzyme betaine, which nourishes and strengthens the liver and gall bladder. With 8% chlorine, beets are cleansing for the liver, kidney and gall bladder. The pigment that gives beets their rich, purple-crimson color — betacyanin — is also a

powerful cancer-fighting agent. Beets are also a good source of vitamin C, magnesium, tryptophan, iron, copper and phosphorus.

Buying and Storing: Bright glossy, crisp green beet tops or leaves indicate fresh beets. Buy firm, unblemished, small beets with greens intact, if possible. For storing, cut off the tops and treat as leafy greens. Store unwashed beets in a vented plastic bag in the refrigerator. Beets will keep for up to 1½ weeks.

Culinary Use: Grate fresh, raw beets into salads. Roast, steam or boil fresh beets in water for a vegetable side dish. Use cooked canned or frozen beets when fresh are not available. For using beet tops as a leafy vegetable, see page 124.

Broccoli

Brassica oleracea

Actions: Antioxidant, anticancer, promotes healing, prevents cataracts.

Uses: Like other cruciferous vegetables, broccoli contains cancer-fighting indoles, glucosinolates and dithiolthiones. A 1-cup (250 mL) serving of broccoli packs over 200% of the body's daily requirement of vitamin C and over 190% of vitamin K. It is high in vitamin A and is one of only four vegetables with vitamin E. It has a fair amount of folate, manganese, tryptophan and potassium. Vitamin B_6 (pyridoxine), B_2 (riboflavin), phosphorus, magnesium, protein, omega-3 fatty acids, vitamin B_5, iron, calcium, vitamins B_1 (thiamin) and B_3 (niacin) and zinc are also present in broccoli. Purple sprouting broccoli is an excellent source of lignans, believed to help protect against hormone-related cancers and may help relieve symptoms associated with menopause.

Buying and Storing: Broccoli yellows as it ages. Deep green color and firm tight buds are a sign of freshness. Thin stalks are more tender than thick, woody stems that tend to be hollow. Store in a vented plastic bag in the produce drawer of the refrigerator for up to 3 days.

Culinary Use: Raw broccoli is eaten with dips and sauces. Fresh broccoli may be boiled, steamed or stir-fried. Cooked broccoli should retain some crunch and bright green color. Use frozen broccoli when fresh is not available.

Brussels Sprouts

See Cabbage

Cabbage

Brassica oleracea var. *capitata*
green, red, Savoy, bok choy, Chinese, kohlrabi, Brussels sprouts

Actions: Immune building, antibacterial, anticancer, helps memory, antioxidant, promotes healing, prevents cataracts, detoxifying, diuretic, anti-inflammatory, tonic, antiseptic, restorative, prevents ulcers.

Uses: Cruciferous vegetables, of which cabbage is one, appear to lower our risk of cancer more effectively than any other vegetable or fruit. Cabbage is high in cancer-fighting indoles and a good source of choline, which improves mental functioning. It is also an excellent source of vitamins K and C. A very good remedy for anemia, cabbage has also been used as a nutritive tonic to restore strength in debility and convalescence. Of benefit to the liver, cabbage is also effective in preventing colon cancer and may help diabetics by reducing blood sugar. Cabbage juice is significant in preventing and healing ulcers. Cabbage contains manganese, vitamins B_1 (thiamin), B_2 (riboflavin), B_6 (pyridoxine), folate, omega-3 fatty acids, calcium, potassium, vitamin A, tryptophan, protein and magnesium.

Buying and Storing: Fresh cabbage has loose outer leaves around a firm center head. Older, stored cabbage does not have the outer wrapper leaves and tends to be paler in color. Cabbage will keep for up to 2 weeks in a vented plastic bag in the refrigerator. Wash and cut or slice just before using.

Culinary Use: Fresh cabbage is available year-round and is an excellent vegetable to have on hand at all times. It is an essential ingredient in vegetable stock. Steam, broil or stir-fry cabbage with other vegetables, legumes and grains or slice thin and serve raw in salads.

Carrots

Daucus carota ssp. *sativus*

Actions: Antioxidant, anticancer, artery protecting, expectorant, antiseptic, diuretic, immune boosting, antibacterial, lower blood cholesterol, prevent constipation.

Uses: Carrots have a cleansing effect on the liver and digestive system, help counter the formation of kidney stones and relieve arthritis and gout. Their antioxidant properties from carotenoids (including beta-carotene) have been shown to cut cancer risk, protect against arterial and heart disease and lower blood cholesterol. Carrots enhance mental functioning, decrease the risk of cataracts and promote good vision. Carrots are extremely nutritious and rich in vitamins A (1 cup/ 250 mL supplies over 600% of our daily requirement), K and C. Potassium, some B vitamins, manganese and folate are also present.

Buying and Storing: The inedible green tops continue to draw nutrients out of the carrot so choose fresh carrots that are sold loose with the tops removed or remove and discard the tops immediately. Choose firm, well-shaped carrots with no cracks. The deeper the the carrot's color, the higher the concentration of carotene. If stored unwashed in a cold but moist place, carrots should not shrivel. Keep for up to 2 weeks in a vented plastic bag in the produce drawer of the refrigerator.

Culinary Use: Carrots are a versatile vegetable with natural sweetness that can be used in almost any vegetable recipe. Cooking frees up carotenes (precursors to vitamin A), the anticancer agents in carrots. Steam, roast, stir-fry or simmer carrots just until tender. Grated carrots are used raw in salads and grain and pasta dishes.

Cauliflower

Brassica oleracea var. *botrytis*

Actions: Antioxidant, anticancer.

Uses: As are all cruciferous vegetables (cabbage, Brussels sprouts, broccoli, collard greens, kohlrabi), cauliflower is rich in indoles, the cancer preventing phytonutrients. Cauliflower is an excellent source of

vitamin C. It is a good source of vitamin K, folate and vitamin B$_6$ (pyridoxine). Potassium and some protein and iron are also present.

Buying and Storing: Fresh cauliflower has dense, tightly packed florets and crisp, green leaves surround the head. Keep loosely covered in the refrigerator for no longer than 1 week.

Culinary Use: Wash and cut away outer leaves, save and use them as you would any leafy green vegetable. Cut the head into florets, discarding the woody core and stems. Use cauliflower raw in salads and appetizers with dips and sauces. Cauliflower is very good in soups, curries, stir-fries and chutneys. Steam or boil cauliflower or bake with other ingredients.

Celery

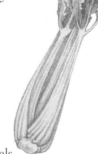

Apium graveolens var. *dulce* and *Celeriac Apium graveolens* var. *rapaceum*

Actions: Mild diuretic, anticancer.

Uses: Sometimes used as a treatment for high blood pressure (two to four stalks per day). The coumarins in celery help prevent free radicals from damaging cells, thus helping to prevent cell mutation, a pre-cancer condition. Coumarins also boost immune responses. The acetylenic compounds in celery have been found to stop the growth of tumorous cells. For the healing properties of celery seeds, see page 146.

Buying and Storing: Fresh celery has some crisp green leaves and firm crisp ribs. Older stalks have had the leaves removed. Celery varieties range in color from very light to dark green and as the color darkens, the taste gets stronger. Store for up to 2 weeks in a vented plastic bag in the refrigerator.

Culinary Use: Use celery (stalks and leaves) when making salads, appetizers and vegetable cocktails to add a natural saltiness. Celery combines well with eggs, apples and walnuts. The light, almost white inner stalks are tender and serve well with dips. Pan-fry, include in stir-fries, braise or chop and include celery in baked dishes.

Celeriac is the root of a different variety of celery than the common table celery. It adds a stronger celery flavor to dishes. Scrub and cut celeriac into wedges. Peel the tough outer skin of celeriac and slice or chop. To prevent browning, drop the pieces into a bowl of water with a squeeze of lemon juice added. Steam, broil, stir-fry or cook celeriac au gratin with other vegetables.

Celeriac

See Celery

Chile Peppers

Capsicum annuum

Actions: Stimulant, tonic, diaphoretic, stimulates blood flow to the skin, antiseptic, antibacterial, expectorant, prevents bronchitis, prevents emphysema, decongestant, blood thinner, carminative.

Uses: Chiles are hot peppers (including cayenne, jalapeño, ancho/poblano, habanero, serrano and pasilla to name only a few) that contain the active element capsaicin. They are high in vitamin A and contain some vitamin C, iron, magnesium, phosphorus and potassium. Chile peppers help people with bronchitis and related problems by irritating the bronchial tubes and sinuses by causing the secretion of a fluid that thins the constricting mucus and helps move it out of the body. Capsaicin also blocks the pain message from the brain, making it an effective pain reliever. In addition, it also has clot-dissolving properties that make it useful if taken on a consistent basis. See also Cayenne Pepper (page 146).

Buying and Storing: Look for firm, crisp peppers with smooth skin and no blemishes. Store peppers in a paper bag in the produce drawer of the refrigerator for up to 4 days. Peppers freeze easily and may be added to sauces, soups and stews without thawing. Buy clean, fully dried chile peppers and store in a cool dry place.

Culinary Use: Wash and handle chile peppers carefully and wash hands thoroughly after handling because capsaicin will irritate skin and eyes. Remove the stem and inside pulp including seeds (seeds do not contain the fire). When first using chile peppers add half of the recommended amount to the recipe. Taste and add more, if desired.

Use fresh, reconstituted dried or canned chiles in recipes. Whisk in a drop of hot or jerk sauce or a quarter teaspoon (1 mL) of powdered cayenne to sauces, dips, dressings, soups or smoothies to substitute for fresh chiles.

Collard Greens

See Leafy Greens

Corn

Zea mays

Actions: Anticancer, antiviral, raises estrogen level, neutralizes stomach acid, high fiber helps with kidney stones and water retention.

Uses: Corn is a good source of B_1 (thiamin) and B_6 (pyridoxine). Corn adds roughage to the diet.

Caution: Corn and corn products (cereals, corn chips or foods with cornstarch) may trigger food intolerances that lead to chronic conditions, including rheumatoid arthritis, headaches and irritable bowel syndrome.

Buying and Storing: Fresh corn is best if cooked within minutes of picking. When that is not possible, buy fresh corn that has been kept cold and use as soon as possible.

Culinary Use: Corn is sweet and blends with most vegetables. It is added to soups, risottos, egg dishes, salads, grains and baked vegetable dishes. Use leftover cooked fresh corn by slicing kernels off the cob with a sharp knife. Frozen or canned whole-kernel corn packed in water can be used when fresh is not available.

Cucumbers

Cucumis sativus

Actions: Diuretic, anti-inflammatory.

Uses: The ascorbic and caffeic acids in cucumbers help soothe skin irritations and reduce swelling.

Cucumbers are moderate sources of vitamins C and A, potassium, manganese and folate. They are high in water, making cucumbers refreshing vegetables for summer salads. Cucumbers contain sterols, which may help the heart by reducing cholesterol.

Buying and Storing: Choose bright shiny green-skinned, firm cucumbers. Avoid yellow spots (although this is a sign of ripeness, the seeds will be bitter and the flesh too soft) and wax on the skin. Store in the produce drawer of the refrigerator for 4 to 5 days.

Culinary Use: Wash before using, peel (especially if skin has been waxed or if not organic), cut into cubes and leave seeds intact. Shred into salads and sauces. Use thinly sliced fresh cucumbers to replace greens in some salads.

Eggplant

Solanum melongena

Actions: Antibacterial, diuretic, may lower blood cholesterol, may prevent cancerous growths.

Uses: Now used topically to treat skin cancer, eggplant's terpenes may also work internally to deactivate steroidal hormones that promote certain cancers. A fair amount of potassium in eggplant normalizes blood pressure. They are a good source of folate, vitamin B_6 (pyridoxine) and vitamin C. Eggplant is low in fat and calories.

Buying and Storing: Choose small, heavy, deep purple eggplants with firm, smooth skin that have no scrapes, cuts or bruises. Use immediately or keep for 1 to 2 days in the produce drawer of the refrigerator.

Culinary Use: Wash before using, peel (if not organic), cut into cubes and leave seeds intact. Salting is not as important now because the varieties sold today are not as bitter, but it can prevent the absorption of oil in recipes in which they are fried. The meaty texture and subtle, earthy flavor are what makes eggplant popular in vegetarian dishes. Eggplants are used in dips, appetizers and baked vegetable dishes such as moussaka, ratatouille and curries. Garlic, onions, tomato sauce and mozzarella cheese enhance eggplant in baked dishes.

Fennel

Foeniculum vulgare

Actions: Antioxidant, anti-inflammatory, anticancer. For the medicinal benefits of fennel seeds, see page 150.

Uses: A bulb-like vegetable similar to celery, but with a distinctly sweet anise taste, fennel is a good source of vitamin C. Fennel also contains potassium, manganese, folate, phosphorus and calcium.

Buying and Storing: Avoid bulbs with wilted or browning stalks or leaves. The bulb should be firm and white with a light green tinge. Remove leaves and keep for up to 1 week in the refrigerator.

Culinary Use: Use the leaves in recipes if they are still attached to the stalks. Use raw fennel with vegetables for dipping or in a salad. Soups and stews and all baked vegetable dishes are enhanced by fennel. One-quarter fennel bulb measures about 1 cup (250 mL) when chopped.

Garlic

See Herbs

Jerusalem Artichoke

Helianthus tuberosus

Actions: Antibacterial.

Uses: Jerusalem artichokes are the tuberous roots of a plant related to the sunflower (which is why they are often sold as "sunchokes.") Their sweet, nutty flavor blends well in juices. People with diabetes easily digest the inulin, a type of carbohydrate, found in Jerusalem artichokes. They are also a source of calcium, iron and magnesium.

Buying and Storing: Since Jerusalem artichoke is not a commercial crop, it is unlikely that it will be widely available. Should you find some at a local farmers' market or grow the plants, treat them as

you would sweet potatoes. Store in a cool dry place for 1 or 2 weeks.

Culinary Use: Boil and steam with other fresh garden vegetables or use in a scallop or gratin dish. Jerusalem artichokes go best with potatoes, carrots, parsnips and onions.

Kale

See Leafy Greens

Kohlrabi

See Cabbage

Leafy Greens

kale, Swiss chard, collard greens, mustard greens, turnip greens, lettuce

Actions: Antioxidant, anticancer.

Uses: Although the nutrient amounts change with each green, in general it can be said that leafy greens are excellent sources of vitamin A and chlorophyll, and good sources of vitamin C, with some calcium, iron, folic acid and potassium.

Buying and Storing: Buy bright green, crisp (not wilted) greens and store them unwashed in a vented plastic bag in a cold spot in the refrigerator. Leafy greens are very tender and will go limp and turn yellow (or brown) when not stored or handled properly. Store away from fruits and wash just before using.

Culinary Use: Remove tough spine and stem, and shred or chop leafy greens or tear the tender greens for salads. The stronger-tasting greens (kale, Swiss chard, collard, mustard, turnip) work well in hearty dishes like curries, legumes and spicy Indian and Moroccan dishes. Use the milder flavored greens in salads, with grains and as garnishes.

Leeks

Allium ampeloprasum var. *porrum*

Actions: Expectorant, diuretic, relaxant, laxative, antiseptic, digestive, hypotensive.

Uses: Leeks are easily digested and often used in tonics, especially during convalescence from illness. They can be blended in toddies for relief from sore throats due to their warming, expectorant and stimulating qualities. Leeks are good sources of folate and contain some vitamin C, B_2 (riboflavin), allicin, quercetin and magnesium.

Buying and Storing: Choose leeks with firm white bulbs with white roots still intact and crisp, bright green tops. Leeks with the base removed will deteriorate quickly. Unwashed and kept in a plastic bag in the refrigerator, leeks should last from 1 to 2 weeks.

Culinary Use: Trim white roots and outer dark green leaves, split and wash under running water to remove grit or soil trapped between the layers. Slice, chop or cut into chunks. Leeks may be used raw but mellow and soften when cooked. Savory tarts, casseroles, soups, stuffing, egg dishes, pasta and baked vegetable dishes make good use of the milder onion-like taste of leeks.

Lettuce

See Leafy Greens

Mushrooms

Actions: see Maitake and Shiitake, left and page 126.

Uses: Used and thought of as a vegetable, mushrooms are actually fungi living off other host organisms. Mushrooms reproduce by spores and have no roots, leaves, flowers or seeds, as do plants.

Buying and Storing: Look for mushrooms that are firm, plump and clean. Mushrooms should be free of any signs of softness, deterioration or mold. Common button mushrooms are widely available. Fresh mushroom varieties such as portobello, oyster, cremini, shiitake and maitake, and dried whole or cut mushrooms are available in Oriental markets, whole or natural food stores and some supermarkets. Store fresh mushrooms, loosely covered, in a paper bag for up to 5 days. Dried mushrooms keep for up to 6 months if stored in a cool dry place.

Caution: Always purchase mushrooms from reliable sources such as supermarkets and food markets. Many mushroom varieties are toxic and eating varieties from the wild may be fatal.

Raw mushrooms contain hydrazines, potentially toxic substances that are destroyed in cooking or drying. Do not eat fresh, raw mushrooms — always cook them.

Culinary Use: Clean mushrooms using a minimum amount of water or wipe with a clean, damp cloth. Cooking with shiitake and maitake mushrooms at least three times per week (more if possible) will contribute to overall immune and cardiovascular health and may lower your risk of cancer.

Whole, fresh mushrooms are roasted or grilled. Halved or chopped mushrooms are used in stews, broths and soups. Sliced mushrooms for rice (risotto) and grain dishes, stir-fries and roasted vegetable dishes. Shredded mushrooms complement cooked salads and sandwich fillings.

Dried mushrooms are added to soups and stews or reconstituted by soaking them in water or other liquids. Save the soaking water and use it in soups, stews, gravies and sauces or add to other cooking liquids in recipes.

Maitake Mushroom

Grifola frondosa

Maitake means dancing mushroom in Japan because it is made up of many overlapping, fan-shaped fruit bodies that resemble butterflies dancing. In North America, maitake mushrooms are referred to as "hen of the woods" because they grow at the base of trees or stumps in big clusters resembling a hen's tail feathers.

Actions: Liver protective, lowers blood pressure, protect against breast and colorectal cancers, antioxidant.

Uses: In the late 1980s, Japanese scientists identified the maitake mushroom as being more potent than any mushroom previously studied. Maitake has remarkable tonic effects, especially on the immune system. It is used in the prevention of some cancers and may help protect against high blood pressure, constipation, diabetes and HIV.

Maitake's polysaccharide compound, known as beta 1,6 glucan (or D-fraction) is recognized by researchers as the most effective active agent stimulating cellular immune responses and inhibiting tumors.

Shiitake Mushroom

Lentinula edodes

Amber to brown, medium in size and traditional mushroom shaped. Shiitake have a flat, leathery cap, with a tough, woody stem.

Actions: Recognized as a symbol of longevity in Asia, shiitake mushrooms have long been used in traditional Chinese medicine. They have proven immune-boosting, antitumor, anticancer, antiviral, anti-AIDS, antibacterial, cholesterol lowering, hepato-protective and liver-protective properties.

Uses: A strengthened immune response due to the action of shiitake mushrooms means increased body resistance to bacterial, viral, fungal and parasitic infections. Shiitake is beneficial in soothing bronchial inflammation, regulating urinary incontinence, reducing chronic high cholesterol and inhibiting cancer metastasis. It is used to treat arthritis and chronic fatigue syndrome.

Lentinan in shiitake mushrooms has been shown to enhance immunity cells in clearing the body of tumor cells and in fighting HIV and hepatitis B viruses. Lentinan is one of three different anticancer drugs extracted from mushrooms approved by Japan's Health and Welfare Ministry. According to Dr. Moss, an expert in cancer treatment, incorporating fresh or dried shiitake into a diet rich in whole grains, vegetables and fruits is a low-cost cancer prevention strategy.

One 8 oz (250 g) serving yields 20% of the body's daily requirement of iron. Shiitake mushrooms are high in vitamin C, protein, dietary fiber and calcium.

Caution: Shiitake mushrooms contain uric acid forming purines and individuals with kidney problems or gout may wish to limit or avoid them.

Mustard Greens

See Leafy Greens

Onions

Allium species

Actions: Antibacterial, anticancer, antioxidant, circulatory and digestive stimulant, antiseptic, lower cholesterol, hypotensive, hypoglycemic, diuretic, heart protective.

Uses: Onions help prevent thrombosis, reduce high blood pressure, lower blood sugar, prevent inflammatory responses and prohibit the growth of cancer cells. Shallots and yellow or red onions are the richest dietary source of quercetin, a potent antioxidant and cancer-inhibiting phytochemical. Onions are good sources of vitamin B_1 (thiamin), vitamin B_6 (pyridoxine) and vitamin C.

Buying and Storing: Choose onions that feel firm and have dry, tight skins. Avoid onions with woody centers in the neck and black powdery patches. If stored in a cool dry place with good air circulation, onions will keep for up to 1 month or more.

Culinary Use: Vidalia, red and Spanish onions are milder in flavor than yellow cooking onions. Shallots have a mild delicate flavor and are used whole in some dishes. Use onions raw in salads, sandwich fillings and for toppings. Include onions in stir-fries, salsas and other sauces, pasta, stuffing, baked vegetable dishes, soups and stews. They caramelize and sweeten when roasted.

Parsnips

Pastinaca sativa

Actions: Anti-inflammatory, anticancer.

Uses: Parsnips are best fresh, after frost has concentrated the carbohydrate into sugar, making them sweeter. They are a good source of vitamin C and E, as well as potassium with some protein, iron and calcium. Like other root vegetables, parsnips store well and are an excellent fresh winter vegetable.

Buying and Storing: Look for firm flesh with no shriveling, soft spots or cuts. Parsnips should snap when bent. Small thin parsnips with tops still intact are best (remove and discard the tops before storing). Keep in a vented plastic bag in the refrigerator for up to 1½ weeks.

Culinary Use: Small, fresh parsnips are surprisingly sweet and roasting brings out the sugars even more. Parsnips add natural sweetness to baked goods, soups, sauces, stir-fries, baked vegetable dishes and jams. Pair older parsnips with apples and/or carrots for a more pleasant taste. To cook parsnips, wash and peel if not organic, roughly chop, place in a small saucepan, cover with water and simmer until soft.

Peas

See Beans and Peas

Peppers

Capsicum annuum
green, red, yellow, orange and purple bell peppers

Actions: Antioxidant, anticancer, heart protective.

Uses: Red peppers are high in vitamins C and A (supplying over 100% of the Daily Recommended Amounts of each) and are good sources of vitamin B_6 (pyridoxine), with some manganese, folate and potassium.

Buying and Storing: Look for firm, crisp peppers with smooth skin and no blemishes. Avoid waxed peppers because the wax can accelerate bacteria growth. Store peppers in a paper bag in the crisper drawer of the refrigerator for up to 4 days. Peppers freeze easily and may be added to soups and stews without thawing.

Culinary Use: Peppers are versatile vegetables, used raw in appetizers, salads and fillings. Mediterranean cooking relies on peppers for vegetable dishes. Orange, red and yellow varieties are sweeter in flavor than the green and purple types.

Potatoes

Solanum tuberosum
white, yellow, red, purple

Actions: Anticancer, heart protective.

Uses: Potatoes are high in potassium, which may help prevent high blood pressure and strokes. Potatoes are an excellent source of vitamin B_6 (pyridoxine) and are good sources of vitamins C and B_1 (thiamin), folate and fiber. They are a low

fat, satisfying vegetable but cooking and garnishing methods determines how nutritious they are.

Buying and Storing: Select clean, smooth, well-shaped potatoes. Wrinkled skin, soft spots and bruises should be avoided. One medium potato weighs about 8 oz (250 g) and dices into about 1 cup (250 mL). If kept in a dry cool and frost-free place (cellar or porch), potatoes will last for 2 to 3 weeks. Keep covered with a brown paper or burlap bag because light causes potatoes to form chlorophyll and turn green. The green itself is not harmful but it is a sign that there is an increase in solanine, a glycoalkaloid that can cause allergic reactions and illness.

Culinary Use: Fresh potatoes are a versatile staple, cooked in gratins, soups, stews, and salads and baked vegetable dishes. They are mashed, boiled, roasted, sautéed, baked or deep-fried. Always use fresh potatoes.

Pumpkin

See Squash

Radishes

Raphanus sativum
red, white and Japanese daikon

Uses: A good source of potassium and iron, radishes lend a pleasantly hot taste to juices.

Buying and Storing: Small, firm radishes with dark green leaves showing no signs of wilting or yellow are best. Radishes keep for up to 1 week in a vented plastic bag in the refrigerator.

Culinary Use: Radishes are usually eaten raw in salads and as a garnish for summer dishes. If known to be organic, the leaves may be used as a salad ingredient or used to make pesto.

Rutabagas

Brassica napo brassica

See Turnips

Spinach

Spinacea oleracea

Actions: Anticancer, helps memory, antioxidant, promotes healing, prevents cataracts, anti-anemia.

Uses: A good source of choline, which improves mental functioning, and folic acid (a heart protector), spinach is one of only four vegetables high in vitamin E. It is also high in cancer-fighting lutein, as well as chlorophyll and vitamins C and A. Spinach is a good source of calcium, iron, protein and potassium.

Buying and Storing: Choose loose spinach instead of packaged whenever available. Look for broad, crisp leaves with deep green color and no signs of yellow, wilting or softness. Spinach keeps for up to 3 days in a vented plastic bag in the produce drawer of the refrigerator. Pick over and remove yellow or wilted leaves of pre-packaged spinach and rewrap in a vented plastic bag for storing.

Culinary Use: Wash fresh leaves well, remove tough spine and stem and shred or coarsely chop the leaves. Spinach is served raw in salads and appetizers. It may be added to soups, sauces, stuffing, risottos, vegetable dishes and pasta. To measure, tightly pack torn or chopped spinach into a dry measuring cup. Use frozen, or canned spinach when fresh is not available.

Squash

Cucurbita species
acorn, butternut, Hubbard, pumpkin, turban

Actions: Antioxidant, anticancer.

Uses: A good winter vegetable, squash is high in vitamins A and C and potassium. Squash is also a good source of manganese, folate and omega-3 fatty acids.

Buying and Storing: Summer squash, such as zucchini, pattypan, cocozelle and the marrows, are small and tender with pliable skin and seeds. Winter squash, such as acorn, spaghetti, butternut, hubbard and pumpkin, have matured on the vine and their rind and seeds are tough and woody. Keep whole squash in a cold moist place or in the produce drawer of the refrigerator. Winter squash may keep as long as 1 month if stored properly. Cooked squash freezes well for use in recipes.

Culinary Use: Squash is often baked whole or split, seeded and baked. Acorn squash is often stuffed with a variety of savory fillings and baked. Use squash in soups, stews, pasta sauces and some baked goods. To bake, wash and prick with a sharp knife. Arrange whole squash on a baking dish and bake at 375°F (190°C) for 40 to 45 minutes or until tender.

Sweet Potatoes

Ipomoea batatas

Actions: Antioxidant, anticancer, heart protective.

Uses: Sweet potatoes are high in vitamin A (retinol), beta-carotene, vitamin C and fiber. They are a good source of copper and potassium and they also contain some calcium, iron, magnesium and zinc.

Buying and Storing: Select clean, smooth, well-shaped and firm sweet potatoes. Wrinkled skin, soft spots and bruises should be avoided. If kept in a cool dry and frost-free place (cellar or porch), sweet potatoes will last for up to 1 month.

Culinary Use: Although not related to the ordinary potato, sweet potatoes are often prepared in the same way, with baking as the most common method. Mashed sweet potatoes make a good topping for baked vegetable dishes. One medium sweet potato weighs about 10 ounces (300 grams) and dices into about 1 cup (250 mL).

Swiss Chard

See Leafy Greens

Tomatoes

Lycopersicon esculentum

Actions: Antioxidant, anticancer.

Uses: High in lycopene and glutathione, two powerful antioxidants, raw tomatoes reduce the risk of many cancers. Lycopene is also thought to help maintain mental and physical functioning and is absorbed by the body more efficiently when tomatoes are juiced. Tomatoes also contain glutamic acid that is converted in the human system to gamma-amino butyric acid (GABA), a calming agent, known to be effective for kidney hypertension. Drink tomato juice or smoothies made with tomatoes to relax after a stressful day. Tomatoes are also good sources of vitamins B_6 (pyrodoxine) and C.

Buying and Storing: Vine-ripened heritage varieties have the best flavor. Tomatoes are best bought fresh only when in season (use canned or reconstituted dried at other times). Local tomatoes are not treated with ethylene gas to force reddening. Plump, heavy, firm skinned, bright red tomatoes keep for 2 to 3 days at room temperature. When almost over-ripe, store tomatoes in the refrigerator for 1 or 2 more days only.

Culinary Use: Raw fresh tomatoes are used in salads, sandwiches and as a side dish in the summertime. Fresh tomatoes are stuffed and eaten raw or baked. To remove the skin, cut a cross in the skin of each tomato using a paring knife. Place in a heatproof bowl and cover with boiling water. Leave for 30 seconds and drain. The skins will easily slip off. To remove the seeds, cut tomatoes in half and gently squeeze the seeds out. Use canned tomatoes in sauces, soups, stews and baked vegetable dishes.

Turnips

Brassica rapa

Actions: Tonic, decongestant, antibacterial, anticancer, diuretic.

Uses: Turnips have a beneficial effect on the urinary system. They purify the blood and aid in the elimination of toxins. For this reason, they make a good addition to recipes. Both the root and the green tops are high in glucosinolates, which are thought to block the development of cancer. Good sources of calcium, iron and protein, small fresh tender turnips are available in the spring and sometimes in the fall.

Buying and Storing: Small, firm turnips with dark green leaves showing no signs of wilting or yellow are best. Rutabagas (similar to turnips but a different species in the cabbage family) may be waxed to hold in their moisture and are generally a lot bigger than the young fresh turnip. Turnips keep for up to 1 week in a vented plastic bag in the refrigerator. Rutabagas will keep longer.

Culinary Use: Fresh turnips can be hot and peppery in taste. They may be steamed, boiled or shredded and added raw to salads. Treat young turnips as you would parsnips — add to soups, stews and baked vegetable dishes. For using the green leafy turnip tops, see Leafy Greens, page 124.

Watercress

Nasturtium officinale

Actions: Antioxidant, diuretic, anticancer, tonic, antibiotic, cleansing.

Uses: High in fiber and vitamin C, and a good source of vitamin A. Purchase from farmers' markets in spring. Watercress grows wild around streams and wet areas, but be careful not to harvest in areas where fields drain directly into streams.

Buying and Storing: Pick watercress just before using. If purchasing, choose bright green, crisp sprigs with leaves intact. Sort through and remove any yellow or wilted stems. Watercress is fragile and should be used immediately or wrapped in a towel in the produce drawer of the refrigerator for 1 or 2 days.

Culinary Use: Watercress adds a hot and peppery bite to salads and baked dishes. Use watercress to replace spinach, parsley or other greens in sauces, soups, fillings and egg dishes.

Wild Greens

dandelion leaves, mustard, sorrel, turnip, wild garlic mustard, wild leeks or ramps

See Leafy Greens

Zucchini

Cucurbita pepo
Italian, yellow straightneck, yellow crookneck

Actions: Antioxidant.

Uses: A good source of vitamins A and C, folate, potassium and B$_3$ (niacin), zucchini is mild tasting and blends well with stronger vegetables.

Buying and Storing: Although zucchini grows quite large, the smaller fruit are tender and less woody. Look for soft thin skin with no cuts or bruises and stem end intact.

Culinary Use: The fresh flowers may be stuffed and baked. Zucchini are eaten raw in salads, often mixed with carrot. They are steamed, stir-fried or added to soups, sauces, stews and baked vegetable dishes.

Legumes

Definition: Leguminous plants include 10,000 plant species. Peas and beans, along with clover, alfalfa, wisteria and lupines all produce their seeds in pods. The term "legume" is applied to the plant, the pods or the seeds. "Pulse" is a common term in Asia that means fresh or dry edible leguminous seeds. The words "pulse" and "legume" may be interchanged. "Dal" is a Middle Eastern term applied to lentils, mung beans and split peas. The word "dal" also refers to a puréed dish made from lentils, mung beans or split peas.

Actions/Uses: The high levels of fiber in legumes work to lower cholesterol in the body and prevent blood sugar levels from rising too rapidly after a meal. This makes legumes a good choice for individuals with diabetes, insulin resistance or hypoglycemia.

Legumes help to control weight by retaining water in the digestive tract, giving the feeling of fullness. Legumes flush fats rather than allowing the body to store them. The oils in legumes are rich in linoleic and linolenic acids, two of the three essential fatty acids, which help the immune system. The fiber in legumes is a valuable tool for preventing colon cancer.

The amino acids (protein) in beans and peas make them a valuable food for vegetarians. Legumes are low in the amino acid methionine and high in lysine. Cereals are high in methionine and low in lysine. When legumes are combined with cereals in a dish (for example Red Beans and Rice), the combined amino acids make up complete, high-quality protein, an important issue for vegetarians.

A 1-cup (250 mL) serving of most legumes delivers 100% or more of the Recommended Daily Amounts of molybdenum, a trace mineral responsible for detoxifying damaging sulfites in the body.

Legumes are high in most B vitamins — 1 cup/ 250 mL cooked beans yields 40% of the daily requirement of B_1 (thiamin) and B_6 (pyridoxine). A good source of iron and choline, which improves mental functioning, legumes also contain vitamin A and potassium as well as calcium and vitamin C.

Buying and Storing: Whole or natural food stores and ethnic (Middle Eastern, Indian, Caribbean) stores carry a wide selection of legumes both prepackaged and in bulk. Look for clean dried peas and beans with no signs of wrinkling or mildew. Dried legumes will keep for a very long time if kept in a clean glass container away from heat and light.

Culinary Use: Grain and legume dishes are especially important for vegetarians, who benefit from the complete proteins formed when grains and legumes are combined. Lentils and split peas may be added to soups and stews without soaking but all other legumes must be soaked to soften and rehydrate them. Soaking reduces the cooking time by half. Cooked canned peas, beans and lentils are an excellent and easy way to use legumes when time does not permit soaking and cooking the dried beans. When using canned legumes, if the recipe calls for them to be drained, reserve the liquid and use it in soups and stock recipes because it retains many of the water-soluble nutrients.

To Soak Legumes: Place washed beans in a large saucepan and cover with 2 inches (5 cm) of water. Bring to a boil over high heat. Reduce heat and gently simmer for 2 minutes. Leave the pan on the element and turn off the heat. Let stand 1 hour or overnight. Discard the soaking water and rinse the beans. Legumes have now been rehydrated and are ready to cook.

To Cook Legumes: Place soaked, drained, rinsed beans in a large saucepan. Cover with 2 inches (5 cm) of fresh water. Cover the pan and bring to a boil. Reduce heat and simmer for 45 minutes to 2 hours (cooking times differ for the varieties), or cook until tender. Add salt or other seasonings after legumes have been cooked because if added before, salt toughens the beans.

Adzuki Beans

Phaseolus angularis

Native of Asia, the small, oval, dark red adzuki beans grow on bushes rather than vines, as do most legumes. They are eaten fresh, dried or sprouted and ground into flour. The taste is mild, slightly nutty. Adzuki beans have a thick skin and take up to 2 hours to cook.

Black Beans

Phaseolus vulgaris

Large, shiny black, kidney-shaped beans from South America, black beans are a staple in South and Central American and Caribbean dishes. In traditional dishes, they are boiled and fried and often paired with rice for complete protein. The taste is earthy, with overtones of mushroom. Cook black beans for 1 hour.

Black-Eyed Peas

Vigna unguiculata

Originating in China, black-eyed peas traveled the Silk Route to Arabia and from there to Africa. Slaves carried them to America where they became an important part of "soul food" dishes.

Kidney-shaped and smooth, with thin skin, black-eyed peas are cream-colored with a definite black or brown spot or eye. They are smooth and buttery in texture and the taste is subtle. Black-eyed peas may be cooked in soups or stews without soaking. Check for doneness after 30 minutes and do not overcook, which will cause them to loose their texture. Substitute black-eyed peas for flageolets in any recipe.

Cannellini Beans

Phaseolus vulgaris

See also Haricot Beans

Cannellini beans are a member of the haricot bean family and are used extensively in Italian cooking. Cannellini beans are white, oval and medium size. Their tough skin means that cannellini beans will take 1 to 1½ hours to soften. Their texture is smooth and buttery and the taste is subtle, making them a good bean for soups and spreads.

Chickpeas

Cicer arietinum

(also known as Garbanzo)

The Roman word, arietinum means "like a ram." Arietinum is an apt name for chickpeas because they resemble a ram's head with horns curling around the sides. Large, round and tan-colored, chickpeas are nutty in flavor and firm in texture. Chickpeas require up to 1½ hours to cook. They are very versatile, used in salads, soups, stews, sauces, spreads and dips.

Fava Beans

Vicia faba

(also known as broad beans)

Used in European soups and stews since before medieval times, the fava bean has been an important staple throughout history. Fava beans are large, light brown or taupe in color with wrinkled skin and a strong, earthy flavor. They are usually tender after 1 hour of cooking. Fava beans can overwhelm some dishes and are at their best in hearty soups and stews.

Flageolets

Phaseolus vulgaris

See also Haricot Beans

Popular in French and Mediterranean dishes, flageolets are immature kidney beans, picked before they ripen and considered a delicacy. Smaller than mature kidney beans, flageolets are pale green, tender and very mild tasting. Salads are the best way to feature the subtle taste and texture of flageolets.

Haricot Beans

Phaseolus vulgaris

The Haricot family of beans includes cannellini beans, great Northern beans, white kidney, navy beans, flageolets and small whites. They are the mature (except in the case of flageolets), dried white, small round or oval seeds of the green bean (string bean), known as *haricot vert* in France. These beans are common beans, easily found in most supermarkets and in dried soup packets. Haricot beans take about 1 hour to cook but stand up to long, slow simmering. They are the beans used in the fabulous French cassoulet and the popular Boston Baked Bean dish that originated in the city still known as Beantown.

Red Kidney Beans

Phaseolus vulgaris

Native to Mexico, red kidney beans (sometimes called kidney) are now used throughout the world in ethnic dishes such as Chile con Carne and Three-Bean Salad. Also known as red beans, they have evolved into many different varieties. Kidney-shaped and usually deep red in color, kidney beans also come in brown, black and white varieties. The texture is mealy and the taste is rich and unique. Check for doneness after 1 hour of simmering because red kidney beans will start to loose their texture if cooked too long.

Lentils

Lens esculenta and *L. culinaris*

Dating from about 8000 BC, lentils are believed to be the first legumes to be cultivated. They originated in Asia and spread to India and the Middle East and are still very popular in dishes from those areas, where they play an important role in providing protein to the diet.

Lentils range in color from a tan and gray-brown, to dark brown, green, red, yellow and blue. They are small flat disks that can be very small ($1/8$ inch/0.25 cm) or larger ($1/4$ inch/0.5 cm). Lentils do not need to be presoaked and cook in 10 to 15 minutes. They should not be overcooked because they will loose their texture and turn to mush. Lentils are used in soups, baked vegetable dishes, stews and purées.

Lima Beans

Phaseolus lunatus

There are two main species of lima bean, the large lima from Central America and the smaller variety originating in Mexico. The name actually comes from the capital city of Peru. American Indians used lima beans as part of their three sisters dishes. Corn and squash were the other sisters. They have traveled around the world and are now the most important bean in Africa.

Lima beans are flat, white to pale green seeds with a mealy texture when cooked. Cook lima beans for 1 to $1\frac{1}{2}$ hours. They are available fresh, dried, canned and frozen and can be added to soups and stews and baked grain and vegetable dishes.

Mung Beans

Vigna radiata

Mung beans are sold with or without their husk. They can be whole or split. Native to India, they are known as *moong dal*. Mung beans are the variety of legume that the Chinese sprout (they are five times richer in vitamins A and B and contain vitamins C and B_{12} when sprouted). Each of the many varieties of mung beans are small, round and most often yellow inside a dull green skin. There are brown and black varieties but the green or yellow (when hulled) mung beans are the most common. Cook mung beans for less than 1 hour or add directly to soups and other dishes that will simmer for at least that long.

Peas

Pisum sativum

Peas originated in the Middle East and spread to China, the Mediterranean, India and Europe. A staple in Greece, Rome and ultimately Great Britain, peas were the perfect food to grow in earlier times because they would keep all winter. Small, round, bright green when fresh, dried peas are usually split. Dried split peas are green or yellow. Use fresh, dried, canned or frozen peas. Fresh peas have a fresh, sweet taste. All dried split peas cook quickly without soaking and have a deeper, richer flavor than fresh.

Soybeans

Glycine max

Soybeans are the only known vegetable source of complete protein, meaning they contain all of the essential amino acids in the appropriate proportions essential for the growth and maintenance of body cells. In addition to being an excellent source of fiber, the fat in soybeans (34%) is polyunsaturated, lower than animal fat in calories and rich in linolenic fatty acids. See Caution, page 88.

Whole and Ancient Grains

Definition: Cereal grains are part of the grass family of plants. Whole grains have not been refined and stripped of their outer bran and inner germ. Whole grains supply complex carbohydrates and nutrients to the body because the whole seed package, with its three major sections and their nutrients, is intact.

Ancient is a term that is often used to describe grains (spelt, kamut) and herb seeds (quinoa, amaranth, teff) that have survived thousands of years without hybridization or significant genetic modification. They are much the same now as when prehistoric man gathered them. Ancient grains have largely been introduced to the Western world within the last half of the twentieth century and enjoy limited availability.

The outer layer, called bran, protects the life force and nourishment of all grains. Bran contains fiber, some minerals and protein. It is always removed when grains are refined. The largest part of grain is the endosperm, which provides a storehouse of food in the form of carbohydrate intended for the growing seed. The third, perhaps most important section of whole grains, the germ, is the life-spark of the grain. It is a rich source of protein, antioxidant vitamin E, phytate, iron, zinc and magnesium.

Actions/Uses: Whole grains supply fiber, which helps prevent against colon cancer. They are rich in phytoestrogens that halt the early stages of breast cancer and protect against cancer of the large intestine. The vitamin E in grains has an antioxidant effect. Whole grains protect against heart disease, fight obesity and lower blood sugar levels. Whole grains supply selenium, potassium and magnesium to the body. Each grain or seed listed below has its own nutrient quota.

Buying and Storing: Whole or natural food stores carry a wide selection of whole and ancient grains both packaged and in bulk. Purchase small quantities of ground grain and a wide variety of whole grains. Use them often, and store in glass containers below 65°F (18°C) or in the refrigerator.

Flavor: The presence of the outer bran makes whole grains chewier and more flavorful. A nutty flavor is evident, yet each grain species has its own characteristic flavor.

Culinary Use: Whole grains are sprouted, toasted, used with dried fruit as a breakfast cereal or casserole topping, cooked and added as an ingredient in baked products, soups, salads and stir-fries and baked with custard and fruit for desserts.

To Wash Whole Grains: Place whole grains in a sieve and swish in cool water. Whole grains benefit from presoaking for up to several hours before cooking. Whole grains double their bulk when cooked.

To Cook Whole-Grain Berries: Measure berries into a medium-size pot. Cover with twice the amount of water, place over medium-high heat and bring to a boil. Cover pot with a lid, turn heat off and set aside overnight or for a minimum of 2 to 3 hours. Most of the liquid will be absorbed. Test to see if the grain is tender. If not, add enough water to cover and simmer until tender (whole grains retain a chewy texture and never get soft like processed grain). Drain and store in a tightly covered glass jar in the refrigerator until ready to use. Cooked whole grains keep 2 to 3 days in the refrigerator.

Amaranth

Amaranthus cruentus

The only seed to provide humans with the most effective balance of protein matched only by milk, amaranth plays an important role in dairy-reduced diets. Lysine is higher in amaranth than any other complex carbohydrate. The ancient Aztecs revered amaranth as a "wonder food," not knowing that science would show it to be lean and high in vitamins and minerals and calcium.

Forms Available: Whole seed, flour and sometimes mixed with other grains in whole-grain blends.

Barley

Hordeum vulgare

Barley is one of the oldest domesticated crops. The gummy fiber in barley is thought to be what is responsible for its ability to reduce high serum cholesterol levels in the body. Barley is a source of potassium, magnesium and B_3 (niacin).

Forms Available: Pot barley is the preferred form because it is milled just enough to remove the inedible hull. Scotch barley is coarsely ground hulled barley and has as many of the nutrients as pot barley. Not really a whole food, pearl barley is whiter than pot barley because more of the hull and bran layers are stripped along with much of the protein, fiber, vitamins and minerals. Rolled barley is pot barley that has been sliced, steamed, and rolled into flakes.

Buckwheat

Fagopyrum esculentum

Buckwheat is not related to wheat, but is a plant in the same family as rhubarb. Buckwheat is an excellent source of antioxidants and it increases the quality of protein in the diet because it is higher in the amino acid lysine.

Forms Available: Whole kernel, white hulled buckwheat (called groats), kasha (hulled, crushed and toasted white buckwheat), flour and noodles (called soba).

Bran

Bran is the outer layer of grains and contains fiber, protein and other nutrients. The easiest way to cook with bran is to buy whole grains with the bran still attached. Bran may be purchased at most supermarkets and whole or natural food stores. Store bran in the refrigerator and use it to add fiber and nutrients to most recipes or to enrich milled flour. Use 1 to 2 tbsp (15 to 25 mL) in baked goods, toppings, stir-fries and legume and vegetable dishes.

Forms Available: Oat, wheat and rye bran is available in flakes or buds.

Corn

Zea mays

Commonly called maize, corn is the only widely used grain that is native to the Western hemisphere. It has been proven that corn was grown and used some 80,000 years ago.

Forms Available: Whole corn kernels (see Corn, page 123) are dried and ground into other products. Corn flour is ground from a variety of corn with a soft starch that makes it easy to grind. Hard shell flint corn is ground to a coarse meal called polenta — very deep yellow-orange polenta is highest in beta-carotene. The Algonquin Indians discovered that soaking fresh corn with wood ashes until the kernels burst out of their skins and drying and grinding the inner corn kernels produces hominy and grits. Hominy and grits are not exactly whole foods, but they do deliver fiber and some protein

and are usually combined with eggs, vegetables, cheese or legumes for balanced dishes. Cornmeal, polenta, hominy or grits that are processed by the old, traditional stone-ground method retain more of the bran and germ.

Kamut

Triticum polonicum

A non-hybrid form of wheat originating in the Fertile Crescent between Egypt and the Tigris-Euphrates region, kamut is truly an ancient grain. It is a good source of calcium, magnesium, phosphorus and potassium and supplies 12% of the body's daily protein requirements. Kamut is a much larger grain than wheat, with a mild, sweet, buttery and nutty flavor. Substitute kamut for wheat or spelt in any recipe.

Forms Available: Whole kernel and flour.

Millet

Panicum miliaceum

Native to Africa and Asia, millet is the round yellow seed of an annual grass. Millet is not a true cereal but related to sorghum, a type of millet. A good source of protein, millet is an excellent source of the B vitamins, magnesium, zinc, copper and iron. Combine millet in vegetarian dishes with a good source of vitamin C such as carrots, oranges or broccoli.

Forms Available: Whole seed often mixed with other grains in whole-grain blends.

Oats

Avena sativa

Oats are higher in protein and essential fatty acids than other cereals because when hulled, the bran and germ remain intact with the groat. Oats are an excellent source of B vitamins and minerals.

Forms Available: Steel-cut oats contain the bran and germ while Scotch-cut (also known as Irish oats) are ground with stones and may be missing some nutrients. Steamed oat groats are sliced and rolled to make rolled oats. Whole rolled oats (also known as old-fashioned oats) are higher in nutrients than quick-cooking oats and the even thinner instant oats, which are partially cooked and may cook faster but are not considered whole foods.

Quinoa

Chenopodium quinoa

Actually an herb seed, quinoa is protein rich and extremely high in calcium (1 cup/250 mL of cooked quinoa equals the amount of calcium found in 1 quart/liter of milk). Gluten-free and easily digested, quinoa is classed as an ancient grain. Rinse thoroughly before using to remove the bitter saponin coating.

Forms Available: Whole seed.

Rice

Oryza sativa var.

A cereal originating in Asia, rice has been a staple there since about 5000 BC. Brown rice, or rice with the bran intact, is rich in B vitamins, protein, magnesium and fiber and that is why it is considered whole. Eat rice with a fruit or vegetable high in vitamin C.

Forms Available: More than 25 varieties of rice are available — basmati, Wehani, black and red rice are a few — and most can be purchased in the following forms: brown (missing only the hull and the most nutritious); polished white rice, which lacks the protein and other nutrients in brown rice; parboiled rice is steamed white rice; quick-cooking or instant brown rice has been partially cooked and slit to make it cook faster; brown rice farina (stone-ground brown rice); and rice flour, which is usually made by grinding white rice. See also Wild Rice (page 137).

Rye

Secale cereale

Rye originated in Southwest Asia and is similar in nutrients to wheat but with more of the lysine amino acid. When rye is crossed with wheat, the hybrid triticale is the result.

Forms Available: Whole kernel called rye berries, rolled, cracked and flour.

Spelt

Triticum aestivum spelta

One of the original natural grains known to man, spelt was grown in Europe more than 9,000 years ago. It contains more protein, fats and crude fiber than wheat, and is high in mucopolysaccharides. Spelt is usually organically grown because it is hardier, resistant to pests and diseases and therefore doesn't require fertilizers, pesticides or insecticides.

Caution: Spelt may be tolerated by people with wheat allergies, but should be avoided by people with celiac disease or gluten intolerance.

Forms Available: Whole kernel called spelt berries, rolled spelt or flakes and flour.

Teff (or Tef)

Eragrostis abyssinica

Grown by Ethiopians for centuries, teff means "lost" in reference to the tiny seeds that are hard to harvest. Now available in limited supply in the West, teff is a good wheat substitute for some dishes because it does not contain gluten. However, the lack of gluten means that teff will not hold the structure for baked products. The seed is so small it cannot be refined so all the nutrients are intact.

Forms Available: Whole grains.

Wheat

Triticum aestivum

Wheat may have been one of the first cultivated plants 11,000 years ago. There are two main types of wheat — hard (with a higher protein and gluten content) and soft. The berry contains both insoluble and soluble fiber, vitamins, minerals, protein, carbohydrates and phytochemicals. Eating whole wheat with legumes and seeds helps to enrich the incomplete proteins in vegetarian dishes.

Forms Available: Whole kernels called wheat berries are the most nutritious form. Bulgur is wheat that has been steamed, dried and crushed. Couscous is a processed flour product made from cracked wheat that cooks faster than berries but does not have their nutrients. Farina (a fine cracked wheat), rolled wheat or flakes, whole and crushed germ and bran (see page 135) are the other semi-whole wheat forms. Whole unbleached flour is preferred to refined white wheat flour and udon noodles are more nutrient-rich than pasta made from refined white flour. Seitan is a high-protein food made from the gluten in wheat flour and for wheat grass in cereal grasses.

Wild Rice

Zizania palustris

Wild rice is not rice at all, but is an aquatic grain harvested from the brown and green reeds of a long-stemmed annual plant that grows primarily in the shallow waters of northern Ontario, Manitoba and Minnesota. It is a sacred plant, central to the Ojibwe religion and the foundation of their belief system. At the same time, it was a staple food, one that can be stored for years against times of famine. The taste of wild rice is nutty and pleasant and the texture is chewy. Wild rice has more protein than wheat and brown or white rice, less fat than corn and is high in B_1 (thiamin), B_2 (riboflavin), B_3 (niacin) and potassium. Substitute wild rice for brown rice in recipes. Use cooked wild rice in soups, salads, breads and cakes and as a breakfast cereal.

Forms Available: Whole grain and mixed with other rice varieties in gourmet blends.

Nuts and Seeds

Definition: The term nut describes any seed or fruit of a plant that has an edible kernel and is found in a hard shell. Seeds are found in the fruit of plants or growing on the stalk after the flower dies. Unless they are salted, spiced or treated with additives, preservatives or dyes, most raw or dry-roasted nuts are considered whole foods.

Actions/Uses: Because they contain all that is necessary for a plant's new life, nuts and seeds are extremely nutritious, supplying protein, vitamin E and fiber along with essential minerals. Five human epidemiological studies found that nut consumption is linked to a lower risk for heart disease. This is likely due to their monounsaturated fats and the antioxidant action of vitamin E found in most nuts.

Most nuts (with the exception of coconut and pine nuts) contain linoleic acid and alpha-linolenic acid. These essential fatty acids are associated with decreased risk of tumor formation and heart disease and are also essential for healthy skin, hair, glands, mucus membranes, nerves and arteries. Although their fat is polyunsaturated or monounsaturated, which may actually help decrease blood cholesterol levels, nuts and seeds should be used regularly but in moderation.

Buying and Storing: Whole food stores carry a wide selection of whole raw nuts and seeds packaged and in bulk. Unshelled nuts will keep in a cool place for up to 6 months. Purchase small quantities of shelled whole nuts in the fall when they are harvested and store in a cool place or the refrigerator for up to 2 months. Due to their high oil content, chopped nuts will go rancid quickly and should be stored in the refrigerator for up to 6 weeks.

Culinary Use: Nuts and seeds are best eaten raw (or lightly toasted). They can be used whole or chopped as snacks, in salads, casseroles, stuffing, cereals and baked goods, as a topping for baked vegetable and fruit dishes, as well as in grain and lentil dishes. Whole shelled nuts may retain their skins, which do not need to be removed unless the taste is just too bitter.

To Blanch Nuts: To remove skins from almonds, pistachios and walnuts, cover with boiling water, let cool and rub or pinch skins off. Dry on absorbent towels. To blanch hazelnuts: Place in a single layer in a baking pan in a 350°F (180°C) oven for about 15 minutes or until skins dry and rub off easily.

To Toast Nuts or Seeds: Preheat the oven to 375°F (190°C). Spread nuts or seeds in one layer on an ungreased baking sheet and bake for 3 minutes.

Turn nuts/seeds over and toast for 1 to 3 minutes more, watching closely. Nuts/seeds are done when they color slightly. Let cool before using. Seeds take much less time to toast than nuts. Store toasted nuts in an airtight container in a cool, dry place for up to 1 week.

Almonds

Prunus amygdalus

Of the two types of almonds — bitter and sweet — only the sweet is edible in the raw state. The poisonous prussic acid in bitter almonds is removed by heating. Bitter almonds are used mainly in the production of almond oil and almond essence and are not readily available to consumers. Jordan and Valencia varieties of sweet almonds from Spain and Portugal are widely available. The flat, medium-size Californian almonds are used mostly for processing but may be available to home cooks in North America.

One-quarter cup (60 mL) of almonds supplies the body with 45% of its daily requirements of manganese and vitamin E. Almonds are high in protein, potassium, magnesium and phosphorus and they have the highest calcium content of all nuts.

Forms Available: Whole unshelled, whole shelled with skin, whole shelled and blanched, blanched halves, blanched slivers, flaked, roasted, chopped and ground (almond meal). Marzipan is a confectionary paste made from ground almonds, sugar and egg whites often used as an icing base for fruitcakes.

Brazil Nuts

Bertholettia excelsa

Native to the tropical regions of Brazil, Venezuela and Bolivia, Brazil nuts are rich and sweet tasting. The meat is found inside a coconut-like shell that is larger than most nuts. The taste lends itself to sweet dishes but Brazil nuts may also be used in savory dishes where nuts are called for. Brazil nuts are the best source of selenium, a trace mineral that reduces the risk of cancer and arthritis. They are also high in protein and exceptionally high in potassium, manganese and phosphorus. They are a good source of calcium and sodium, with small amounts of B vitamins.

Forms Available: Whole unshelled, whole shelled with skin, whole shelled and blanched, chopped and roasted.

Cashews

Anacardium occidentale

Originating in Brazil, cashews now grow in many other tropical areas. Often eaten as a snack, the buttery taste of cashews also complements grain and baked vegetable dishes, stuffing and salads. Cashew nuts contain some protein but have high oil content. Cashews are high in copper and have significant amounts of magnesium, tryptophan and phosphorus and are the only nuts that contain a small amount of vitamin C.

Forms Available: All forms of cashews come shelled. They are available whole raw or roasted, in halves, pieces and chopped, and salted.

Chestnuts

Castanea sativa

Sweet chestnuts grow on wild trees in Britain, Europe and North America and are cultivated in Italy, France and Spain. Raw chestnuts do not keep long before the flesh deteriorates and so are usually cooked before they are sold. If fresh, chestnuts should be bought in the shell and cooked or used right away. They can be boiled, steamed, roasted or stewed. Chestnuts are low in oils and high in carbohydrates. They are high in potassium, are good sources of calcium, magnesium and phosphorus and have small amounts of the B vitamins.

Forms Available: Cooked whole, usually peeled, dried and ground or canned chestnut purée.

Note: The water chestnut is unrelated to chestnuts. Water chestnuts are the edible fruit from an herbaceous water plant.

Coconuts

Cocos nucifera

The coconut, largest of all nuts, is the fruit of the coconut palm that grows on tropical islands. Coconuts may be eaten fresh along with their milk or the flesh is dried and usually sweetened. Coconuts are rich in potassium and have significant amounts of phosphorus and magnesium. They are a good source of protein. Both the coconut flesh and milk are used in curries, fruit dishes, sauces and desserts.

Forms Available: Whole (fresh) in the shell and dried, grated, shredded, flaked or desiccated. Canned coconut milk and coconut oil are also available.

Flaxseeds

Linum usitatissimum

Flaxseed oil is the best vegetable source of essential omega-3 fatty acids, which help lubricate the joints and prevent absorption of toxins by stimulating digestion. They contain 30% of the body's daily requirement of manganese and are high in dietary fiber. Flaxseeds also contain magnesium, folate, copper, phosphorus and vitamin B_6 (pyridoxine).

Flaxseeds must be ground for the body to absorb and benefit from the oils. Once ground, the seeds deteriorate rapidly. Buy in small amounts and store whole, ground seeds and flaxseed oil in refrigerator.

Forms Available: Whole, ground and flax meal. Flaxseed oil is also available.

Peanuts

Arachis hypogaea

Widely available, peanuts are an important food staple in some areas, a snack in others. Peanuts are actually legumes encased in a dry, fibrous pod. High in manganese and protein and containing tryptophan, vitamin B_3 (niacin), folate and copper, peanuts also have significant amounts of vitamin E.

Caution: Many individuals experience an allergic reaction when exposed to peanuts and peanut products. Peanuts that have been deep-fried, battered, candied or combined with additives, dyes, fats or sugars have no place in a whole foods diet.

Forms Available: Whole unshelled, shelled raw with skin, shelled and blanched, roasted and salted. Also available chopped.

Pecans

Carya pecan

Native to North America, pecans are sweetly pleasant tasting. Grafting techniques developed thin-shelled varieties in the 19th century. This was crucial to their widespread use. Pecans lend texture and interest to salads, fruit dishes, baked vegetables and grains and can replace most nuts in recipes. They are well used in sweets, pies and fruitcakes. Pecans are high in protein with significant amounts of B vitamins. They have some iron, calcium, potassium and phosphorus.

Forms Available: Whole unshelled, shelled raw with skin, shelled blanched and roasted whole, halves and chopped.

Pine Nuts

Pinus pinea

Pine nuts are the edible seed of just over a dozen varieties of pine tree. Pine nuts are probably the most expensive of all the edible nuts. They are small, creamy-colored and buttery in texture. Their oil-rich flesh is what contributes to their taste and texture. High in protein and carbohydrate, they are also good sources of B vitamins. Keep pine nuts in the refrigerator for up to 1 month.

Forms Available: Except when purchased directly from harvesters, pine nuts always come shelled and are usually whole. They may be raw or roasted and salted.

Pistachio Nuts

Pistacia vera

Small, green pistachio nuts are native to the Middle East, where they are a symbol of happiness. Pistachio nuts have a soft texture and mild flavor which makes them versatile in cooking. They are used in salads and as a topping for vegetables, grains and legume dishes. Pistachio nuts are also used in sweet dishes.

Forms Available: Whole unshelled raw and salted, shelled raw and salted.

Pumpkin Seeds

The pumpkin's small, flat green seeds are used to treat and prevent parasites as well as to nourish and restore the prostate gland. They are high in manganese, magnesium, phosphorus and tryptophan and contain iron, copper, vitamin K, zinc and essential fatty acids.

Forms Available: Whole unshelled raw, unsalted and salted, shelled raw, unsalted and salted or toasted and salted.

Sesame Seeds

Sesamum indicum

Tiny, cream-colored and almond-shaped, sesame seeds are widely available. They originate from Africa, where they are called *benne*. Sesame seeds are high in copper and manganese and are a good source of protein. They work well with legumes or whole grains. They have high levels of tryptophan, calcium,

magnesium and iron and some phosphorus, zinc and vitamin B_1 (thiamin). Sesame seeds and oil lend a nutty taste to breads, vegetables, grains and beans.

Tahini is a thick paste made from ground sesame seeds. It is used in dips, spreads and falafel dishes. Halva is a sweet sesame cake made with honey.

Forms Available: Whole with hulls, raw, hulled and polished, hulled and roasted. Sesame seed oil is available raw and toasted. Tahini paste is available in Middle Eastern stores and natural food stores.

Sunflower Seeds

Helianthus annuus

Sunflowers most probably originated in Mexico. The long, flat, gray or black-striped seeds are cultivated for oil as well as for eating. One-quarter cup (50 mL) of sunflower seeds supply 90% of the body's daily requirement of vitamin E and almost 55% of vitamin B_1 (thiamin). Sunflower seeds are high in protein, manganese, magnesium, copper, trypotophan and selenium. They also contain significant amounts of phosphorus, vitamin B_5 (pantothenic), folate and potassium. They may be used to replace the more expensive pine nuts in pesto recipes and salads. Sunflower oil is polyunsaturated and has a light, nutty taste, making it a popular salad oil.

Forms Available: Whole and raw with hulls, hulled raw, roasted and salted.

Walnuts

Juglans regia (English) or *J. nigra* (black)

There are two main varieties of walnut, the English (or Persian) walnut, and the Black walnut (native to North America). Walnuts are widely available and used often in a wide variety of dishes, both savory and sweet. Walnuts are high in oil, protein, potassium and phosphorus. They contain some vitamin B_6 (pyridoxine), and folic acid, which is not found in other nuts. Eaten as a snack or used in stuffing, salads, cakes, vegetable and grain dishes, $1/4$ cup (60 mL) supplies 90% of the body's requirement of omega-3 fatty acids and 40% of manganese. They also contain copper and tryptophan.

Forms Available: Whole unshelled raw, whole shelled raw, halves, pieces, chopped and ground. Walnut oil is available.

Sea Vegetables

Definition: Often called seaweeds or sea herbs, sea vegetables are edible, wild plants that grow abundantly in the oceans. They are primitive plants with blades for leaves, stipes for stems and holdfasts for roots. Sea vegetables have been honored by cultures of the Far East and harvested by seaside communities around the world for food, salt, medicine and fertilizer for many thousands of years.

Actions/Uses: Sea vegetables are rich in minerals and trace elements, particularly iodine, calcium, potassium and iron. They contain small amounts of protein, but their protein includes essential amino acids, unlike most plants that only contain incomplete amino acids. They have a significant amount of vitamins A, B, C and D, including vitamin B_{12}, which is only found in three other plant foods (alfalfa, comfrey and fermented soybean products). Most sea vegetables have anticancer properties.

Caution: Do not consume sea vegetables if you have a hyperthyroid condition.

Buying and Storing: Whole or natural food stores carry a selection of packaged dried sea vegetables. Some supermarkets offer a few dried and prepackaged sea vegetables for sale. Store unopened dried sea vegetables indefinitely and once opened, keep in an airtight container for up to 3 months.

Culinary Use: Most dried sea vegetables require a quick rehydration by soaking in cool water for 10 to 15 minutes. Shredded dried sea vegetables, such as arame, wakame and hijiki, may be added to soups, broths, sauces and stews without soaking but will need to simmer for 20 to 30 minutes to cook and may require slightly more liquid depending on the dish. Finely chopped or powdered dried sea vegetables are almost always used with other herbs as a salt substitute.

Arame

Eisenia bicyclis

Arame appears as short, thin, curled strands. It is dark yellow-brown when growing, black when dried. Arame grows off Japan's northern and southern coasts. It is soft with a slightly resistant texture and sweet, delicate flavor.

Actions/Uses: Alleviates high blood pressure and builds strong bones and teeth. Arame is one of the richest sources of iodine and is highly concentrated in iron and calcium.

Culinary Use: Add to curries, salads, soups, stews, and tomato sauce and baked vegetable and grain dishes. Soak in water for 3 to 5 minutes, then cook as directed in recipe or add to long-simmering soups and stews directly.

Dulse

Palmaria palmata

Dulse has large, dark red fronds. Found off North Atlantic waters, it has a chewy texture that is salty and nutlike.

Actions/Uses: Prevents scurvy, induces sweating, is a remedy for seasickness and treats symptoms of the herpes virus. Dulse is exceptionally concentrated in iodine, which is important to the thyroid gland. It is rich in manganese, which activates the enzyme system. Dulse is a good source of phosphorus, B vitamins, vitamins E and C, bromine, potassium, magnesium, sulfur, calcium, sodium, radium, boron, rubidium, manganese, titanium and other trace elements.

Culinary Use: Use dulse in the same way as spinach — chopped, in stuffing, relishes, salad dressings, grain and vegetable bakes. Toast and eat dulse as a snack. It thickens gravies and sauces. Soak in water for 20 minutes, then cook as directed in recipe, or add to long-simmering soups and stews directly.

Hijiki

Hizikia fusiforme

Brown when fresh and black when dried, hijiki has short, thin, curled strands. It is harvested off the northern and southern coasts of Japan, Korea and China. The sweet, delicate flavor and crisp texture of hijiki make it very popular in vegetarian dishes.

Actions/Uses: Diuretic, resolves heat-induced phlegm, helps remove toxins, benefits thyroid, helps normalize blood sugar levels, aids weight loss, soothes nerves, supports hormone functions, builds bones and teeth. Hijiki is an excellent source of calcium, iron and iodine, and is abundant in vitamin B_2 (riboflavin) and B_3 (niacin).

Caution: Canadian, Hong Kong, UK and New Zealand government food safety agencies advise consumers to avoid consumption of hijiki seaweed. Test results have indicated that levels of inorganic arsenic were significantly higher in hijiki than in other types of seaweed. Inorganic arsenic, which can occur naturally in some foods, is known to add to the risk of people developing cancer.

Culinary Use: Hijiki adds interest and texture to salads and rice dishes, soups, stews, stuffing and stir-fries. Soak in water for 15 to 20 minutes, then cook as directed in recipe, or add to long-simmering soups and stews directly.

Kelp

Pleurophycus gardneri

Kelp's broad light brown to light olive-brown leaf-like fronds are found off the Pacific coast of North America. The fresh or dried frond has a delicate, mild taste when cooked. Kelp is usually available in granular, powdered or tablet form. However, the dried and shredded or long strips may be available in whole or natural food stores.

Actions/Uses: Antibacterial, antiviral (herpes), may lower blood pressure and cholesterol, high in calcium, phosphorus and iodine.

Culinary Use: Wrap fresh kelp fronds (if you can find them) around rice or other fillings, or steam, chop and add to stir-fries, salads or stuffing. Use the dried whole or strips of kelp in the same way as fresh but rehydrate first. Sprinkle the powder or granules into soups, stews, salads and stir-fries, or mix with dry ingredients in breads, pancakes and muffins. Granular kelp is added to most vegetable and grain dishes, sauces, gravy, dips and spreads. No soaking is needed if the granular or powdered forms are used but rehydrate if using dried whole or strips.

Kombu

Laminaria japonica

Fresh kombu (called sashimi) is a long, thick, dark green frond. Most often kombu is sold dried whole or in strips or shredded. Used for centuries, kombu is found mainly off the coastal waters of China, Korea and Japan, where it's cultivated. Kombu's taste is sweet and yet robust.

Actions/Uses: Rich in protein, calcium, iodine, magnesium, iron and folate.

Caution: Kombu contains significant amounts of glutamic acid, a forerunner of monosodium glutamate (MSG) and so should be used in small quantities.

Culinary Use: Kombu is used to flavor soups, broths, sauces and stews. The Japanese make a soup broth called Dashi using kombu. Kombu is removed and discarded before the soup is served. Soak dried kombu for 10 minutes and simmer for 15 to 20 minutes to soften it.

Nori

Porphyra tenera

Both coasts of North America and the middle and lower tidal zones of Europe's seacoasts grow nori. Called "laver" in Britain, nori is bright pink when young, turning to dark purple as the plant ages. To get a consistent size and thickness that works for rolling rice, the leaves are pressed into thin sheets. Nori tastes like mild, salty corn. The sheets are often toasted before being used in sushi or other dishes.

Actions/Uses: Antibacterial, diuretic, treats painful urination, goiter, edema, high blood pressure, beriberi, appears to heal ulcers, is high in protein and rich in vitamins A, C, B_1 (thiamin), B_3 (niacin) and phosphorus.

Culinary Use: Use green, black or toasted nori sheets to wrap vegetables and rice for sushi. Chopped or crumbled, nori adds interest and texture to salads, stir-fries and vegetable dishes. Toast nori sheets lightly over a low flame or element on high until black and crisp.

Wakame

Undaria pinnatifida

The thin black fronds of the wild wakame grow in Japan's northern seas. Wakame has a softly resistant texture and a strong, sweet flavor.

Actions/Uses: Boosts immune functioning, promotes healthy hair and skin. Wakame is used in Japanese tradition to purify mother's blood after childbirth. It is rich in calcium, B_3 (niacin) and B_1 (thiamin).

Culinary Use: Chop whole fresh wakame and use as any leafy green vegetable in soups, stews, salads, sandwiches, vegetable and stir-fry dishes. The shredded dried wakame strips may be added to most vegetarian dishes. Soak dried wakame in water for 5 minutes, drain and simmer for 45 minutes.

Herbs

Definition: Herbs are defined as plants whose parts are used to enhance our lives. Strictly speaking, an herb (pronounced *herb* or *erb*) is a plant that is used for culinary, medicinal, cosmetic or ornamental purposes. That definition is broad enough to encompass some trees, spices and flowers that we otherwise might not think of as herbs.

Actions/Uses: The vitamins, minerals and phytochemicals found in herbs can make a significant contribution to our health through diet. Generally, most herbs are antioxidant and the green parts supply chlorophyll, which enhances the body's ability to produce hemoglobin and thus to increase the delivery of oxygen to cells. (See the individual herbs for their specific actions.)

Caution: Avoid medicinal doses of all herbs while pregnant unless following advice by a medical herbalist or midwife.

Buying and Storing: As with fruits and vegetables, the whole fresh herb is the best form to use in cooking. Grow your own or look for fresh organic herbs in supermarkets and farmers' markets. Store fresh herbs rolled in a damp tea towel in the produce drawer of the refrigerator.

For teas, beverages and medicinal applications, dried herbs are used. Dry fresh herbs for use over the winter or purchase small quantities of organic dried herbs from a farm or whole or natural food stores. Replace all dried herbs after 8 to 10 months. Use dark-colored glass or ceramic containers with tight-fitting lids to store herbs individually. Label and date and keep in a cool, dark place for no longer than 1 year.

Culinary Use: Herbs are used in both savory and sweet dishes. They enliven and are an integral part of vegetarian recipes. When a smooth texture is desired in sauces, beverages or dressings, it is advantageous to make an herb tea. Strain off the herbs and use the infused liquid to flavor the dish. The recipes in this book call for the use of fresh herbs except where dried are indicated. (See the individual herbs for the specific flavors and combinations that they complement.)

To substitute dried herbs in recipes: Use one-half to one-third less dried herbs than the quantity of fresh called for in the recipe. Crush or grind the dried herb to a powder then add to the recipe.

To Make Herbal Infusion (Tea or Tissane): Bring 1 cup (250 mL) of pure or filtered water to a boil. Measure 1 tsp (5 mL) dried herb into a teapot. Pour boiled water over top. Place a lid on the teapot and a cork in the spout (to prevent steam from escaping). Steep the tea for 10 to 15 minutes. Let the infusion cool before adding to recipes. Strain and discard solids. For convenience, make 1 to 2 cups (250 to 500 mL) medicinal tea and store in a covered jar in refrigerator for use throughout the day.

To Dry Herbs: Most herbs dry well, except for parsley, chives and basil, which are better frozen. To dry well, herbs require a warm, dry, dark atmosphere where air circulates freely, such as an attic, dark corner of a room, basement or a barn.

For long-stemmed herbs (mints, yarrow, sage), gather in small bunches, tie the stems and hang upside down in a warm, dry, dark place. Paper bags may be used to catch the falling bits and to keep the light away. For leaves on short stems (thyme) and flowers (calendula, violets and all others), strip leaves off the stems and the petals off the center of the flower (or dry the flower head whole). Scatter leaves or petals in a single layer on a nylon net or screen. The faster the plant parts dry, the more color and fragrance they will retain. Scrub roots, cut into $\frac{1}{2}$-inch (1 cm) pieces, and place in one layer on a drying rack, screen or suspended fabric to dry. Leave in pieces for longer storage. Grind small amounts to a powder just before using. Bottle and store in dark-colored bottles in a cool, dark place.

Alfalfa

Medicago sativa

A hardy perennial that is easily grown in most parts of North America.

Parts Used: Leaves, flowers and sprouted seeds.

Actions: Tonic, nutritive, lower blood cholesterol, anti-anemia.

Uses: Alfalfa is a cell nutritive and overall tonic for the body. It promotes strong teeth, bones and connective tissue. Alfalfa is one of the best sources of chlorophyll, which has the ability to stimulate new skin growth, heal wounds and burns, diminish the symptoms of arthritis, gout and rheumatism, lower cholesterol levels, reduce inflammation and improve the body's resistance to cancer.

The mature tops and seeds are high in amino acids and chlorophyll, as well as minerals such as calcium, magnesium, phosphorus and potassium and vitamins

K, B and P, which the body uses to repair and build musculoskeletal system structures and tissues.

Sprouted seeds have an enhanced concentration of vitamins. Alfalfa shoots (per 100 g) have 3,410 I.U. of beta-carotene and 162 mg of vitamin C.

Caution: Alfalfa seeds and sprouts are rich in the amino acid canavanine, which can contribute to inflammation in rheumatoid arthritis, systemic lupus erythematosus and other rheumatoid and inflammatory conditions. Alfalfa leaf is NOT a source of canavanine and can be used in inflammatory and rheumatic conditions.

Availability: Whole or cut dried leaf is available in whole or natural food stores. Sprouted seeds are readily available.

Culinary Use: Alfalfa has a light, grassy taste to the fresh flowers and leaves and a stronger, also grassy taste to the dried aerial parts. Add fresh or dried whole sprigs to soups and stews during the last hour of cooking, then remove. Fresh leaves are perfect in salads, rice and vegetable dishes. Use a generous handful of fresh or dried alfalfa in vegetable stock. Add the chopped fresh leaf to soups and stews during the last 10 minutes of cooking.

Fresh flowers and sprouts work well in salads, stir-fries and sandwiches. Add them when juicing vegetables and include alfalfa tea with liquids in breads.

Astragalus

Astragalus membranaceus

Astragalus is a hardy, shrub-like perennial native to eastern Asia but grown in temperate regions including Canada and the United States.

Parts Used: Root.

Actions: Immune stimulant, antimicrobial, heart tonic, diuretic, promotes tissue regeneration.

Uses: Used throughout the Orient as a tonic, astragalus is a safe and powerful immune system stimulator for virtually every phase of immune system activity. It also has been shown to alleviate the adverse effects of steroids and chemotherapy on the immune system and can be used during traditional cancer treatment.

Availability: While more and more North American herb farms are growing this exceptional medicinal herb, the most reliable sources for the

dried, sliced root are Oriental herb stores centered in large urban areas. However, whole or natural food stores do carry cut or powdered astragalus and the tincture form.

Culinary Use: The mild, slightly sweet, earthy taste of astragalus is so subtle it can be used in soups and vegetable stocks without detection. Add one or two pieces of the dried root to soups or vegetable stock or grind and include in root beverages and seasoning blends. Astragalus tincture may be added to smoothies and soups just before serving.

Basil

Oscimum basilicum

A bushy annual with large, waxy, deep green leaves and small tubular flowers that grow in long spikes.

Parts Used: Leaves and flowering tops.

Actions: Antispasmodic, soothing digestive, antibacterial, antidepressant, adrenal stimulant.

Uses: To relieve indigestion, nervous tension, stress and tension headaches.

Availability: Fresh sprigs are sold in season at farmers' markets and supermarkets. Dried, cut and sifted leaves are available in whole or natural food stores.

Culinary Use: Slightly nutmeg and clove with citrus undertones, each variety has a variation of the spicy basil taste. Use about three to six large fresh basil leaves for baked vegetable, legume and grain dishes. Wash, pat dry and strip leaves from stem (discard stem) and roughly chop leaves or cut in chiffonade.

Burdock

Arctium lappa

A hardy biennial that produces fruiting heads covered with hooked burrs that catch on clothing and the fur of animals. Grows wild extensively in North America.

Parts Used: Root, stalk, leaves and seeds.

Actions: Leaves are a mild laxative, diuretic. The root is also a mild laxative, antirheumatic, antibiotic, promotes sweating, diuretic, cleansing, stimulating efficient removal of waste production, a skin and blood cleanser. Burdock also stimulates urine flow. Root and seeds are a soothing demulcent and

tonic. They soothe kidneys and relieve lymphatics. The seeds prevent fever, are anti-inflammatory, antibacterial and reduce blood sugar levels.

Uses: Leaves may be used in the same way as roots although they are less effective. Burdock root is a cleansing, eliminative remedy. It helps to remove toxins causing skin problems (including eczema, acne, rashes, boils), digestive sluggishness or arthritic pains. It supports the liver, lymphatic glands and digestive system. Burdock seeds relieve lymphatics, are a soothing demulcent tonic, and soothe the kidneys.

For every 1 cup (250 mL) of boiled burdock root, there is 61 mg calcium, 450 mg potassium and 116 mg phosphorus.

Availability: Fresh root is available seasonally at Asian food markets. Due to its extensive growth habit in rural and urban waste areas, burdock can be easily foraged. Dig roots from the wild in the fall. Scrub and chop, then dry for storage. Cut dried leaves and root and tinctures are available in whole or natural food stores.

Culinary Use: Fresh burdock leaves have a taste similar to spinach or Swiss chard. Roots are nutty and pleasant tasting when cooked. Use fresh burdock leaves as you would spinach and other leafy greens. In the summer, use the large fresh leaves to wrap vegetables, fish and meat for grilling. In the spring, use the tender young sprouts and smaller leaves in salads and soups or cooked as a vegetable. The fresh leaf stalks may be peeled and roasted or boiled. They are a delicate vegetable, much like asparagus when cooked.

Use fresh burdock roots and stalks in soups instead of potatoes, roast or grill them as a vegetable, grate and mix with potatoes for latkes. Roasted, dried burdock roots are a good coffee substitute.

Use fresh or dry burdock seeds in tea blends or as seasonings, in the same way you would use sesame seeds.

Calendula

Calendula officinalis

A prolific annual (easily grown from seed) with bright yellow to orange marigold-like flowers, calendula's common name is pot marigold.

Parts Used: Petals.

Actions: Astringent, antiseptic, antifungal, anti-inflammatory, heals wounds, menstrual regulator, stimulates bile production.

Uses: Calendula acts as an aid to digestion and as a general tonic. It is taken to ease menopausal problems, period pain, gastritis, peptic ulcers, gall bladder problems, indigestion, and fungal infections.

Availability: Calendula is widely used in gardens and in vegetable gardens. Whole dried flower heads are available in whole or natural food stores.

Culinary Use: Formerly used to color cheese, calendula adds a soft, flecked yellow color to baked products, rice and sauces. Calendula petals have a delicate floral taste and smell. The flavor and aroma strengthens upon drying, but is still overpowered by other robust ingredients in food. Use calendula as a substitute for saffron and as a natural food coloring. Use fresh petals chopped in salads, soups, stews, rice, egg dishes, custards and puddings. The fresh or dried petals add color as a garnish for all main or dessert dishes, cakes, breads and muffins. They are also used for color in non-alcoholic punches and frozen ices.

Cardamom

Elettaria cardamomum

Originally from Indian rainforests, cardamom is a rhizomatous perennial with large lanceolate leaves. For centuries it has been exported to Europe mainly for its fragrance. When coaxed into blooming, the flowers are white with a dark pink-striped lip.

Parts Used: Seeds.

Actions: Antispasmodic, carminative, digestive stimulant, expectorant.

Uses: Cardamom is a pungent herb with stimulating, tonic effects that work best on the digestive system. It relaxes spasms, stimulates appetite and relieves flatulence.

Availability: The whole dried (white or green) pods are preferred because they keep up to 1 year. Whole pods are available at Asian, Indian or Middle Eastern markets. Hulled seeds are widely available in supermarkets and whole or natural food stores. As with all hulled seeds, buy in small quantities and use frequently.

Culinary Use: Used ground or as whole seeds, the lemon and floral taste of cardamom is slightly similar to nutmeg with camphor and smoky notes. Toasting cardamom brings out its complex flavors. It is used in sweet and savory dishes and in many spice blends and some teas. Cardamom is especially good in custards, puddings, with apples and pears, and in rice pilafs. Cardamom combines well with coffee, chiles, coriander, cumin, ginger, pepper, saffron, basil and yogurt.

Cayenne Pepper

Capsicum annuum and *Capsicum frutescens*

A tropical perennial, grown as an annual in temperate zones. (See also Chile Peppers, page 122)

Parts Used: Fruit

Actions: Stimulant, tonic, carminative, induces perspiration, rubefacient, antiseptic, antibacterial.

Uses: Cayenne stimulates blood circulation, purifies the blood, promotes fluid elimination and sweat, and is most often used as a stimulating nerve tonic. Over-the-counter creams and ointments containing the active capsaicin extract are applied externally and are often effective in relieving the pain of osteoarthritis and rheumatoid arthritis, shingles infection, as well as the burning pain in the toes, feet, and legs of diabetic neuropathy and fibromyalgia. The capsaicin in cayenne works by blocking a protein that normally relays pain messages from nerve endings to the brain.

Cayenne supplies 7.8 mg calcium, 0.4 mg iron, 8 mg magnesium, 15.5 mg phosphorus, 107 mg potassium, 4 mg vitamin C and a whopping 2,205 I.U. vitamin A for every 1 tbsp (15 mL).

Caution: Cayenne has an irritating property that heals unbroken inflammations by bringing the blood to the surface when applied externally. Use on unbroken skin or it will irritate and not be as effective. Natural practitioners often advise that capsaicin should not be used internally in cases of chronic inflammation of the intestinal tract, such as in irritable bowel syndrome, ulcerative colitis and Crohn's disease.

Availability: Fresh, whole chile peppers are available in some ethnic markets, supermarkets and whole or natural food stores. Dried whole chiles and powdered cayenne pepper are widely available.

Culinary Use: To enjoy the health benefits of the hot and biting cayenne, start with small doses. Experts say that virtually everybody can gradually build up a tolerance to the hot taste and learn to love it. Milk, yogurt and ice cream soothe the tongue. Cayenne pepper is the principal ingredient of hot pepper sauce.

Use chopped fresh chiles in tomato sauces, soups and stews, and preserved in chili sauce and in raw or cooked salsas. Roasted, peeled and chopped fresh chiles are excellent in sauces, especially barbecue sauces. Dried, whole chiles complement soups, soup stocks, and may be crushed as a garnish for salads, cooked dishes and blended in teas.

Dried powdered cayenne pepper serves as a garnish for main dish meals and in spice blends and rubs for roasted or grilled vegetables.

Celery Seeds

Apium graveolens

The celery plant is a biennial with a bulbous root and thick, fleshy grooved stems. The leaves are pinnately divided. Small gray-brown seeds follow umbels of tiny green-white flowers. Medicinal celery seeds are collected from wild celery.

Parts Used: Seeds (for medicinal purposes). For Celery stalk, see page 122.

Actions: Anti-inflammatory, antioxidant, carminative, reduce blood pressure, sedative, urinary antiseptic.

Uses: Aromatic, tonic, relieve muscle spasms and are used to treat gout, inflammation of the urinary tract, cystitis, osteoarthritis and rheumatoid arthritis.

Caution: Do not use seeds in pregnancy.

Availability: Dried seeds should be purchased from herbalists or whole or natural food stores. The dried seeds found in supermarkets do not have the medicinal value because they are not gathered from the wild plant.

Culinary Use: Medicinal celery seeds have a mild celery taste and can be used in the same ways as other seeds such as sesame or poppy. Crush and add to ingredients in seasonings, soups, baked vegetables, legumes and grain dishes, and use in blended drinks.

Chamomile

See German Chamomile

Cinnamon

Cinnamomum zeylanicum and *c. cassia*

Cinnamon is the dried, smooth inner bark of an evergreen tree indigenous to Sri Lanka and cultivated in hot, wet tropical regions of Mexico, India, Brazil, East and West Indies and Indian Ocean islands.

Parts Used: Bark.

Actions: Carminative, diaphoretic, astringent, stimulant, antimicrobial.

Uses: Cinnamon is a warming carminative used to promote digestion and relieve nausea, vomiting and diarrhea. It is used for upset stomach and irritable bowel syndrome. Recent research has shown that cinnamon helps the body use insulin more efficiently.

Availability: Most of the cinnamon available in supermarkets is *Cinnamomum cassia*, a harder, darker and slightly more bitter-tasting variety of cinnamon. True cinnamon, *C. zeylanicum*, is softer, paler and sweeter in taste. Dried, rolled sticks, called quills may be sold in 2- to 18-inch (5 to 45 cm) lengths in specialty food stores and whole or natural food stores. The ground cinnamon and cinnamon powder widely available is *C. cassia*.

Culinary Use: Fragrant and warm with tones of clove and citrus, cinnamon's sweetly spicy flavor blends well with apples, chile pepper and chocolate. Cinnamon is one of the spices in Garam Masala Spice Blend, an Indian seasoning used for savory dishes, rice and curries. Cinnamon is usually used as a carminative with other herbs and spices. It may be used freely to flavor other herbal teas.

Whole quills are used to flavor syrups, sauces, custards, drinks and other liquids. The woody sticks are usually removed after imparting flavor. Crushed sticks are toasted and added to herbal spice and tea blends.

Sweet milk, cream and rice puddings and desserts take advantage of powdered cinnamon and it is widely used in cakes and biscuits, pastries, doughnuts and sweet fritters. Ground cinnamon is mixed with brown or white sugar and sprinkled on porridge, cereal, coffee and toast. Apple crisp, apple pie and pickled dishes are traditional foods that use cinnamon for a dominant flavor.

Cloves

Syzygium aromaticum

Once exotic and only for royalty, cloves are the pink, unopened flower buds of an evergreen tree native to Indonesia, now grown in Zanzibar, Madagascar, West Indies, Brazil, India and Sri Lanka.

Parts Used: Dried buds.

Actions: Antioxidant, anesthetic, antiseptic, anti-inflammatory, anodyne, antispasmodic, carminative, stimulant, prevents vomiting, antihistamine, warming.

Uses: Used for asthma, bronchitis, nausea, vomiting, flatulence, diarrhea and hypothermia. Some studies indicate that cloves may have anticoagulant properties and stimulate the production of enzymes that fight cancer. Clove oil, which is 60 to 90% eugenol, is the active ingredient in some mouthwashes, toothpastes, soaps, insect repellents, perfumes, foods, various veterinary medications and many over-the-counter toothache medications.

Availability: Whole, dried buds and powder widely available.

Culinary Use: Cloves are fragrantly pungent and hot with strong camphor that can leave numbness on the tongue. Their unique flavor is used in spiced or mulled wines, liqueurs, pickles, vegetable stock, sauces and other liquids and studded in fruit and baked goods.

Ground cloves are added to sweet and savory sauces and glazes, fruit dishes, curries, rice, soups and stews, mincemeat, traditional fruit puddings, cakes and stewed fruit dishes. Cloves complement apples, pears, figs and eggplant and they blend well with coriander, cumin, nutmeg, allspice and mace.

Coriander Seeds

Coriandrum sativum

A hardy annual with slender, erect, branched stems that bear pinnate, parsley-like aromatic leaves. Small, flat umbels of tiny white to pale mauve flowers yield round green berries (seeds) that ripen to a brownish yellow.

Parts Used: Seeds.

Actions: Soothing digestive, stimulates appetite, improves digestion and absorption.

Uses: Digestive problems, flatulence.

Availability: Whole dried seeds are readily available in whole or natural food stores and Indian markets. Ground seeds are common at supermarkets.

Culinary Use: Not at all similar in taste to the green leaves (cilantro) that grow on the same plant, coriander seeds are warm, sweet and mild with citrus and floral notes. Coriander seeds are used in most curry seasonings and they are often added to coffee and dessert dishes. Sweet-and-sour dishes and pickles make use of coriander's sweet floral flavors. Coriander complements mushrooms, onions, cinnamon, fennel, nutmeg, plums, apples and pears.

Cumin Seeds

Cuminum cyminum

Cumin seeds are taken from a slender annual plant with dark green leaves that is found wild from the Mediterranean to the Sudan and central Asia. Bristly oval seeds follow umbels of tiny white or pink flowers.

Parts Used: Seeds.

Actions: Stimulant, soothing digestive, antispasmodic, diuretic, increase milk in breastfeeding.

Uses: Indigestion, flatulence.

Availability: Whole dried seeds are readily available in whole or natural food stores and Indian markets. Usually supermarkets only carry the ground seeds.

Culinary Use: Toasting the seeds in a dry skillet brings out a nutty sweetness to the seeds that, without toasting, are pungent, sharp and bitter with earthy spice. Cumin seeds are combined with coriander, cardamom, allspice and anise in spice blends. They are one of the main spice flavors in chili con carne.

Dandelion

Taraxacum officinale

A low-growing, common, hardy and herbaceous perennial, dandelion develops from a long, thick, dark brown taproot with white and milky flesh. One brilliant yellow round flower head sits atop a smooth, hollow stem. Oblong, bright green, deeply toothed leaves grow in a basal rosette directly from the root.

Parts Used: Roots, stems, leaves and flowers.

Actions: Dandelion leaves are diuretic and a tonic for the liver and digestive system. The root is a liver tonic, promotes bile flow, diuretic, mildly laxative and antirheumatic.

Dandelion is highest in lecithin (29,700 ppm) of any of the plant sources. Lecithin is important for cell membrane protection and replacement, reducing cholesterol, converting fat into energy, prevention of strokes and heart attacks and is used in treating Alzheimer's disease.

Uses: Leaves are used specifically to support the kidney. The root works to support the liver. Dandelion is used for gall bladder, kidney and bladder ailments. It is used for liver ailments, including hepatitis and jaundice to promote the liver's processing of toxins for elimination. It also provides important nutrients for storage or release into the system. It's used in skin problems and rheumatism and increases the flow of urine. As a diuretic, dandelion is important for its high potassium content since many other diuretics deplete the body's supply of potassium. Related disorders of digestion, such as dyspepsia, have also been shown to benefit from the ingestion of dandelion.

Dandelion is high in inulin, a form of carbohydrate easily assimilated by diabetics and hence is a potential source of nutritional support for diabetics. It is one of the best food sources of vitamin A (8,400 I.U. beta-carotene per 100 g). The greens yield 187 mg calcium, 66 mg phosphorous, 3 mg iron, 397 mg potassium and 35 mg vitamin C per 100 grams.

Availability: The whole plant is easily foraged spring through fall. Fresh leaves are found in some supermarkets, farmers' markets and whole or natural food stores. The chopped, dried leaf is available in whole or natural food stores.

Culinary Use: Dandelion leaves are tart, bitter and somewhat lemon-like in taste. The fresh root is similar to parsnip but not as strong and the roasted, dried root has a nutty, earthy flavor. Treat the fresh, peeled root in the same way as any root vegetable. Chop and use the fresh root to make a decoction for spring tonic or grate it into salads to help the transition from winter to spring. The dried root is excellent in teas, broths, soups, sauces, stews or any other long-simmering dish. Roasted roots are used as a coffee substitute, often blended with roasted chicory and/or burdock roots.

The fresh, young spring leaves are used as a salad staple or steamed, braised or sautéed as greens, with pasta, in soups and stocks.

Dandelion flower has traditionally been used to flavor wine. The fresh or dried leaves add color to sauces, butter, dips and cheese mixtures. They may be added to baked products, rice dishes or chopped in salads, soups, egg dishes, custards and puddings. Dandelion flowers make a healthy substitute for saffron and may be used as a garnish for all main or dessert dishes, in cakes, breads and muffins. The unopened buds are steamed or sautéed with vegetables. Dried leaves and flowers are combined with other herbs, such as nettles, burdock and yellow dock, to make herb beer or a healing tea blend.

Dill Seeds

Anethum graveolens

Dill is a tall top-heavy, annual plant with a long hollow stem growing out of a spindly taproot. Terminal flowers appear in a wide, flat umbel with numerous yellow flowers. Branches along the stem support feathery blue-green leaflets.

Parts Used: Seeds.

Actions: Soothing digestive, antispasmodic, increase milk in breastfeeding.

Uses: Flatulence, infant's colic, bad breath.

Availability: Dill is easy to grow. Harvest seeds in late summer, early fall. Dried seeds are readily available in whole or natural food stores and supermarkets.

Culinary Use: Dill seeds combine well with potatoes, rye, squash and sweet potatoes, cabbage, onion and vinegar, lending a warm, pleasantly anise

and citrus flavor. Salad dressings, sauces and some seasonings use dill seeds.

Echinacea

Echinacea angustifolia or *E. purpurea*

The bright purple petals surrounding a brown cone make echinacea a top choice for perennial beds. A hardy perennial native to North America, its common name is purple coneflower.

Parts Used: Root, leaves and flowers with the root being the most potent.

Actions: Immune stimulating, anti-inflammatory, antibiotic, antimicrobial, antiseptic, analgesic, antiallergenic, lymphatic tonic.

Uses: Studies have shown that echinacea works best at the first sign of cold or flu, taken in 4 to 6 doses daily for not more than 10 days. It has interferon-like actions, helping to prevent and control viral infections. It hastens the healing of tissue and also fights viruses and candida. Echinacea root is more potent than the leaves.

Availability: Dried root, dried stems and leaves are available whole or cut in whole or natural food stores. Echinacea is also available in tincture and tablet form.

Culinary Use: The root is sweet and pleasantly aromatic while the flowers and stems are faintly aromatic. Using echinacea in cooking may aid in general well being and help head off minor illnesses if taken in a soup for 2 or 3 days following bouts of stress or excessive fatigue. Echinacea root combines well with garlic for fighting colds and flu.

Petals and leaves enliven salads, vegetable dishes and stir-fries, as garnish. Dried petals are used in seasonings.

Whole, fresh or dried echinacea root is added to long-simmering soups and stews. Fresh roots are grated into salads and vegetable and grain dishes. Ground root is dried and combined with other spices or added to sauces, dips, puddings and desserts.

Dried echinacea leaves, petals and finely chopped dried root may be blended with other herbs, such as hyssop, peppermint and thyme, for an effective cold remedy tea blend.

Add 1 tsp (5 mL) echinacea tincture to stocks, soups and stews when colds and flu threaten.

Fennel Seeds

Foeniculum vulgare

Fennel grows wild in Mediterranean Europe and Asia and has naturalized in many other parts of the world where the fleshy bulb is harvested and used as a vegetable. Fennel looks like a larger version of the dill plant. Stout, solid stems support bright yellow, large umbel clusters of flowers. Thread-like and feathery green leaves alternately branch out from joints of the stem. Flowers appear in summer, followed by gray-brown seeds.

Parts Used: Seeds. For the fennel bulb, see page 124.

Actions: Soothing diuretic, anti-inflammatory, antispasmodic, soothing digestive, promote milk flow, mild expectorant.

Uses: Indigestion, flatulence, increase milk flow in breastfeeding, relieve colic in babies when taken by the nursing mother and used directly for colic and coughs.

Caution: Avoid high doses in pregnancy, as it is a uterine stimulant.

Availability: Harvest fennel seeds in late summer, early fall. Dried seeds are readily available in whole or natural food stores and supermarkets.

Culinary Use: Fennel seeds are lightly anise-flavored, with astringent citrus tones. They are often combined with cinnamon, cumin, allspice, fenugreek, thyme and cumin for spice blends. The anise flavor complements both sweet and savory dishes, especially custards, rice and egg dishes. Cabbage, lentils, beets and potatoes go well with fennel seeds.

Fenugreek

Trigonella foenum-graecum

Grown as a fodder crop in southern and central Europe, fenugreek is widely naturalized from the Mediterranean to southern Africa and Australia. This annual legume has aromatic trifoliate leaves and solitary or paired yellow-white flowers, followed by beaked pods with yellow-brown seeds shaped like a pyramid.

Parts Used: Aerial parts and seeds.

Actions: Expectorant, soothing digestive, protects intestinal surfaces, reduces blood sugar and increases milk in breastfeeding.

Uses: Bronchitis, coughs, diabetes, diverticular disease, ulcerative colitis, Crohn's disease, menstrual pain, peptic ulcer, stomach upsets.

Availability: Dried seeds are found in whole or natural food stores and some supermarkets. The dried (and rarely fresh) leaves may be found in Indian markets when in season.

Culinary Use: Fresh fenugreek leaves are mildly pungent with a hint of lemon. Dried seeds are pungent, bitter and give the "curry" aroma to spice blends. Toasting the seeds brings out a slightly sweeter, nutty taste with maple overtones. For a nutritious soup stock, simmer 1 to 2 tsp (5 to 10 mL) lightly crushed seeds and 1 cup (250 mL) water for 10 minutes. Let cool. Strain and discard seeds. Add to the liquid in the recipe. Fenugreek seeds are combined with cumin, cinnamon, coriander, allspice, fennel, chiles and garlic in seasonings. Toasted fenugreek works well with other sweet spices (cinnamon and nutmeg) in sweet custards and desserts.

Garlic

Allium sativum

A hardy perennial plant with an edible root bulb made up of four to 15 cloves enclosed in a white, tan or pinkish papery skin. At the tip of the round, hollow and sturdy stem, white flowers appear encased in a teardrop-like membrane that tapers to a sharp, green point. Just before the flowers open, the bud causes the stem to curl and the flower stalk forms a twisted shape. The edible green flower stalks with unopened buds are called "scapes." Flowers form a round ball when in full bloom.

Parts Used: Bulb or head, sometimes called "bud" at the root of the plant. Fresh scapes (the green tops) are eaten as green vegetables.

Actions: Antimicrobial, antibiotic, cardioprotective, hypotensive, anticarcinogen, promotes sweating, reduces blood pressure, anticoagulant, lowers blood sugar levels, expectorant, digestive stimulant, diuretic, antihistaminic, antiparasitic.

Uses: Research has shown that garlic inhibits cancer cell formation and proliferation. It lowers serum total and low-density lipoprotein cholesterol in humans and reduces the tendency of the blood to clot, thereby reducing the risk of blocked arteries and heart disease. Garlic is an antioxidant and helps stimulate the immune system. It has strong antibiotic and anti-inflammatory properties that make it a good wound medicine. Garlic protects organs from damage induced by synthetic drugs, chemical pollutants and the effects of radiation.

One raw garlic clove provides 6 g protein, 29 mg calcium, 202 mg phosphorus, 529 mg potassium and 15 mg vitamin C.

Caution: Dried garlic salt has no medicinal value.

Availability: Fresh whole organic bulbs are found at farmers' markets, food stores and supermarkets. Scapes are found at farmers' markets and Asian markets in mid to late summer.

Culinary Use: Garlic's hot, sharp and strong unique taste is due to the active compound allicin. Fresh cloves have the highest medicinal value. It is beneficial to add half to 1 whole fresh raw clove to ingredients in dips and spreads.

To get reliable medicinal benefit from garlic, it is recommended that about two medium-size whole garlic bulbs (about 2 oz/60 g) be taken per week. That requires that almost every main dish you consume contain a minimum of two cloves each. Start to increase your fresh garlic consumption by blending minced fresh garlic into prepared sauces, dips and salad dressings and adding a minimum of one garlic clove to every main dish you make.

The whole head or bulb is often roasted to caramelize the sugars for use in spreads, dips, sauces, vegetable and pasta dishes and spreads. (For Roasted Garlic, see page 206.) Whole, blanched (boiled 30 seconds in water) cloves add subtle flavor to dressings or stir-fries, spiced oils and vinegars. Puréed blanched cloves are used to thicken sauces. Slivered whole garlic works in stir-fries, rice, legume and grain dishes. Chopped, fresh, raw cloves are combined with other herbs and spices for salad dressings, aïoli, pesto, hummus, salsas and seasonings.

Fresh, chopped scapes are mixed into dips, salads, sauces, salad dressing, used as a garnish, stir-fried with butter and lemon or added to grilled or baked vegetable and rice dishes.

Garlic's flower is a beautiful garnish and enlivens vinegars and oils, salads, stir-fries and other main dishes.

German Chamomile

Matricaria recutita

A low-growing hardy annual easily grown in North America. Flowers have daisy-like petals surrounding rounded yellow centers.

Parts Used: Flower heads and petals.

Actions: Gentle sedative, anti-inflammatory, mild antiseptic, prevents vomiting, antispasmodic, carminative, nervine, emmenagogue, mild pain reliever.

Uses: Anxiety, insomnia, indigestion, peptic ulcer, travel sickness and inflammations (such as gastritis) and menstrual cramps are often eased with chamomile. Chamomile also reduces flatulence and pain caused by gas.

Phytonutrients: To date, more than 120 chemical components have been identified from chamomile's clear blue essential oil. Chamazulene, alpha-bisabolol and matricinare have been evaluated individually and found to reduce inflammation. Alpha-bisabolol is also strongly antispasmodic, antimicrobial and mildly sedative.

Availability: Whole dried flower heads and chamomile tincture are available in whole or natural food stores.

Culinary Use: Use fragrant, apple-tasting chamomile to flavor jams, jellies, syrups and sauces. Fresh or dried petals may be used in salads and as an edible garnish, in baked goods and other desserts such as puddings. To relieve an acute upset stomach, take chamomile tea between meals on an empty stomach so the tea will have direct contact with the mucous lining.

Ginger

Zingiber officinale

The fleshy root we use in cooking is the edible rhizome of a tender perennial plant that is native to Southeast Asia.

Parts Used: Root.

Actions: Antinausea, relieves headaches and arthritis, anti-inflammatory, circulatory stimulant, expectorant, antispasmodic, antiseptic, diaphoretic, guards against blood clots, peripheral vasodilator, prevents vomiting, carminative, antioxidant.

Uses: Ginger root calms nausea and morning sickness and prevents vomiting. Take ¼ to ½ tsp (1 to 2 mL) ground ginger in water every 3 to 4 hours to relieve nausea and motion sickness. It is a cleansing herb with warming effects. Ginger is used to stimulate blood flow to the digestive system and to increase absorption of nutrients and increases the action of the gall bladder, while protecting the liver against toxins and preventing the formation of ulcers. Studies show that ginger offers some relief from the pain and swelling of arthritis without side effects. Ginger is also used in flatulence, circulation problems, impotence, and to prevent nausea after chemotherapy.

Caution: Ginger can be irritating to the intestinal mucosa, and should be taken with or after meals. Ginger is contraindicated in kidney disease.

Availability: Fresh gingerroot and dried powdered ginger are widely available in supermarkets, Asian and Indian markets and whole or natural food stores.

Culinary Use: Fresh gingerroot is hot and pungent with a sweet, spicy-citrus bite. The dried powder has a stronger, more bitter taste. Both fresh and dried ginger possess therapeutic properties, so use fresh or dried, ground ginger liberally in cooking, as a general tonic (hormone balancer) and to ward off colds and flu. Cook with fresh and dried ginger daily if you or someone in your family suffers from migraine headaches, influenza threatens, rheumatoid arthritis is diagnosed, joint stiffness is a problem, or embarking on a weight loss program.

Fresh and clean tasting with a hot bite, fresh ginger blends well with most fruits and many vegetables. Add sliced fresh ginger to vinegars, oils or stocks. Use julienned ginger in stir-fries and vegetable dishes. Chop or grate raw ginger into salad dressings, marinades, Asian sauces and spreads. Ginger enhances all main dishes, stir-fries, cakes, baked goods, preserves and pickles. Use ginger juice to flavor salad dressings, marinades or sauces and candied ginger in fruit salads, desserts, salad dressings and sauces. Peel and chop fresh ginger, dry and blend with other herbs for teas.

To store fresh gingerroot: If left in a cool, dry place, fresh ginger will only keep for several days. Wrap fresh root in a paper towel and set in an open plastic bag to keep for several weeks in the refrigerator or seal in a plastic bag, freeze and cut off as needed. Fresh ginger keeps indefinitely when peeled, sliced, placed in a glass jar, covered with vodka, sealed and refrigerated.

Use candied or preserved ginger where fresh ginger is called for, especially in desserts and drinks. Candied ginger keeps for a year or longer, and is easy to use in cooking.

If fresh leaves are available, use them as a decorative plate liner, to wrap fish for the grill or to serve finger foods and hors d'oeuvres. If fresh flowers are available, use for salads and as an edible garnish.

Dried ground or powdered ginger is used in cooking as you would fresh.

Ginseng

Siberian *Eleutherococcus senticosis,* North American *Panax quinquefolius,* Asian *Panax ginseng*

A hardy perennial, native to cool, wooded areas of Eastern and Central North America.

Parts Used: Root (from plants older than 4 years) and leaves if organic.

Actions: Antioxidant, adaptogen, tonic, stimulant, regulates blood sugar and cholesterol levels, stimulates immune system.

Uses: Ginseng helps the body resist and adapt to stress. It is a mild stimulant and as a tonic, it promotes long-term overall health. Along with increasing the body's resistance to diabetes, cancer, heart disease and various infections, the medical literature claims that ginseng can improve memory, increase fertility, protect the liver against many toxins and protect the body from radiation. It is also used in impotence and depression.

Caution: Avoid ginseng if you have a fever, asthma, bronchitis, emphysema, high blood pressure or cardiac arrhythmia. Avoid in pregnancy and with hyperactivity in children. Do not take with coffee. Do not take continuously for periods of longer than one month.

Availability: Dried root (whole or chopped), tea, powder and tincture are all found in whole or natural food stores and Asian markets. Fresh ginseng is sometimes found in Chinese and Asian markets. While native to North American woodlands, ginseng has been harvested to near extinction. Please do not collect from the wild or purchase wild crafted North American ginseng.

Culinary Use: The flavor of ginseng is pungent, bitter and astringent with notes of lime but when cooked in dishes, ginseng imparts only a slight flavor to the food. Use in the same way as ginger. Dried ginseng root is very hard and brittle. A good grater, such as those used for nutmeg, will shred the root fine. Whole fresh or dried root is excellent in soups, stocks and stews. Dried whole, grated or flaked ginseng is used in long-simmering soups and stews, and strained off.

Chopped fresh or dried ginseng is added to muesli and granola and dessert bars, whole-grain toppings for desserts and mixed with other herbs for tea blends.

Ground dried ginseng is more bitter than the fresh and works best in milkshakes and smoothies, salad dressings, puddings and other cooked desserts, as part of an antibiotic herbal seasoning, chili pastes and roux. The dried organic leaves are brewed into teas, then added to soups, broths, stews and puddings.

Hemp

Cannabis sativa

A tall woody plant that grows on multi-cellular stalks. Leaves consist of five, deeply cut lobes.

Parts Used: Leaves, stalks, seeds, flowering tops and fruit.

Actions: Promotes healthy menstruation, carminative, treats glaucoma, anti-emetic, aids breathing and inhibits lung tumor growth.

Uses: Hemp has been used to treat digestive disorders, neuralgia, insomnia, depression, migraines, asthma and inflammation.

Tetrahydrocannabinol (THC), cannabinol (CBN) and cannabidiol (CBD) are the active compounds in hemp. Hemp seed contains 26 to 31% pure protein with the essential amino acids and fatty acids.

Availability: Seeds low in THC and hemp oil are available in Canada and Europe. Medicinal use of marijuana is still controversial, but available with prescription in some Canadian provinces, and is legislated in 12 states in the United States.

Culinary Use: Hemp oil is thick and green with a rich, pleasant earthy taste. Hemp oil is rich in linoleic and linolenic fatty acids. It is used without

heating, in dressings, sauces, dips and spreads. Hemp seeds are used in commercial snacks and a tahini-like paste and may be used in desserts, soups, baked vegetable and grain dishes and stews. In the Middle East a nutritious drink called Bhang is made using hemp leaves, black pepper, cloves, nutmeg and mace as the seasoning base. Water, watermelon juice or cucumber juice is added to the spices for a refreshing drink.

Hyssop

Hyssopus officinalis

An evergreen, bushy, woody perennial, hyssop is native to central and southern Europe, western Asia and northern Africa. The square, upright stem bears linear, opposite leaves an purple flowers in whorls from the dense spikes at the top of the stems.

Parts Used: Leaves and flowering tops.

Actions: Antispasmodic, expectorant, promotes sweating, mild painkiller, diuretic, antiviral against herpes simplex, reduces phlegm, soothing digestive.

Uses: Relieves asthma, bronchitis, colds, coughs, influenza, fevers and flatulence. The green tops, boiled in soup, have actually been used in the treatment of asthma. Caffeic acid and unspecified tannins in extracts of hyssop have been shown to have strong anti-HIV activity.

Availability: Hyssop is easy to grow and is harvested from May through fall. Dried leaves are available from whole or natural food stores.

Culinary Use: A fresh, minty, peppery, slightly bitter and pungent taste makes the fresh leaves and flowers excellent additions to salads, fruit cocktails and wraps. The fresh or dried leaves and/or flowers are added to baked goods (especially brownies and date squares), fruit flans and pies, dessert and cough syrups, jams, jellies, sauces, dessert dishes, soups, stews, stocks and stuffing. Hyssop is also dried and mixed with green tea and other herbs for beverages.

Lavender

Lavandula spp

A shrub-like plant with dense, woody stems from which linear, pine-like, gray-green leaves grow. The flowers grow in whorls of tiny flowers on spikes from long stems.

Parts Used: Leaves, stems and flowering tops.

Actions: Relaxant, antispasmodic, antidepressive, nervous system tonic, circulatory stimulant, antibacterial, antiseptic, carminative, promotes bile flow.

Uses: Lavender relieves colic, depression, exhaustion, indigestion, insomnia, and stress and tension headaches.

Laboratory research on the anticancer activity of perillyl alcohol distilled from lavender shows promise in the fight against cancer of the breast, pancreas, colon and prostate.

Caution: Avoid high doses in pregnancy because it is a uterine stimulant.

Availability: Easily grown in temperate climates, harvest lavender from June through fall. Organic, food grade dried flower buds are available in whole or natural food stores.

Culinary Use: Lavender is fragrant and distinctly floral. It can overwhelm the flavors of any dish if over used, so it is best to start with small amounts and increase in very small increments. Dried lavender is three times as potent as the fresh. Fresh or dried flowers are best in baked goods such as cookies, cakes, scones, quick breads, sauces, jellies, sorbets and vinegars. They can also be used as a garnish, to flavor honey and vinegar and in jams, jellies and candies. Dried flowers and leaves are often included in Herbes de Provence spice blend and in sugar substitutes or blended with other herbs and green tea. Lavender teams nicely with lemon in tarts and other desserts and was used to flavor condiments.

Lemon Balm

Melissa officinalis

Opposite, oval, strongly lemon-scented leaves grow on thin, square stems. Flowers are tubular, white or yellow, growing in clusters, at the base of the leaves.

Parts Used: Leaves and flowering tops.

Actions: Antioxidant, antihistamine, carminative, antispasmodic, antiviral, antibacterial, nerve relaxant, antidepressive, stimulates bile flow, lowers blood pressure.

Uses: Lemon balm eases anxiety, depression, stress, flatulence, indigestion and insomnia.

Availability: An easily grown perennial, harvest leaves and flowers from June through autumn. Organic dried leaves are available in whole or natural food stores.

Culinary Use: Lemon balm is distinctly lemon flavored but it can have a slightly soapy taste. For this reason, it is usually blended with other lemon herbs such as lemon thyme and lemon verbena. Dried lemon balm blends are used in teas or the teas are used in sauces, custards and puddings. The fresh leaves are added to salads and dressings, puddings, egg dishes and rice pilafs. Lemon balm may be added in small amounts to recipes whenever lemon juice is an ingredient but it does not replace the lemon juice.

Lemon Verbena

Aloysia triphylla

A fast-growing, deciduous shrub, and native to South America, lemon verbena grows to over 6 feet (1.8 m) in zones 8 to 10. Long, pointed green leaves grow on erect stems with green to brown bark that turn woody with maturity. Lavender-colored flowers are tiny and grow in spikes.

Parts Used: Leaves.

Actions: Antispasmodic, digestive.

Uses: Indigestion, flatulence.

Availability: Dried leaves may be available in whole or natural food stores.

Culinary Use: Lemon verbena imparts a clear, strong, sweetly lemon taste to foods. Dried lemon verbena leaves are combined with fennel seeds for a refreshing pre- or after dinner tonic beverage that aids digestion and helps to reduce gas. Fresh or dried leaves are blended with thyme, basil, mint and chives for seasoning. Lemon verbena leaves are used with whole grains, baked vegetables and desserts.

Licorice

Glycyrrhiza glabra

A tender perennial, hardy in zones 7 to 9, native to the Mediterranean region and southwest Asia.

Parts Used: Root.

Actions: Gentle laxative, tonic, anti-inflammatory, antibacterial, anti-arthritic, soothes gastric and intestinal mucous membranes, expectorant.

Uses: Licorice root is considered to be one of the best tonic herbs because it provides nutrients to almost all body systems. It detoxifies, regulates blood sugar levels and recharges depleted adrenal glands. It has also been shown to heal peptic ulcers and is used to soothe irritated membranes and loosen and expel phlegm in the upper respiratory tract. It is also used to treat sore throat, urinary tract infections, coughs, bronchitis, gastritis and constipation.

Caution: Large amounts taken over long periods of time may cause fluid retention and a reduction in blood potassium levels. Avoid or use sparingly if you have high blood pressure. Extracts lack the tonic action.

Availability: Whole or powdered dried root available in whole or natural food stores.

Culinary Use: Licorice has a sweet, earthy flavor. Although we think of licorice as a flavor, the taste most people associate with licorice is actually anise. The terms anise and licorice are commonly interchangeable now, however, the medicinal qualities are not. Licorice root is 50 times as sweet as table sugar. Brewers use licorice because it gives port and stout their characteristic black color and thick consistency. It can also be used in cooking for the same purpose in sauces, puddings and gravies.

To use licorice in desserts and sauces, make a tea by simmering 1 tsp (5 mL) of the cut and sifted dried root in a cup of boiling water for 5 minutes. Strain the tea and use for sauces and in baked goods such as cookies and puddings.

Linden Flower

(Lime Flowers) *Tilia cordata* or *T.* x *europaea*

Found throughout northern temperate regions, common linden is a deciduous tree with dark green, shiny, heart-shaped leaves and yellow-white flowers that appear in mid-summer. It is often grown as an ornamental in North American cities.

Parts Used: Flowering tops.

Actions: Antispasmodic, promotes sweating when taken as a hot tea, diuretic when taken as a warm tea, lowers blood pressure, relaxant, mild astringent.

Uses: Linden flower tea is a pleasant-tasting, relaxing remedy for stress, anxiety, tension headache and insomnia. It relaxes and nourishes blood vessels, making it useful in high blood pressure and heart disease. In promoting sweating, it is useful in colds, flu and fevers. The tea can be given to children as a calming remedy or to reduce fevers.

Availability: Harvest leaves and flowers in mid-June and leaves from early summer through autumn. Dried aerial parts are available in whole or natural food stores. Linden tea bags are often found in supermarkets.

Culinary Use: The actions in linden is partially due to its essential oils, which are only released with heat. For this reason, dried or fresh linden is not added to raw dishes. The easiest method to incorporate the pleasant and mildly lime taste of linden into recipes is by making a tea with the fresh or dried leaves. Use the strained infusion to replace some or all of the liquid in grains, sauces, puddings and desserts.

Mustard

Brassica spp

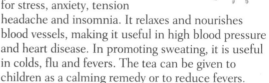

A hearty annual indigenous to North America, the mustard plant is tall with bright green oval leaves. Yellow flowers appear in mid-summer and seedpods develop late summer to early fall.

Parts Used: Seeds (and leaves for cooking) (see Leafy Greens, page 124).

Actions: Blood cholesterol regulator, blood sugar regulator, heartbeat regulator, reduces flatulence.

Uses: Mustard seeds are a good source of magnesium. (1 tbsp/15 mL ground mustard seed contains 33 mg magnesium) which helps regulate cholesterol, blood sugar and heartbeat. Native Americans used it to treat asthma, bronchitis, congestion, constipation, dropsy, fever, indigestion, sore muscles and toothache. It has been found to boost energy levels of people with chronic fatigue syndrome.

Availability: Yellow, white, black or brown dried mustard seeds are widely available in food stores. Easily grown from seed.

Culinary Use: Dried mustard seeds are sharp, hot and biting. They are ground into a paste and combined with other spices, vinegar and liquids to make a pungent and hot paste. Mustard seeds or paste may be added to soups, stews, legume and baked vegetable dishes. Use mustard leaves as you would other green leafy vegetables.

Nutmeg

Myristica fragrans

Native to tropical rainforest in the Moluccas and the Banda Islands, the bushy evergreen nutmeg tree is now grown for commercial production in Asia, Australia, Indonesia and Sri Lanka. Pale yellow flowers are followed by fleshy, yellow, round or pear-shaped fruits (generally called seeds).

Parts Used: Dried kernel of the nutmeg fruit.

Actions: Anti-inflammatory, antispasmodic, carminative, digestive stimulant, sedative.

Uses: Nutmeg relieves colic, diarrhea, flatulence, nausea, vomiting and muscle tension.

Caution: Do not use in pregnancy.

Availability: Whole, dried nutmeg seeds are available in whole or natural food stores. Ground nutmeg is widely available.

Culinary Use: Sweetly aromatic with a woodsy clove tone, nutmeg adds depth to savory dishes such as soups, stews, sauces and grain and pasta dishes. It is equally good in desserts and milk puddings. Nutmeg combines well with cinnamon, cloves, allspice, cardamom, coriander, fennel and ginger.

Parsley

Petroselinum crispum

A hardy biennial, native to the Mediterranean and grown as an annual in colder climates.

Parts Used: Leaves, stems and roots.

Actions: Antioxidant, tonic, digestive, diuretic.

Uses: As a diuretic, parsley helps the body expel excess water and flushes the kidneys. Always look for and treat underlying causes of water retention. As a nutrient, it is one of the richest food sources of vitamin C. Parsley's chlorophyll and myristicin may also inhibit the development of some cancers.

Parsley is an excellent source of vitamin A. One hundred grams of fresh parsley contains 3,200 I.U. beta-carotene along with 390 mg calcium, 281 mg vitamin C, 200 mg phosphorus and 17.9 mg iron.

Caution: Parsley should not be used in high doses during pregnancy because it stimulates the womb. Parsley is contraindicated in kidney inflammation.

Availability: Fresh sprigs are found in most supermarkets year-round.

Culinary Use: Parsley's fresh citrus taste has a hint of anise to it. It has the unique ability to enhance the flavors of other ingredients and so it is widely used in vegetarian cooking. One-third to ½ cup (75 to 125 mL) chopped fresh parsley may be added to soups, stews, legume and grain dishes and baked vegetables.

Peppermint

Mentha x piperita

An invasive, hardy perennial, native to Europe and Asia but easily grown in North America, peppermint supports bright green, oval aromatic leaves on purple stems. Small pink, white or purple flowers form elongated conical spikes at the tops of the stems.

Parts Used: Leaves and flowers.

Actions: Antispasmodic, digestive tonic, prevents vomiting, carminative, peripheral vasodilator, promotes sweating, promotes bile flow, analgesic.

Uses: Taking peppermint before eating helps stimulate liver and gall bladder function by increasing bile flow to the liver and intestines. Peppermint is well known for its ability to quell nausea and vomiting. Peppermint is used in ulcerative colitis, Crohn's disease, diverticular disease, travel sickness, fevers, colds, flu and to improve the appetite.

Menthol is the constituent that gives peppermint its antiseptic, decongestant, analgesic and mildly anesthetic (the cooling, numbing sensation) properties.

Caution: Do not use during pregnancy or give to children.

Availability: Fresh sprigs in some markets and supermarkets year-round. Dried leaves are found in whole or natural food stores. Peppermint teas in bulk and bags are widely available.

Culinary Use: Whole fresh sprigs are used in sauces, as a garnish and in teas or drinks. Fresh or dried leaves are great in jellies, sauces, teas, beverages, desserts, salads, marinades, and vegetable and fruit dishes. Fresh flowers enhance salads, stir-fries, and vegetable and fruit dishes. Peppermint tea from fresh or dried leaves and flowers is delicious hot or iced. Blend peppermint with other tea herbs to lend its characteristic fresh and minty flavor.

Purslane

Portulaca oleracea

A wild, low-growing and sprawling perennial that grows throughout much of the world. Leaves are oval, thick (almost succulent) and grow opposite along the horizontal stem. Purslane is considered a weed in North America but eaten as an important food in Europe and the Middle East.

Parts Used: Leaves and tender stems.

Actions: Antioxidant, anti-inflammatory, heart protective.

Uses: Medicinal doses are used to treat heart disease, arthritis and other inflammatory diseases.

Low in saturated fat, purslane is a good source of vitamins B_1 (thiamin), B_3 (niacin) and B_6 (pyridoxine), and a very good source of vitamin A, C, B_2 (riboflavin), calcium, iron, magnesium, phosphorus, potassium, copper and manganese. It is also high in pectin and essential fatty acids.

Caution: Purslane contains oxalic acid and if consumed in very large doses, may be toxic.

Availability: The plant often appears unwanted in gardens and cultivated plots. Fresh leaves may

be found in some Greek and Turkish markets but otherwise, must be harvested from the wild.

Culinary Use: Purslane is a very good addition to fresh green salads because of its fresh, astringent citrus taste and juicy leaves that add crunch. Fresh leaves complement beets, zucchini, tomato sauces, beans, and spinach and potato dishes.

Red Clover

Trifolium pratense

A perennial with tubular pink to red flowers throughout the summer, red clover grows in fields throughout North America. Its three long oval leaflets distinguish it as a clover.

Parts Used: Flowering tops.

Actions: Antispasmodic, expectorant, hormone balancing, nutrient, blood thinning, lymphatic cleanser.

Uses: Coughs, bronchitis, whooping cough, menstrual problems.

Caution: Because it contributes to blood thinning, avoid red clover in times of heavy menstrual flow.

Availability: The flowering tops can be harvested May through September from the wild or cultivated gardens. Dried flowers are available in whole or natural food stores. Dried clover that has turned brown is of little use; be sure that the flowers are still pink.

Culinary Use: Fresh red clover leaves and buds are pleasantly green and woodsy and are added to summer salads. Remove the bitter green centers from the flowers before using. Blend dried red clover with other herbs for a medicinal tea.

Red Raspberry

Rubus idaeus

A deciduous shrub with prickly stems and pinnately divided leaves, widespread in Europe, Asia and North America. Small white flowers appear in clusters with aromatic, juicy red fruit following in early summer.

Parts Used: Leaves (see Fruits for berry information, page 116).

Actions: Antispasmodic, astringent, promotes milk in breastfeeding.

Uses: Red raspberry leaves have long been used to tone the uterus during pregnancy and labor, resulting in less risk of miscarriage, relief of morning sickness and a safer, easier birth. As an astringent, raspberry leaf is useful in sore throat and diarrhea.

Availability: Harvest leaves from early summer through autumn. Dried leaves are available in whole or natural food stores.

Culinary Use: The leaves have a slight raspberry taste but with astringent and lemon tones. Fresh raspberry leaves may be included in fresh green salads or chopped and added to soups and baked vegetable dishes. Dried leaves are blended with thyme or sage for a soothing tea that eases coughs. Red raspberry tea is easy to make and take during pregnancy.

Rose

Rosa species

Cultivation of roses dates back thousands of years with *R. rugosa*, *R. gallica*, *R. rubra* and *R. damascena* being among the oldest varieties. *Rosa rugosa* is a deciduous shrub with thorny stems and dark green, oval leaves. Dark pink or white flowers appear in summer and are followed by large, globular, bright red hips (fruit). Wild roses (including the dog rose of North America) grow all over northern temperate regions throughout the world.

Parts Used: Petals and rose hips.

Actions: Rose hips from *Rosa canina* contain vitamin C and are diuretic, astringent and a mild laxative. Rose petals from *Rosa gallica*, *R. damascena*, *R. centifolia*, *R. rugosa* are antidepressant, anti-inflammatory, astringent, blood tonic.

Uses: Their nutrient value makes rose hips useful in prevention of the common cold and as a tasty addition to herbal teas used to improve immune functioning. As an astringent, they are used in diarrhea. Rose petals can be added to teas for their relaxing and uplifting fragrance. Used in a bath, they have been known to ease the pains of rheumatoid arthritis.

Availability: Harvest fresh petals from organic bushes from mid-summer through autumn and hips in the fall. Dried edible rose petals and rose water are available in Middle Eastern markets. Do not use petals from roses purchased from florist shops.

Culinary Use: Rose petals are perfumed and pleasantly fragrant. Use fresh or dried rose petals to flavor syrups and sauces. Because hips are an important source of vitamin C, use fresh or dried rosehips in teas, syrups and fruit drinks, steep in water, then add to stocks, soups, sauces and gravy. Rose water can replace some of the liquid in desserts and dessert sauces.

Rosemary

Rosmarinus officinalis

An evergreen shrub that grows to 6 feet (180 cm) in warm climates, rosemary is native to the Mediterranean.

Parts Used: Leaves and flowers.

Actions: Antioxidant, anti-inflammatory, astringent, nervine, carminative, antiseptic, diuretic, diaphoretic, promotes bile flow, antidepressant, circulatory stimulant, antispasmodic, nervous system and cardiac tonic.

Uses: An effective food preservative. Rosemary may be effective in preventing breast cancer, and it fights against the deterioration of brain functions (improves memory). It is also useful in treating migraine and tension headaches, nervous tension, flatulence, depression, chronic fatigue syndrome and joint pain.

Caution: Avoid large amounts of rosemary during pregnancy.

Availability: Fresh sprigs found in some ethnic markets and supermarkets year-round. Dried whole and powdered leaf found in supermarkets, whole or natural food stores.

Culinary Use: Rosemary is used in smaller amounts than other culinary herbs due to its resinous pine and citrus taste with camphor and spice tones. A combination of rosemary, thyme, garlic and sea salt makes an excellent rub for roasted vegetables and a versatile seasoning for dressings, stuffing and sauces. Rosemary is very good in baked goods such as scones, cookies, focaccia and quick breads. Use a whole sprig the same way you would whole vanilla beans, to impart the spicy essence to egg dishes, syrups and puddings and then remove.

Sage

Salvia officinalis

A hardy, woody perennial evergreen shrub that is native to western United States and Mexico. Tender and hardier varieties of sage grow easily all over Mexico, the United States and southern Canada. Sage has wrinkled, gray-green, oval leaves and purple, pink or white flowers.

Parts Used: Leaves and flowers.

Actions: Antioxidant, antimicrobial, antibiotic, antiseptic, carminative, antispasmodic, anti-inflammatory, circulatory stimulant, estrogenic, peripheral vasodilator, reduces perspiration, uterine stimulant.

Uses: Sage's volatile oil kills bacteria and fungi, even those resistant to penicillin. It is very good as a gargle for sore throat, laryngitis and mouth ulcers. Also used to reduce breast milk production, and to relieve night sweats and hot flashes of menopause.

Caution: Sage can cause convulsions in very high doses. Do not use where high blood pressure or epilepsy is evident, or during pregnancy. Sage should not be consumed during pregnancy. Sage contains steroid-like factors and can encourage miscarriage.

Availability: Fresh sprigs are found at some supermarkets and farmers' markets. Dried, whole, cut, rubbed or ground sage is available at most supermarkets.

Culinary Use: Sage is pungent with balsamic and camphorous notes. Dried sage is often bitter and more potent than the fresh leaves. Small amounts of fresh or dried sage leaves enhance apples, cheese, whole grains, potatoes, tomatoes and legumes. Sage combines well with thyme, garlic, bay, oregano and marjoram, parsley and savory. It is used in stuffing, sauces, and baked vegetable dishes and with legumes and pasta. For a throat-soothing tea, blend sage with thyme, sweet cicely, peppermint and/or licorice. The flower is used chopped fresh in salads, vegetable dishes and as a garnish.

Spearmint

Mentha spicata

Spearmint is a hardy perennial found growing wild in wet soil in most of North America. It is invasive and, like all mints, has a square stem with bright green, lanceolate leaves, lilac, pink, or white flowers borne on a terminal, cylindrical spike.

Parts Used: Leaves and flowering tops.

Actions: Antispasmodic, digestive, induces sweating.

Uses: To relieve the common cold, influenza, indigestion, flatulence and lack of appetite. Spearmint is milder than peppermint, so is often used in treating children's colds and flu.

Availability: The leaves are best harvested just before the flowers open. Dried leaves are available in health food stores.

Culinary Use: Spearmint has a milder, sweeter mint flavor than peppermint and for cooking, fresh spearmint sprigs are preferred. Fresh spearmint leaves are used with potatoes, zucchini and peas. While mint jelly and sauce are usually made with peppermint, salsas are made with the sweeter spearmint. Spearmint combines well with cardamom, coriander, cumin, marjoram and thyme. Spearmint is the mint most often used in Mint Juleps. Lentil and whole grain dishes and some stews can benefit from dried spearmint.

Stevia

Stevia rebaudiana

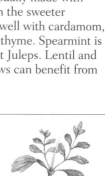

A small, tender shrub, native to northeastern Paraguay and adjacent sections of Brazil.

Parts Used: Leaves.

Actions: Energy booster, natural, low caloric sweetener, tonic, digestive, diuretic.

Uses: Stevia's main benefit is in its use as a safe sweetener and sugar alternative. With its powerful sweet, licorice taste (stevia is 200 to 300 times sweeter than sugar), stevia prevents cavities and does not trigger a rise in blood sugar. It increases energy and improves digestion by stimulating the pancreas without feeding yeast or fungi.

Availability: Dried, cut and powdered leaves and liquid extract available in whole or natural food stores.

Culinary Use: Fresh stevia leaves are sweet with a slight citrus taste. They are best used in cooking if made into an infusion. Make a tea from a handful of fresh stevia sprigs and 2 cups (500 mL) boiling water, let steep overnight. Strain and add the liquid to sauces, syrups, dressings, puddings and other desserts.

Substitute 2 tbsp (25 mL) stevia powder for 1 cup (250 mL) sugar in recipes. Add stevia liquid drops to tea, juices, desserts, syrups and other beverages to sweeten.

Note: Some sugar is required for the success of baked goods, so stevia cannot be substituted for sugar in all recipes.

Stinging Nettle

Urtica dioica

Widespread in temperate regions of Europe, North America and Eurasia, this perennial has bristly, stinging hairs on the stem and ovate, toothed leaves that cause minor skin irritation when touched. Minute green flowers appear in clusters during the summer.

Parts Used: Leaves.

Actions: Leaves and flowers are astringent, blood tonic, circulatory stimulant, diuretic, eliminate uric acid from the body, high in iron, chlorophyll and vitamin C, promote milk in breastfeeding. Fresh stinging nettle root is astringent, diuretic.

Uses: A valuable herb, stinging nettle leaves and flowers are useful as a general, daily nourishing tonic, as well as specifically to treat iron-deficiency anemia, gout, arthritis, kidney stones and as a blood tonic in pregnancy, diabetes, poor circulation and chronic skin disease such as eczema.

The fresh root has a strong action on the urinary system. It is useful in water retention, kidney stones, urinary tract infection, cystitis, prostate inflammation and swelling.

Availability: Gather leaves and flowers while flowering in summer, and harvest the root in autumn. Use gloves to protect bare skin from uric acid. Dried leaves and flowers are available in whole or natural food stores.

Culinary Use: Enjoy the peppery and slightly citrus taste of stinging nettle in soups and salads and add to recipes as you would fresh spinach. Cooking and drying neutralizes the uric acid in the hairs on the leaves and stems that causes the sting.

Tea

Camellia sinensis

Green and black tea comes from the shrub or small tree indigenous to the wet forests of Asia and cultivated commercially in Asia, Africa, South America, and North Carolina.

Green tea is heated and dried after harvesting and undergoes no further processing. Black tea is dried, exposed to air (and fermented) before it is heated, causing the antioxidant catechins to oxidize and form equally potent antioxidants called theaflavins.

Parts Used: Leaves.

Actions: Antioxidant, stimulant, astringent, antibacterial, diuretic, antitumor, anti-obesity, prevents gum disease and cavities, lowers blood pressure and blood sugar levels, lowers cholesterol.

Uses: Green tea is a good tonic beverage and can be mixed with other herbs for teas.

Epidemiological studies of Japanese people, heavy consumers of green tea, show that they have lower death rates from cancer of all types, especially cancer of the stomach. A recent Swedish study revealed that women who drank a minimum of two cups of tea daily developed 46% less ovarian cancer than non-tea drinkers.

Catechins in green tea and theaflavins in black tea are strongly antioxidant, protect against cancer, fight viral infection, streptococcus mutans and lower LDL or low-density lipoprotein. The fluoride content in green tea prevents cavities. Vitamins B and C, proanthocyanidins and phenolic compounds are potent antioxidants in green tea.

Caution: Tea (both green and black) contains caffeine — about 3 to 4%, about one-quarter to one-third the amount in coffee and the stronger the tea, the greater the quantity of caffeine in the drink.

Tea interferes with iron intake from foods of plant origin and vegetarians in particular should take tea between meals and not with them.

Availability: Dried green tea in bulk is found in Oriental markets and whole or natural food stores or individually wrapped in supermarkets.

Culinary Use: Green tea is astringent, some are strong tasting while others are refreshingly sweet and mild. Use green tea for syrups, dressings and puddings. Blend dried green tea with other dried herbs for a beverage.

Thyme

Thymus species

A bushy, low-growing shrub easily grown in North America.

Parts Used: Leaves.

Actions: Antioxidant, expectorant, antiseptic, antispasmodic, astringent, tonic, antimicrobial, antibiotic, heals wounds, carminative, calms coughs, nervine.

Uses: Thyme is ideal for deep-seated chest infections such as chronic coughs and bronchitis. It is also used for sinusitis, laryngitis, asthma and irritable bowel syndrome.

Thyme is high in calcium (1,890 mg in 100 mg fresh leaves), phosphorus, potassium and beta-carotene (3,800 I.U.).

Caution: Avoid in pregnancy. Children under 2 years of age and people with thyroid problems should not take thyme.

Availability: Fresh sprigs available in farmers' markets in season and most supermarkets year-round. Dried whole leaves in whole or natural food stores.

Culinary Use: The taste of thyme is peppery, pungent, slightly sweet and clove-like. It is extremely versatile and can be added to most dishes. It stands up to long cooking in soups, stews, tomato sauces, gumbos and chowders. Used daily, thyme's antioxidant effect is beneficial. Use thyme in canning and preserving because of its antibacterial, antifungal activity.

Fresh flowering sprigs are great in fruit and vegetable preserves, to flavor vinegar, oils and wine, in long-simmering dishes. Dried sprigs are used in bouquet garni and to release flavor when burned with coals for grilling foods.

Fresh thyme leaves are added to salads, vegetable dishes, soups, casseroles, stuffing, vegetable pâtés, breads, spreads, dips, vinegars, mustards and herb blends. Use lemon thyme with sea vegetables, lemon-flavored baked goods, syrups, puddings and desserts.

The fresh flowers lend a mild taste and rosy color to vinegar, butter and sauces or can be used as a garnish on soups, pasta, rice and desserts. Dried leaves and flowers are blended with other tea herbs.

Turmeric

Curcuma longa

A deciduous tender perennial belonging to the ginger family, hardy to zone 10 and native to southeast Asia. The long rhizome resembles ginger but is thinner and rounder with brilliant orange flesh.

Parts Used: Fleshy root.

Actions: Antioxidant, anti-inflammatory, antimicrobial, antibacterial, antifungal, antiviral, anticoagulant, analgesic, reduces cholesterol, reduces post-exercise pain, heals wounds, antispasmodic, protects liver cells, increases bile production and flow.

Uses: Turmeric appears to inhibit colon and breast cancer and is used in hepatitis, nausea, digestive disturbances, and where gall bladder has been removed. It boosts insulin activity and reduces the risk of stroke. Turmeric is also used in rheumatoid arthritis, cancer, candida, AIDS, Crohn's disease, eczema and digestive problems.

Availability: Asian stores stock fresh or frozen whole rhizomes at times when it is seasonal in the countries where it grows. Oriental markets or whole or natural food stores offer the dried, whole rhizomes, and supermarkets sell ground turmeric.

Culinary Use: The flavor of turmeric is pungent and charged with a fresh, peppery, camphorous, slightly acrid taste and is at its peak in freshly grated turmeric. Dried, whole rhizomes retain a warm, sweetish, woody character. Dried, powdered turmeric is weaker and slightly bitter in taste but still gives a yellow color to foods. Turmeric is one of the ingredients in traditional Indian curries. Use the fresh root whenever possible, cutting or grating it as required. Use turmeric to add warmth and a bright yellow hue to rice dishes, cheeses, lentils, pickles, chicken, fish, salsas and liqueurs. The fresh chopped root is also added to stocks, soups, sauces and stews. Fresh sliced root is used to flavor vinegar, oils soups or stocks and the julienne strips are added to stir-fries. Finely chopped or grated, raw fresh turmeric is excellent in salad dressings, marinades, baked vegetable or legume dishes, stir-fries, preserves and pickles. Turmeric juice is used to flavor salad dressings, marinades or sauces. Candied turmeric is used much like candied ginger in fruit salads, salad dressings, syrups and sauces.

Blend fresh or dried turmeric with other spice or herbs such as sweet cinnamon or cloves, hot pepper or mustard, earthy cumin or fenugreek and sharp dill, bay or thyme.

To store fresh root: Wrap the whole fresh root in a dry towel and set in an open plastic bag to keep for several weeks in the refrigerator. To keep longer, seal the fresh root in a plastic bag, freeze and cut off as needed. To keep fresh turmeric indefinitely, peel and slice, place in a glass jar, cover with vodka, seal and refrigerate.

Cooking with Yogurt

How Do I Cook with Yogurt?

The proteins in yogurt make it tricky for cooking. Like sour cream, it will separate when boiled, so we use emulsifiers — such as flour, cornstarch and arrowroot — to help prevent it from separating in dishes that are cooked in the oven. In sauces cooked on top of the stove, I add yogurt at the end of the cooking, and gently cook over low heat to heat it through.

Substitute yogurt for sour cream in recipes for a lower-calorie result. In baked goods, yogurt may be substituted for milk or for part of the milk, producing a richer, moist product. It is common practice to add $\frac{1}{2}$ tsp (2 mL) baking soda to the flour in a recipe for every 1 cup (250 mL) yogurt used to replace 1 cup (250 mL) milk in baked goods.

When the recipes in this book call for "yogurt," I mean either homemade or store-bought fresh, unflavored yogurt with live, active bacterial cultures. Unless otherwise indicated, you may use any of the yogurt recipes in Basic Yogurt-Making Recipes (page 19) or store-bought in these recipes.

How Do I Drain Yogurt?

To produce a thick and creamy yogurt, the watery whey from the milk may be drained away. The longer the yogurt drains, the thicker the yogurt will be.

To Drain Yogurt: Set a strainer or colander (preferably stainless-steel) over a bowl large enough to hold 2 cups (500 mL) liquid. Line the strainer with a double layer of clean cheesecloth. Pour 2 cups (500 mL) fresh unflavored yogurt into the lined strainer and cover the strainer with plastic wrap or fold up the edges of the cheesecloth to enclose the yogurt. Set the bowl and strainer in the refrigerator, and let the watery whey drain away from the yogurt solids. Much of the liquid will drain away in the first 10 minutes.

To indicate how long to let the yogurt drain, I use the following terms in the recipes in this book:

Drained Yogurt: Follow the directions above, and allow yogurt to drain for 10 minutes.

The yogurt will be thick and creamy, with a soft texture. Drained homemade fresh yogurt will resemble the Bulgarian or Balkan-style yogurt made using special strains of bacteria. 2 cups (500 mL) yogurt yield about $1\frac{1}{2}$ cups (375 mL) drained yogurt.

Honey Yogurt: This sweet and creamy yogurt can be used as a dressing for fruit salads or drizzled over desserts. To make honey yogurt, stir 3 tbsp (45 mL) liquid honey, maple syrup, brown rice syrup or agave nectar into $1\frac{1}{2}$ cups (375 mL) drained yogurt.

Yogurt Cheese: If you allow yogurt to drain for 8 hours or overnight, the result is a very thick, soft product that resembles cream cheese. Yogurt cheese is used in dips and spreads, and can replace the same quantity of cream cheese in some recipes. 4 cups (1 L) yogurt yield about $1\frac{1}{3}$ cups (325 mL) yogurt cheese.

Yogurt Cream: For a pourable, fresh-tasting cream that closely resembles crème fraîche, stir 1 tsp (5 mL) yogurt into 2 cups (500 mL) heavy or whipping (35%) cream and let stand for 15 minutes.

Note: If you want 2 cups (500 mL) drained yogurt to use in a recipe or to make honey yogurt, use a 750 g container of plain yogurt and set it over a cheesecloth-lined strainer. You will get roughly 2 cups (500 mL) drained yogurt.

Yogurt is healthy and nutritious, and consuming 1 cup (250 mL) a day is a delicious way to achieve almost 60% of your recommended daily allowance (RDA) of iodine and almost 50% of your RDA of calcium, along with significant amounts (25% of your RDA or higher) of phosphorus, vitamin B_2, protein and vitamin B_{12}. Canada's Food Guide and the USDA Food Pyramid include yogurt as part of essential, everyday foods. For more on the health benefits of yogurt, see pages 12 and 69.

Dips, Spreads, Snacks and Starters

Dips and Spreads

Use this delicious spread as an all-purpose substitute for commercial mayonnaise, as a dip or spread for sandwiches, or to accompany raw or lightly steamed vegetables, grilled fish or poultry. If you omit the garlic, the taste is refreshing and lends itself to fruit salads and dessert topping. You can add a spoonful of liquid honey to the non-garlic version.

Tzatziki

1	English cucumber	1
1⅓ cups	Yogurt Cheese (page 162)	325 mL
1	clove garlic, finely chopped	1
2 tbsp	chopped fresh mint	30 mL
2 tsp	freshly squeezed lemon juice	10 mL
	Sea salt and freshly ground pepper	

1. Shred cucumber (peel first, if not organic) into a colander. Let stand in the sink or over a bowl for 30 minutes. Press or squeeze lightly to expel excess liquid.

2. In a bowl, combine cucumber, yogurt cheese, garlic, mint and lemon juice. Stir to mix well. Season to taste with salt and pepper. Use immediately or store, tightly covered, in the refrigerator for up to 2 days.

Cheesy, flavorful and creamy, this dip has all the characteristics of a commercial dip and yet it is not loaded with the calories and chemicals. Use it on baked potatoes, soups and bagels or anytime you would use sour cream.

Herbed Feta Dip

½	English cucumber	½
1⅓ cups	Yogurt Cheese (page 162)	325 mL
1 cup	crumbled feta cheese	250 mL
2 cups	packed fresh spinach leaves, chopped	500 mL
¼ cup	chopped fresh chives or green onions	60 mL
2	cloves garlic, minced	2

1. Shred cucumber (peel first, if not organic) into a colander. Let stand in the sink or over a bowl for 30 minutes. Press or squeeze lightly to expel excess liquid.

2. In a bowl, combine cucumber, yogurt cheese, feta cheese, spinach, chives and garlic. Stir to mix well. Use immediately or store, tightly covered, in the refrigerator for up to 2 days.

There are some great brands of commercial hummus on the market today, and yet most of them contain chemical additives and preservatives. I still make my own hummus to use as a spread with sandwiches and a sauce for raw or cooked vegetables because I prefer to eliminate as many additives as possible from my diet. In this version, yogurt replaces most of the traditional olive oil, making this hummus a lower-calorie alternative.

Hummus

• *Food processor or blender*

1	can (14 to 19 oz/398 to 540 mL) chickpeas, drained and rinsed, or 2 cups (500 mL) cooked chickpeas	1
2	cloves garlic	2
2 tbsp	tahini paste or peanut butter	30 mL
1 to 2 tbsp	olive oil	15 to 30 mL
1½ cups	Drained Yogurt (page 162)	375 mL
3 tbsp	freshly squeezed lemon juice	45 mL
½ tsp	salt	2 mL
½ tsp	ground cumin	2 mL

1. In a food processor or blender, combine chickpeas and garlic and process until chopped. Stop and add tahini paste and olive oil to taste. With motor running, add drained yogurt through opening in lid and process until well mixed. Stop and scrape down sides of bowl. Add salt and cumin and process until mixed into the hummus. Use immediately or store, tightly covered, in the refrigerator for up to 1 week.

The "good" fat in avocados makes guacamole a healthy choice instead of butter, mayonnaise or other spreads filled with saturated fats.

Variation

• Add a tomato, skinned, seeded and chopped, in Step 2.

Guacamole

I	large ripe avocado	I
I tbsp	freshly squeezed lemon juice (approx.)	15 mL
3 tbsp	Yogurt Cheese or Drained Yogurt (page 162)	45 mL
2	green onions, finely chopped	2
I	clove garlic, minced	I
	Salt and freshly ground pepper	
	Tortilla chips	

1. Slit avocado in half lengthwise from stem end around base and back to stem. Twist the two halves apart. Remove pit from one half and skin from both halves. Coarsely chop flesh into a bowl. Using a fork, mash lemon juice into avocado.

2. Stir in yogurt cheese, green onions and garlic. Taste and add more lemon juice, salt and pepper as required. Spoon into a small bowl and serve with tortilla chips. Use immediately or store, tightly covered, in the refrigerator for up to 2 days.

I love the striking color of this spread. It is very dramatic when used in appetizers.

Creamy Red Pepper Spread

• *Food processor or blender*

2	red bell peppers, seeded and thinly sliced	2
I	clove garlic, minced	I
I tbsp	olive oil	15 mL
I ⅓ cups	Yogurt Cheese (page 162)	325 mL
2 tbsp	freshly squeezed lemon juice	30 mL
I tbsp	tahini paste	15 mL
I tbsp	pure maple syrup or liquid honey	15 mL

1. In a large skillet, combine bell peppers, garlic and oil. Sauté over medium heat for 7 minutes or until tender. Transfer to a bowl and let cool.

2. In a food processor or blender, combine pepper mixture, yogurt cheese, lemon juice, tahini and maple syrup and process for about 30 seconds or until smooth. Transfer to a bowl or serving dish. Use immediately or store, tightly covered, in the refrigerator for up to 3 days.

Blue Cheese Spread

1 ⅓ cups	Yogurt Cheese (page 162)	325 mL
2 to 4 tbsp	heavy or whipping (35%) cream	30 to 60 mL
1 cup	crumbled blue cheese	250 mL

This makes a fairly stiff spread for hors d'oeuvres or to stuff into cherry tomatoes. If you would like a softer, creamier spread, use 1½ cups (375 mL) Drained Yogurt (page 166) and process it with the blue cheese in a food processor or blender and omit the cream altogether.

1. In a bowl, mix yogurt cheese with as much cream as needed to make a firm spread. Fold in blue cheese. Use immediately or store, tightly covered, in the refrigerator for up to 3 days.

Makes 1½ cups (375 mL)

Roasted Garlic and Artichoke Dip

With its taste of the Mediterranean, this spread adds flavor to an impromptu sauce for steamed vegetables, as a substitute for mayonnaise, as a dip for raw vegetables, or as a spread for crackers and breads. It is easy to make, and may be made up to 3 days in advance.

- *Preheat oven to 400°F (200°C)*
- *Small heatproof baking dish with lid or foil*
- *Blender or food processor*

3	whole heads garlic, excess skin removed	3
2 tbsp	olive oil	30 mL
1 1/3 cups	Yogurt Cheese (page 162)	325 mL
1	can (14 oz/398 mL) artichoke hearts, drained	1
1 tbsp	chopped fresh rosemary	15 mL
	Sea salt and freshly ground pepper	

1. Cut a ¼-inch (0.5 cm) slice off the tops of garlic. Place heads, root end down on baking dish. Drizzle oil over garlic cloves. Place lid on dish or cover with foil. Bake in preheated oven for 45 minutes to 1 hour or until garlic is tender. Let cool.

2. Squeeze garlic flesh out of skins into blender or food processor. Add yogurt cheese, artichokes and rosemary and process until soft and creamy. Season to taste with salt and pepper. Use immediately or store, tightly covered, in the refrigerator for up to 3 days.

Makes 2½ cups (625 mL)

Avocado Aïoli

Creamy and just as tasty as the traditional egg-and-oil Mediterranean sauce called "aïoli," this spread is great on steamed vegetables — especially asparagus and artichokes.

2	ripe avocadoes, seeded and peeled	2
1 tbsp	freshly squeezed lemon juice	15 mL
1½ cups	Drained Yogurt (page 162)	375 mL
2	cloves garlic, minced	2
¼ tsp	sea salt	1 mL

1. In a bowl, using a fork, mash avocadoes with lemon juice. Whisk in drained yogurt, garlic and sea salt. Use immediately or store, tightly covered, in the refrigerator for up to 5 days.

I like the nutty flavor
of the roasted eggplant.
You can try roasting a
whole head of garlic at
the same time as the
eggplant for a more
mellow garlic dip.

Baba Ghanouj

- *Preheat oven to 400°F (200°C)*
- *Rimmed baking sheet, lightly oiled*
- *Food processor*

1	large eggplant (about 1 lb/500 g)	1
2	cloves garlic	2
½ cup	fresh parsley leaves	125 mL
1 tbsp	freshly squeezed lemon juice	15 mL
½ cup	Yogurt Cheese (page 162)	125 mL
	Sea salt and freshly ground pepper	

1. Using a fork, prick eggplant in several places. Place on
prepared baking sheet and bake in preheated oven for
30 minutes or until flesh is soft inside. Let cool. Cut eggplant
in half and scoop out and discard seeds. Let eggplant
drain in a colander over the sink.

2. In a food processor, combine garlic and parsley and process
until finely chopped. Using a large spoon, scoop eggplant
flesh from skin and add to food processor; discard skin.
Add lemon juice and yogurt cheese and and process
until smooth. Season to taste with salt and pepper. Use
immediately or store, tightly covered, in the refrigerator for
up to 5 days.

Creamy Spinach Dip

Using yogurt in dips cuts the fat and yet keeps the texture and flavor of full-fat mayonnaise or sour cream.

• *Food processor or blender*

2	cloves garlic	2
¼ cup	fresh parsley leaves	60 mL
2 cups	packed spinach leaves or I package (10 oz/300 g) frozen spinach, thawed and drained	500 mL
3 tbsp	snipped fresh dill leaves	45 mL
I tbsp	freshly squeezed lemon juice	15 mL
1⅓ cups	Yogurt Cheese (page 162)	325 mL

I. In a food processor or blender, combine garlic and parsley and process until finely chopped. Add spinach, dill and lemon juice and process until chopped. Add yogurt cheese and process until mixed into the greens. Use immediately or store, tightly covered, in the refrigerator for up to 5 days.

Caponata

Known as *Caponata Siciliana* in Italy and not usually made with yogurt as it is here, this thick dip is delicious with garlic bread as antipasto but can be spread on vegetables in hors d'oeuvres or served with greens as a starter. I find that it is also very good when tossed with cooked pasta or rice.

Tip

- If you cut ½-inch (1 cm) wide lengthwise strips from the eggplant skin before dicing, the pieces with some peel won't shrink.

3 tbsp	olive oil, divided	45 mL
1	onion, chopped	1
1	small eggplant, cut into ½-inch (1 cm) dice (see Tip, left)	1
1	clove garlic, crushed	1
½ cup	chopped red bell pepper	125 mL
1½ cups	chopped fresh Roma (plum) tomatoes	375 mL
½ cup	chopped black olives, optional	125 mL
3 tbsp	shredded fresh basil or flat-leaf parsley	45 mL
1 tbsp	chopped drained capers	15 mL
½ cup	Drained Yogurt (page 162)	125 mL

1. In a skillet, heat 2 tbsp (30 mL) of the oil over medium-high heat. Add onion and eggplant. Cook, stirring constantly, for 3 to 5 minutes or until vegetables are soft. Add remaining oil, garlic and bell pepper. Cook, stirring frequently, for 5 minutes or until pepper is soft. Add tomatoes and cook, stirring frequently, for about 7 minutes or until mixture is soft and liquid has evaporated.

2. Remove from heat and let cool. Stir in olives, if using, basil, capers and drained yogurt. Use immediately or store, tightly covered, in the refrigerator for up to 5 days.

Serves 4 to 6

This tart makes a
versatile light meal
and an any-season
nutritious snack.
Serve it with grilled or
sliced fresh tomatoes
in the summer and
steamed vegetables in
the winter.

Artichoke and Leek Tart

- *Preheat oven to 375°F (190°C)*
- *10-inch (25 cm) springform pan or round tart pan,
  lightly oiled*

Potato Base

3 cups	thinly sliced potatoes	750 mL
I cup	sliced leek, white and light green parts	250 mL
3 tbsp	honey mustard	45 mL
2 tbsp	olive oil	30 mL
½ tsp	salt	2 mL
	Freshly ground pepper	

Topping

2 tbsp	olive oil	30 mL
½ cup	chopped onion	125 mL
I	clove garlic, chopped	I
4	eggs	4
I	can (14 oz/398 mL) artichoke hearts, drained and diced	I
I cup	shredded Cheddar cheese	250 mL
½ cup	plain yogurt	125 mL
¼ cup	bread crumbs	60 mL
¼ cup	chopped fresh parsley	60 mL
½ tsp	sea salt	2 mL
¼ cup	freshly grated Parmesan cheese	60 mL

I. *Potato Base:* In a large bowl, toss potatoes and leek with
   mustard and oil. Spread in bottom of prepared pan. Press
   potatoes with the back of a spoon to compress. Sprinkle
   salt and pepper over top. Bake in preheated oven for 25 to
   30 minutes or until potatoes are just tender but not soft. Let
   cool slightly. Reduce oven to 325°F (160°C).

2. *Topping:* Meanwhile, in a skillet, heat oil over medium-high heat. Add onion and cook, stirring frequently, for 7 minutes or until soft. Add garlic and cook, stirring occasionally, for 3 minutes. Onion and garlic should be soft and slightly browned. Let cool.

3. In a bowl, beat eggs. Add artichokes, Cheddar, yogurt, bread crumbs, parsley and salt. Stir in onion and garlic and mix well. Pour over potato base. Sprinkle Parmesan over top and bake for 25 to 30 minutes or until a knife inserted in the middle comes out clean and cheese is lightly browned. Transfer to a wire cooling rack and let stand for 10 minutes before serving.

Makes 18 pieces

Black Bean Quesadillas

These quesadillas are perfect for appetizers when cut into small wedges or you can serve the larger size for a light lunch. Make double batches and freeze these tasty Mexican-inspired sandwiches to use as quick snacks or light main meals.

Variation

• Use cooked or canned black-eyed peas, fava beans or kidney beans in place of the black beans.

• *Food processor or blender*

2	cloves garlic	2
1⅓ cups	Yogurt Cheese (page 182)	325 mL
1 cup	cooked or canned black beans, rinsed and drained	250 mL
½ cup	sliced black or green olives	125 mL
¼ cup	chopped sunflower seeds	60 mL
1 tbsp	chopped fresh oregano	15 mL
½ cup	tomato sauce or salsa, divided	125 mL
6	7-inch (18 cm) flour tortillas	6
1 cup	shredded Swiss or mozzarella cheese, divided	250 mL

1. In a food processor or blender, process garlic until finely chopped. Add yogurt cheese, black beans, olives, sunflower seeds and oregano and process just until mixed. Set aside.

2. Spread 1 tbsp (15 mL) of the tomato sauce over one half of each tortilla to within ½ inch (1 cm) of the edge. Spoon one-sixth of the bean filling over tomato sauce and sprinkle one-sixth of the cheese over the filling. Moisten tortilla edges with water. Fold each tortilla in half over filling and press edges lightly to seal.

3. In a lightly oiled large skillet, cook quesadillas over medium heat, 2 or 3 at a time, for 3 to 5 minutes on each side, until lightly browned on each side. Cut each quesadilla into 3 triangles for appetizers, or serve whole for a light lunch. Serve warm, garnished with extra yogurt cheese or yogurt, if desired.

Makes twelve
3-inch (7.5 cm) or
about thirty-six
1-inch (2.5 cm)
falafel "cookies"

Baked Vegetable Falafel

- *Preheat oven to 400°F (200°C)*
- *2 baking sheets, lightly oiled*
- *Food processor*

Make these small falafel "cookies" to use as a base for canapés with spreads or salsas. If you make large falafels, they are perfect for filling wraps or pita pockets. Baking the seasoned chickpea disks is much healthier than deep-frying them. Serve large falafel over shredded lettuce with Creamy Spinach Dip (page 172) or Caponata (page 173).

Tips

- For this amount of beans, use 1 can (14 to 19 oz/398 to 540 mL) chickpeas or fava beans, drained and rinsed.

- In Step 3, drop falafel mixture by 1 tbsp (15 mL) for smaller, canapé-size falafel "cookies" and reduce baking time to 12 to 17 minutes.

Variation

- Substitute grated sweet potato, parsnip or carrot for the zucchini.

2 cups	cooked drained chickpeas or fava beans (see Tips, left)	500 mL
2 tbsp	freshly squeezed lemon juice	30 mL
2 tbsp	olive oil	30 mL
I tbsp	curry powder	15 mL
I	egg, beaten	I
2 cups	coarsely grated zucchini or yellow summer squash	500 mL
1/4 cup	finely chopped green onions	60 mL
1/4 to 1/2 cup	toasted chickpea flour or brown rice flour	60 to 125 mL
3/4 tsp	baking powder	3 mL
I cup	Yogurt Cheese (page 162) or store-bought or homemade Tzatziki (page 164)	250 mL

1. In a food processor, combine chickpeas, lemon juice, oil and curry powder and process for 30 seconds or until smooth. Transfer to a bowl.

2. Stir egg into chickpea purée and mix well. Stir in zucchini and green onions. Sprinkle 1/4 cup (60 mL) of the flour and baking powder over mixture and stir to make a moist, thick batter. If too thin to hold together, add more flour, 1 tbsp (15 mL) at a time, until the desired consistency is achieved.

3. Using a 1/4 cup (60 mL) measure, drop falafel mixture onto prepared baking sheets, about 1 inch (2.5 cm) apart, and flatten slightly with the back of a spoon. Continue to form falafels until sheets are full. Place one baking sheet on the left-hand side of the top oven rack and one baking sheet on the right-hand side of the lower oven rack and bake in preheated oven for 15 to 20 minutes or until bottoms are lightly browned. Serve immediately, garnished with a dollop of yogurt cheese.

Vegetable Frittata Bites

This makes a great company brunch dish because it can be made the night before and refrigerated. If made on Sunday morning, leftovers serve as nutritious after-school snacks for the beginning of the week.

Variation

• Add ¼ cup (60 mL) milk and 1 cup (250 mL) stale bread cubes in Step 3.

• *Preheat oven to 375°F (190°C)*
• *9-inch (23 cm) square baking dish, lightly oiled*

2 cups	trimmed fresh spinach	500 mL
2 tbsp	olive oil	30 mL
⅔ cup	sliced leek, white and light green parts	150 mL
½ cup	chopped onion	125 mL
½ cup	chopped red bell pepper	125 mL
½ cup	shredded carrot	125 mL
6	eggs	6
⅓ cup	plain yogurt	75 mL
¼ cup	shredded Swiss cheese	60 mL
¼ cup	shredded Cheddar cheese	60 mL
1 tbsp	chopped fresh basil	15 mL
2 tsp	chopped fresh sage	10 mL
2 tsp	fresh thyme leaves	10 mL
½ tsp	salt	2 mL
	Freshly ground pepper	

1. Wash spinach, drain and transfer wet leaves to a saucepan. Cover and cook on medium-high heat for about 2 minutes or until spinach is wilted. Remove from heat, drain and cool. Squeeze out excess moisture and coarsely chop.

2. Meanwhile, in a large skillet, heat oil over medium heat. Add leek, onion, bell pepper and carrot. Cook, stirring, for 7 minutes or until soft. Stir in spinach and distribute it evenly. Set aside and let cool.

3. In a large bowl, beat together eggs and yogurt. Add Swiss cheese, Cheddar, vegetable mixture, basil, sage, thyme, salt, and pepper to taste. Pour into prepared baking dish. Mixture may be prepared to this point, covered and refrigerated for several hours or overnight. Return to room temperature before baking.

4. Bake in preheated oven for 25 to 30 minutes or until lightly browned and set. Let cool for 10 minutes before cutting. Serve warm or at room temperature.

The unusual combination of pear and caramelized onion is slightly sweet and very pleasant in this elegant easy appetizer. It complements Middle Eastern naan bread, lavash or artisanal flatbread. If the flatbread is more than 1-inch (2.5 cm) thick, cut it in half lengthwise to make two bases. Double this recipe, or use a different spread for the second half of the loaf.

Caramelized Pear and Onion Flatbread

- *Preheat broiler (475°F/240°C if possible)*
- *Rimmed baking sheet*

2 tbsp	olive oil	30 mL
1 tbsp	butter	15 mL
2	red onions, thinly sliced	2
1	pear, thinly sliced	1
4	cloves garlic, thinly sliced	4
2 tbsp	lightly packed brown sugar	30 mL
2 tbsp	balsamic vinegar	30 mL
1 1/3 cups	Yogurt Cheese (page 162)	325 mL
1/2 cup	crumbled feta cheese	125 mL
1 tbsp	fresh thyme leaves	15 mL
1	large naan bread or flatbread	1

1. In a skillet, heat oil and melt butter over medium-high heat. Add red onions and pear and bring to a light simmer, stirring constantly. Reduce heat to medium-low and cook, stirring occasionally, for 10 minutes or until onions are soft. Add garlic, brown sugar and vinegar and cook, stirring occasionally, for 3 to 5 minutes. Garlic should be soft and the liquid should have evaporated, leaving a soft and sticky (caramelized) mixture. Let cool slightly.

2. Meanwhile, in a bowl, combine yogurt cheese, feta and thyme. Spread evenly over naan and place on baking sheet. Spread onion mixture over yogurt mixture and place under broiler for 30 seconds or until bread warms through. Transfer to a cutting board and cut into appetizer-size pieces.

Potato and Onion Fritters

• *Preheat oven to 325°F (160°C)*

If you make the fritters small, you can serve them as appetizers; if they are shaped a bit bigger, they make a fast and nutritious meal. The egg holds the ingredients together and the flour absorbs the liquid from the freshly grated vegetables to keep the pancakes from falling apart.

2	medium potatoes, shredded and drained	2
1 cup	cooked or canned black or kidney beans, drained, rinsed and chopped	250 mL
1	carrot, shredded	1
½	onion, chopped or shredded	½
½ cup	shredded Swiss or Cheddar cheese	125 mL
1	clove garlic, minced	1
1 tbsp	chopped fresh savory	15 mL
1 tbsp	chopped fresh oregano	15 mL
½ tsp	salt	2 mL
1	egg, beaten	1
¼ cup	all-purpose or whole wheat flour (approx.)	60 mL
2 to 4 tbsp	olive oil, divided	30 to 60 mL
1⅓ cups	Yogurt Cheese (page 162)	325 mL

1. In a large bowl, combine potatoes, beans, carrot, onion, cheese, garlic, savory, oregano and salt, mixing well. Stir in egg. Sprinkle in flour, 1 tbsp (15 mL) at a time, stirring until the mixture holds together well.

2. In a large skillet, heat 1 tbsp (15 mL) of the oil over medium heat. Drop 2 tbsp (30 mL) or ¼ cup (60 mL) of the potato mixture into the skillet and flatten lightly with a fork (keep fritter compact and at least ½-inch/1 cm thick). Repeat to make 1 or 2 more fritters. Cook for 4 minutes on one side. Flip and cook for 3 to 4 minutes on the other side or until browned. Using a slotted lifter, transfer to a paper towel to drain and then to a baking sheet and keep warm in preheated oven. Repeat with remaining oil and vegetable mixture. Serve hot with a dollop of yogurt cheese.

The traditional way to make this Turkish delicacy is to bread and deep-fry stuffed eggplant "sandwiches," but I prefer to skip the last steps and serve this lighter version warm or at room temperature.

Variation

• Arrange stuffed eggplant rolls in a lightly greased 11- by 7-inch (28 by 18 cm) baking dish. Cover with 2 cups (500 mL) tomato sauce. Bake in preheated 350°F (180°C) oven for 15 to 20 minutes or until sauce is bubbling and rolls are heated through. Serve warm with rice or couscous for a light meal.

Cheese-Stuffed Eggplant Rolls

• *Preheat oven to 375°F (190°C)*
• *2 baking sheets, lightly oiled*

2	long thin eggplants, ends trimmed	2
3 tbsp	salt	45 mL
3 tbsp	olive oil (approx.)	45 mL
1½ cups	Cheese Filling (below)	375 mL

1. Slice eggplants lengthwise ⅛-inch (3 mm) thick. Place one layer in a large colander set in the sink or over a bowl and sprinkle slices with salt. Repeat until all eggplant slices have been salted. Let drain for 1 hour. Rinse and pat dry.

2. Place eggplant slices on prepared baking sheets in a single layer, working in batches, as necessary. Brush lightly with oil. Bake in preheated oven for 7 to 10 minutes or until lightly browned. Remove from oven, flip slices over and bake for another 3 minutes to brown the other sides. Using tongs, lift slices from pan and transfer to drain on paper towels. Repeat with remaining slices.

3. Place 1 tbsp (15 mL) of the filling on one end of an eggplant slice and roll eggplant around it. Continue until all slices are rolled. Serve warm or cover and refrigerate overnight and reheat in a 350°F (180°C) oven for 2 to 3 minutes or until warmed through.

To make entertaining easier, make the Cheese Filling ahead and the eggplant strips ahead to the end of Step 2. Be sure to wrap tightly and refrigerate overnight and bring them back to room temperature before continuing with Step 3 above.

Cheese Filling

1⅓ cups	Yogurt Cheese (page 162)	325 mL
4 oz	cream cheese, softened	125 g
2	cloves garlic, minced	2
1	egg, lightly beaten	1
2 tbsp	chopped fresh cilantro or flat-leaf parsley	30 mL
1 tsp	garam masala spice blend (see Tip, page 219)	5 mL

1. In a bowl, combine yogurt cheese, cream cheese, garlic, egg, cilantro and garam masala. Stir to mix well.

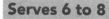

Herbed Yogurt, Prosciutto and Cherries on Rye

Easy to make and a very nice flavor combination, this unusual appetizer is not only tasty, but also a healthy start to any meal.

1 ⅓ cups	Yogurt Cheese (page 162)	325 mL
2 tbsp	finely chopped green onions	30 mL
1 tbsp	finely chopped fresh basil or oregano	15 mL
1 cup	chopped dried cherries	250 mL
2 tbsp	liquid honey	30 mL
6	slices dense rye bread, crusts removed	6
6	slices prosciutto, each slice cut into 3 lengthwise pieces	6
	Freshly ground black pepper	

1. In a bowl, combine yogurt cheese, green onions and basil. In a separate bowl, combine dried cherries and honey. Set both aside.

2. Cut each slice of rye bread into 3 fingers. Spread about 1 tbsp (15 mL) of the yogurt mixture over each finger. Top yogurt mixture with a slice of prosciutto and a scant tablespoon (15 mL) of the honeyed cherries. Grind fresh pepper over top and serve immediately.

Roasting both the mushrooms and the garlic gives a nutty flavor to this delicious warm starter.

Roasted Portobello Mushrooms on Toast Points

- *Preheat oven to 400°F (200°C)*
- *Rimmed baking sheet, lightly oiled*

2	whole heads garlic	2
5	portobello mushrooms, stems trimmed	5
3 tbsp	olive oil	45 mL
1⅓ cups	Yogurt Cheese (page 162)	325 mL
¼ cup	toasted pine nuts or sunflower seeds	60 mL
¼ cup	chopped flat-leaf parsley	60 mL
1 tbsp	balsamic vinegar	15 mL
4	slices whole wheat bread	4
	Soft butter	
¼ cup	shaved Parmesan cheese	60 mL

1. Cut a ¼-inch (0.5 cm) slice off the tops of garlic. Arrange garlic heads, root end down, and mushrooms, stem side up, on prepared baking sheet. Drizzle oil over all. Roast in preheated oven for 30 minutes. Check mushrooms and, when tender, transfer to a large bowl. Garlic should be very soft and, if not, roast for another 10 minutes or until soft. Transfer pan to a wire cooling rack and let cool.

2. In a bowl, combine yogurt cheese, pine nuts and parsley. Squeeze roasted garlic cloves into yogurt mixture and, using a fork, mash until well mixed into yogurt mixture.

3. Slice mushrooms into the bowl they have been cooling in and toss with any accumulated juices and balsamic vinegar. Fold yogurt mixture into mushrooms.

4. Toast bread slices and butter lightly. Cut into points by slicing from each bottom corner to diagonally opposite corner in an "X". Arrange 4 points on each plate. Divide mushroom mixture into 4 portions and place each portion over toast points. Top with shaved Parmesan.

Mushroom Bruschetta

The combination of yogurt and mushrooms lends a unique taste twist to the classic tomato topping for Italian garlic bread.

2 tbsp	olive oil	30 mL
2 cups	sliced mushrooms	500 mL
½ cup	chopped onion	125 mL
1 tbsp	freshly squeezed lemon juice	15 mL
1⅓ cups	Yogurt Cheese (page 162)	325 mL
¼ cup	crumbled goat cheese	60 mL
1 tbsp	chopped fresh parsley	15 mL
2 tsp	fresh thyme leaves	10 mL
16	slices crusty white Italian-style bread (½-inch/1 cm slices)	16
4	cloves garlic, halved	4
¼ cup	olive oil	60 mL
	Sea salt and freshly ground pepper	

1. In a skillet, heat 2 tbsp (30 mL) of the oil over medium-high heat. Add mushrooms and onion. Cook, stirring frequently, for 6 minutes or until vegetables are tender. Transfer to a bowl. Toss with lemon juice and let cool slightly. Add yogurt cheese, goat cheese, parsley and thyme and mix well.

2. Meanwhile, toast bread in batches. While still hot, rub both sides with the cut side of a garlic clove and place on a serving platter or individual serving plates. Drizzle oil over each slice of bread and season with salt and pepper. Divide mushroom topping evenly among toasted bread slices and spread over top.

Soups

Broccoli and Orange Soup

The sweet-tart of the citrus complements the broccoli in this light soup. You can save four orange segments and use to garnish the soup or serve with Yogurt Gremolata (page 248).

• *Blender*

I tbsp	olive oil	15 mL
I tbsp	butter	15 mL
I	onion, chopped	I
I	head broccoli, chopped	I
3 cups	chicken broth	750 mL
2 cups	plain yogurt	500 mL
2	oranges, segmented	2

1. In a large saucepan, heat oil and melt butter over medium-high heat. Add onion and cook, stirring frequently, for 7 to 10 minutes or until soft. Add broccoli and cook, stirring constantly, for 2 to 3 seconds. Add broth and bring to a boil. Cover and reduce heat to medium-low. Gently simmer for 20 minutes or until broccoli is tender. Transfer mixture to a bowl.

2. In a blender, purée half of the broccoli mixture with half of the yogurt and half of the orange segments. Return to saucepan. Purée remaining broccoli mixture, yogurt and orange segments and add to saucepan. Heat puréed soup over medium heat, stirring constantly (do not let boil).

Curried Sweet Potato Soup

2 tbsp	olive oil	30 mL
I cup	chopped onion	250 mL
I tbsp	curry powder	15 mL
2	sweet potatoes, peeled and cut into large dice	2
I cup	chopped carrot	250 mL
3 cups	vegetable broth	750 mL
¼ cup	chopped raisins	60 mL
I tsp	salt	5 mL
I	can (14 oz/400 mL) coconut milk	I
½ cup	Drained Yogurt (page 162)	125 mL
⅓ cup	chopped red bell pepper	75 mL

1. In a large saucepan, heat oil over medium-low heat. Add onion and curry powder and cook, stirring occasionally, for 6 minutes. Stir in sweet potatoes and carrot. Cook, stirring constantly, for 3 minutes.

2. Stir in broth. Increase heat and bring to a boil. Reduce heat and simmer, stirring occasionally, for 15 minutes. Add raisins and salt and cook for 5 minutes or until all vegetables are soft. Remove from heat.

3. Using a potato masher, roughly mash sweet potato mixture. Stir in coconut milk and drained yogurt. Return to medium-high heat and heat through (do not let boil). Ladle soup into 4 bowls. Divide bell pepper evenly over each bowl. Serve immediately.

Cheddar Cheese and Parsnip Soup

This soup can simmer for as long as several hours (before the yogurt, cheese and milk are added) or it can be ready in less than an hour. If you wish, simmer it for a while, keep an eye on the liquid and add more water or broth when required.

3 tbsp	olive oil	45 mL
I	leek, white and light green parts, chopped	I
I cup	chopped onion	250 mL
2	cloves garlic, minced	2
2 cups	chicken broth	500 mL
2	parsnips, chopped	2
I cup	chopped potato	250 mL
I cup	chopped rutabaga	250 mL
I tbsp	fresh thyme leaves	15 mL
I tbsp	chopped fresh sage	15 mL
I tsp	salt	5 mL
I ½ cups	shredded Cheddar cheese	375 mL
I cup	plain yogurt	250 mL
I cup	milk	250 mL

1. In a large saucepan, heat oil over medium-high heat. Add leek and onion and cook, stirring frequently, for 10 minutes or until vegetables are soft. Add garlic and cook, stirring frequently, for 3 minutes or until lightly golden. Stir in broth and bring to a boil.

2. Add parsnips, potato, rutabaga, thyme, sage and salt. Reduce heat to medium and gently simmer, stirring occasionally, for 15 to 20 minutes or until tender. Remove from heat.

3. Using a slotted spoon, transfer about 1 cup (250 mL) of the vegetables to a bowl. Using a potato masher, roughly mash and return to saucepan. Stir in cheese, yogurt and milk. Heat over medium heat, stirring constantly, for 2 to 3 minutes or until cheese is melted (do not let boil). Serve immediately.

This is a winter soup —
its comforting tomato
taste is welcome on
those days when most
dinners come from a
can and whatever the
pantry holds.

Creamy Tomato Soup

• *Food processor or blender*

1 tbsp	olive oil	15 mL
1 cup	finely chopped onion	250 mL
1	clove garlic, finely chopped	1
1 cup	shredded carrot or rutabaga	250 mL
½ cup	finely chopped celery or kohlrabi	125 mL
1	can (28 oz/796 mL) tomatoes with juice	1
1 cup	chicken broth	250 mL
2 tbsp	blackstrap molasses	30 mL
1 tbsp	apple cider vinegar	15 mL
1 tbsp	dried thyme	15 mL
½ tsp	salt	2 mL
½ tsp	ground nutmeg	2 mL
1 cup	Drained Yogurt (page 162)	250 mL

1. In a large saucepan, heat oil over medium heat. Add onion and cook, stirring frequently, for 7 minutes. Stir in garlic, carrot and celery. Cook, stirring occasionally, for 5 minutes.

2. Add tomatoes with juice, broth, molasses, vinegar, thyme, salt and nutmeg. Bring to a gentle boil. Cover, reduce heat and simmer for 35 minutes.

3. Using a slotted spoon, lift out half of the vegetables and transfer to a food processor or blender. Process for 30 seconds or until smooth. Pour into a bowl. Repeat with remaining vegetables. Keep remaining cooking liquids hot in the saucepan over low heat. Return purée to saucepan and stir in drained yogurt.

4. Taste and add more vinegar, thyme, salt or nutmeg, if required. Heat through (do not let boil) and serve immediately.

Creamed Scallop Soup

Gently poached scallops in a flavorful broth make this a special starter. Straining the leek and thyme in Step 2 gives the soup its silky smooth texture, but the straining is optional. You can use bay scallops, but they are smaller and cook faster than sea scallops, so reduce cooking time in Step 3, if necessary.

Variation

* Instead of scallops, you can also make this with the same amount of shrimp, lobster or crabmeat.

12 oz	sea scallops	375 g
1 tbsp	olive oil	15 mL
2 tsp	butter	10 mL
1	leek, white and light green parts, finely chopped	1
1 cup	fish stock or chicken broth	250 mL
½ cup	dry white wine	125 mL
1 tbsp	fresh thyme leaves	15 mL
½ tsp	salt	2 mL
½ cup	heavy or whipping (35%) cream	125 mL
2 tbsp	Drained Yogurt (page 162)	30 mL
2 tbsp	finely chopped fresh chives	30 mL

1. Trim off the tough ligament, if still attached, from the side of each scallop. Rinse scallops and pat dry. Set aside.

2. In a heavy-bottomed saucepan, heat oil and melt butter over high heat. Add leek and cook, stirring constantly, for 5 minutes or until soft. Add fish stock, wine, thyme and salt. Cover and bring to a boil. Reduce heat and gently boil for 5 minutes. Strain through a fine mesh sieve into a bowl, pressing on solids to release liquids. Discard solids and return strained soup broth to saucepan.

3. Bring broth to a simmer over medium-high heat. Using a slotted spoon, lower scallops into broth. Reduce heat, cover and gently simmer for about 2 minutes or just until scallops are a milky-opaque color. Using a slotted spoon, lift out scallops and transfer to a pie plate. Cover to keep warm. Keep soup broth warm in saucepan over low heat.

4. Meanwhile, in a bowl, combine cream and drained yogurt, whisking until blended. Whisk cream mixture into broth in saucepan.

5. Divide scallops and chives evenly among 4 warmed soup bowls. Ladle soup over and serve immediately.

Chipotle peppers add a mysteriously smoky flavor to this robust soup. Serve it with nacho chips or a salad for a complete meal. You can substitute flat-leaf parsley for the cilantro.

Chipotle Corn and Black Bean Soup

4	slices side bacon	4
1 tbsp	olive oil	15 mL
2 cups	chopped red onion	500 mL
2	cloves garlic, chopped	2
1	can (28 oz/796 mL) stewed tomatoes with juice	1
1 cup	chicken broth	250 mL
2	chipotle peppers in adobo sauce	2
1	cayenne pepper, chopped	1
2 cups	fresh or frozen corn kernels	500 mL
2 cups	cooked black turtle beans or 1 can (14 to 19 oz/398 to 540 mL), rinsed and drained	500 mL
1 cup	cooked red or brown rice	250 mL
1 cup	plain yogurt	250 mL
1/4 cup	chopped fresh cilantro	60 mL
1/4 cup	shredded Cheddar cheese	60 mL

1. In a skillet over high heat, cook bacon until crisp. Transfer to paper towels and set aside. Drain skillet and discard bacon fat. In same skillet, heat oil over medium-high heat. Add red onion and cook, stirring frequently, for 8 minutes or until onion is soft and translucent. Add garlic and cook, stirring frequently, for 3 minutes.

2. Add tomatoes with juice, broth, chipotle peppers with adobo sauce, cayenne pepper, corn and black beans. Bring to a boil, reduce heat and simmer, stirring occasionally, for 20 minutes. Crumble bacon and add to soup with rice and yogurt. Heat through (do not let boil). Ladle soup into 4 bowls and garnish with cilantro and shredded cheese.

Coconut Chicken Soup

4	boneless skinless chicken breasts (each about 7 oz/210 g)	4
2 tbsp	olive oil	30 mL
I	onion, chopped	I
I tbsp	Thai-inspired Red Curry Paste (page 257 or store-bought) or curry powder	15 mL
I tbsp	chopped candied ginger	15 mL
2 cups	chicken broth	500 mL
I	can (14 oz/400 mL) coconut milk	I
8 oz	rice vermicelli noodles	250 g
I cup	Cultured Coconut Milk "Yogurt" (page 23 or store-bought coconut-flavored yogurt) or plain yogurt	250 mL
I	hot chile pepper, chopped, optional or to taste	I

1. Trim off all visible fat from chicken breasts and discard. In a saucepan, heat oil over medium heat. Add chicken and onion and cook, turning chicken and stirring onions frequently, for 8 to 10 minutes or until chicken is browned and onion is tender. Stir in curry paste and ginger and cook, stirring constantly, for 1 minute.

2. Add chicken broth and coconut milk and bring to a boil over high heat. Reduce heat and simmer, turning chicken at least once, for about 20 minutes or until chicken is no longer pink inside. Remove chicken and shred. Set aside.

3. Add noodles to soup and simmer for 5 minutes or until al dente. Using tongs, lift noodles into 4 bowls. Ladle soup over. Top with shredded chicken, yogurt, and chopped chile pepper, if using.

Beet Soup

This soup has a dual personality. If made following the method at right, it is thick and chunky, very much a peasant-style soup. Yet if the cooked vegetables are strained and blended in a food processor and returned to the pot with the cooking liquid and drained yogurt, a smooth and creamy sophisticated texture is achieved.

I lb	beets, peeled and finely chopped	500 g
I	onion, finely chopped	I
I	stalk celery, finely chopped	I
I	apple, finely chopped	I
I	carrot, shredded	I
I	parsnip, shredded	I
5 cups	vegetable broth, divided	1.25 L
I tbsp	olive oil	15 mL
I tbsp	butter	15 mL
2 tbsp	freshly squeezed lemon juice	30 mL
I tbsp	fresh thyme leaves	15 mL
I tsp	salt	5 mL
I ½ cups	Drained Yogurt (page 162)	375 mL

1. In a large saucepan, combine beets, onion, celery, apple, carrot, parsnip, 1 cup (250 mL) of the broth, oil and butter. Bring to a gentle boil over medium-high heat. Cover, reduce heat to medium and gently simmer for 15 minutes.

2. Stir in remaining 4 cups (1 L) of broth, lemon juice, thyme and salt. Bring to a boil over high heat. Cover, reduce heat and gently simmer for 30 minutes or until vegetables are soft. Remove from heat and stir in drained yogurt.

Mushroom Noodle Soup

Earthy and rich with the down-to-earth flavor of mushrooms, this soup is easy and yet so so good. Cremini mushrooms are related to the common white (or button) mushrooms but are more flavorful. Wild mushrooms or a mixture of wild and cultivated mushrooms lend a richer flavor to the soup. You could use a combination of mushrooms for this soup or just one variety.

2 tbsp	olive oil	30 mL
2	onions, chopped	2
3	cloves garlic, finely chopped	3
3 tbsp	white or red wine	45 mL
4 cups	sliced mushrooms	1 L
4 cups	chicken broth	1 L
1/2 tsp	sea salt	2 mL
4 oz	spaghetti, broken into 2-inch (5 cm) pieces	125 g
1 1/2 cups	Drained Yogurt (page 162)	375 mL

1. In a large saucepan, heat oil over medium heat. Add onions and cook, stirring occasionally, for 5 minutes or until soft. Add garlic and cook, stirring frequently, for 2 minutes. Stir in wine and mushrooms and cook, stirring occasionally, for 10 minutes. Add broth and salt and bring to a boil over high heat. Reduce heat and simmer for 15 minutes.

2. Add spaghetti and gently boil, for about 7 minutes or until al dente. Remove from heat and stir in drained yogurt.

Carrot and Squash Soup

Brightly colored and packed with vitamin A, this soup is a great fall dish. Use any winter squash or pumpkin.

2 tbsp	olive oil	30 mL
2 cups	chopped onions	500 mL
1 tbsp	packed brown sugar	15 mL
1 tsp	ground coriander seeds	5 mL
4 cups	chicken broth	1 L
2 cups	diced squash or pumpkin	500 mL
2 cups	shredded carrots	500 mL
1 1/2 cups	Drained Yogurt (page 162)	375 mL

1. In a saucepan, heat oil over medium heat. Add onion and cook, stirring frequently, for 8 minutes or until soft. Stir in brown sugar and coriander. Cook, stirring constantly, for 1 minute. Add broth and bring to a boil.

2. Add squash, reduce heat and gently boil, for 5 minutes. Add carrots and gently boil, stirring, 10 to 12 minutes or until tender. Remove from heat and stir in drained yogurt.

Easy to make, this soup is nutritious and filling enough for a light winter lunch.

Curried Vegetable and Lentil Soup

2 tbsp	curry powder	30 mL
I tbsp	olive oil	15 mL
I tsp	toasted sesame oil	5 mL
I cup	chopped onion	250 mL
4 cups	vegetable broth	I L
I cup	dried red or green lentils, rinsed and drained	250 mL
I cup	chopped green cabbage	250 mL
I	zucchini, finely chopped	I
I	carrot, finely chopped	I
I	parsnip, finely chopped	I
I	stalk celery, finely chopped	I
	Salt and freshly ground pepper	
I cup	plain yogurt	250 mL
¼ cup	freshly chopped parsley leaves, optional	60 mL

1. In a large saucepan, stir curry with olive oil and sesame oil to make a paste. Heat gently over medium-low heat. Cook, stirring constantly, for 1 minute. Add onion and cook, stirring constantly, for 3 minutes.

2. Add broth. Bring to a boil over high heat. Reduce heat, add lentils, cover and simmer for 45 minutes or until lentils are tender.

3. Add cabbage, zucchini, carrot, parsnip and celery. Cover and simmer, stirring occasionally, for 25 minutes. Add salt and pepper to taste. Remove from heat and stir in yogurt. Ladle into 4 soup bowls and garnish with parsley, if using.

Potato Leek Soup

I particularly like this soup in the winter when a hearty and chunky soup is most welcome. This one makes a satisfying meal and it is very easy to prepare.

Tip

* You can use pork loin (or shoulder), cut into cubes as listed in the ingredients, or you could use $1\frac{1}{4}$ lbs (625 g) of 1-inch (2.5 cm) thick pork chops with the bone attached. Using meat with the bone in soups and stews adds more flavor.

2 tbsp	olive oil	30 mL
I	onion, chopped	I
8 oz	mushrooms, chopped	250 g
2	cloves garlic, chopped	2
2	leeks, white and light green parts, sliced	2
1 lb	boneless pork, trimmed and cut into 1-inch (2.5 cm) cubes (see Tip, left)	500 g
3 cups	beef or chicken broth	750 mL
1 lb	potatoes, cut into 1-inch (2.5 cm) cubes	500 g
1 cup	chopped cauliflower florets	250 mL
$\frac{1}{4}$ cup	Drained Yogurt (page 162)	60 mL
$\frac{1}{2}$ tsp	ground nutmeg	2 mL

1. In a saucepan, heat oil over medium-high heat. Add onion and mushrooms and cook, stirring frequently, for 4 minutes. Add garlic, leeks and pork and cook, stirring frequently, for about 6 minutes or until vegetables are soft and pork is browned on all sides.

2. Add broth and bring to a boil. Add potatoes and cauliflower, cover, reduce heat and simmer for 15 minutes or until potatoes and cauliflower are tender. Remove from heat and stir in drained yogurt. Ladle into bowls and garnish with nutmeg.

Salads and Dressings

Salads

Mâche (*Valerianella locusta*), also known as "lamb's lettuce" and "corn salad," is often one of the greens in a mesclun blend. The small, dark green leaves have a fine, silky texture and a slightly sharp, nutty taste.

Tip
* Use ¼ cup (60 mL) chopped dried figs or dates when fresh figs are not available.

Variation
* Use spinach, watercress or mesclun greens in place of the mâche greens.

Fruited Mâche with Blue Cheese Dressing

2	soft ripe pears	2
2 tbsp	freshly squeezed lemon juice	30 mL
4 cups	mâche greens	1 L
¼ cup	Blue Cheese Dressing (page 204) or store-bought	60 mL
4	soft ripe figs, halved lengthwise (see Tip, left)	4
2 tbsp	coarsely chopped hazelnuts	30 mL

1. Halve and core pears. Slice lengthwise and place in a small bowl. Sprinkle with lemon juice and toss to coat. Set aside.

2. In a large bowl, toss mâche with dressing.

3. Divide fig halves and pear slices evenly over greens. Garnish with hazelnuts.

A simple, raw and nutritious salad, this dish can become a staple in the winter when fresh carrots are still plentiful.

Variations
* *Grated Apple with Ginger-Spiked Citrus Sauce:* Add shredded apple instead of the carrots.
* *Grated Turnip with Ginger-Spiked Citrus Sauce:* Add shredded turnip instead of the carrots.

Grated Carrots with Ginger-Spiked Citrus Sauce

4	carrots, grated	4
2	green onions, thinly sliced diagonally	2
⅓ cup	chopped dates	75 mL
¼ cup	coarsely chopped walnuts or other favorite nuts and/or seeds	60 mL
⅓ cup	Ginger-Spiked Citrus Sauce (page 250)	75 mL

1. In a large bowl, combine carrots, green onions, dates and walnuts. Toss with sauce to coat. Serve immediately.

Mediterranean Bean Salad

Make this salad your own by adding your favorite vegetables. In the winter, 1 cup (250 mL) shredded cabbage or root vegetables adds texture and vitamins. Summer squash, peas or beans, steamed until they are slightly softened but still crunchy, make great warm-weather ingredients.

Variations

• *Mediterranean Bean and Nut Salad:* Use chopped nuts in place of the lentils, but add just before serving.

• Chopped red or green bell pepper may replace the olives.

• Add any of the following: 1 cup (250 mL) cooked green beans, 2 chopped hard-boiled eggs, 3 oz (90 g) crumbled feta cheese or ½ cup (125 mL) cherry tomato halves.

• Add 1 to 2 oz (30 to 60 g) cooked fresh tuna or other cold water fish.

1	can (14 to 19 oz/398 to 540 mL) cannellini beans, rinsed and drained, or 2 cups (500 mL) cooked navy beans or Great Northern beans	1
½ cup	cooked red lentils	125 mL
½ cup	coarsely chopped drained canned artichokes or hearts of palm	125 mL
½ cup	diced red onion	125 mL
¼ cup	chopped fresh parsley	60 mL
¼ cup	coarsely chopped black or green olives	60 mL
¼ cup	Mediterranean Dressing (page 204)	60 mL

1. In a large bowl, combine beans, lentils, artichokes, red onion, parsley and olives. Toss with dressing to coat. Cover and let stand for at least 30 minutes or refrigerate overnight. Serve at room temperature.

Chickpea, Potato and Chicken Salad

Use a commercial mayonnaise or the Yogurt Hollandaise Sauce for this recipe.

Poached Chicken

• You can use leftover baked chicken for this recipe, but poaching helps to retain the moisture in the meat.

• *To poach chicken:* Place the trimmed boneless skinless breasts in a saucepan or skillet with a mixture of half wine, half water — enough to cover. Add several sprigs of fresh parsley, 4 peppercorns, a bay leaf and a pinch of dried thyme. Bring to a boil over high heat. Cover, reduce heat to low to medium and simmer gently for about 20 minutes or until no longer pink inside. Drain and let cool. Chicken may be poached the day before, then cooled, covered and refrigerated until ready to cube and add to the salad.

1 cup	Yogurt Hollandaise Sauce (page 252) or store-bought mayonnaise	250 mL
½ cup	chopped fresh basil	125 mL
2 tbsp	freshly squeezed lemon juice	30 mL
1½ cups	Drained Yogurt (page 162)	375 mL
2 cups	cubed poached chicken breast (see Poached Chicken, left)	500 mL
1 cup	cubed cooked potatoes	250 mL
1 cup	chopped red bell pepper	250 mL
1	can (14 to 19 oz/398 to 540 mL) chickpeas, rinsed and drained, or 2 cups (500 mL) cooked chickpeas	1
½ cup	sliced black olives	125 mL
¼ cup	capers, rinsed and drained	60 mL
¼ cup	chopped red onion	60 mL
	Salt and freshly ground black pepper	

1 In a large bowl, combine sauce and basil. Stir in lemon juice and drained yogurt. Fold in chicken, potatoes, bell pepper, chickpeas, olives, capers and red onion. Season to taste with salt and pepper. Cover and refrigerate for at least 3 hours to allow flavors to develop.

This basic cabbage salad may be changed significantly with the addition of chopped fresh vegetables, chopped apple, shredded chicken or fish, chopped dried fruit or other types of nuts or seeds.

Coleslaw with Creamy Basil Dressing

½	large cabbage, shredded	½
1	large carrot, shredded	1
¼ cup	chopped red onion	60 mL
¼ cup	chopped celery	60 mL
¼ cup	golden raisins	60 mL
¼ cup	chopped walnuts, optional	60 mL
	Creamy Basil Dressing (page 205)	

1. In a bowl, combine cabbage, carrot, red onion, celery, raisins, and walnuts, if using. Stir dressing into salad.

This is such a favorite yogurt recipe, it had to be included. I added the carrot and green onion for a slight twist.

Tip

• *To drain shredded cucumber:* Set the cucumber in a colander over a bowl and let drain out. This will take about 30 minutes. (Alternatively, cover the colander and let stand overnight in the refrigerator.) Draining the cucumber keeps the dip from separating.

Cucumber Raita

1	cucumber, shredded and drained (see Tip, left)	1
1	carrot, shredded	1
2	green onions, thinly sliced	2
2 cups	Drained Yogurt (page 162)	500 mL

1. In a bowl, combine drained cucumber, carrot, green onions and drained yogurt. Stir well to mix.

2. Transfer mixture to a clean container with lid. Store, tightly covered, in the refrigerator for up to 3 days.

Tunisian Carrot Feta Salad

Colorful, lightly spiced and delicious, this recipe can be used as a stuffing for steamed whole tomatoes, peppers or eggplant.

6 oz	feta cheese	175 g
1/3 cup	olive oil	75 mL
1/4 cup	chopped fresh parsley	60 mL
2 tbsp	white wine vinegar	30 mL
1	clove garlic, minced	1
1 tbsp	chopped fresh marjoram	15 mL
1 tsp	ground cumin	5 mL
1/4 tsp	ground cinnamon	1 mL
1/4 cup	plain yogurt	60 mL
4 cups	shredded carrots	1 L
1/2 cup	sliced black olives	125 mL

1. Cut feta into small cubes and place in a large bowl. In a jar with tight-fitting lid, combine oil, parsley, vinegar, garlic, marjoram, cumin and cinnamon. Shake well to combine and pour over feta. Cover and let stand for 30 minutes, stirring occasionally.

2. Using a fork, stir yogurt into feta mixture. Add carrots and toss well. Divide salad evenly among 4 plates and garnish with black olives.

Green beans and
cannellini beans
combine in this
flavorful summer salad.
For a change, add
nuts or grated summer
zucchini or beets.

Tip

* I like to use fresh
  whole mint leaves
  in salads but if you
  prefer to chop the
  mint by all means
  do so.

Summer Beans with Pappardelle

4 oz	green beans, trimmed	125 g
14 oz	pappardelle or rigatoni pasta	400 g
1/4 cup	olive oil	60 mL
2 tbsp	freshly squeezed lemon juice	30 mL
10	fresh mint leaves (see Tip, left)	10
2	green onions, thinly sliced	2
1	clove garlic, minced	1
4	Roma (plum) tomatoes, seeded and chopped	4
1	can (14 to 19 oz/398 to 540 mL) cannellini beans, rinsed and drained, or 2 cups (500 mL) cooked navy beans or Great Northern beans	1
2 oz	creamy goat cheese	60 g
1/2 cup	plain yogurt	125 mL

1. In a large pot of boiling salted water, blanch green beans for 5 minutes. Using tongs or a slotted spoon, lift beans out of the boiling water. Plunge into ice cold water. Drain and set aside.

2. Return pot to the heat and bring water back to a boil. Add pappardelle and cook for 8 to 12 minutes or until al dente. Drain and rinse under cold water. Set aside.

3. In a bowl, whisk together oil and lemon juice. Using a fork, mix in mint leaves, green onions, garlic and tomatoes. Add green beans, pappardelle and cannellini beans. Toss to coat beans and pasta with oil mixture. Divide salad evenly among 4 plates.

4. In a bowl, combine goat cheese and yogurt. Spoon a dollop over top of each salad.

Dressings

Yogurt lightens up this classic dressing without sacrificing flavor and texture. Try this dressing with fresh fruit salad.

Blue Cheese Dressing

3 tbsp	hazelnut oil	45 mL
1 tbsp	balsamic vinegar	15 mL
3 oz	blue cheese, crumbled	90 g
¼ cup	Drained Yogurt (page 162)	60 mL
	Salt and freshly ground pepper, optional	

1. In a small bowl, combine oil, vinegar and blue cheese. Whisk to mix well. Fold in drained yogurt. Taste and add salt and pepper, if required. Use immediately or store, tightly covered, in the refrigerator for up to 3 days.

Olive oil, lemons, garlic and fresh yogurt are classic ingredients of the Mediterranean region. Yogurt takes what would be essentially a vinaigrette and turns it into a creamy dressing. This light and zippy dressing complements other ingredients of the area such as olives, artichokes, legumes and red pepper.

Mediterranean Dressing

2 tbsp	olive oil	30 mL
2 tbsp	apple cider vinegar	30 mL
1 tbsp	freshly squeezed lemon juice	15 mL
1	clove garlic, minced	1
2	anchovy fillets, drained and chopped, optional	2
	Freshly ground pepper	
3 tbsp	plain yogurt	45 mL

1. In a jar with a tight-fitting lid or a small bowl, combine oil, vinegar, lemon juice, garlic, anchovies, if using, and pepper. Shake or whisk to mix well. Transfer to a bowl and stir in yogurt. Use immediately or store, tightly covered, in the refrigerator for up to 3 days.

Lemon and ginger
make a refreshing
combination in this
dressing. Use it with
grilled vegetables and
even fruit.

Creamy Gingered Lemon Dressing

¼ cup	olive oil	60 mL
3 tbsp	tamari or soy sauce	45 mL
2 tbsp	freshly squeezed lemon juice	30 mL
1 to 2	cloves garlic, minced	1 to 2
1 tbsp	chopped candied ginger	15 mL
¼ cup	Drained Yogurt (page 162)	60 mL

1. In a bowl, combine oil, tamari, lemon juice, garlic and ginger. Whisk to mix well. Fold in drained yogurt. Use immediately or store, tightly covered, in the refrigerator for up to 2 days.

Basil lends a spicy
nutmeg essence, while
yogurt lightens this
dressed-up mayonnaise.

Creamy Basil Dressing

1½ cups	Drained Yogurt (page 162)	375 mL
¼ cup	mayonnaise	60 mL
1 tsp	liquid honey	5 mL
3 tbsp	apple cider vinegar	45 mL
¼ cup	shredded fresh basil	60 mL

1. In a bowl or jar with tight-fitting lid, combine drained yogurt, mayonnaise, honey, vinegar and basil. Whisk or shake until smooth. Use immediately or store, tightly covered, in the refrigerator for up to 3 days.

Smoky Garlic Dressing

The "smoke" comes from smoked Spanish paprika or pimentón. In its place, you can use chopped chipotle chile peppers. How much you use is up to your taste for heat. This makes a delicious spread for sandwiches, pitas and wraps.

* *Food processor or blender*

1 cup	Drained Yogurt (page 162)	250 mL
2	cloves garlic	2
1 tbsp	freshly squeezed lemon juice	15 mL
1 tbsp	smoked Spanish paprika (pimentón) or chipotle flakes	15 mL

1. In a food processor, combine yogurt, garlic, lemon juice and paprika. Process until smooth. Use immediately or store, tightly covered, in the refrigerator for up to 3 days.

Roasted Garlic Dressing

Creamy and thick and with a slight sweetness, this dressing may serve as an alternative to the traditional Caesar salad dressing.

1	head roasted garlic (below)	1
¼ cup	plain yogurt	60 mL
1 tbsp	rice vinegar	15 mL
¼ tsp	salt	1 mL
¼ to ½ tsp	cayenne pepper	1 to 2 mL

1. Squeeze roasted garlic cloves from skins into a small bowl.

2. Add yogurt, vinegar and salt to garlic. Using a fork, whisk to mix well and add cayenne to taste, ¼ tsp (1 mL) at a time, tasting after each addition. Use immediately or store, tightly covered, in the refrigerator for up to 2 days.

Roasted Garlic

When roasted, garlic is mellow and sweet.

* *Preheat oven to 400°F (200°C)*

1	whole head garlic	1
1 tsp	olive oil	5 mL

1. Remove loose, papery skin from garlic head. Cut ¼ inch (0.5 cm) off tips of cloves in entire head. Place garlic head, cut side up, in small baking dish and drizzle with oil. Cover with a lid or foil. Bake in preheated oven for about 40 minutes or until garlic is quite soft. Transfer to a cooling rack. If using a clay garlic roaster with a lid, roast at 375°F (190°C) for 35 to 40 minutes. When cool enough to handle, squeeze cloves from skins.

Rich Ranch Dressing

• *Food processor*

¾ cup	plain yogurt	175 mL
½ cup	mayonnaise	125 mL
I	roasted red bell pepper, drained and chopped	I
2 tbsp	chopped fresh parsley	30 mL
I tbsp	Dijon mustard	15 mL
I tbsp	chopped chives or green onions	15 mL
¼ tsp	celery seeds	I mL

I keep a jar of roasted red peppers in my pantry just for making this dressing. Once the jar is opened, the remaining peppers keep in their brine for up to 3 weeks in the refrigerator, and I add them to salads, stir-fries and other vegetable dishes.

I. In a food processor, combine yogurt, mayonnaise, roasted pepper, parsley, mustard, chives and celery seeds and process until smooth. Use immediately or store, tightly covered, in the refrigerator for up to 3 days.

Caesar Dressing

• *Blender*

3	anchovy fillets, drained	3
3	cloves garlic	3
3 tbsp	olive oil	45 mL
I tbsp	freshly squeezed lemon juice	15 mL
2 tsp	Dijon mustard	10 mL
I tsp	Worcestershire sauce	5 mL
¼ cup	plain yogurt	60 mL

Most often, Caesar dressing is loaded with calories from the oil. In this recipe, the yogurt cuts the amount of oil required without sacrificing flavor and texture.

I. In a blender, combine anchovies and garlic and process until finely chopped. Add oil, lemon juice, mustard and Worcestershire sauce and process until combined. Add yogurt and process until smooth. Use immediately or store, tightly covered, in the refrigerator for up to 3 days.

Honey Mustard Dressing

Makes ⅓ cup (75 mL)

This light and fresh dressing is very good with stone fruits, steamed or raw cabbage, and other fruit and vegetable salads.

¼ cup	Drained Yogurt (page 162)	60 mL
2 tbsp	liquid honey	30 mL
1 tbsp	Dijon mustard	15 mL
2 tsp	white wine vinegar	10 mL

1. In a bowl, using a fork, combine drained yogurt, honey, mustard and vinegar. Use immediately or store, tightly covered, in the refrigerator for up to 3 days.

Fruit-Bottom Dressing

Makes ⅔ cup (150 mL)

It's fun to try different fruit in the Fruit-Bottom Yogurt recipe and you can use any of them, or a store-bought fruit yogurt here.

⅔ cup	Fruit-Bottom Yogurt (6 oz/175 g) (page 25)	150 mL
1 tbsp	freshly squeezed lemon juice	15 mL
1	large clove garlic, minced	1

1. In a small bowl, combine yogurt, lemon juice and garlic. Stir well. Use immediately or store, tightly covered, in the refrigerator for up to 3 days.

Mains

Serve this robust chili over baked potatoes for a main dish or with whole-grain nachos for an appetizer or party dish. Because many of the water-soluble nutrients are in the canned liquid, try to use both the beans and the liquid from the tin (if using home-cooked dried beans, do not use cooking liquid).

Tip

* Freezing tofu overnight or for a few hours, and then thawing, gives it a meaty texture. It crumbles nicely and seems to absorb more of the cooking liquid. Omit this step if time does not permit.

Variation

* Use chickpeas or black-eyed peas in place of either the black or kidney beans.

Black Bean Chili

1 cup	chopped onion	250 mL
1 ½ cups	chopped red bell pepper	375 mL
2 tbsp	olive oil	30 mL
½ cup	chopped celery	125 mL
3	cloves garlic, finely chopped	3
2	dried cayenne chiles, crushed	2
1 ½ tbsp	Cajun seasoning	22 mL
1 lb	firm tofu, frozen, thawed and crumbled (see Tip, left)	500 g
1	can (28 oz/796 mL) tomatoes with juice	1
1	can (14 to 19 oz/398 to 540 mL) black beans with liquid	1
1	can (14 to 19 oz/398 to 540 mL) dark red kidney beans with liquid	1
¼ cup	chopped fresh parsley	60 mL
1 tbsp	chopped fresh savory	15 mL
1 tbsp	blackstrap molasses, optional	15 mL
	Salt and freshly ground pepper	
½ cup	Drained Yogurt (page 162)	125 mL

1. In a large saucepan, combine onion, bell pepper and oil. Sauté over medium heat for 7 minutes. Add celery, garlic, chiles, Cajun seasoning and tofu. Reduce heat and gently simmer, stirring occasionally, for 5 minutes.

2. Add tomatoes with juice. Increase heat and bring to a boil, stirring up browned bits from bottom of the pan. Reduce heat and simmer for 10 minutes. Add black and red beans with liquid, parsley and savory. Simmer for 5 to 10 minutes or until heated through. Add molasses, if using. Season to taste with salt and pepper. Garnish each serving with drained yogurt.

Swiss Chard and Feta Soufflé

Separating the eggs and beating air into the whites makes this soufflé rise beautifully. Don't be disappointed if it falls before you can get it to the table. It will be light and delicious all the same.

- *Preheat oven to 375°F (190°C)*
- *2-quart (2 L) soufflé dish, lightly oiled*

2 cups	lightly packed chopped Swiss chard or spinach	500 mL
2 tbsp	olive oil	30 mL
2 tbsp	butter	30 mL
½ cup	all-purpose flour	125 mL
1½ cups	milk	375 mL
½ cup	plain yogurt	125 mL
6	eggs, separated	6
8 oz	crumbled feta cheese	250 g
¼ tsp	ground nutmeg	1 mL
	Salt and freshly ground pepper	
⅓ cup	shredded Cheddar cheese	75 mL

1. In a saucepan, bring 3 tbsp (45 mL) water to a boil over high heat. Add Swiss chard. Cover, reduce heat and simmer, stirring occasionally, for about 6 minutes or until tender. Drain and let cool.

2. In the same saucepan, heat oil and melt butter over medium-high heat. Reduce heat to low and stir in flour. Slowly add milk, whisking constantly. Cook, stirring, for about 4 minutes or until sauce has thickened. Remove pan from heat and whisk in yogurt. Whisk in egg yolks, one at a time, whisking in each before adding the next yolk. Fold drained Swiss chard, feta cheese and nutmeg into the egg yolk mixture. Season to taste with salt and pepper and mix well.

3. In a bowl, beat egg whites until soft peaks form. Fold whites into egg yolk mixture. Use light strokes and do not overmix. Turn into prepared soufflé dish and bake in preheated oven for 30 minutes. Remove from oven and sprinkle Cheddar over top. Return to oven and bake for 3 to 5 minutes more or until cheese is melted and soufflé is firm in the center.

Usually called "orzo" in North America, *risone* is Italian for "barley," from which it was originally made. The pasta we call risone (orzo) is now made from hard winter flour like all other pasta. Its shape is similar to a giant grain of rice, and risone may be available in various vegetable colors.

Variation

- You can substitute small shell pasta (orecchiette), or vermicelli pasta, broken into $1/2$-inch (1 cm) pieces, for the risone.

Spinach and Artichoke Risone

I tbsp	olive oil	30 mL
I tbsp	butter	30 mL
I	onion, halved and sliced	I
I	fennel bulb, sliced	I
2 cups	risone	500 mL
2 cups	lightly packed chopped spinach	500 mL
I	can (14 oz/398 mL) artichoke hearts, drained and chopped	I
¾ cup	plain yogurt	175 mL
½ cup	heavy or whipping (35%) cream	125 mL
2 tbsp	dry white wine	30 mL
I tbsp	Dijon mustard	15 mL

1. In a skillet, heat oil and melt butter over medium-high heat. Add onion and fennel. Reduce heat to medium-low and cook, stirring occasionally, for 20 minutes or until soft and caramelized.

2. Meanwhile, in a pot of boiling salted water, cook risone for 5 to 6 minutes or until al dente. Drain and rinse under cool water.

3. When vegetables are soft, remove pan from heat and add spinach, artichokes, yogurt, cream, wine and mustard. Return to medium-low heat and simmer gently, stirring frequently, for 5 minutes or until spinach is wilted and artichokes heated through. Add risone and simmer for 1 minute or until heated through.

Leeks, onion and garlic combine in this savory gratin, for a filling and yet meatless entrée.

Zucchini and Leek Gratin

- *Preheat oven to 375°F (190°C)*
- *8-cup (2 L) baking dish, lightly oiled*

2	zucchini, cut into 4 lengthwise slices	2
3	leeks, white and light green parts, sliced in half lengthwise	3
I	onion, cut into eighths	I
3 tbsp	olive oil	45 mL
4	cloves garlic, finely chopped	4
2 tbsp	chopped fresh basil or oregano	30 mL
I tbsp	fresh thyme leaves	15 mL
1/3 cup	sliced green or black olives	75 mL
I tsp	cornstarch	5 mL
I tsp	granulated sugar	5 mL
2 tbsp	vegetable broth or water	30 mL
I cup	plain yogurt	250 mL
I cup	shredded Cheddar cheese	250 mL
1/2 cup	grated Parmesan cheese	125 mL

1. Arrange zucchini and leeks in prepared baking dish. In a bowl, toss together onion, oil, garlic, basil and thyme. Spoon over zucchini and leeks. Bake, uncovered, in preheated oven for 35 minutes or until vegetables are just tender. Remove from oven and sprinkle olives over vegetables. Leave oven on.

2. Meanwhile, in a bowl, combine cornstarch and sugar. Drizzle with broth and stir with a fork until smooth. Stir in yogurt. Spread yogurt mixture over vegetables. Sprinkle Cheddar and Parmesan over top. Cover dish with a lid or foil and bake for 15 minutes.

This meal can be on the table in less than 30 minutes and, apart from the mushrooms and yogurt, is made with items that may already be in the pantry. It can serve as a light main dish, especially with cooked beans, nuts or seeds added for protein, but it can also serve as a side dish.

Mushroom Noodles with Green Curry Sauce

2 tbsp	olive oil	30 mL
I	onion, chopped	I
I4 oz	assorted mushrooms (shiitake, oyster, enoki, button), sliced	400 g
2½ cups	vegetable broth	625 mL
I tbsp	freshly squeezed lime juice	I5 mL
I tsp	toasted sesame oil	5 mL
8 oz	soba noodles, broken into thirds	250 g
2 cups	Cultured Coconut Milk "Yogurt" (page 23) or store-bought coconut yogurt	500 mL
I tbsp	Green Curry Paste (page 255) or store-bought, or to taste	I5 mL
2 tsp	tamari sauce	I0 mL
I tsp	freshly grated gingerroot	5 mL

1. In a wok or saucepan, heat olive oil over high heat. Add onion and mushrooms and cook, stirring constantly, for 4 minutes. Add broth, lime juice and sesame oil and bring to a boil. Add noodles. Cover and boil gently for 6 to 8 minutes or until al dente.

2. Meanwhile, in a bowl, combine yogurt, green curry paste, tamari sauce and ginger. Stir into mushroom and noodles and heat through.

Eggplant and Lentil Stir-Fry

I have made this without the rice and served it as a warm salad. With the addition of the rice, it becomes a whole meal delivering complete protein.

Variation

- Use mushrooms, leeks, bell peppers or zucchini, or a combination of any, in place of the eggplant.

3 tbsp	olive oil, divided	45 mL
2 cups	chopped onions	500 mL
1	red bell pepper, chopped	1
3	cloves garlic, finely chopped	3
1	small eggplant, cut into $1/2$-inch (1 cm) cubes	1
$2\frac{1}{2}$ cups	vegetable broth (approx.)	625 mL
$\frac{1}{2}$ cup	red or brown lentils	125 mL
$\frac{1}{2}$ cup	brown or red rice	125 mL
1 tbsp	rice vinegar	15 mL
1 tsp	freshly grated gingerroot	5 mL
1 tbsp	garam masala spice blend (see Tip, page 219)	15 mL
1 cup	plain yogurt	250 mL
$\frac{1}{4}$ cup	chopped fresh parsley	60 mL

1. In a skillet with a lid, heat 2 tbsp (30 mL) of the oil over medium-high heat. Add onions and bell pepper and cook, stirring constantly, for 5 minutes. Add remaining oil, garlic and eggplant. Cook, stirring constantly, for 5 minutes or until vegetables are soft.

2. Stir in broth, lentils, rice, vinegar, ginger and garam masala. Stir well and bring to a boil. Cover, reduce heat and simmer gently for 40 minutes, stirring once or twice, and adding more broth and reducing heat slightly if the liquid has evaporated too quickly. Cook until lentils and rice are tender and liquid has all but evaporated. Stir in yogurt and parsley.

Sweet Potato Vindaloo

Using yogurt in the sauce is a great way to moderate the spicy flavor of this classic Indian dish.

You can substitute commercial curry powder for the Vindaloo Spice Blend, but toasting and grinding fresh spices adds authenticity to Sweet Potato Vindaloo and other Indian dishes.

Tips

* You can use curry powder instead of spice blend.

* Store spice blend in a dark glass jar with a lid, tightly covered, in a cool, dry place for up to 4 months.

* If you can find Brazilian green peppercorns, use them in this spice blend — they impart a sharp, tangy flavor that delivers bite to the blend.

* You don't have to toast the spices before grinding them, but that step adds to the richness and depth of the blend.

Vindaloo Spice Blend

I tbsp	each cumin seeds and coriander seeds	15 mL
I tbsp	green or black peppercorns	15 mL
I tsp	yellow or brown mustard seeds	5 mL
8	cardamom pods	8
3	whole cloves	3
I	fresh or dried cayenne pepper, cut into pieces	I
I tsp	each ground turmeric and cinnamon	5 mL

Sweet Potato Vindaloo

2 tbsp	olive oil	30 mL
I	onion, coarsely chopped	I
I	red bell pepper, coarsely chopped	I
I tbsp	freshly chopped or candied gingerroot	15 mL
2 cups	vegetable broth	500 mL
2	sweet potatoes, cut into 1-inch (2.5 cm) cubes	2
2	yellow, white or red potatoes, cut into 1-inch (2.5 cm) cubes	2
I cup	plain yogurt	250 mL

1. *Vindaloo Spice Blend:* In a small skillet, dry-roast cumin and coriander seeds, peppercorns, mustard seeds and cardamom pods over medium-high heat, stirring constantly, until they begin to pop. Do not let spices smoke. Let cool and transfer cardamom pods to a mortar. Using a pestle, pound pods and release seeds into mortar, discarding pods. Add remaining toasted spices along with cloves and cayenne, and use pestle to grind to a coarse or fine powder as desired. Add turmeric and cinnamon, mix well and set aside.

2. *Sweet Potato Vindaloo:* In a Dutch oven or saucepan, heat oil over medium heat. Add onion and bell pepper and cook, stirring frequently, for 5 minutes. Stir in 2 tbsp (30 mL) spice blend and ginger. Cook, stirring frequently, for 1 minute.

3. Add broth and bring to a boil. Add sweet and yellow potatoes. Reduce heat and simmer, stirring occasionally, for 20 minutes or until potatoes are tender. Remove from heat and let stand for 5 minutes. Stir in yogurt.

This delicious meatless oven casserole combines classic Greek flavors of spinach, leek, dill and feta cheese. It can also be made with frozen spinach or Swiss chard.

Tip
- When fresh tomatoes are not available, 1 can (14 oz/398 mL) diced tomatoes, drained, may be substituted.

Baked Spinach, Beans and Feta Cheese

- *Preheat oven to 350°F (180°C)*
- *13- by 9-inch (33 by 23 cm) baking pan, lightly oiled*

1 lb	large lima or yigandes beans	500 g
2¼ lbs	fresh spinach or 1½ lbs (750 g) frozen chopped spinach (thawed)	1.125 kg
4 oz	feta cheese, crumbled, divided	125 g
1 cup	plain yogurt	250 mL
4	green onions, chopped	4
1	leek, white and light green parts, chopped	1
½ cup	chopped fresh dill	125 mL
½ cup	shredded Cheddar cheese	125 mL
3	Roma (plum) tomatoes, peeled, seeded and chopped (see Tip, left)	3
2 tsp	sea salt	10 mL
¼ tsp	freshly ground pepper	1 mL
⅓ cup	olive oil	75 mL
¾ cup	dry bread crumbs	175 mL

1. In a large pot, soak beans in water overnight. Drain, rinse well and transfer to a large pot. Cover with cold water (at least 3 times as much water as beans) and bring to a boil over high heat. When a full boil is reached, reduce heat and gently boil for 1 hour or until tender. Transfer to a colander. Drain, rinse well and set aside.

2. Meanwhile, trim, rinse and squeeze excess water from spinach. Coarsely chop and transfer to a colander to drain.

3. In a large bowl, combine feta with yogurt. Add spinach, green onions, leek and dill. Mix well. Distribute half of the spinach mixture evenly over bottom of prepared pan. Spread an even layer of beans over spinach mixture and top with remaining spinach mixture. Spread Cheddar and chopped tomatoes evenly over top. Sprinkle with salt and pepper. Drizzle with oil and spread an even layer bread crumbs over top.

4. Bake in preheated oven for about 1½ hours. Vegetables should be soft and their liquid almost evaporated. Let stand for 15 to 20 minutes before serving.

Hot Corn Cakes

Like crab cakes or
bean cakes, these
all-vegetable versions
may be served as
appetizers and starters
or as a main dish
light meal.

1	can (14 oz/398 mL) creamed corn	1
1 cup	shredded zucchini	250 mL
1/2 cup	cornmeal	125 mL
1/2 cup	shredded Cheddar cheese	125 mL
1/4 cup	chopped fresh cilantro or flat-leaf parsley	60 mL
3	jalapeño peppers, chopped	3
1/4 cup	all-purpose flour (approx.)	60 mL
1 tsp	baking powder	5 mL
1	egg, beaten	1
2 tbsp	plain yogurt	30 mL
1/2 cup	olive oil, divided	125 mL

1. In a bowl, combine corn, zucchini, cornmeal, Cheddar, cilantro and jalapeños. Mix well. Sprinkle with flour and baking powder and mix well. Add egg and yogurt and stir. The batter should be fairly stiff and, if not, add flour in 2 tbsp (30 mL) additions until it holds together.

2. In a skillet, heat 2 tbsp (30 mL) of the oil over medium heat. Drop 2 tbsp (30 mL) of the batter onto the pan for each corn cake and cook for 3 minutes per side or until golden and crispy. Transfer to a warmed plate and continue cooking remaining batter, adding oil to pan as needed.

Coconut Squash Curry

For this easy skillet dinner, use butternut, acorn or any other variety of winter squash or pumpkin. You can use plain yogurt with $1/4$ cup (60 mL) desiccated unsweetened coconut added, in place of the coconut yogurt.

Tip

• Garam masala is a blend of Indian spices that usually includes cinnamon. It can be found in most spice sections or specialty food stores.

2 tbsp	olive oil	30 mL
1 tbsp	butter	15 mL
1	onion, chopped	1
1	red bell pepper, chopped	1
3	cloves garlic, chopped	3
1 tbsp	garam masala spice blend (see Tip, left) or curry powder	15 mL
2 tsp	curry powder	10 mL
1 tsp	ground cumin	5 mL
2 cups	diced squash	500 mL
2 cups	chopped cauliflower	500 mL
1	can (14 oz/398 mL) chopped tomatoes with juice	1
$1/2$ cup	Cultured Coconut Milk "Yogurt" (page 23) or store-bought coconut yogurt	125 mL

1. In a skillet, heat oil and melt butter over medium-high heat. Add onion and bell pepper and cook, stirring frequently, for 7 minutes or until onion is soft. Add garlic, garam masala, curry powder and cumin. Cook, stirring constantly, for 1 minute. Add squash and cauliflower and stir to coat vegetables with spice mixture.

2. Add tomatoes with juice and bring to a boil. Cover, reduce heat and simmer gently, stirring occasionally, for 35 minutes or until vegetables are tender. Remove from heat and stir in yogurt.

Yellow Curry Dal

Look for small yellow lentils in Middle Eastern supermarkets or use the widely available red lentils in this dish. Save leftover Yellow Curry Dal for use in soups.

2 tbsp	olive oil	30 mL
1 cup	chopped onion	250 mL
2	cloves garlic, finely chopped	2
1 tbsp	curry powder	15 mL
1 tsp	grated fresh gingerroot	5 mL
1¼ cups	dried yellow lentils, rinsed	300 mL
2 cups	vegetable broth or water	500 mL
½ cup	plain yogurt	125 mL
	Sea salt and freshly ground pepper	

1. In a saucepan, heat oil over medium heat. Add onion and garlic and cook, stirring occasionally, for 6 to 8 minutes or until soft. Stir in curry powder and ginger. Cook, stirring frequently, for 1 minute.

2. In a strainer, pick over and remove any small stones or grit from lentils. Add lentils and broth to saucepan. Stir well and bring to a boil. Reduce heat and simmer for 15 minutes, stirring occasionally for the first 10 minutes and frequently during the last 5 minutes of cooking. Cook only until water is absorbed and lentils are soft. Add yogurt and season to taste with salt and pepper. Serve warm or at room temperature.

Fish and Seafood

The coating keeps the fish moist as it bakes in the oven, so the coating works particularly well with salmon steaks.

Variation

- Pine nuts, pecans, walnuts or sunflower seeds may be used in place of the almonds.

Crispy Baked Fish

- *Preheat oven to 375°F (190°C)*
- *Rimmed baking sheet, lightly oiled*
- *Food processor*

4	fish fillets, such as salmon, perch, trout, cod or sole	4
¼ cup	all-purpose flour	60 mL
¼ cup	Drained Yogurt (page 162)	60 mL
2	cloves garlic, optional	2
¼ cup	almonds	60 mL
3 tbsp	chopped fresh herbs, such as parsley, oregano, sage, thyme and rosemary	45 mL
2	fresh crusts or slices whole wheat bread, torn into pieces	2

1. In a shallow pan, dredge fish in flour to coat both sides. Arrange on prepared baking sheet, skin side down (if skin still attached), leaving about 1 inch (2.5 cm) between the fillets. Spread yogurt over top of fish.

2. In a food processor, combine garlic, if using, and almonds and process until chopped. Add herbs and bread crusts and process until finely chopped. Pat over fish, covering yogurt completely and forming a crust over entire tops and sides of fish. Bake in preheated oven for 15 to 20 minutes or until fish has turned opaque and flakes easily with a fork.

This is an impressive presentation for dinner and yet very easy to prepare, with no pots for cleanup. The coconut sauce permeates the fish and vegetables as they steam in their own paper pocket. Serve rice or noodles to finish off the meal.

Whitefish and Vegetables with Curry Sauce in Parchment

- *Preheat oven to 350°F (180°C)*
- *2 rimmed baking sheets*
- *4 sheets (each 15 by 12 inches/38 by 30 cm) parchment paper*

4	whitefish fillets	4
2	onions, quartered	2
I	red bell pepper, sliced	I
I	leek, white and light green parts, sliced	I
I cup	Coconut Curry Sauce (page 253)	250 mL

1. Fold each sheet of parchment paper in half lengthwise, then open up like a book. Lay one whitefish fillet alongside the fold of each sheet. Divide onions, bell pepper and leek evenly into 4 portions and arrange each portion on top of 1 fillet, then spoon $\frac{1}{4}$ cup (60 mL) of the curry sauce over top of vegetables. Fold the top free half of the "book page" over the fish and vegetables. Roll up the long edge of parchment towards the fish and vegetables and press as you roll the 2 edges to seal the edges together. Roll up the 2 short edges of parchment to make a sealed pocket.

2. Place 2 pockets on each baking sheet and bake in preheated oven for 10 to 15 minutes or until fish has turned opaque and flakes easily with a fork and vegetables are tender. Plate and serve in the parchment paper.

Mediterranean Fish Stew

Rich, hearty and very flavorful, this stew is often my choice for winter meals. It is on the table in less than an hour, and makes a fabulous weekday dinner with some leftovers for a lunch or two. Pacific cod is my first choice in fish for this dish, but any fish works. Check the sustainable fish lists or what looks the freshest that day you're at the market.

1 lb	skinless fish fillets	500 g
3 tbsp	freshly squeezed lemon juice	45 mL
8 oz	rice vermicelli noodles	250 g
1 tbsp	olive oil	15 mL
1 tbsp	butter	15 mL
1	onion, chopped	1
2	cloves garlic, chopped	2
3	carrots, sliced	3
3	stalks celery, sliced	3
2 cups	Caponata (page 173) or 1 can (14 to 19 oz/398 to 540 mL) diced tomatoes with juice	500 mL
3 cups	water or fish stock	750 mL
1	bay leaf	1
¼ cup	chopped fresh parsley	60 mL
2 tbsp	chopped fresh oregano	30 mL
1 tbsp	fresh thyme leaves	15 mL
1 cup	Creamy Salsa Verde (page 258) or Drained Yogurt (page 162)	250 mL

1. Cut fish into 2-inch (5 cm) chunks and arrange in a pie plate. Drizzle with lemon juice. Cover and set aside.

2. Bring a large saucepan of salted water to a gentle boil. Remove from heat and stir in vermicelli noodles, pressing them into the water. Set pot with water and noodles aside.

3. In another pot, heat oil and melt butter over medium heat. Add onion and cook, stirring frequently, for 6 minutes or until soft. Add garlic, carrots and celery and cook, stirring, for 1 minute. Add Caponata, water and bay leaf and bring to a boil. Reduce heat and simmer gently for 15 minutes or until vegetables are tender-crisp. Add parsley, oregano, thyme and fish chunks and cook for 10 to 15 minutes or until fish has turned opaque and flakes easily with a fork. Discard bay leaf.

4. Drain noodles and add to stew. Stir for 1 minute to heat through. Serve with salsa verde.

Sole in Spinach Sauce

Surprisingly easy and very fast, this dish works for weekday dinners but is impressive enough for company. Fresh catfish, whitefish or cod also work well in this recipe because their firm texture stands up in the spinach sauce. Use fresh fish and fresh spinach whenever possible.

Tip

• A 12-oz (375 g) package of fresh spinach yields 6 cups (1.5 L), which is ideal, but you can use an 8- or 10-oz (250 or 300 g) package in the sauce with good results.

2 tbsp	olive oil	30 mL
1	onion, chopped	1
4	fresh sole fillets (about 1 ½ lbs/750 g)	4
	Sea salt and freshly ground pepper	
2 tbsp	freshly squeezed lemon juice	30 mL
¼ to ½ cup	water	60 to 125 mL
2 tbsp	freshly squeezed lemon juice	30 mL
6 cups	packed coarsely chopped spinach leaves (see Tip, left)	1.5 L
⅔ cup	Drained Yogurt (page 162)	150 mL

1. In a large deep-sided skillet, heat oil over medium heat. Add onion and cook, stirring occasionally, for 5 minutes or until soft. Add fish to skillet and season to taste with salt and pepper. Add lemon juice and enough water to come slightly more than halfway up the sides of fish. Bring to a gentle simmer over medium-low heat. Cover and simmer gently, turning fish once, for 10 minutes or until fish has turned opaque and flakes easily with a fork.

2. Transfer fish to a platter and keep warm. Add spinach to skillet, increase heat to medium and cook, stirring occasionally, for 2 to 3 minutes or until wilted and liquid has evaporated. Drain excess liquid if spinach is cooked before liquid has evaporated. Stir in drained yogurt. Return fish to sauce and heat through.

Tzatziki (page 164), Avocado Aïoli (page 170)
and Creamy Spinach Dip (page 172)

Caramelized Pear and Onion Flatbread (page 179)

Curried Sweet Potato Soup (page 187)

Summer Beans with Pappardelle (page 203)

Baked Chicken and Mushroom Risotto (page 231)

Lamb Tagine with Plums and Apricots (page 245)

Raspberry Fudge Cookies (page 273)

Lemon Yogurt Cake (page 274)

In the summer I serve this cold with a noodle or rice salad on the side or simply over salad greens. If you use a roasting pan or large wok, the salmon does not need to be cut and keeping it whole makes a beautiful presentation on a platter.

Poached Salmon with Caper Sauce

Poached Salmon

1 ½ cups	chicken broth	375 mL
1	salmon filet (about 1 ¼ lbs/625 g)	1
2	stalks celery, chopped	2
1	onion, quartered	1
¼ cup	dry white wine	60 mL
2 tbsp	freshly squeezed lemon juice	30 mL

Caper Sauce

2 tsp	cornstarch	10 mL
1 tsp	granulated sugar	5 mL
1 tbsp	chopped drained capers	15 mL
2 tsp	Dijon mustard	10 mL
½ cup	Drained Yogurt (page 162)	125 mL

1. *Poached Salmon:* In a roasting pan, wide pot or wok, bring broth to a boil over medium-high heat. Add salmon, celery, onion, wine and lemon juice. Cover, reduce heat and gently simmer for 10 to 15 minutes or until the salmon has turned opaque and flakes easily with a fork. Transfer salmon to a warmed platter and keep warm. If you plan to serve it cold, lift salmon out of poaching liquid onto a platter. Let cool, cover tightly and refrigerate for 1 hour or overnight.

2. Increase heat to high and boil poaching liquid for 10 minutes or until reduced to about 1 cup (250 mL).

3. *Caper Sauce:* Meanwhile, in a small bowl, combine cornstarch and sugar. Stir in 2 tbsp (30 mL) water to form a smooth paste. Add to reduced poaching liquid and cook, stirring constantly, for 2 to 3 minutes or until sauce has thickened. Remove from heat and stir in capers, mustard and drained yogurt. Pass sauce separately at the table or drizzle over salmon on the platter. Sauce may be kept, covered, in the refrigerator until ready to use. Serve hot with hot salmon or at room temperature with chilled salmon.

Shrimp Creole

A wok is the perfect tool for cooking this dish but if you do not have one, use a large saucepan. The seasoned rice is exceptional with the shrimp and snow peas. I sometimes add 2 tbsp (30 mL) Red or Green Curry Paste (page 255 or store-bought) for a spicy creole flavor. The recipe uses uncooked shrimp but if you use cooked shrimp, stir them into the hot mixture at the last minute to heat through.

• *Wok*

24	large shrimp	24
2 tbsp	freshly squeezed lemon juice	30 mL
2 tbsp	olive oil	30 mL
1	onion, chopped	1
1	small zucchini, coarsely chopped	1
½	red bell pepper, chopped	½
1 tbsp	chopped fresh oregano	15 mL
1 tbsp	fresh thyme leaves	15 mL
1	can (28 oz/796 mL) diced tomatoes with juice	1
1½ cups	water	375 mL
1 tsp	salt	5 mL
¾ cup	long-grain white rice	175 mL
2 cups	snow peas	500 mL
1 cup	plain yogurt	250 mL

1. Peel, rinse and devein shrimp. Set in a shallow dish, sprinkle with lemon juice and cover. Set aside in the refrigerator.

2. In a wok, heat oil over medium-high heat. Add onion and stir-fry for 3 minutes or until soft. Add zucchini, bell pepper, oregano and thyme and stir-fry for 2 minutes. Add tomatoes with juice, water and salt. Bring to a boil and stir in rice. Cover, reduce heat and simmer gently for 20 minutes or until rice is tender.

3. Add shrimp and snow peas and cook, stirring frequently, for 3 minutes or until shrimp have turned a bright pink and peas are tender-crisp. Remove from heat and stir in yogurt.

Seafood is tender protein and is usually cooked gently by poaching, baking in sauce or steaming. If cooked too long or over high heat, scallops and other shellfish will turn rubbery. This rich mushroom sauce is perfect for cooking shrimp, scallops, lobster or crab and is very versatile. Serve it over rice or noodles or in puff-pastry shells (vol-au-vents); stuffed into giant pasta shells, tomatoes or roasted peppers; or spooned over roasted vegetables.

Seared Scallops in Mushroom Yogurt Sauce

2 tbsp	butter	30 mL
1 tbsp	olive oil	15 mL
1/2 cup	chopped green onions or shallots	125 mL
2 cups	sliced mushrooms	500 mL
1 tbsp	all-purpose flour	15 mL
1 cup	chicken broth	250 mL
1/2 cup	dry white wine	125 mL
1 lb	scallops	500 g
1/2 cup	Drained Yogurt (page 162)	125 mL

1. In a saucepan, melt butter and heat oil over medium-high heat. Add green onions and cook, stirring frequently, for 4 minutes. Add mushrooms and cook, stirring constantly, for 4 minutes or until vegetables are soft. Reduce heat to medium and stir in flour. Slowly whisk in broth and wine and cook, whisking constantly, for 3 minutes or until sauce thickens. Add scallops and simmer gently for about 3 minutes or until flesh turns opaque and scallops are firm but not rubbery. Remove from heat and stir in drained yogurt.

The sauce is easy to pull together using canned shrimp, lobster or crabmeat in place of the fresh or frozen shellfish listed here. Smoked salmon or trout is also an alternative or an addition to the shrimp and crabmeat. I have served this over toast points in place of the noodles.

Fettuccine with Crab and Shrimp Sauce

10 oz	fettuccine	300 g
2 tbsp	olive oil	30 mL
2 tbsp	butter	30 mL
8 oz	fresh or frozen (thawed) shrimp	250 g
8 oz	fresh or frozen (thawed) crabmeat	250 g
¼ cup	all-purpose flour	60 mL
1½ cups	milk	375 mL
	Sea salt and freshly ground pepper	
½ cup	plain yogurt	125 mL
3 tbsp	chopped fresh parsley	45 mL
2 tbsp	chopped fresh basil or oregano	30 mL
½ cup	grated Parmesan cheese	125 mL

1. In a large pot of boiling salted water, cook fettuccine for about 8 minutes or until al dente. Drain and rinse.

2. Meanwhile, in a saucepan, heat oil and melt butter over medium-high heat. Reduce heat to medium and add shrimp and crabmeat and cook, stirring constantly, for 3 to 4 minutes or until shellfish turns bright pink. Using a slotted spoon, lift shellfish out and set aside.

3. Using a whisk, blend flour into oil in pan. Add milk and cook, whisking constantly, for 4 minutes or until sauce has thickened. Season to taste with salt and pepper. Add shellfish to sauce and stir to heat through. Remove from heat and stir in yogurt, parsley and basil. Serve over fettuccine and pass Parmesan at the table.

Poultry

Basque Chicken Sauté

Serves 6

The flavor is rich and complex — truly Mediterranean in its origins. For best results, remove skin and all traces of fat from the chicken but, for optimum flavor, use cuts with the bone in for this dish. I have used two containers (each 6 oz/175 g) fruit-bottom yogurt in this dish with good results.

2 to 4 tbsp	olive oil, divided	30 to 60 mL
6	chicken legs or breasts or 12 thighs	6
	Sea salt and freshly ground pepper	
1	red bell pepper, coarsely chopped	1
1	red onion, coarsely chopped	1
3	large garlic cloves, minced	3
2 tbsp	fresh thyme leaves	30 mL
½ cup	chicken broth or water	125 mL
½ cup	white or red wine	125 mL
2 tbsp	freshly squeezed lemon juice	30 mL
1 cup	cherry tomatoes	250 mL
½ cup	green or black olives, halved	125 mL
1 tsp	hot pepper flakes	5 mL
1 cup	Drained Yogurt (page 162)	250 mL

1. In a large skillet or Dutch oven, heat 2 tbsp (30 mL) of the oil over medium heat. Add half of the chicken, season with salt and pepper and cook over medium-low heat, turning once, for 15 minutes or until well browned. Transfer to a large plate and brown remaining chicken, adding more oil to pan as needed. Transfer second batch of chicken to plate and set aside.

2. Add bell pepper, red onion, garlic and thyme to skillet and cook over medium heat, stirring frequently, for 5 minutes or until vegetables are soft and onions are transparent. Stir in broth, wine and lemon juice and simmer for 1 minute, stirring and scraping up all the bits from bottom of the pan. Add tomatoes, olives and hot pepper flakes and cook, stirring constantly, for 1 minute.

3. Return chicken and juices to skillet. Cover and simmer over medium-low heat, stirring occasionally and turning chicken once, for about 25 minutes or until juices run clear when chicken legs or thighs are pierced or breasts are no longer pink inside. Let stand for 10 minutes. Stir yogurt into sauce.

This is a dish with Mediterranean roots. You can add ¹/₂ cup (125 mL) pitted green or black olives or chopped roasted red pepper to the couscous in Step 3 to add a sunny Basque flavor.

Baked Chicken with Couscous and Pesto Yogurt

- *Preheat oven to 400°F (200°C)*
- *8-cup (2 L) baking dish, lightly oiled*

2 to 3 tbsp	olive oil, divided	30 to 45 mL
4	skinless boneless chicken breasts	4
1	onion, sliced	1
1	jar (6 oz/170 mL) marinated artichoke hearts with liquid	1
2 cups	chicken broth	500 mL
2 cups	couscous (10-oz/340 g box)	500 mL
	Sea salt and freshly ground pepper	
1¹/₂ cups	Pesto Yogurt (below)	375 mL

1. In a skillet, heat 2 tbsp (30 mL) of the oil over medium-high heat. Add chicken and cook for 2 minutes per side or until golden. Add more oil to the skillet, if required. Using tongs, transfer chicken to a plate and set aside.

2. Reduce heat to medium-low. Add onion to pan and cook, stirring frequently, for 12 minutes or until soft and lightly golden. Add artichoke hearts with liquid. Stir well and remove from heat.

3. Scrape onion mixture and liquid into bottom of baking dish. Stir in broth. Add couscous and stir well. Season to taste with salt and pepper. Arrange browned chicken on top of couscous, adding any liquids that have collected on the plate. Spread pesto yogurt over chicken. Cover dish with a lid or tented foil and bake in preheated oven for 20 minutes or until chicken is no longer pink inside.

You can use pesto made with any combination of herbs — basil, parsley, rosemary, sage, thyme and garlic scapes when in season. I prefer homemade pesto.

Pesto Yogurt

1 cup	Drained Yogurt (page 162)	250 mL
¹/₂ cup	pesto, homemade or store-bought	125 mL

1. In a bowl, combine drained yogurt and pesto. Stir well to mix.

You could serve this easy chicken and creamy risotto as a luncheon dish or as a main-course dinner dish with a green salad or steamed vegetables. Don't be tempted to omit the grated lemon zest because it really sets up the taste.

Baked Chicken and Mushroom Risotto

- *Preheat oven to 400°F (200°C)*
- *8-cup (2 L) baking dish, lightly oiled*

3	skinless boneless chicken breasts (about 1 lb/500 g)	3
2 tbsp	olive oil	30 mL
1 tbsp	butter	15 mL
1	leek, white and light green parts, sliced	1
1 cup	coarsely chopped mushrooms	250 mL
1 1/2 cups	Arborio rice	375 mL
4 cups	chicken broth	1 L
1 tbsp	grated lemon zest	30 mL
1/2 cup	frozen peas	125 mL
1 cup	plain yogurt	250 mL
1/2 cup	crumbled goat's cheese	125 mL

1. Slice chicken breasts into 1/2-inch (1 cm) wide strips. In a skillet, heat oil and melt butter over medium-high heat. Add chicken and cook, stirring frequently, for 3 minutes or until lightly browned on all sides. Using tongs, transfer to a plate and set aside.

2. Add leek and mushrooms to pan and cook, stirring frequently, for 5 minutes or until leek has softened. Add rice and cook, stirring constantly, for 2 to 3 minutes or until transparent. Scrape vegetables, rice and browned bits from bottom of pan into prepared baking dish. Stir in broth and lemon zest. Cover and bake in preheated oven for 20 minutes.

3. Add browned chicken pieces and peas to rice mixture and stir well. Cover and bake for 15 to 20 minutes or until rice is tender and chicken is no longer pink inside. Remove from oven and stir in yogurt and goat's cheese.

One dish and little mess make this a convenient weeknight dish. Serve over cooked whole grains for a complete meal.

Tip

• Use tender fresh greens, such as collard, kale, Swiss chard, beet tops or spinach.

Chicken and Roasted Vegetable Gratin

• *Preheat oven to 400°F (200°C)*
• *10-cup (2.5 L) casserole dish*

2	Vidalia onions, quartered	2
4	parsnips, quartered lengthwise and cut into 2-inch (5 cm) pieces	4
4	whole cloves garlic, peeled	4
3 tbsp	olive oil	45 mL
8 oz	ground chicken, crumbled	250 g
1 cup	dry whole wheat bread crumbs	250 mL
4 cups	greens, torn (see Tip, left)	1 L
2 cups	Yogurt Cheese Sauce (page 250)	500 mL

1. In casserole dish, toss onions, parsnips and garlic with oil. Stir in crumbled ground chicken. Roast in preheated oven, stirring once or twice, for 30 minutes. Add bread crumbs and toss to combine. Reduce oven temperature to 350°F (180°C) and bake for 10 minutes more or until vegetables are tender.

2. Remove casserole from oven. Stir in greens. Pour yogurt cheese sauce over top and return to oven. Bake for 15 minutes or until sauce is bubbling. Serve immediately.

This light salad is meant to be served at room temperature, and could be used as a starter or a luncheon dish.

Shredded Chicken with Minted Lime Yogurt Dressing

Salad

10 oz	wide rice noodles	300 g
3	skinless boneless cooked chicken breasts, shredded	3
1 cup	shredded carrot	250 mL
½ cup	shredded cucumber	125 mL
3 tbsp	sunflower seeds	45 mL

Minted Lime Yogurt Dressing

3 tbsp	Drained Yogurt (page 162)	45 mL
3 tbsp	freshly squeezed lime juice	45 mL
1 tbsp	peanut oil	15 mL
3 tbsp	chopped fresh mint	45 mL
2 tbsp	sesame seeds	30 mL

1. *Salad:* In a heatproof bowl, cover rice noodles with boiling water. Let stand for 7 to 10 minutes or until al dente. Drain and rinse.

2. In a separate bowl, combine chicken, carrot, cucumber and sunflower seeds.

3. *Minted Lime Yogurt Dressing:* In a bowl, whisk together drained yogurt, lime juice and oil. Stir in mint. Drizzle over chicken and vegetables. Divide noodles among 4 plates. Top noodles with shredded chicken and dressing. Sprinkle sesame seeds over top.

Roasted Chicken with Spicy Red Pepper Sauce

With its coating of yogurt, the chicken is insulated from the drying heat of the oven and actually steams as it would if it were cooked in a tagine. The meat will be so moist and tender, you might think it isn't cooked but if the juices run clear and the flesh is opaque and no longer pink inside, it is done. Letting the chicken rest after removing it from the oven completes the cooking.

Tip

* You can use pizza sauce or spaghetti sauce in place of the tomato sauce in this recipe. When tomatoes are in season, I use 2 cups (500 mL) chopped fresh Roma (plum) tomatoes, instead.

* *Preheat oven to 375°F (190°C)*
* *8-cup (2 L) baking dish, lightly oiled*

Chicken

¾ cup	plain yogurt	175 mL
1	can (14 oz/400 mL) tomato sauce, divided (see Tip, left)	1
2	cloves garlic, minced	2
1 tbsp	finely chopped candied ginger	15 mL
1 tbsp	hot smoked Spanish paprika (Pimentón)	15 mL
1 tsp	ground cumin	5 mL
1 tsp	ground coriander	5 mL
½ tsp	salt	2 mL
4	skinless boneless chicken breasts	4

Spicy Red Pepper Sauce

3 tbsp	olive oil, divided	45 mL
1	onion, chopped	1
1	red bell pepper, chopped	1
1 tbsp	Thai-inspired Red Curry Paste (page 257) or store-bought, or curry powder	15 mL
2	cloves garlic, finely chopped	2
1	jar (6 oz/175 mL) roasted sweet red peppers, drained	1
4 cups	cooked jasmine rice	1 L

1. *Chicken:* In a bowl, combine yogurt, 3 tbsp (45 mL) of the tomato sauce, garlic, ginger, paprika, cumin, coriander and salt. Set aside remaining tomato sauce for Step 2. Arrange chicken breasts in prepared dish. Spread half of the yogurt mixture evenly over chicken to coat. Reserve remaining yogurt mixture for red pepper sauce. Bake chicken in preheated oven for 30 to 40 minutes or until no longer pink inside. Remove from oven and let stand for 5 to 10 minutes.

2. *Spicy Red Pepper Sauce:* Meanwhile, in a skillet, heat 2 tbsp (30 mL) of the oil over medium heat. Add onion and cook, stirring frequently, for 5 minutes. Reduce heat to medium-low. Add remaining oil, bell pepper and curry paste and cook, stirring frequently, for 4 minutes. Add garlic and cook, stirring constantly, for 1 minute. Increase heat to high. Add remaining tomato sauce and roasted red peppers and bring to a boil. Reduce heat to medium-low and simmer gently, stirring occasionally, for 15 minutes. Keep warm over low heat until chicken is cooked and has stood for 5 to 10 minutes. Stir in remaining yogurt mixture.

3. To serve, spoon rice into 4 serving bowls and top each with a chicken breast. Spoon Spicy Red Pepper Sauce over chicken.

Using yogurt with spicy foods is a time-honored technique that cools the fire.

Tandoori Turkey

- *10-cup (2.5 L) baking dish or casserole, lightly oiled*
- *Instant-read thermometer*

2 tbsp	olive oil	30 mL
1 cup	chopped onion	250 mL
6	cloves garlic, minced	6
1 tbsp	freshly grated gingerroot	15 mL
2 tbsp	Red or Green Curry Paste (page 255) or store-bought tandoori paste	30 mL
1 cup	plain yogurt	250 mL
4 tbsp	freshly squeezed lime juice, divided	60 mL
2 tsp	salt	10 mL
1	turkey breast, skin removed and trimmed of excess fat (about 8 oz/250 g)	1

1. In a skillet, heat oil over medium heat. Add onion and cook, stirring frequently, for 6 minutes or until soft. Add garlic and ginger and cook, stirring constantly, for 1 minute. Add curry paste and cook, stirring constantly, for 1 minute. Remove from heat and transfer half to a bowl. Stir yogurt and 2 tbsp (30 mL) of the lime juice into onion-spice mixture in bowl and set aside.

2. Transfer remaining onion-spice mixture to a large bowl. Add remaining 2 tbsp (30 mL) of lime juice and salt. Using a sharp knife, lightly score outside of turkey breast (make slits about ⅛-inch/3 mm deep and about 1-inch/2.5 cm apart). Place turkey breast in the large bowl of onion-spice mixture. Using a spatula, rub onion-spice mixture into turkey. Cover and let stand at room temperature for 30 minutes.

3. Meanwhile, preheat oven to 350°F (180°C).

4. Place turkey in prepared baking dish and spoon reserved yogurt mixture over top, so that it is evenly coated with a thick layer. Cover with a lid or foil. Bake in preheated oven for 45 to 60 minutes or until a thermometer inserted into thickest part registers 165°F (74°C).

Easy and fast, the cream sauce teams well with rice or egg noodles, and the whole dish can be on the table in less than an hour. This dish is foolproof. Try it with carrots or celery, or cauliflower slices instead of the zucchini. Layering and cooking the vegetables with the meat in one dish makes preparation easy. Serve it with couscous, or with rice or egg noodles.

Variation

• When I am really pressed for time, I use 1 can (10 oz/284 mL) cream of mushroom soup mixed with 1 cup (250 mL) plain yogurt in place of the Yogurt Cheese Sauce.

Turkey Breasts in Tarragon Cream Sauce

• *Preheat oven to 375°F (190°C)*
• *10-cup (2.5 L) baking dish, lightly oiled*

2	small onions, halved and sliced	2
1	zucchini, diced	1
8	dried apricots, sliced	8
2 tbsp	olive oil	30 mL
	Sea salt and freshly ground pepper	
1 lb	skinless boneless turkey or chicken breasts, cut into 1-inch (2.5 cm) wide strips	500 g
1 cup	Yogurt Cheese Sauce (page 250)	250 mL
1 tbsp	chopped fresh tarragon	15 mL

1. Spread onions over bottom of prepared dish. Sprinkle zucchini and apricots over onions. Drizzle with oil. Season with a few grinds of salt and pepper. Spread turkey strips evenly over vegetables.

2. In a bowl, whisk together yogurt cheese sauce and tarragon. Pour over turkey. Cover and bake in preheated oven for 30 minutes or until vegetables are soft and turkey is no longer pink inside.

A classic dish served
throughout America's
South, red beans and
rice are traditionally
flavored with sausage
or ham.

Variation

• Use black beans
  in place of the
  red beans.

Turkey, Red Beans and Rice

2 tbsp	olive oil	30 mL
1 cup	chopped onion	250 mL
2	cloves garlic, finely chopped	2
1 cup	coarsely chopped green bell pepper	250 mL
¼ cup	chicken broth	60 mL
1 tbsp	Red or Green Curry Paste (page 255) or store-bought	15 mL
1	can (28 oz/796 mL) tomatoes, drained	1
2 cups	cubed poached turkey or chicken	500 mL
2 cups	cooked red or brown rice	500 mL
1	can (14 to 19 oz/398 to 540 mL) red or kidney beans, drained and rinsed, or 2 cups (500 mL) cooked red or kidney beans	1
1 cup	plain yogurt	250 mL
¼ cup	chopped fresh parsley	60 mL

1. In a large saucepan, heat oil over medium-high heat. Add
onion, garlic and bell pepper and cook, stirring constantly,
for 7 minutes or until vegetables are tender.

2. Add broth and curry paste and cook, stirring constantly, for
1 minute. Add tomatoes and bring to a boil. Reduce heat
and simmer, stirring occasionally, for 10 minutes. Stir in
turkey, rice and beans and simmer for 5 minutes or until
heated through. Remove from heat and add yogurt and
parsley. Serve immediately.

Serves 6

Great for a traditional Sunday meal, this tougher cut of beef is transformed into a meltingly delicious meal.

Tip

- Use any combination of herbs such as oregano, basil, thyme, sage, rosemary and parsley.

Boneless Beef Chuck Pot Roast

- *Preheat oven to 350°F (180°C)*
- *Dutch oven or roasting pan*

2 tbsp	olive oil	30 mL
2	onions, quartered	2
4	cloves garlic, thickly sliced	4
2 lbs	boneless beef chuck pot roast or boneless beef bottom blade roast	I kg
4 cups	beer or chicken broth	I L
2 tbsp	Dijon mustard	30 mL
I tbsp	crushed dried Mediterranean herbs (see Tip, left)	I5 mL
3	carrots, cut in half lengthwise	3
3	parsnips, cut in half lengthwise	3
3	potatoes, cut into chunks	3
¾ cup	Drained Yogurt (page 162)	175 mL

1. In bottom of a Dutch oven or roasting pan, heat oil over high heat. Add onions and garlic and sauté, stirring constantly, for 4 minutes until lightly browned. Add roast and brown on all sides, turning often.

2. Add beer, mustard and herbs and bring to a boil. Cover and bake in preheated oven for $2\frac{1}{2}$ hours. Add carrots, parsnips and potatoes. Cover and bake for 30 minutes or until vegetables are tender and beef is fork-tender. Transfer roast and vegetables to a warmed platter. Drain away any fat and stir drained yogurt into pan juices. Slice roast and serve with vegetables and yogurt sauce either drizzled over meat on platter or in a separate bowl on the side.

I have found that there are some very good store-bought, low-fat chicken and beef meatballs already precooked and frozen. If you prefer to make and cook your own meatballs, they may be made ahead of time and added to the sauce just to warm through prior to serving.

Meatballs in Mushroom Cream

Mushroom Cream

2 tbsp	olive oil	30 mL
1	onion, cut in half and sliced	1
2 cups	sliced mushrooms	500 mL
1 tbsp	Red or Green Curry Paste (page 255) or store-bought	15 mL
1 tbsp	butter	15 mL
3 tbsp	all-purpose flour	45 mL
2 cups	beef or chicken broth	500 mL
¼ cup	red wine or sherry	60 mL
24	cooked fresh or frozen (thawed) meatballs	24
1 cup	plain yogurt	250 mL

1. *Mushroom Cream:* In a skillet, heat oil over medium-high heat. Add onion and cook, stirring frequently, for 5 minutes. Add mushrooms and curry paste and cook, stirring frequently, for 5 minutes or until vegetables are soft. Using a slotted spoon, transfer onions and mushrooms to a bowl.

2. Add butter to skillet and let melt. Blend flour into butter. Gradually whisk in broth and cook, stirring constantly, for about 3 minutes or until smooth and slightly thickened. Reduce heat to low. Add onion mixture, wine and meatballs and cook, stirring frequently, for about 8 minutes or until meatballs are heated through. Remove from heat and stir in yogurt.

Hungarian Goulash is known today as a paprika-flavored stew, but the original dish is actually more of a soup than a thick stew. This dish is an easy version of the stew.

Tip

- Paprika is a ground red spice made from either red bell peppers or hot red chile peppers. Use either the sweet or spicy paprika in this stew.

Gulyás

¼ cup	all-purpose flour	60 mL
1 tbsp	paprika (see Tip, left)	15 mL
½ tsp	salt	2 mL
8 oz	boneless beef top round or outside round steak, cut into 1-inch (2.5 cm) cubes	250 g
8 oz	lean boneless pork chops or loin, cut into 1-inch (2.5 cm) cubes	250 g
3 tbsp	olive oil, divided	45 mL
2	onions, quartered	2
1	can (28 oz/796 mL) tomato pasta sauce or spaghetti sauce	1
1 cup	beef broth or water	250 mL
4	potatoes, cut into wedges	4
2 cups	homemade or canned sauerkraut	500 mL
1 cup	plain yogurt	250 mL

1. In a bowl, combine flour, paprika and salt. Toss beef and pork cubes in flour mixture to coat.

2. In a large saucepan, heat 2 tbsp (30 mL) of the oil over medium-high heat. Add onions and meat and cook, stirring constantly, for 8 minutes or until meat is browned and onions are soft. Add remaining oil to pan, as needed, to keep meat from sticking. Add any remaining flour mixture, tomato sauce and broth. Bring to a boil, stirring and scraping up any brown bits from bottom of pan. Cover, reduce heat and simmer for 1½ hours, adding more water, if necessary, to keep stew from scorching.

3. Add potatoes and sauerkraut and simmer gently for 15 to 20 minutes or until meat is fork-tender and potatoes are tender. Remove from heat and stir in yogurt.

Serves 6

Short-grain Italian
Arborio rice works best
for this recipe. Brown
rice does not absorb the
broth in the same way.

Ground Beef, Leek and Mushroom Pilaf

• *Heated serving bowl*

1 tbsp	olive oil	15 mL
8 oz	lean ground beef	250 g
1	leek, white and light green parts, sliced	1
2 cups	coarsely chopped shiitake mushroom caps	500 mL
3 tbsp	white or red wine	45 mL
2 tbsp	fresh thyme leaves	30 mL
1 cup	Arborio rice	250 mL
2 cups	beef or chicken broth, divided	500 mL
1	head roasted garlic (page 206)	1
1/2 cup	plain yogurt	125 mL
1/2 cup	freshly grated Parmesan cheese	125 mL

1. In a large skillet, heat oil over medium-high heat. Add beef and cook, stirring constantly and breaking up with a spoon, for 5 minutes or until lightly browned. Add leek, mushrooms and wine. Reduce heat to medium and gently simmer for 5 minutes or until mushrooms are soft. Stir in thyme and rice. Cook, stirring constantly, for 3 minutes.

2. Stir in 1/2 cup (125 mL) of the broth and squeeze roasted garlic cloves into rice mixture. Increase heat to high. Bring to a boil and stir up any brown bits from bottom of skillet. Add the remaining 1 1/2 cups (375 mL) of broth. Cover and bring to a boil. Reduce heat and simmer for 20 minutes or until rice is tender. Remove from heat and stir in yogurt, then sprinkle Parmesan over top.

Peppered Pork

Have the butcher cut four slices from a boneless loin of pork or use four bone-in pork chops in this recipe.

1 tbsp	olive oil	15 mL
2	slices bacon, coarsely chopped	2
4	slices pork loin (each about 1½-inches/4 cm thick)	4
1	onion, halved and sliced	1
1	green bell pepper, cut into large chunks	1
3 cups	chopped fresh tomatoes (or one 28 oz/796 mL can diced tomatoes) with juices	750 mL
1 tbsp	paprika	15 mL
½ tsp	salt	5 mL
½ cup	plain yogurt	125 mL

1. In a saucepan, heat oil over medium-high heat. Add bacon and pork slices and cook, stirring bacon and turning pork frequently, for 4 to 5 minutes or until bacon is crisp and pork is browned. Transfer to a plate.

2. Add onion to pan and cook, stirring frequently, for 4 minutes. Add bell pepper and cook, stirring frequently, for 3 to 4 minutes or until vegetables are soft. Add tomatoes with juices, paprika and salt and bring to a boil. Return pork slices to pan and simmer gently, stirring occasionally, for 15 to 20 minutes or until just a hint of pink remains in pork. Remove from heat and stir in yogurt and bacon.

Pork Cutlets with Tarragon Yogurt

Because the meat is simmered gently, this is a tenderizing method of cooking some of the tougher cuts of meat such as shoulder blade cuts.

Be sure to gauge the size of the pan with the size of the cutlets. If you cook the meat in one layer in the pan, it will cook more evenly. If you must layer the meat, transfer the onions and mushrooms to a bowl, then brown the meat on both sides and return all the meat and vegetables to the pan and continue with the recipe, turning the meat occasionally and allowing extra time.

* *Large heavy-bottomed skillet or Dutch oven*

2 tbsp	olive oil	30 mL
1	onion, halved and thinly sliced	1
2 cups	sliced mushrooms	500 mL
4	boneless pork shoulder blade cutlets (each 1/2-inch/1 cm thick), trimmed of excess fat	4
1/4 tsp	sea salt	1 mL
1 cup	chicken or beef broth	250 mL
1/4 cup	white or red wine	60 mL
1/2 cup	plain yogurt	125 mL
2	egg yolks	2
2 tbsp	chopped fresh tarragon	30 mL

1. In a large skillet or Dutch oven, heat oil over medium heat. Add onion and cook, stirring frequently, for 5 minutes. Reduce heat to medium-low. Stir in mushrooms and cook for 5 minutes or until onions and mushrooms are soft. Add pork cutlets and brown on both sides. Season with salt.

2. Add broth and wine to the pan and bring to a boil over high heat. Cover, reduce heat to low and simmer for 30 minutes or until meat is fork-tender. Transfer meat to a warmed platter.

3. Meanwhile, in a small bowl, combine yogurt, egg yolks and tarragon. Stir yogurt mixture into onion-mushroom mixture. Increase heat to medium and gently simmer sauce, stirring constantly, for 4 to 6 minutes or until sauce thickens (do not let boil).

Moroccan and Persian dishes favor fruited meats slowly cooked in clay tagines. The conical shape of the tagine lid keeps the dish very moist and renders the meat very tender. You can intensify the fruit flavor by using Fruit-Bottom Yogurt (page 25). Serve with cooked rice or couscous.

Lamb Tagine with Plums and Apricots

- *Preheat oven to 350°F (180°C)*
- *Tagine or 12-cup (3 L) casserole dish with lid, lightly oiled*

12 oz	boneless lamb leg or shoulder, cut into 1-inch (2.5 cm) cubes	375 g
1	small eggplant, diced	1
1 cup	coarsely chopped onion	250 mL
½ cup	coarsely chopped pitted plums or prunes	125 mL
½ cup	coarsely chopped fresh or dried apricots	125 mL
½ cup	applesauce	125 mL
2 tbsp	freshly squeezed lemon juice	30 mL
½ tsp	salt	2 mL
2 tbsp	olive oil	30 mL
½ cup	plain or Fruit-Bottom Yogurt (page 25)	25 mL

1. In base of tagine, combine lamb, eggplant, onion, plums, apricots, applesauce, lemon juice and salt. Drizzle oil over top. Cover and bake in preheated oven for 1 to 1½ hours or until lamb is tender. Let stand for 10 minutes with lid on. Stir in yogurt and serve immediately.

In this recipe, yogurt is used in place of rich cream in the meat sauce and again for butter and cream in the mashed potato topping. You can use a less tender cut of meat such as pork shoulder or lamb shanks. Cut the meat off the bone and then into cubes because this is a tenderizing method of cooking the meat.

Shepherd's Pie with Garlic Mashed Potatoes

- *Preheat oven to 350°F (180°C)*
- *Dutch oven or flameproof casserole dish*

3 tbsp	olive oil, divided	45 mL
I	onion, chopped	I
2	cloves garlic, finely chopped	2
2 cups	sliced mushrooms	500 mL
I	leek, white and light green parts, sliced	I
2 lbs	boneless pork or lamb, trimmed and cut into I-inch (2.5 cm) cubes	I kg
2 cups	beef or chicken broth	500 mL
I	zucchini, diced	I
2 cups	sliced cauliflower	500 mL
I cup	fresh or canned (drained) corn kernels	250 mL
I tsp	ground nutmeg	5 mL
I cup	plain yogurt	250 mL
	Garlic Mashed Potatoes (right)	

1. In Dutch oven or flameproof casserole dish, heat 2 tbsp (30 mL) of the oil over medium heat. Add onion and cook, stirring occasionally, for 5 minutes. Add garlic, mushrooms and leek and cook, stirring frequently, for about 5 minutes or until vegetables are tender. Add remaining oil to dish. Add pork cubes and brown on all sides, stirring frequently.

2. Increase heat to high. Stir in broth and bring to a boil. Add zucchini and cauliflower. Cover and bake in preheated oven for 2 hours or until meat is very tender. Remove from oven and stir in corn, nutmeg and yogurt. Make ahead and keep in the refrigerator for up to 1 day. Bring to room temperature and heat gently over medium heat, stirring frequently.

3. Prepared garlic mashed potatoes. Spoon mashed potatoes over meat stew in casserole dish and pass family style or serve individual servings of stew with mashed potatoes.

Garlic Mashed Potatoes

6	medium potatoes (1 $\frac{1}{2}$ lbs/750 g)	6
1 tsp	salt	5 mL
$\frac{1}{4}$ cup	milk	60 mL
6	cloves roasted garlic (page 206)	6
3 tbsp	plain yogurt	45 mL

1. In a saucepan, cover potatoes with water. Add salt and bring to a boil over high heat. Reduce heat to medium and simmer for 12 minutes or until potatoes are tender. Drain.

2. In same saucepan, heat milk over medium heat. Add drained potatoes and garlic and mash using a potato masher. Add yogurt.

The nice thing about this dish is that it is easy to prepare and frees up all your time while it cooks in the oven. This is a great entrée for Sunday family dinner or entertaining friends on a Saturday night. Serve with buttered egg noodles, boiled new potatoes or rice.

Lamb Shanks with Squash and Yogurt Gremolata

- *Preheat oven to 400°F (200°C)*
- *Roasting pan, lightly oiled*
- *Small food processor or blender*

Lamb

3 cups	cubed squash	750 mL
4	onions, quartered	4
4	cloves garlic, halved	4
1	carrot, cut into chunks	1
1	parsnip, cut into chunks	1
4	sprigs fresh thyme	4
4	lamb shanks	4
2 cups	beef or chicken broth	500 mL
¼ cup	red wine	60 mL

Yogurt Gremolata

½ cup	packed flat-leaf parsley leaves	125 mL
1	clove garlic	1
2 tbsp	salted roasted sunflower seeds	30 mL
1 tbsp	capers, rinsed and drained	15 mL
	Zest of half a lemon	
½ cup	Drained Yogurt (page 162)	125 mL

1. *Lamb:* In bottom of prepared pan, toss together squash, onions, garlic, carrot, parsnip and thyme. Arrange shanks over top. Pour broth over top, cover and bake in preheated oven for 1 hour. Stir in wine and bake, uncovered, for 30 minutes or until vegetables are tender and meat is pulling away from the bones.

2. *Yogurt Gremolata:* In a small food processor or blender, combine parsley, garlic, sunflower seeds, capers and lemon zest. Process until finely chopped. Transfer to a bowl and mix with drained yogurt. Serve separately to garnish lamb shanks and vegetables.

Sauces

Ginger-Spiked Citrus Sauce

Makes 1½ cups (375 mL)

This is a sweet and tangy sauce for fruit and desserts, waffles and pancakes. Make it the night before, and serve with granola and banana or other fruit. Use Yogurt Cheese (page 162), in place of the drained yogurt, for a thicker topping.

1½ cups	Drained Yogurt (page 162)	375 mL
2 tbsp	packed brown sugar, or to taste	30 mL
1 tsp	grated orange zest	5 mL
1 tsp	finely chopped candied ginger	5 mL

1. In a bowl, combine drained yogurt, brown sugar, orange zest and ginger. Cover and refrigerate for at least 1 hour for flavors to develop or overnight.

Yogurt Cheese Sauce

Makes 1 cup (250 mL)

The "classic" cheese sauce is made with a white sauce (butter, flour, milk) and grated cheese. My yogurt version uses whole wheat flour, rice milk instead of cow's milk, oil in place of the butter, and adds some not-so-classic but flavorful ingredients, such as tamari and nutmeg.

Tip
* Increase or reduce the milk by 3 tbsp (45 mL) to achieve either a thinner or a thicker sauce.

1	clove garlic, chopped	1
2 tbsp	olive oil	30 mL
3 tbsp	whole wheat or spelt flour	45 mL
1 tsp	brewer's yeast	5 mL
1 cup	rice milk or soy milk	250 mL
¼ cup	shredded Swiss or Cheddar cheese	60 mL
2 tbsp	grated Parmesan cheese	30 mL
¼ cup	Drained Yogurt (page 162)	60 mL
1 tsp	tamari or soy sauce	5 mL
¼ tsp	ground nutmeg	1 mL

1. In a saucepan, combine garlic and oil. Sauté over medium heat for about 3 minutes or until garlic is fragrant and soft. Add flour and yeast and stir to make a paste. Gradually whisk in rice milk and cook, stirring constantly, for 5 to 6 minutes or until thickened.

2. Stir in Swiss and Parmesan cheeses and cook, stirring, for 1 to 2 minutes or until melted. Remove from heat and stir in drained yogurt, tamari and nutmeg. Serve immediately.

Mushroom Sauce

Make this sauce for any dish that requires a white or béchamel sauce. It contains no fat, and flour or eggs are not used to thicken it.

Tip

- For a smooth sauce, purée in a blender or food processor before adding the drained yogurt.

Variation

- Use a whole head of roasted garlic (page 206) in place of the raw garlic cloves.

1 oz	dried mushrooms, whole or sliced	30 g
1 cup	boiled water	250 mL
1 cup	chopped onion	250 mL
3	cloves garlic, finely chopped	3
1	stalk celery, chopped	1
1/4 cup	ground almonds	60 mL
1/4 cup	white wine	60 mL
1 cup	rice milk or soy milk, divided	250 mL
1 tbsp	chopped fresh parsley	15 mL
1 tbsp	chopped fresh oregano	15 mL
1/2 tsp	salt	2 mL
1/2 cup	Drained Yogurt (page 162)	125 mL

1. In a small heatproof bowl, pour boiled water over mushrooms. Set aside and let stand for 15 minutes. Strain mushrooms and reserve 1/2 cup (125 mL) of the soaking liquid. Set aside. Chop mushrooms and set aside.

2. In a saucepan, combine onion, garlic, celery, almonds and wine. Sauté gently over medium-low heat for 10 minutes. If mixture gets too dry, add a little of the rice milk.

3. Stir in remaining rice milk, parsley, oregano, salt and reserved mushrooms and soaking liquid. Increase heat to high and bring to a boil. Reduce heat and simmer, stirring occasionally, for 30 to 45 minutes or until sauce is thick. Let cool. Stir in drained yogurt. Use immediately or cover tightly and refrigerate until needed or for up to 24 hours. Bring to room temperature and stir well before using in recipes.

Dill Sauce

This is a classic white sauce with dill and yogurt for extra flavor. Serve it with poached or grilled fish and chicken. Any fresh herbs — such as chives, oregano, sage, thyme, rosemary, or a combination of these — may be used in place of the dill.

2 tbsp	butter or olive oil	30 mL
2 tbsp	all-purpose flour	30 mL
1 cup	milk	250 mL
2 tbsp	chopped fresh dill	30 mL
2 tsp	white wine vinegar	10 mL
1 tsp	granulated sugar	5 mL
½ cup	plain yogurt	125 mL

1. In a saucepan, melt butter over medium heat. Stir in flour. Cook, stirring constantly, for 1 minute or until flour thickens slightly. Gradually whisk in milk. Cook, whisking constantly, for 4 to 5 minutes or until sauce thickens. Stir in dill, vinegar and sugar and cook, stirring constantly, for 1 minute. Remove from heat and stir in yogurt.

Yogurt Hollandaise Sauce

• *Double boiler*

Using yogurt in this versatile sauce makes it healthier and easier to make, while the taste and texture is still excellent. Use it for poached eggs or over smoked salmon and poultry or steamed asparagus, fiddleheads and Brussels sprouts.

1 tbsp	butter	15 mL
¾ cup	Drained Yogurt (page 162)	175 mL
2 tsp	freshly squeezed lemon juice	10 mL
3	egg yolks	3
1 tsp	Dijon mustard (approx.)	5 mL
¼ tsp	salt (approx.)	1 mL
Pinch	freshly ground black pepper	Pinch

1. In the top of double boiler over lightly simmering water, melt butter. Whisk in drained yogurt, lemon juice, egg yolks, mustard, salt and pepper. Cook over simmering water, stirring constantly, for 8 to 12 minutes or until sauce thickens. Taste and add more mustard or salt, if required.

Coconut Curry Sauce

Use this mildly spicy sauce with stir-fried or roasted vegetables and grilled meats. For a spicier kick, use Red or Green Curry Paste (page 255) in place of the curry powder.

2 tbsp	olive oil	30 mL
1 cup	chopped onion	250 mL
1 tbsp	curry powder or to taste	15 mL
2 tsp	garam masala spice blend (see Tip, page 219)	5 mL
1 cup	coconut milk	250 mL
1 tbsp	cornstarch	15 mL
1 tbsp	granulated sugar	15 mL
1 cup	Cultured Coconut Milk "Yogurt" (page 23) or store-bought, or plain yogurt	250 mL
2 tbsp	fruit chutney, optional	30 mL
1 tbsp	unsweetened desiccated coconut, optional	15 mL

1. In a saucepan, heat oil over medium heat. Add onion and cook, stirring frequently, for 6 minutes or until soft and translucent. Stir in curry powder and garam masala. Add coconut milk and simmer gently, stirring occasionally, for 10 minutes or until slightly thickened.

2. Meanwhile, in a bowl, combine cornstarch and sugar. Slowly add to onion mixture in pan and cook, stirring constantly, for 3 to 5 minutes or until sauce is thick and smooth. Remove from heat and stir in yogurt, and chutney and coconut, if using.

Green Thai Yogurt Sauce

| 1½ cups | Drained Yogurt (page 162) | 375 mL |
| 2 tbsp | Green Curry Paste (page 255) or store-bought (approx.) | 30 mL |

To save time, purchase green curry paste (widely available at Asian markets), but be aware that most are made with shrimp paste. This is one sauce that starts out with a small amount of the paste and is tasted after each addition, so that it is not overpowering and yet hot enough for you.

1. In a small bowl, combine drained yogurt and 1 tbsp (15 mL) of the curry paste. Taste and add more paste until the desired heat is reached. Cover and refrigerate until ready to use or for up to 2 days.

Of all the different spice and chile combinations, this is one that I particularly like because of the cinnamon. You may double the recipe to make more of the paste.

Variation

* *Red Curry Paste:* Add red cayenne peppers and use red onions in place of the green onions.

Green Curry Paste

* *Small food processor or blender*

1 tbsp	pure creamed coconut (see page 31)	15 mL
½ tsp	ground cumin	2 mL
½ tsp	ground coriander	2 mL
½ tsp	ground turmeric	2 mL
¼ tsp	ground cinnamon	1 mL
1 tsp	brown sugar	5 mL
8	hot green chile peppers, coarsely chopped	8
4	green onions or ¼ onion, coarsely chopped	4
½ cup	fresh cilantro or flat-leaf parsley leaves	125 mL
2	cloves garlic	2
2 tsp	freshly grated gingerroot	10 mL
1 tsp	peanut oil or toasted sesame oil	5 mL
	Sea salt and cracked peppercorns	

1. In a spice wok or small heavy skillet, combine creamed coconut, cumin, coriander, turmeric and cinnamon. Heat over medium-low heat, stirring constantly, for 30 seconds or until coconut softens and spices release their fragrance. Do not allow spices to burn or smoke. Remove from heat and mash creamed coconut with the back of a wooden spoon to melt and break it up. Add brown sugar and let cool.

2. In a small food processor or blender, combine chile peppers, green onions, cilantro, garlic and ginger. Process until finely chopped. Add cooled spices. With motor running, add oil through the feed tube and process until well blended. Add salt and peppercorns to taste. Cover and refrigerate until ready to use or for up to 3 weeks.

Red Thai Coconut Sauce

This is a hot, but not
blistering, hot sauce.
Use it in stir-fried
vegetable dishes and
as a garnish for soup.
You can use plain
yogurt and add 2 tbsp
(15 mL) unsweetened
desiccated coconut,
if you do not have
coconut yogurt.

| 1 cup | Cultured Coconut Milk "Yogurt" (page 23) or store-bought coconut yogurt | 250 mL |
| 2 tbsp | Thai-Inspired Red Curry Paste (page 257) | 30 mL |

1. In a bowl, combine yogurt and 1 tbsp (15 mL) of the curry paste. Taste and add more paste, if desired.

Thai-Inspired Red Curry Paste

This paste is similar to the traditional Thai red curry paste, but uses North American ingredients. The Asian ingredients are given in brackets should you wish to use them, instead.

Tip

• If you can only get dried cayenne peppers, slit them in half and soak in warm water for 20 minutes. Drain and use as directed in Step 1.

Variation

• Use 1 tbsp (15 mL) grated lemon or lime zest in place of the lemon verbena leaves.

• Food processor

3	cloves garlic	3
1	slice candied ginger (1 tbsp/15 mL freshly grated gingerroot)	1
½	red onion	½
2	anchovy fillets, optional (1 tsp/5 mL shrimp paste)	2
15	fresh red cayenne peppers (see Tip, left)	15
12	fresh or dried lemon verbena leaves (4 stalks lemongrass, minced)	12
6	sprigs fresh cilantro or flat-leaf parsley	6
2 tbsp	fresh rosemary leaves (1 tbsp/15 mL minced lime leaves)	30 mL
1 tsp	cracked black peppercorns	5 mL
1 tsp	ground coriander	5 mL
1 tsp	ground cumin	5 mL
½ tsp	salt	2 mL
1 tsp	toasted sesame oil	5 mL

1. In a food processor, combine garlic and ginger. Process until finely chopped. Add red onion and anchovies, if using. Process until finely chopped. Add cayenne peppers and process until finely chopped. Add lemon verbena, cilantro, rosemary, peppercorns, coriander, cumin and salt. Process and with motor running, add sesame oil through the feed tube. Process until a smooth paste is achieved.

2. Cover tightly or spoon into a sterilized jar and cap. Store in the refrigerator for up to 3 weeks.

Any culinary herb will work, so use what you have available. Use salsa verde as an accompaniment for nachos or a sauce for fish.

Tip

* To use fresh herbs in recipes, wash and pat dry. Snip or pull whole leaves from the stem and lightly pack into a dry measure.

Creamy Salsa Verde

* *Food processor*

¼ cup	sunflower seeds	60 mL
4	anchovy fillets	4
2	cloves garlic	2
2 tbsp	drained capers	30 mL
1 cup	fresh flat-leaf parsley leaves (see Tip, left)	250 mL
½ cup	fresh oregano leaves	125 mL
½ cup	fresh cilantro leaves	125 mL
½ cup	fresh mint leaves	125 mL
¼ cup	fresh dill leaves	60 mL
3 tbsp	olive oil	45 mL
2 tbsp	freshly squeezed lemon juice	30 mL
1½ cups	Drained Yogurt (page 162)	375 mL

1. In a food processor, combine sunflower seeds, anchovies, garlic and capers. Process for about 30 seconds or until uniformly chopped. Add parsley, oregano, cilantro, mint and dill leaves. Pulse until uniformly chopped. With motor running, add oil and lemon juice through the feed tube and process until smooth.

2. In a bowl, combine herb mixture with drained yogurt. Cover and refrigerate until ready to use or for up to 2 days.

Garlic White Sauce

Many casseroles, soups and pasta dishes rely on a white sauce to bind all of the ingredients. Here is a basic white sauce to have in your recipe toolbox.

Tip

- *To roast eggplant:* Roast whole, pricked eggplant on a baking sheet in a preheated 400°F (200°C) oven for 45 to 60 minutes or until tender.

1 tbsp	olive oil	15 mL
½	onion, finely chopped	½
3 tbsp	finely chopped fresh parsley	45 mL
1	clove garlic, finely chopped	1
1 cup	rice milk	250 mL
½ cup	plain yogurt	125 mL
1	roasted eggplant, peeled (see Tip, left)	1
1	head roasted garlic (page 206)	1

1. In a saucepan, heat oil over medium heat. Add onion and cook, stirring occasionally, for 5 minutes or until slightly softened. Add parsley and garlic and cook, stirring frequently, for 3 to 4 minutes or until onion is soft.

2. In a blender, combine onion mixture, rice milk, yogurt, eggplant and garlic. Process until liquefied. Use immediately or store, tightly covered, in the refrigerator for up to 3 days.

Creamy White Sauce

A very easy sauce that is useful in main-course dishes, this basic white sauce is light and silky, with a roasted, nutty taste. Use it in pasta and roasted vegetable dishes as you would a béchamel or Mornay sauce made with cream.

- *Preheat oven to 400°F (200°C)*
- *Rimmed baking sheet*
- *Blender or food processor*

½	eggplant	½
½	butternut squash	½
I	apple, halved	I
4 tbsp	olive oil, divided	60 mL
I	whole head garlic, ¼ inch (0.5 cm) trimmed from top	I
I cup	rice milk	250 mL
½ cup	plain yogurt	125 mL

1. Arrange eggplant, squash and apple, cut side down, on baking sheet and drizzle with 3 tbsp (45 mL) of the oil. Place garlic head, cut side up, on same baking sheet. Drizzle with remaining oil.

2. Bake in preheated oven for 30 minutes. Using a slotted spoon, remove apple halves and transfer to a bowl. Bake remaining vegetables for another 15 minutes or until eggplant is tender. Transfer eggplant to a bowl. Continue to bake squash and garlic for another 15 minutes, for a total of 1 hour, or until tender. Let cool slightly. Scoop apple, eggplant and squash flesh out of their skins and discard skins.

3. In a blender or food processor, combine rice milk, yogurt, apple, eggplant and squash. Squeeze garlic flesh out of the skin and add to the blender. Blend until sauce is liquefied and smooth. Use immediately or store, tightly covered, in the refrigerator for up to 3 days.

Avocado Sauce

This versatile, creamy sauce can be used for pasta sauces, in casseroles and sometimes in desserts (see Tip, below).

Tip

• If the sauce is intended for desserts or sweet dishes, use vanilla-flavored soy milk or rice milk and omit the garlic.

• Blender or food processor

2 tbsp	olive oil	30 mL
3 tbsp	all-purpose flour	45 mL
1 cup	rice milk or soy milk	250 mL
3 tbsp	freshly squeezed lemon juice	45 mL
1	ripe avocado	1
1	clove garlic	1
1/4 cup	plain yogurt	60 mL
	Sea salt and freshly ground pepper	

1. In a saucepan, heat oil over medium heat. Stir in flour and cook, stirring constantly, for 1 minute. Whisk in rice milk. Cook, stirring, for about 4 minutes or until thickened. Let cool slightly.

2. In a blender or food processor, combine lemon juice, avocado and garlic. Process for 20 seconds. With the motor running, add rice milk mixture and yogurt through the opening in the lid. Blend until sauce is liquefied and smooth. Season to taste with salt and pepper.

Cashew Curry Sauce

With their delicate taste and creamy texture, cashews make this sauce very different from a peanut sauce. Use it with pasta and rice, or with milder tasting vegetables.

• *Blender or food processor*

4 tsp	olive oil, divided	20 mL
I	onion, cut in half and sliced	I
I	leek, white and light green parts, sliced	I
2 tsp	cumin seeds	10 mL
2 tsp	coriander seeds	10 mL
1/3 cup	whole cashews	75 mL
1/2 cup	soy milk	125 mL
1/2 cup	plain yogurt	125 mL
8	cloves roasted garlic (see Tip, page 206)	8
I tsp	chipotle flakes or hot pepper flakes	5 mL
1/2 tsp	ground cinnamon	2 mL
	Sea salt and freshly ground pepper	

1. In a skillet, heat 1 tbsp (15 mL) of the oil over high heat. Add onion and leek. Reduce heat to medium-low and cook, stirring occasionally, for 10 minutes or until soft.

2. In a small skillet over medium-high heat, toast cumin and coriander seeds, stirring constantly, for 2 to 3 minutes or until lightly colored or until the seeds begin to pop and their fragrance is released. Stir into onion-leek mixture. Let cool.

3. Add remaining 1 tsp (5 mL) of oil to the skillet used for toasting seeds. Heat oil over medium-high heat. Add cashews and toast, stirring frequently, for 5 minutes or until lightly browned.

4. In a blender or food processor, combine soy milk, yogurt, toasted cashews and roasted garlic. Process until smooth. Add onion-leek mixture, chipotle flakes and cinnamon and process until smooth. Season to taste with salt and pepper. Use immediately or store, tightly covered, in the refrigerator for up to 3 days.

Cashew Cream Mushroom Sauce

Makes 3 cups (750 mL)

It may seem as though there are too many mushrooms but, as they cook, their volume will be reduced by about half. A saucepan or deep, wide-bottomed skillet will reduce the cooking time. The wider the pan, the faster the mushrooms will cook.

2 tbsp	olive oil	30 mL
4 cups	sliced mushrooms	1 L
1	small onion, chopped	1
1	clove garlic, finely chopped	1
1 cup	vegetable broth or water	250 mL
½ cup	Cashew Cream (below)	125 mL
½ cup	plain yogurt	125 mL

1. In a saucepan, heat oil over high heat. Add mushrooms, onion and garlic. Reduce heat to medium-low and cook, stirring frequently, for 10 to 20 minutes or until mushrooms are reduced and tender.

2. Add broth and increase heat to bring the mixture to a gentle boil. Boil gently, stirring occasionally, for 5 minutes or until broth is reduced by about half. Stir in Cashew Cream and yogurt and heat through. Use immediately or store, tightly covered, in the refrigerator for up to 3 days.

Cashew Cream

Makes 1⅓ cups (325 mL)

Use this wherever half-and-half (10%) cream is called for. You can make the sauce thicker by using another ½ cup (125 mL) cashews. It can then substitute for heavy or whipping (35%) cream in recipes. Only one other nut may be substituted for the cashews in this versatile cook's tool, and that is macadamia.

• *Blender*

⅓ cup	cashew nuts	75 mL
½ cup	rice milk or soy milk	125 mL
½ cup	plain yogurt	125 mL

1. In a blender, combine cashews, rice milk and yogurt. Blend until nuts are completely puréed and cream is smooth.

2. Use immediately or store, tightly covered, in the refrigerator for up to 4 days. Shake well before using.

Put this easy-to-make sauce to work with steamed vegetables, or use it with pasta or rice, or with stir-fried vegetables.

Yellow Coconut Curry Sauce

• *Blender*

½ cup	coconut milk	125 mL
¼	onion	¼
6	dried apricots	6
2	cloves garlic or 8 cloves roasted garlic (page 206)	2
1 tsp	grated lemon zest	5 mL
2 tbsp	freshly squeezed lemon juice	30 mL
1 tbsp	coarsely chopped galangal or gingerroot	15 mL
2 tsp	miso	10 mL
1 tsp	hot pepper flakes	5 mL
1 tsp	coriander seeds	5 mL
½ tsp	caraway seeds	2 mL
½ tsp	fennel seeds	2 mL
½ tsp	fenugreek seeds	2 mL
1 tbsp	finely chopped fresh turmeric root or 1 tsp (5 mL) ground turmeric	15 mL
½ cup	Cultured Coconut Milk "Yogurt" (page 23) or store-bought, or plain yogurt	125 mL
½ cup	unsweetened desiccated coconut, optional	125 mL

1. In a blender, combine coconut milk, onion, apricots, garlic, lemon zest and juice, galangal, miso and hot pepper flakes. Process until blended.

2. In a saucepan, combine coriander, caraway, fennel and fenugreek seeds and turmeric root. Toast over medium-high heat, stirring constantly, for 2 to 3 minutes or until seeds begin to pop and their fragrance is released. Scrape coconut-milk mixture into saucepan and simmer, stirring occasionally, for 10 minutes. The sauce should be thick and creamy.

3. Strain into a bowl and stir in yogurt, and coconut, if using. Use immediately or store, tightly covered, in the refrigerator for up to 5 days.

Desserts and Frozen Yogurts

Desserts

Use fresh peaches, nectarines, apricots or cherries or berries (fresh or drained frozen blackberries, black currants, blueberries or elderberries), when they're in season, for this great breakfast dish.

Tip

• Two cans (each 14 oz/398 mL) low-sugar fruit (drained) works when fresh local fruit is not available.

Roasted Fruit with Custard

• *Preheat oven to 350°F (180°C)*
• *10-inch (25 cm) pie plate, lightly oiled*
• *Blender*

4 cups	pitted peeled sliced soft fruit or berries (see Intro and Tip, left)	1 L
2 tbsp	granulated sugar	30 mL

Custard

½ cup	all-purpose flour	125 mL
¼ cup	packed brown sugar	60 mL
Pinch	salt	Pinch
2	eggs, lightly beaten	2
1 cup	rice milk or soy milk	250 mL
1 tsp	vanilla extract	5 mL
¼ tsp	ground nutmeg	1 mL
1 cup	Drained Yogurt (page 162)	250 mL

1. Spread fruit evenly over bottom of prepared pie plate. Sprinkle with granulated sugar.

2. *Custard:* In a blender or large bowl, combine flour, brown sugar, salt, eggs, rice milk, vanilla and nutmeg. Process for 15 seconds or whisk until batter is smooth. Pour over fruit. Bake in preheated oven for 45 minutes or until puffy and golden brown. Serve warm with a dollop of drained yogurt.

Creamy and thick, this is a classic cheesecake. Serve it with any of the fruit or dry toppings found on pages 46 through 58. If you don't have lemon yogurt, use plain yogurt and ¼ cup (60 mL) Lemon Sauce (page 55) instead.

Variation

• *Raspberry Lemon Cheesecake:* Use raspberries instead of blueberries.

Blueberry Lemon Cheesecake

• *Preheat oven to 300°F (150°C)*
• *9-inch (23 cm) springform pan, ungreased*

Crust

1 ½ cups	shortbread cookie or graham cracker crumbs	375 mL
¼ cup	butter, melted	60 mL

Cheesecake

2	packages (each 8 oz/250 g) cream cheese, at room temperature	2
½ cup	granulated sugar	125 mL
3	eggs	3
1 cup	Lemon Yogurt (page 29) or store-bought	250 mL
¼ cup	sweetened condensed milk	60 mL
1 tbsp	grated lemon zest	15 mL
1 tsp	vanilla extract	5 mL
2 cups	fresh blueberries or Berries in Syrup (page 53)	500 mL

1. *Crust:* In a bowl, combine cookie crumbs and butter. Press into bottom and ½ inch (1 cm) up sides of springform pan. Bake in preheated oven for 6 minutes or until firm but not browned. Let cool for 10 minutes or longer.

2. *Cheesecake:* In a large bowl, combine cream cheese and sugar. Using an electric mixer, beat on low speed for 3 to 4 minutes or until light and fluffy. Add eggs, one at a time, beating for about 30 seconds after each addition. Beat for 2 to 3 minutes on low to medium speed until well combined. Add yogurt, condensed milk, lemon zest and vanilla and beat for 2 to 3 minutes on medium speed.

3. Scrape cheesecake mixture over crust in springform pan. Bake in preheated oven for 50 to 60 minutes or until the edge is firm. The center may be cracked and slightly wobbly. Turn off the oven and let cheesecake cool for 30 minutes in the oven with the door ajar. Transfer to a wire cooling rack and let cool completely. Cover and refrigerate for at least 2 hours or overnight. Serve garnished with fresh berries.

Pumpkin Cheesecake

This is a delicious cheesecake and perfect for a different Thanksgiving dessert. Pay attention to the size of the pan and the amounts because the springform pan is filled to within $\frac{1}{4}$ inch (0.5 cm) of the top. You don't need a baking sheet under the cake pan because, although the cake puffs up a bit, it won't overflow the pan as it bakes.

- *Preheat oven to 350°F (180°C)*
- *9-inch (23 cm) springform pan, ungreased*

Crust

I cup	gingersnap cookie crumbs (about 18 to 24 cookies)	250 mL
2 tbsp	butter, softened	30 mL

Cheesecake

2	packages (each 8 oz/250 g) cream cheese, at room temperature	2
I¼ cups	packed brown sugar	300 mL
2	eggs (see Tips, right)	2
I	can (28 oz/796 mL) pure pumpkin purée, divided	I
I cup	plain yogurt	250 mL
⅔ cup	evaporated milk	150 mL
I tsp	ground cinnamon	5 mL
½ tsp	ground nutmeg	2 mL

Topping (see Tips, right)

	Reserved pumpkin purée and cheesecake mixture	
I cup	confectioner's (icing) sugar	250 mL
½ tsp	ground cinnamon	2 mL

1. *Crust:* In a bowl, combine cookie crumbs and butter. Press into bottom and $\frac{1}{2}$ inch (1 cm) up sides of springform pan. Bake in preheated oven for 6 minutes or until firm but not browned. Let cool for 10 minutes or longer.

2. *Cheesecake:* In a large bowl, combine cream cheese and brown sugar. Using an electric mixer, beat on low speed for 3 to 4 minutes or until light and fluffy. Add eggs, one at a time, beating for about 30 seconds after each addition. Beat for 2 to 3 minutes on low to medium speed until well mixed. Transfer $\frac{1}{2}$ cup (125 mL) of the pumpkin purée to a bowl and set aside. Add remaining pumpkin purée, yogurt, evaporated milk, cinnamon and nutmeg and beat for 2 to 3 minutes on medium speed.

- This recipe contains raw eggs. If you are concerned about the safety of using raw eggs, use pasteurized eggs in the shell or pasteurized liquid whole eggs, instead.

- If you choose not to make the pumpkin topping, use a whole 15-oz (425 mL) can of pumpkin (or 1¾ cups/425 mL).

3. Transfer ½ cup (125 mL) of the cheesecake mixture to the reserved pumpkin purée in the bowl. Cover and reserve in the refrigerator for topping. Pour remaining cheesecake mixture over crust in springform pan. Bake for 55 to 65 minutes or until the edge is firm. The center may be cracked and slightly wobbly. Turn off the oven and let cheesecake cool for 30 minutes in the oven with the door ajar. Transfer to a wire cooling rack and let cool completely. Cover and refrigerate for at least 2 hours or overnight.

4. *Topping:* Add confectioner's sugar and cinnamon to reserved pumpkin purée and cheesecake mixture and mix until well blended. Remove ring from springform pan. Spread topping over top of chilled cheesecake. Serve immediately or store in the refrigerator for up to 24 hours until ready to serve.

Blackberry Sabayon

2 cups	fresh or frozen (drained) blackberries	500 mL
⅔ cup	granulated sugar, divided	150 mL
½ cup	milk	125 mL
2	eggs, separated	2
1 tbsp	crème de cassis or blackberry syrup	15 mL
¾ cup	plain yogurt	175 mL

1. In a large bowl, toss together blackberries and ¼ cup (60 mL) of the sugar. Set aside.

2. In a saucepan, combine milk with ¼ cup (60 mL) of sugar. Heat gently over medium heat, stirring constantly, for 2 minutes or until bubbles form around side of pan. In a bowl, beat egg yolks together. Drop a spoonful of the hot milk mixture into yolks and stir. Add more hot milk to yolks, by the spoonful, until yolks are warm. Add yolks to milk mixture in pan. Heat over medium heat, stirring constantly, for 4 minutes or until custard thickens and coats the back of a metal spoon. Remove from heat, stir in crème de cassis and let cool.

3. Meanwhile, in a bowl, using a rotary or electric mixer, beat egg whites until soft peaks form. Sprinkle with remaining sugar and beat until stiff peaks form. Fold yogurt and meringue into custard. Pour over blackberries and stir lightly to mix.

Not too sweet, this dish is very good for brunch or breakfast. The Almond Pie Crust is a healthier alternative to traditional pastry.

Tip

* Make the crust and line the pan up to 2 days in advance. Cover tightly and store in the refrigerator until ready to fill and bake.

Variation

* For a savory twist, add 1 tbsp (15 mL) finely chopped onion in Step 2.

Apple and Cheddar Cheese Flan

* *Preheat oven to 400°F (200°C)*
* *9-inch (23 cm) flan or pie pan*
* *Food processor or blender*

6	apples	6
1 cup	Drained Yogurt (page 162)	250 mL
¼ cup	creamed cottage cheese	60 mL
1	egg, beaten	1
2 cups	finely shredded Cheddar cheese	500 mL
½ cup	organic cane sugar	125 mL
1 tbsp	chopped fresh sweet cicely or mint	15 mL

Almond Pie Crust

20	arrowroot or vanilla cookies	20
½ cup	whole almonds (unblanched)	125 mL
⅓ cup	butter	75 mL
2 tbsp	organic cane sugar	30 mL

1. Peel, core and slice 5 of the apples. In a large bowl, mix drained yogurt and cottage cheese together. Beat in egg. Add sliced apples, Cheddar cheese, sugar and sweet cicely and stir well.

2. *Almond Pie Crust:* In a food processor or blender, combine cookies and almonds. Process for 20 seconds or until medium-fine.

3. In a saucepan, melt butter over medium heat. Remove from heat, stir in almond mixture and sugar. Press crumb crust into pan. Chill until ready to fill.

4. Spoon cheese mixture over crust, spreading to level the top. Core and thinly slice remaining apple, leaving the peel on. Arrange over top of cheese mixture. Bake in preheated oven for 1 hour or until crust is lightly browned and apples are tender. Let stand for 10 minutes before serving.

Lemon Soufflé

This is an easy and light dessert. Serve it warm, right out of the oven.

- *Preheat oven to 325°F (160°C)*
- *Double boiler*
- *7-inch (18 cm) soufflé dish, buttered*

⅓ cup	all-purpose flour	75 mL
1½ cups	plain yogurt	375 mL
3	eggs, separated	3
¾ cup	granulated sugar, divided	175 mL
	Grated zest and juice of 1 lemon	

1. In a bowl, sprinkle flour over yogurt and mix well with a fork. Set aside.

2. In the top of a double boiler, beat egg yolks with ½ cup (125 mL) of the sugar. Stir in lemon zest and juice. Set over double boiler of simmering water. Add yogurt mixture and cook, stirring constantly, until custard thickens and coats the back of a metal spoon. Remove from heat and let cool.

3. In a bowl, using a rotary or electric mixer, beat egg whites until soft peaks form. Sprinkle with remaining sugar and beat until stiff peaks form. Fold meringue into cooled custard and scrape into prepared dish. Bake in preheated oven for 40 minutes or until soufflé is puffed and lightly browned.

Raspberry Fudge Cookies

Soft, moist and chewy, these cookies are as close as you can get to fudge in a lower-fat baked product. They are mixed right in a saucepan, so cleanup is easy. Be sure to bake these cookies until they firm up because they will be soft and fall apart if you undercook them. To serve, layer crumbled Raspberry Fudge Cookies with homemade fruit yogurt or Blackberry Sabayon (page 270) in parfait glasses for a quick and elegant dessert.

- *Preheat oven to 350°F (180°C)*
- *2 baking sheets, lightly coated with cooking spray*

⅓ cup	coconut oil, softened, or butter	75 mL
⅔ cup	granulated sugar	150 mL
½ cup	unsweetened cocoa powder	125 mL
⅓ cup	packed brown sugar	75 mL
⅔ cup	Fruit-Bottom Yogurt with raspberry preserves (page 25) or 1 container (6 oz/175 g) store-bought	150 mL
1 tsp	vanilla extract	5 mL
1¼ cups	all-purpose flour	300 mL
¼ tsp	baking soda	1 mL
⅛ tsp	salt	0.5 mL

1. In a saucepan, melt coconut oil over medium heat. Turn heat off but keep pan on the warm element. One at a time, stir in granulated sugar, cocoa powder and brown sugar, mixing well after each addition. Add yogurt and vanilla and stir to mix well.

2. Set a sieve over the pan and sift in flour, baking soda and salt. Mix well. Drop by level tablespoonful, 2 inches (5 cm) apart, onto prepared baking sheets. Bake in preheated oven for 9 to 10 minutes or until puffed and set. Let cool on pans for 2 minutes, then transfer to wire cooling racks to cool completely. Store in an airtight container for up to 5 days.

Lemon Yogurt Cake

Very similar to a pound cake, but with less butter, this is a cake with substance. Use lemon yogurt if you have it.

- *Preheat oven to 350°F (180°C)*
- *10-inch (25 cm) springform pan, lightly oiled*

I cup	butter, softened	250 mL
I cup	granulated sugar	250 mL
3	large eggs	3
I tbsp	grated lemon zest	15 mL
I tsp	vanilla extract	5 mL
2½ cups	all-purpose flour	625 mL
I tsp	baking powder	5 mL
I tsp	baking soda	5 mL
½ tsp	salt	2 mL
I cup	Lemon Yogurt (page 29) or plain yogurt	250 mL

Lemon Icing

¾ cup	confectioner's (icing) sugar	175 mL
½ cup	freshly squeezed lemon juice	125 mL
3 tbsp	plain yogurt	45 mL

1. In a bowl, using a wooden spoon, cream together butter and sugar. Beat in eggs, one at a time, until smooth. Stir in lemon zest and vanilla. In a separate bowl, sift together flour, baking powder, baking soda and salt. Stir flour mixture into butter mixture alternately with lemon yogurt, making three additions of flour mixture and two of yogurt, mixing well after each addition.

2. Scrape batter into prepared springform pan and bake for 1 hour or until a cake tester comes out clean when inserted into middle of cake. Let cake cool in pan for 5 minutes.

3. *Lemon Icing:* Meanwhile, in a bowl, combine sugar and lemon juice and mix well. Add yogurt. Remove ring from the pan and invert cake onto a serving plate. Spoon lemon icing over warm cake, allowing syrup to soak into the top and down the sides of the cake.

Makes about 3 cups (1 L)

Use French Vanilla Yogurt (page 24) or store-bought vanilla yogurt for this simple and delicious frozen yogurt. Chilling the yogurt mixture in the refrigerator before freezing it in the ice cream maker shortens the freezing time.

Tip

* Be sure to use a good-quality yogurt and drain it for at least 4 hours because draining makes the frozen yogurt creamier.

Vanilla Frozen Yogurt

* *Ice cream maker*

5 cups	plain yogurt (see Tip, left)	1.25 mL
¾ cup	granulated sugar	175 mL
1 tsp	vanilla extract	5 mL

1. Place yogurt in a cheesecloth-lined stainless-steel strainer or colander set over a bowl. Cover the yogurt with plastic wrap. Set the bowl and strainer in the refrigerator and let the watery whey drain away from the yogurt solids for 4 hours. Measure 3 cups (750 mL) drained yogurt, reserving any extra for another use.

2. In a bowl, combine drained yogurt, sugar and vanilla. Chill in the refrigerator for at least 1 hour. Churn in an ice cream maker, following manufacturer's instructions. Store in a container with tight-fitting lid in the freezer for up to 2 weeks.

Strawberry Frozen Yogurt

Use this basic recipe for other fresh or frozen berries or stone-fruit frozen yogurt.

Tip

* Be sure to use a good-quality yogurt and drain it for at least 4 hours because draining makes the frozen yogurt creamier.

* *Ice cream maker*

4 cups	plain yogurt (see Tip, left)	I L
½ cup	crushed fresh or frozen strawberries	125 mL
¼ cup	liquid honey or corn syrup	60 mL

1. Place yogurt in a cheesecloth-lined stainless-steel strainer or colander set over a bowl. Cover the yogurt with plastic wrap. Set the bowl and strainer in the refrigerator and let the watery whey drain away from the yogurt solids for 4 hours. Measure 2½ cups (625 mL) drained yogurt, reserving any extra for another use.

2. In a bowl, combine drained yogurt, strawberries and honey. Chill in the refrigerator for at least 1 hour. Churn in an ice cream maker, following manufacturer's instructions. Store in a container with tight-fitting lid in the freezer for up to 2 weeks.

Lemon Frozen Yogurt

Everyone loves this lightly flavored lemony treat. You can increase the amount of grated lemon zest for a tarter taste, but try it my way first.

* *Ice cream maker*

I ½ cups	heavy or whipping (35%) cream	375 mL
I tbsp	finely grated lemon zest	15 mL
I cup	granulated sugar	250 mL
I cup	plain yogurt	250 mL
¼ cup	freshly squeezed lemon juice	60 mL

1. In a saucepan, combine cream and lemon zest. Heat over medium-low heat, stirring frequently, for about 4 minutes or until small bubbles form around side of pan. (Do not let boil.) Remove from heat and stir in sugar until dissolved. Let cool to room temperature.

2. Add yogurt and lemon juice and stir well. Refrigerate for 2 hours or until well chilled. Churn in an ice cream maker, following manufacturer's instructions. Store in a container with tight-fitting lid in the freezer for up to 2 weeks.

Tropical Frozen Yogurt

The fresh tropical fruit blended with coconut and cream make this an exotic frozen dessert. You can use fresh or frozen or canned (drained) fruit. If you have Coconut Yogurt (page 30), use it here.

Tip

* Be sure to use a good-quality yogurt and drain it for at least 4 hours because draining makes the frozen yogurt creamier.

• *Ice cream maker*

2 cups	plain yogurt (seeTip, left)	500 mL
1½ cups	table (18%) cream	375 mL
3 tbsp	chopped pineapple	45 mL
3 tbsp	chopped mango	45 mL
1 tbsp	pure creamed coconut (page 31) or unsweetened desiccated coconut	15 mL
⅔ cup	liquid honey	150 mL
1 tbsp	freshly squeezed lemon juice	15 mL

1. Place yogurt in a cheesecloth-lined stainless-steel strainer or colander set over a bowl. Cover the yogurt with plastic wrap. Set the bowl and strainer in the refrigerator and let the watery whey drain away from the yogurt solids for 4 hours. Measure 1 cup (250 mL) drained yogurt, reserving any extra for another use.

2. In a saucepan, combine cream, pineapple, mango and creamed coconut. Heat over medium-low heat, stirring frequently, for about 4 minutes or until small bubbles form around side of pan. (Do not let boil.) Remove from heat and stir in honey until dissolved. Let cool to room temperature.

3. Add drained yogurt and lemon juice and stir well. Refrigerate for 2 hours or until well chilled. Churn in an ice cream maker, following manufacturer's instructions. Store in a container with tight-fitting lid in the freezer for up to 2 weeks.

Mocha Frozen Yogurt

- *Ice cream maker*

1 ½ cups	heavy or whipping (35%) cream	375 mL
¼ cup	granulated sugar	60 mL
2 tbsp	instant coffee granules	30 mL
1 cup	plain yogurt	250 mL
¼ cup	chocolate syrup	60 mL

1. In a saucepan, heat cream over medium-low heat, stirring frequently, for about 4 minutes or until small bubbles form around side of pan. (Do not let boil.) Remove from heat and stir in sugar and coffee granules until dissolved. Let cool to room temperature.

2. Add yogurt and chocolate syrup and stir well. Refrigerate for 2 hours or until well chilled. Churn in an ice cream maker, following manufacturer's instructions. Store in a container with tight-fitting lid in the freezer for up to 2 weeks.

Orange Cream Frozen Yogurt

- *Ice cream maker*

1 ½ cups	heavy or whipping (35%) cream	375 mL
2 tbsp	finely grated orange zest	30 mL
½ cup	liquid honey or corn syrup	125 mL
1 cup	plain yogurt	250 mL
¼ cup	freshly squeezed orange juice	60 mL

1. In a saucepan, combine cream and orange zest. Heat over medium-low heat, stirring frequently, for about 4 minutes or until small bubbles form around side of the pan. (Do not let boil.) Remove from heat and stir in honey until dissolved. Let cool to room temperature.

2. Add yogurt and orange juice and stir well. Refrigerate for 2 hours or until well chilled. Churn in an ice cream maker, following manufacturer's instructions. Store in a container with tight-fitting lid in the freezer for up to 2 weeks.

This is loaded with fruit and yogurt, with a little table cream. You can use whole, chopped, diced, puréed or strained frozen fruit for this easy and lower-fat frozen yogurt. There's no need to thaw the fruit before blending and churning.

Berries and Cream Frozen Yogurt

• *Ice cream maker*

½ cup	table (18%) cream	125 mL
¼ cup	granulated sugar	60 mL
2 cups	plain yogurt	500 mL
1 cup	chopped fresh or frozen (drained) berries	250 mL

1. In a saucepan, heat cream over medium-low heat, stirring frequently, for about 4 minutes or until small bubbles form around side of pan. (Do not let boil.) Remove from heat and stir in sugar until dissolved. Let cool to room temperature.

2. Add yogurt and berries and stir well. Refrigerate for 2 hours or until well chilled. Churn in an ice cream maker, following manufacturer's instructions. Store in a container with tight-fitting lid in the freezer for up to 2 weeks.

Chocolate Frozen Yogurt

Try adding ½ cup
(125 mL) chopped
bittersweet chocolate
near the end of
churning for extra
chocolate punch.

Tip

• Be sure to use a
good-quality yogurt
and drain it for at
least 4 hours because
draining makes
the frozen yogurt
creamier.

• *Ice cream maker*

3 cups	plain yogurt (see Tip, left)	750 mL
½ cup	granulated sugar	125 mL
3 tbsp	unsweetened cocoa powder	45 mL
I tbsp	cornstarch	15 mL
I cup	2% milk	250 mL
½ cup	table (18%) cream	125 mL
½ cup	chocolate syrup	125 mL
¼ cup	light (white) corn syrup	60 mL
½ tsp	vanilla extract	2 mL

1. Place yogurt in a cheesecloth-lined stainless-steel strainer or colander set over a bowl. Cover the yogurt with plastic wrap. Set the bowl and strainer in the refrigerator, and let the watery whey drain away from the yogurt solids for 4 hours. Measure 1½ cups (375 mL) drained yogurt, reserving any extra for another use.

2. In a saucepan, combine sugar, cocoa powder and cornstarch. Stir in milk and cream. Heat over medium-low heat, stirring constantly, for 2 to 4 minutes or until thickened. Remove from heat and stir in chocolate syrup and corn syrup. Let cool to room temperature.

3. Stir in drained yogurt and vanilla. Refrigerate for 2 hours or until well chilled. Churn in an ice cream maker, following manufacturer's instructions. Store in a container with tight-fitting lid in the freezer for up to 2 weeks.

Beverages

Grapefruit Lassi

Yogurt-based drinks are a popular and cooling drink from South Asia. Spices and herbs are often used to flavor these drinks, but I like to use fresh fruit in them.

• *Blender*

½ cup	grapefruit juice	125 mL
I	orange, segmented	I
⅓ cup	plain yogurt	75 mL
I tbsp	liquid honey, or to taste	15 mL

I. In a blender, combine grapefruit juice, orange segments, yogurt and honey. Secure lid and blend (from low to high if using a variable speed blender) until smooth. Pour into a glass.

Tropical Lassi

This is definitely a sweet treat for a midday snack.

• *Blender*

½ cup	pineapple juice	125 mL
I	fresh mango, seeded	I
I	fresh guava, seeded	I
⅓ cup	plain yogurt	75 mL
⅛ tsp	ground cinnamon, optional	0.5 mL

I. In a blender, combine pineapple juice, mango, guava and yogurt. Secure lid and blend (from low to high if using a variable speed blender) until smooth. Pour into glasses and garnish with cinnamon, if using.

Pear and Basil Lassi

The nutmeg-flavored and spicy basil complements the more delicate pear taste in this drink.

• *Blender*

½ cup	apple juice	125 mL
2	ripe pears	2
I tsp	chopped fresh basil	5 mL
½ cup	Drained Yogurt (page 162)	125 mL

I. In a blender, combine apple juice, pears and basil. Secure lid and blend (from low to high if using a variable speed blender) until smooth. Pour into glasses and spoon drained yogurt into the glass. Serve with spoons.

The yogurt lightens up the drink, making it slightly lower in fat than traditional eggnog. For a festive toast, add a jigger of light or dark rum to each glass before ladling in the eggnog. You can double this recipe for a larger group.

Tip

• This recipe contains raw egg whites. If you are concerned about the safety of raw egg whites, use pasteurized egg whites or you may not wish to make this recipe.

Yogurt Eggnog

3 cups	table (18%) cream	750 mL
½ cup	granulated sugar	125 mL
4	eggs, at room temperature, separated (see Tip, left)	4
1 cup	plain yogurt	250 mL
1 cup	sherry or cognac	250 mL
3 tbsp	confectioner's (icing) sugar	45 mL
1	fresh whole nutmeg or 2 tbsp (30 mL) ground nutmeg	1

1. In a saucepan, heat cream over medium-low heat, stirring occasionally, for 5 minutes or until steam rises from cream. Add granulated sugar, stirring until dissolved.

2. Meanwhile, in a bowl, beat egg yolks. Drop 1 tbsp (15 mL) of the hot cream mixture into yolks and beat in. Keep adding small amounts of the cream mixture until yolks are warmed. Increase heat to medium. Scrape yolk mixture into cream mixture in pan and cook, stirring constantly, for about 10 minutes or until custard has thickened. Remove from heat and let cool to room temperature. Stir in yogurt and sherry and mix well. Cover and refrigerate for 1 hour or overnight, until well chilled.

3. In a deep bowl, using a rotary or an electric mixer, beat egg whites until foamy. Add about 1 tbsp (15 mL) confectioner's sugar at a time, beating well after each addition. Continue beating until soft peaks form. Gently fold meringue into egg yolk mixture. Transfer to a pitcher or punch bowl and keep refrigerated until serving time. Set out whole nutmeg with a small grater (or ground nutmeg and a spoon) for garnishing the drinks.

Moroccan Iced Coffee

This drink is a great summer cooler and after-dinner drink. Try it hot instead of chilled.

2 cups	hot strong brewed coffee	500 mL
I to 2 tbsp	lightly packed brown sugar, or to taste	15 to 30 mL
I tsp	Moroccan Spice Blend (approx.) (below)	5 mL
1/4 cup	plain yogurt	60 mL
3 tbsp	sweetened condensed milk (approx.)	45 mL
1/4 tsp	vanilla extract	I mL
	Ice cubes	

1. In a glass jug or jar with a lid, combine coffee, brown sugar and spice blend. Whisk or shake to dissolve sugar. Let cool.

2. In a bowl, combine yogurt, condensed milk and vanilla. Add to coffee mixture and whisk or shake. Taste and add more sugar, spice blend or condensed milk, if needed. Chill in the refrigerator for several hours or until cold. Whisk or shake and serve over ice.

Makes 2½ tbsp (37 mL)

The spices give an exotic flavor to drink mixtures.

Moroccan Spice Blend

2 tsp	ground ginger	10 mL
2 tsp	whole fennel seeds	10 mL
I tsp	ground cardamom	5 mL
I tsp	ground cinnamon	5 mL
1/2 tsp	ground cloves	2 mL
1/2 tsp	ground black peppercorns	2 mL
1/4 tsp	ground nutmeg	I mL

1. In a bowl, combine ginger, fennel seeds, cardamom, cinnamon, cloves, peppercorns and nutmeg. Stir to mix well. Store in a dark glass jar with lid in a cool dark place.

Serve this feathery light drink (with its papain and bromelain enzymes) to aid in the digestive process.

After Dinner Cocktail

• *Blender*

⅔ cup	mineral water	150 mL
2	papayas, seeded	2
½ cup	plain yogurt	125 mL
½	pineapple, sliced	½
1	piece (½ inch/1 cm) gingerroot, peeled	1
	Ice cubes, optional	

1. In a blender, combine mineral water, papayas, yogurt, pineapple and ginger. Secure lid and blend (from low to high if using a variable speed blender) until smooth. Pour into cocktail glasses over ice, if using.

This is a thick and satisfying drink for mid-morning or in the afternoon when a healthy snack is welcome.

Tip

• Use any berry — raspberry, strawberry, blueberry or blackberry — for this sweet summer drink.

Best Berry Smoothie

• *Blender*

¾ cup	pineapple juice	175 mL
3 tbsp	plain yogurt	45 mL
1 cup	fresh or frozen berries (see Tip, left)	250 mL
1	banana, peeled	1

1. In a blender, combine pineapple juice, yogurt, berries and banana until smooth. Secure lid and blend (from low to high if using a variable speed blender) until smooth. Pour into a glass.

Breakfast Cocktail

Fresh carrot juice is the key to this great-tasting and healthy morning starter.

• *Blender*

½ cup	carrot juice	125 mL
1	mango, halved	1
1	papaya, quartered	1
1	apple, quartered	1
1	piece (½ inch/1 cm) gingerroot, peeled	1
¼ cup	plain yogurt	60 mL

1. In a blender, combine carrot juice, mango, papaya, apple, ginger and yogurt. Secure lid and blend (from low to high if using a variable speed blender) until smooth.

Citrus Cocktail

The yogurt in this drink adds protein to the vitamin C.

Tip

• The sweetness of this smoothie will increase significantly if you use sweetened frozen yogurt rather than plain yogurt.

• *Blender*

½ cup	freshly squeezed orange juice	125 mL
¼ cup	grapefruit juice	60 mL
12	strawberries	12
1	piece (½ inch/1 cm) gingerroot, peeled	1
1 tbsp	wheat germ or chopped almonds	15 mL
¼ cup	plain or frozen yogurt	60 mL

1. In a blender, combine orange juice, grapefruit juice, strawberries, ginger, wheat germ and yogurt. Secure lid and blend (from low to high if using a variable speed blender) until smooth.

Kids love the blue tinge of this healthy drink.

Creamy Pineapple Mocktail

- *Blender*

¹⁄₂	pineapple, sliced	¹⁄₂
I	mango, pitted	I
I cup	blueberries	250 mL
¹⁄₂ cup	plain yogurt	125 mL

I. In a blender, combine pineapple, mango and blueberries. Secure lid and blend (from low to high if using a variable speed blender) until smooth. Whisk together with yogurt and pour into glasses.

High in antioxidants, this drink should be high on your list of healthy menu options.

Granate Berry Smoothie

- *Blender*

¹⁄₂ cup	pomegranate juice	125 mL
¹⁄₂ cup	pomegranate seeds	125 mL
¹⁄₂ cup	raspberries	125 mL
2 tbsp	plain yogurt	30 mL

I. In a blender, combine pomegranate juice, pomegranate seeds and raspberries. Secure lid and blend (from low to high if using a variable speed blender) until smooth. Pour into glass and stir in yogurt.

Orange Slushie

Keep açai berries on hand for an antioxidant boost and delicious flavor.

• *Blender*

¼ cup	plain yogurt	60 mL
3	apricots, halved	3
I	orange, segmented and seeded	I
¼ cup	frozen strawberries	60 mL
¼ cup	frozen açai berries, partially thawed	60 mL

I. In a blender, combine yogurt, apricots, orange, strawberries and açai berries. Secure lid and blend (from low to high if using a variable speed blender) until smooth. Serve with a spoon.

Tropi-Cocktail

Serves 2

Almost as thick as a milk shake, this makes a great after-school snack.

• *Blender*

¼ cup	apricot nectar or freshly squeezed orange juice	60 mL
½ cup	plain yogurt	125 mL
¼	cantaloupe or honeydew melon, cubed	¼
½	mango	½
I	slice papaya	I
I	banana, cut into chunks	I

I. In a blender, combine apricot nectar, yogurt, cantaloupe, mango, papaya and banana. Secure lid and blend (from low to high if using a variable speed blender) until smooth.

The benefit of this fast
breakfast-to-go is its
high nutritional value.

Tips

- Start the prep for
  this in the evening
  for a nutritious
  breakfast drink the
  next day.

- This is a substantial
  and very thick
  mixture that may
  be thinned with
  more juice.

Apricot and Oatmeal Breakfast Special

• Blender or food processor

½ cup	chopped dried apricots	125 mL
1	package (1 oz/30 g) instant oatmeal (about ½ cup/125 mL)	1
1 cup	boiling water	250 mL
1½ cups	orange juice, preferably freshly squeezed	375 mL
2 tbsp	plain yogurt	30 mL
2	pitted dates	2

1. In a small bowl, combine apricots, instant oatmeal and boiling water. Cover and let soak for at least 20 minutes or overnight.

2. In a blender or food processor, combine orange juice, apricot-oatmeal mixture and any soaking liquid, yogurt and dates. Secure lid and blend (from low to high if using a variable speed blender) until smooth.

Fresh or dried apricots
work in this sweet
drink.

Apricot Explosion

• Blender

½ cup	pineapple juice	125 mL
2	apricots, halved	2
1	pineapple wedge, cut into chunks	1
¼ cup	apricot- or peach-flavored frozen yogurt	60 mL

1. In a blender, combine pineapple juice, apricots, pineapple and frozen yogurt. Secure lid and blend (from low to high if using a variable speed blender) until smooth.

Add a dash of almond flavoring for an intense almond taste.

* If using wild elderberries that you have gathered yourself, make absolutely certain you are able to identify it correctly. Raw elderberries can make some people sick. If in doubt, cook first before using in smoothies.

Berry Yogurt Flip

• *Blender*

½ cup	cranberry-raspberry juice	125 mL
1 cup	blueberries or elderberries*	250 mL
½ cup	açai berries, partially thawed	125 mL
6	almonds	6
½ cup	plain yogurt	125 mL

1. In a blender, combine cranberry-raspberry juice, blueberries, açai berries and almonds. Secure lid and blend on low for 30 seconds. Add yogurt and blend on high until smooth.

Use blueberries or black cherries in place of the black currants here.

Black Currant Smoothie

• *Blender*

⅔ cup	apple juice	150 mL
½ cup	black currants	125 mL
1	banana, cut into chunks	1
⅓ cup	plain yogurt	75 mL
2 tbsp	liquid honey, or to taste	30 mL

1. In a blender, combine apple juice, currants, banana, yogurt and honey. Secure lid and blend (from low to high if using a variable speed blender) until smooth.

CocoNog

• *Blender*

½ cup	coconut milk or coconut cream	125 mL
4	frozen banana chunks	4
½ cup	Cultured Coconut Milk "Yogurt" (page 23) or plain yogurt, drained	125 mL
Pinch	ground nutmeg	Pinch
3	ice cubes	3

1. In a blender, combine creamed coconut, banana, yogurt, nutmeg and ice. Secure lid and blend (from low to high if using a variable speed blender) until smooth.

Grapefruit Greetings

• *Blender*

1	can (10 oz/284 mL) mandarin orange segments with juice	1
2 tbsp	freshly squeezed lemon juice	30 mL
1	grapefruit, segmented and seeded	1
1	banana, cut into chunks	1
1	starfruit, halved	1
2	pitted dates	2
½ cup	plain yogurt	125 mL

1. In a blender, combine orange segments with juice, lemon juice, grapefruit, banana, starfruit, dates and yogurt. Secure lid and blend (from low to high if using a variable speed blender) until smooth.

Use fresh figs whenever available.

Maple Ginger Fig Smoothie

• *Blender*

1/4 cup	freshly squeezed orange juice	60 mL
4	fresh or dried figs	4
1/3 cup	plain or fruit-flavored yogurt	75 mL
3 tbsp	pure maple syrup	45 mL
1 tsp	grated gingerroot	5 mL

1. In a blender, combine orange juice, figs, yogurt, maple syrup and ginger. Secure lid and blend (from low to high if using a variable speed blender) until smooth.

Using fresh peppermint adds even more refreshing zing to this cool quencher.

Minty Peach Smoothie

• *Blender*

1/2 cup	peach or apricot nectar	125 mL
1/4 cup	plain yogurt	60 mL
2 tbsp	freshly squeezed lemon juice	30 mL
1 cup	frozen peach slices	250 mL
1	honeydew melon wedge, cubed	1
1 tbsp	chopped fresh peppermint	15 mL

1. In a blender, combine peach nectar, yogurt, lemon juice, peaches, melon and peppermint. Secure lid and blend (from low to high if using a variable speed blender) until smooth.

Serves 3 or 4

This is one drink that can be made with any flavor of yogurt. I particularly like the Strawberry Yogurt (page 26) here.

Peach Paradise Smoothie

• *Blender*

½ cup	evaporated milk	125 mL
¼ cup	blueberries	60 mL
2	peaches, halved	2
3 tbsp	plain or peach-flavored yogurt	45 mL
2 tbsp	chopped almonds	30 mL
¼ tsp	ground cinnamon	1 mL

1. In a blender, combine evaporated milk, blueberries, peaches, yogurt, almonds and cinnamon. Secure lid and process, using the chop or pulse function, until smooth.

Serves 2

Kiwifruit is a great partner for yogurt in this combo.

Pineapple Kiwi Smoothie

• *Blender*

½ cup	pineapple juice	125 mL
2	kiwifruits, quartered	2
2	apricots, halved	2
1	mango, halved	1
½ cup	plain yogurt	125 mL
¼ tsp	ground ginger	1 mL

1. In a blender, combine pineapple juice, kiwis, apricots, mango, yogurt and ginger. Secure lid and blend (from low to high if using a variable speed blender) until smooth.

Tropical in flavor, this can be served in place of dessert.

Tip

• The sweetness of this smoothie will increase significantly if you use sweetened frozen yogurt rather than plain yogurt.

Pineapple Soy Smoothie

• *Blender*

1/4 cup	pineapple juice	60 mL
1/4 cup	unflavored soy milk	60 mL
1	banana, cut into chunks	1
2	pineapple wedges, cut into chunks	2
1/2 cup	plain yogurt or fruit-flavored frozen yogurt, such as Lemon Frozen Yogurt (page 276)	125 mL

1. In a blender, combine pineapple juice, soy milk, banana, pineapple and yogurt. Secure lid and blend (from low to high if using a variable speed blender) until smooth.

As a dessert drink, this is exceptional.

Tip

• Try using homemade frozen yogurt (see recipes, pages 275 to 280) in this smoothie.

Pine-Berry Smoothie

• *Blender*

1	can (14 oz/398 mL) pitted cherries with juice	1
1/4 cup	plain or frozen yogurt	60 mL
2	pineapple wedges, cut into chunks	2
1 cup	blueberries	250 mL
1/2 cup	black currants	125 mL

1. In a blender, combine cherries with juice, yogurt, pineapple, blueberries and black currants. Secure lid and blend (from low to high if using a variable speed blender) until smooth.

Plum Lico

Use black or yellow plums and add honey to taste if using a tart variety.

* Avoid licorice if you have high blood pressure. The prolonged use of licorice is not recommended under any circumstances.

- *Blender*

¼ cup	pineapple juice	60 mL
¼ cup	plain yogurt	60 mL
2	plums, quartered	2
1 cup	pitted cherries	250 mL
½	grapefruit, segmented and seeded	½
¼ tsp	ground licorice*, optional	1 mL

1. In a blender, combine pineapple juice, yogurt, plums, cherries, grapefruit, and licorice, if using. Secure lid and blend (from low to high if using a variable speed blender) until smooth.

Raspberry Smoothie

If you keep fruit in the freezer, you will always have the makings for a great-tasting drink.

- *Blender*

½ cup	freshly squeezed orange juice	125 mL
1 cup	raspberries	250 mL
2	apricots, halved	2
1	peach, halved	1
¼ cup	plain yogurt	60 mL

1. In a blender, combine orange juice, raspberries, apricots, peach and yogurt. Secure lid and blend (from low to high if using a variable speed blender) until smooth.

Rhubarb Pie Smoothie

Strawberry and rhubarb is a delicious combination for pies, and it works beautifully in this drink.

- *Blender*

⅓ cup	raspberry juice	75 mL
1 cup	sweetened cooked rhubarb	250 mL
½ cup	halved strawberries	125 mL
2 tbsp	plain yogurt	30 mL

1. In a blender, combine raspberry juice, rhubarb, strawberries and yogurt. Secure lid and blend (from low to high if using a variable speed blender) until smooth.

Pink and pretty, the
yogurt mixes with the
colorful berries for a
pastel drink.

Sour Cherry Smoothie

• *Blender*

¼ cup	cranberry juice	60 mL
I cup	pitted black cherries	250 mL
½ cup	raspberries	125 mL
⅓ cup	plain yogurt	75 mL

I. In a blender, combine cranberry juice, cherries, raspberries
and yogurt. Secure lid and blend (from low to high if using a
variable speed blender) until smooth.

Using lemon juice in
smoothies or juice lends
a fresh taste.

Strawberry Swirl

• *Blender*

½ cup	cranberry-raspberry juice	125 mL
2 tbsp	freshly squeezed lemon juice	30 mL
10	frozen strawberries	10
¼ cup	frozen raspberries	60 mL
2 tbsp	plain yogurt	30 mL

I. In a blender, combine cranberry-raspberry juice, lemon
juice, strawberries, raspberries and yogurt. Secure lid and
blend (from low to high if using a variable speed blender)
until smooth.

Wake Up and Shine

• *Blender*

1/3 cup	freshly squeezed orange juice	75 mL
1/2 cup	halved strawberries	125 mL
1/2	grapefruit, segmented and seeded	1/2
2 tbsp	plain yogurt	30 mL
1 tsp	blue-green algae, optional	5 mL

1. In a blender, combine orange juice, strawberries, grapefruit, yogurt, and algae, if using. Secure lid and blend (from low to high if using a variable speed blender) until smooth.

Watermelon Smoothie

The yogurt gives substance to this drink.

• *Blender*

1/4 cup	freshly squeezed orange juice	60 mL
1 tbsp	freshly squeezed lemon juice	15 mL
1 cup	chopped watermelon	250 mL
2	plums, quartered	2
1/3 cup	plain yogurt	75 mL

1. In a blender, combine orange juice, lemon juice, watermelon, plums and yogurt. Secure lid and blend (from low to high if using a variable speed blender) until smooth.

Glossary

Adaptogen: A substance that builds resistance to stress by balancing the functions of the glands and immune response, thus strengthening the immune system, nervous system and glandular system. Adaptogens promote overall vitality. Examples: Astragalus and ginseng.

Allylic sulfides: See Organosulfides, page 302.

Alterative: A substance that gradually changes a condition by restoring health.

Amino acid: See Protein, page 302.

Analgesic: A substance that relieves pain by acting as a nervine, antiseptic or counterirritant. *Examples:* German chamomile, meadowsweet and nutmeg.

Anodyne: A substance that relieves pain. *Example:* Clove.

Anthocyanins: See Phenolic compounds, page 302.

Antibiotic: Meaning "against life," an antibiotic is a substance that kills infectious agents, including bacteria and fungi, without endangering health. *Examples:* Garlic, green tea, lavender, sage and thyme.

Anticatarrhal: A substance that reduces the production of mucus. *Examples:* Garlic and marshmallow.

Anti-inflammatory: A substance that controls or reduces swelling, redness, pain and heat, which are normal bodily reactions to injury or infection. *Examples:* German chamomile and St. John's wort.

Antimicrobial: A substance that destroys or inhibits the growth of disease-causing bacteria or other microorganisms.

Antioxidant: A compound that protects cells by preventing polyunsaturated fatty acids (PUFAs) in cell membranes from oxidizing, or breaking down. Antioxidants do this by neutralizing free radicals (see Free radical, page 300). Vitamins C and E and beta-carotene are antioxidant nutrients, and foods high in them have antioxidant properties. *Examples:* Alfalfa, beet greens, dandelion leaf, parsley, garlic, thyme and watercress.

Antipyretic: A substance that reduces fever. *Examples:* German chamomile, sage and yarrow.

Antiseptic: A substance used to prevent or reduce the growth of disease germs in order to prevent infection. Examples: Cabbage, calendula, clove, garlic, German chamomile, honey, nutmeg, onion, parsley, peppermint, rosemary, salt, thyme, turmeric and vinegar.

Antispasmodic: A substance that relieves muscle spasms or cramps, including colic. *Examples:* German chamomile, ginger, licorice and peppermint.

Astringent: A drying and contracting substance that reduces secretions from the skin. Examples: Cinnamon, lemon, sage and thyme.

Beta-carotene: The natural coloring agent (carotenoid) that gives fruits and vegetables (such as carrots) their deep orange color. It converts in the body to vitamin A. Eating foods high in beta-carotene helps prevent cancer, lowers your risk of heart disease, increases immunity, lowers your risk of cataracts and improves mental function. You can get beta-carotene in squash, carrots, yams, sweet potatoes, pumpkins and red peppers.

Betaine: A phytochemical that nourishes and strengthens the liver and gallbladder. It is found in high concentrations in beets.

Boron: A trace mineral that boosts the estrogen level in the blood, boron is also thought to help prevent calcium loss that leads to osteoporosis and to affect the brain's electrical activity. It is found in legumes, leafy greens and nuts.

Carbohydrates: An important group of plant foods that are composed of carbon, hydrogen and oxygen. A carbohydrate can be a single simple sugar or a combination of simple sugars. The chief sources of carbohydrates in a whole-food diet are grains, vegetables and fruits. Other sources include sugars, natural sweeteners and syrups.

Carminative: A substance that relaxes the stomach muscles and is taken to relieve gas and gripe. *Examples:* Clove, dill, fennel, garlic, ginger, parsley, peppermint, sage and thyme.

Carotenoid: See Beta-carotene, page 298.

Catechins: See Phenolic compounds, page 302.

Cathartic: A substance that has a laxative effect. See also Purgative, page 303. *Examples:* Dandelion, licorice and parsley.

Cellulose: See Fiber, page 300.

Chlorophyll: Found only in plants, chlorophyll has a unique structure that allows it to enhance the body's ability to produce hemoglobin, which, in turn, enhances the delivery of oxygen to cells.

Choline: A phytochemical that researchers believe improves mental function, and is therefore helpful for people with Alzheimer's disease. Good sources of lecithin (which contains choline) are dandelion, fenugreek, ginkgo, sage and stinging nettle.

Clabbered milk: Soured milk that has been thickened naturally by allowing it to turn sour. If the milk is clabbered properly, the taste is tangy like yogurt and the texture is rich and creamy.

Cruciferous vegetables: The name given to the Brassica genus of vegetables, which includes broccoli, Brussels sprouts, cabbage, cauliflower, collard greens, kale, bok choy, rutabaga, turnip and mustard greens. The plants in this family were named Cruciferae because their flower petals grow in a cross shape.

Cultured milk products: Produces such as yogurt, sour cream, buttermilk, kefir and crème fraiche that have been fermented by benign bacteria.

Decoction: A solution made by boiling the woody parts of plants (roots, seeds and bark) in water for 10 to 20 minutes.

Demulcent: A soothing substance taken internally to protect damaged tissue. *Examples:* Barley, cucumber, fig, honey, marshmallow and fenugreek.

Diaphoretic: A substance that induces sweating. Examples: Cayenne, cinnamon, German chamomile and ginger.

Digestive: A substance that aids digestion.

Diuretic: A substance that increases the flow of urine. These are intended for use in the short term only. *Examples:* Cucumber, burdock (root and leaf), dandelion (leaf and root), fennel seeds, lemon, linden, parsley and pumpkin seeds.

Dysmenorrhea: Menstruation accompanied by cramping pains that may be incapacitating in their intensity.

Elixir: A tonic that invigorates or strengthens the body by stimulating or restoring health.

Ellagic acid: A natural plant phenol (see Phenolic compounds, page 302) thought to have powerful anticancer and antiaging properties. It is found in cherries, grapes, strawberries, and other red, orange or yellow fruits; nuts; seeds; garlic; and onions.

Emetic: A substance taken in large doses to induce vomiting to expel poisons. Small quantities of some emetics, such as salt, nutmeg and mustard, are used often in cooking with no ill effects.

Emmenagogue: A substance that promotes healthy menstruation. *Examples:* Calendula and German chamomile.

Enzymes: The elements found in food that act as the catalysts for chemical reactions within the body, allowing efficient digestion and absorption of food and enabling the metabolic processes that support tissue growth, give you high energy levels and promote good health. Enzymes are destroyed by heat, but using fruits and vegetables raw in smoothies leaves enzymes intact and readily absorbable.

Essential fatty acids (EFAs): Fat is an essential part of a healthy diet — about 20 fatty acids are used by the human body to maintain normal function. Fats are necessary to maintain healthy skin and hair, transport the fat-soluble vitamins (A, D, E and K) and signal the feeling of fullness after meals. The three fatty acids considered the most important, or essential, are omega-6 linoleic, omega-3 linolenic and gamma-linolenic acids. Evidence suggests that increasing the proportion of these fatty acids in the diet may increase immunity and reduce the risks of heart disease, high blood pressure and arthritis. The best vegetable source of omega-3 EFAs in the diet is flax seeds. Other sources of EFAs are hemp (seeds and nuts), nuts, seeds, olives, avocados and oily fish.

Expectorant: A substance that relieves mucus congestion caused by colds and flu. *Examples:* Elder, garlic, ginger, hyssop and thyme.

Fermenation: When the right conditions are present, namely temperature and benign bacteria, milk coagulates and then ferments (breaks down anaerobically), causing it to become thick and dense in texture and tangy in taste.

Fiber: An indigestible carbohydrate. Fiber protects against intestinal problems and bowel disorders. The best sources are raw fruits and vegetables, seeds and whole grains.

Types of fiber include pectin, which reduces the risk of heart disease (by lowering cholesterol) and helps eliminate toxins. It is found mainly in fruits, such as apples, berries and citrus fruits; vegetables; and dried legumes. Cellulose prevents varicose veins, constipation and colitis and plays a role in deflecting colon cancer. Because cellulose is found in the outermost layers of fruits and vegetables, it is important to buy only organic produce and leave the peels on. The hemicellulose in fruits, vegetables and grains aids in weight loss, prevents constipation, lowers the risk of colon cancer and helps remove cancer-forming toxins from the intestinal tract. Lignin, a fiber known to lower cholesterol, prevent gallstone formation and help people with diabetes, is found only in fruits, vegetables and Brazil nuts.

When raw fresh whole fruits or vegetables are used in smoothies, the pulp, or fiber, is still present in the drink and provides all the health benefits listed above.

Flatulence: Release of gas in the stomach and intestine caused by poor digestion. See also Carminative, page 299.

Flavonoids: These phytochemicals (e.g., genistein and quercetin) are antioxidants that have been shown to inhibit cholesterol production. They are found in cruciferous vegetables (see Cruciferous vegetables, page 299), onions and garlic.

Food combining: A disciplined method of eating foods in a specific order or combination (see page 76). It is used as a short-term aid to solve digestive problems and, in simple terms, requires eating fruit alone and never with meals. At mealtime, protein foods are combined with nonstarchy vegetables (leafy greens, asparagus, broccoli, cabbage, celery, cucumbers, onions, peppers, sea herbs, tomatoes and zucchini) only. Grains are also eaten separately and are combined with nonstarchy vegetables. Health conditions that may benefit from food combining are food allergies and intolerances, indigestion, irritable bowel syndrome, flatulence, fatigue and peptic ulcer.

Free radical: A highly unstable compound that attacks cell membranes and causes cell breakdown, aging and a predisposition to some diseases. Free radicals come from the environment as a result of exposure to radiation, ultraviolet (UV) light, smoke, ozone and certain medications. Free radicals are also formed in the body by enzymes and during the conversion of food to energy. See also Antioxidant, page 298.

Genetically modified organisms (GMO): Foods where the DNA has been modified by genetic manipulation to produce new strains of seeds from which genetically modified foods are grown.

Glutamic acid: A naturally occurring substance that acts as a flavor enhancer. It is found in mushrooms and tomatoes.

Hemicellulose: See Fiber, left.

Homogenization: A mechanical process of breaking up the fat globules in milk (or other liquids) and evenly distributing them so that they do not float to the top of the milk. It is not necessary to use homogenized milk to make yogurt, in fact many artisan yogurt makers use pasteurized but non-homogenized (also known as cream line or standard milk) whole goat's milk for their yogurt products.

Hypotensive: A substance that lowers blood pressure. *Examples:* Garlic, hawthorn, linden flower and yarrow.

Indole: A phytochemical found in cruciferous vegetables (see Cruciferous vegetables, page 299) that may help prevent cancer by detoxifying carcinogens.

Isoflavone: A phytoestrogen, or the plant version of the human hormone estrogen, that is found in nuts, soybeans and legumes. Isoflavones help prevent several types of cancer — including pancreatic, colon, breast and prostate cancers — by preserving vitamin C in the body and acting as antioxidants.

Lacto: The Latin word for milk, lactose is a milk sugar.

Lactose intolerance: Deficiency of the enzyme lactase, which breaks down lactose, the sugar in both cow's and human milk. If you don't have sufficient lactase, milk sugar will ferment in the large intestine, causing bloating, diarrhea, abdominal pain and gas.

Laxative: A substance that stimulates bowel movements. Laxatives are meant to

be used in the short term only. *Examples:* Dandelion root, licorice root, prune, rhubarb and yellow dock.

Lignin: See Fiber, page 300.

Limonene: A type of limonoid (see Limonoid, below) thought to assist in detoxifying the liver and preventing cancer. It is found in lemons, limes, grapefruits and tangerines.

Limonoid: A subclass of terpenes (see Terpene, page 303) found in citrus fruit rinds.

Live bacterial culture: All yogurt is made from live bacterial culture and if the yogurt is not heated, which kills the live bacteria, the yogurt is said to contain live bacterial culture.

Lutein: A carotenoid (see Beta-carotene, page 298) found in beet greens; collard greens; mustard greens; and other red, orange and yellow vegetables.

Lycopene: An antioxidant carotenoid (see Beta-carotene, page 298) that's relatively rare in food. High levels are found, however, in tomatoes, pink grapefruits and watermelon. Lycopene is thought to reduce the effects of aging by maintaining physical and mental function and to reduce the risk of some forms of cancer.

Macrobiotic diet: Eating whole food that is seasonal and produced locally. Whole grains, vegetables, fruits (except tropical fruits), legumes, small amounts of fish or organic meat, sea herbs, nuts and seeds are appropriate foods for North Americans who eat macrobiotically.

Metabolism: The rate at which the body produces energy (or burns calories). It is measured by the amount of heat produced by the body, at rest or engaged in various activities, while maintaining its normal temperature.

Milk allergy: Many individuals, especially babies and young children, have allergic reactions to the protein in cow's milk, which causes wheezing, eczema, rashes, mucus buildup and asthma-like symptoms.

Mucilage: A thick, sticky, glue-like substance found in high concentrations in some herbs, which contains and helps spread the active ingredients of those herbs while soothing inflamed surfaces. *Examples:* Marshmallow and slippery elm.

Nervine: A substance that eases anxiety and stress and nourishes the nerves by strengthening nerve fibers. *Examples:* German chamomile, lemon balm, oats, skullcap, St. John's wort, thyme and valerian.

Nonreactive cooking utensils: The acids in foods can react with certain materials and promote the oxidation of some nutrients, as well as discolor the materials themselves. Nonreactive materials suitable for brewing teas are glass, enameled cast iron or enameled stainless steel. While cast-iron pans are recommended for cooking (a meal cooked in unglazed cast iron can provide 20% of the recommended daily intake of iron), and stainless steel is a nonreactive cooking material, neither is recommended for brewing or steeping teas.

Organosulfides: Compounds that have been shown to reduce blood pressure, lower cholesterol levels and reduce blood clotting. *Examples:* Garlic and onion.

Pasteurization: The actual sterilization of milk (or other liquids) by heating it to 145°F (63°C) and holding it there for at least 30 minutes. Another pasteurization method is "flash" that pasteurizes milk at 161°F (72°C) for a minimum of 16 seconds. Both methods kill harmful bacteria. Almost all milk sold in North America is pasteurized.

Pectin: See Fiber, page 300.

Phenolic compounds: Found in red wine, phenolic compounds, including catechins, anthocyanins, ellagic acid and tannins, can prevent the oxidation of "bad" low-density lipoprotein (LDL) cholesterol, thus reducing the risk of heart disease.

Phytochemicals: Chemicals that come from plants. *Phyto*, from the Greek, means "to bring forth" and is used as a prefix to mean "from a plant."

Probiotic: Literally pro "for" and biotic "life"; live microorganisms, the most common being Lactic acid bacteria (LAB), which because they transform sugars and other carbohydrates into lactic acid, lowers the PH and helps prevent infections. Often prescribed after antibiotics, which kill all bacteria including beneficial gut flora, probiotics help beneficial microbes re-establish, strengthen the immune system, and assist in regular elimination. Common probiotics include *Bifidobacterium bifidum*, *Lactobacillus bulgaricus* (active in yogurt) and *Lactobacillus acidophilus*.

Protein: The building block of body tissues. Protein is necessary for healthy growth, cell repair, reproduction and protection against infection. Protein consists of 22 parts called amino acids. Eight of the 22 amino acids in protein are especially important because they can not be manufactured by the body. Those eight are called essential amino acids.

A food that contains all eight essential amino acids is said to be a complete protein. Protein from animal products — meat, fish, poultry and dairy products — is complete. The only accepted plant sources of complete protein are soybeans and soy products, but research is establishing new theories that the protein content of legumes may be complete enough to replace animal protein.

A food that contains some, but not all, eight essential amino acids is called an incomplete protein. Nuts, seeds, legumes, cereals and grains are plant products that provide incomplete proteins. If your meals include foods from two complementary incomplete protein sources, your body will combine the incomplete proteins in the right proportions to make a complete protein. For example, many cultures have a tradition of using legumes and whole grains together in dishes. Scientifically, this combination provides a good amino-acid (complete protein) balance in the diet, because legumes are low in methionine but high in lysine, and whole grains are high in methionine but low in lysine.

When eaten together, the body combines them to make complete proteins. Nuts and seeds must be paired with dairy or soy proteins in order to provide complete proteins.

Purgative: A substance that promotes bowel movements and increased intestinal peristalsis. *Example:* Yellow dock.

Quercetin: See Flavonoids, page 300.

Resveratrol: A fungicide that occurs naturally in grapes and has been linked to the prevention of clogged arteries by lowering blood cholesterol levels. Resveratrol is found in red wine and, to a lesser extent, in purple grape juice.

Rhizome: An underground stem that is usually thick and fleshy. *Examples:* Ginger and turmeric.

Rubefacient: A substance that, when applied to the skin, stimulates circulation in that area, bringing a good supply of blood to the skin and increasing heat in the tissue. Examples: Cayenne; garlic; ginger; mustard seeds; and oils of rosemary, peppermint and thyme.

Sedative: A substance that has a powerful quieting effect on the nervous system that relieves tension and induces sleep. Examples: German chamomile, lettuce, linden, lavender and valerian.

Stimulant: A substance that focuses the mind and increases activity. *Examples:* Basil, cayenne, cinnamon, peppermint and rosemary.

Tannin: A chemical constituent in herbs that causes astringency (see Astringent, page 298) and helps stanch internal bleeding. See also Phenolic compounds, left. *Examples:* Coffee, tea and witch hazel.

Terpene: A class of phytochemicals found in a wide variety of fruits, vegetables and herbs that are potent antioxidants. Ginkgo biloba is a good source of some terpenes. Limonoids (see Limonoid, page 301), which are found in citrus fruit rinds, are a subclass of terpenes.

Tincture: A liquid herbal extract made by soaking an herb in alcohol and pure water to extract the plant's active components. Some herbalists maintain that tinctures are the most effective way to take herbs, because they contain a wide range of the plant's chemical constituents and are easily absorbed.

Tisane: The "official" term used for a solution made by steeping fresh or dried herbs in boiling water. The term is interchangeable with the word *tea* when herbs are used.

Tonic: An infusion of herbs that tones or strengthens the system. Often tonics act as alteratives (see Alterative, page 298). Taken either hot or cold, tonics purify the blood and are nutritive. Tonic herbs support the body's systems in maintaining health. *Examples:* Alfalfa, astragalus, dandelion (root and leaf) and ginseng.

Vasodilator: A substance that relaxes blood vessels, increasing circulation to the arms, hands, legs, feet and brain. *Examples:* Peppermint and sage.

Volatile oil: Essential component found in the aerial parts of an herb. Often extracted to make essential oils, volatile oils are antiseptic and very effective at stimulating the body parts to which they are applied.

Wildcrafting: The practice of gathering herbs from the wild. Many plants today are endangered because of excessive wildcrafting. To avoid contributing to this problem, buy herbs that are organically cultivated.

Yogurt: When the right conditions are present, namely temperature and benign bacteria, milk coagulates and then ferments, causing it to become thick and dense in texture and tangy in taste. This custard-like fermented milk has come to be known as *yogurt*, the word being a direct derivative of the Turkish word. We call fermented milk products such as yogurt, sour cream, buttermilk, kefir and crème fraîche cultured milk products.

Yogurt cheese: If you allow yogurt to drain for 8 hours or overnight, the result is a very thick, soft product that resembles cream cheese.

Bibliography

Ameye, L.G., et al. *Osteoarthritis and Nutrition. From neutraceuticals to functional foods: a systemic review of the scientific evidence.* Arthritis Research and Therapy 2006 July 19;8(4): R127.

Applegate, L. *101 Miracle Foods That Heal Your Heart.* Paramus, NJ: Prentice Hall Press, 2000.

Balch, P., Balch J. *Prescription for Dietary Wellness.* Greenfield, IN: PAB Books, 1993.

Baumel, S. *Dealing with Depression Naturally.* New Canaan, CN: Keats Publishing, Inc, 1995.

Berkson, D.L. *Healthy Digestion the Natural Way.* New York, NY; John Wiley & Sons, Inc., 2000.

Berman, Connie and Susan Katz. *The Yogurt Book.* New York: Grosset & Dunlap Publishers, 1977.

Boik, J. *Cancer & Natural Medicine (A Textbook of Basic Science and Research).* Princeton MN: Oregon Medical Press, 1995.

Carper, Jean. *Food your Miracle Medicine.* New York NY: Harper Collins Publishers Inc, 1993.

Challem, J., et al. *The Complete Nutritional Program to Prevent and Reverse Insulin Resistance Syndrome X.* New York, NY: John Wiley & Sons Inc, 2000.

Crocker, Pat. *Oregano.* Neustadt ON: Riversong Studios, 2005.

_____*The Vegetarian Cook's Bible.* Toronto ON: Robert Rose, 2007.

_____*Tastes of the Kasbah.* Neustadt ON: Riversong Studios, 2005.

_____*The Smoothies Bible Second Edition.* Toronto ON: Robert Rose, 2010.

_____*The Juicing Bible Second Edition.* Toronto ON: Robert Rose, 2008.

Dalais F.S., et al. *Effects of a diet rich in phytoestrogens on prostate-specific antigen and sex hormones in men diagnosed with prostate cancer.* Urology. 2004 Sept; 64(3): 510-5.

DeBaggio, Thomas and Arthur O. Tucker, Ph.D. *The Big Book of Herbs.* Emmaus, PA: Rodale Press, 1997.

Dikasso D., et al. *Investigation on the antibacterial properties of garlic (Allium sativum) on pneumonia causing bacteria.* Ethiopian Medical Journal 2002 July; 40(3): 241-9.

Duke, James, Ph.D. *The Green Pharmacy.* Loveland, CO: Interweave Press, 2000.

Elkins, Rita. *Depression and Natural Medicine.* Pleasant Grove, UT: Woodland, Publishing Inc., 1995.

Estruch R., et al. *Effects of a Mediterranean-Style Diet on Cardiovascular Risk Factors.* Annals of Internal Medicine. 2006; 145: 1-11.

Fang, N., et al. *Inhibition of growth and induction of apoptosis in human cancer cell lines by an ethyl acetate fraction from shiitake mushrooms.* Journal of Alternative and Complementary Medicine 2006 Mar; 12(2):125-32.

Foster, Steven. *Herbal Renaissance: Growing, Using and Understanding Herbs in the Modern World.* Layton, Utah: Gibbs Smith, 1992.

Foster, Steven and Rebecca Johnson. *National Geographic Desk Reference to Nature's Medicine.* Washington, D.C.: National Geographic, 2006.

Fulghum, Bruce D. and M. Grossan. *The Sinus Cure.* New York, NY: Ballantine Books, 2001.

Goldberg, B. *Alternative Medicine Guide to Heart Disease, Stroke and High Blood Pressure.* Tiburon, CA: Future Medicine Publishing, 1998.

Halyorsen, B.L., et al. *Content of redox-active compounds (ie, antioxidants) in foods consumed in the United States.* American Journal of Clinical Nutrition 2006 Jul; 84(1): 95-135.

Hoffman, D. *Healthy Heart Strengthen your Cardiovascular System Naturally.* Pownal, VT: Storey Books, 2000.

_____*Holistic Herbal.* Boston, MA: Element Books Limited, 1996.

Hudson et al. *Characterization of potentially chemoprotective phenols in extracts of brown rice that inhibit the growth of human breast and colon cancer cells.* Cancer Epidemiology Biomarkers and Prevention 2000 Nov; 9(11): 1163-70.

Hudson, T. *Women's Encyclopedia of Natural Medicine.* Los Angeles, CA: Keats Publishing, 1999.

Ivker, R.S., Nelson, T. *Asthma Survival.* New York, NY: Tarcher/Putman, 2001.

James, M.J., et al. *Dietary polyunsaturated fatty acids and inflammatory mediator production.* American Journal of Clinical Nutrition 2000 Jan; 71(1 Suppl): 343S-8S. Review.

Joseph, James A., Ph.D., Daniel A. Nadeau, M.D., and Anne Underwood. *The Color Code. A Revolutionary Eating Plan for Optimum Health.* New York, NY: Hyperion, 2002.

Judd, J.T., et al. *Dietary trans fatty acids: effect on plasma lipids and lipoproteins of healthy men and women.* American Journal of Clinical Nutrition, April 1994; 59:861-868.

Kaur, S.D. *The Complete Natural Medicine Guide to Breast Cancer.* Toronto, ON: Robert Rose Inc, 2003.

Kendall-Reed, P. and S. Reed. *Healing Arthritis.* Toronto, ON: CCNM Press, 2004.

Kumar, N.B., et al. *The specific role of isoflavones in reducing prostate cancer risk.* Prostate. 2004 May 1; 59(2): 141-7.

Kumar, P., et al. *Effect of quercetin supplementation on lung antioxidants after experimental influenza virus infection.* Experimental Lung Research 2005 June; 31(5): 449-59.

Lanigan, Anne. *The Yogurt Gourmet.* Toronto: Quick Fox, 1978.

Lininger, S., Wright, J., Austin, S., Brown, D., Gaby, A. *The Natural Pharmacy.* Rocklin, CA: Prima Health Division of Publishing, 1998.

Logan, A. *Neurobehavioral Aspects of Omega-3 fatty acids: possible mechanisms and Therapeutic Value in Major Depression.* Alternative Medicine Review 2003;8(4): 410-425.

Lycopene. Alternative Medicine Review 2003; 8(3): 336-342.

Makabe, H., et al. *Anti-inflammatory sesquiterpenes from Curcuma zedoaria.* Journal of Asian Natural Products Research 2006 June; 20(7): 680-5.

Mickleborough, T.D., et al. *Protective effect of fish oil supplementation on exercise-induced bronchoconstriction in asthma.* Chest. 2006 Jan; 129(1): 39-49.

Miller, A.L., et al. *Homocysteine Metabolism: Nutritional Modulation and Impact on Health and Disease.* Alternative Medicine Review 1997; 2(4): 234-254.

Mozaffarian, D., et al. *Fish Consumption and Stroke Risk in Elderly Individuals: The Cardiovascular Health Study.* Archives of Internal Medicine 2005; 165(2): 200-206.

Murray, M. *Diabetes and Hypoglycemia.* Rocklin, CA: Prima Health, 1994.

_____*Natural Alternatives to Prozac.* New York, NY: Quill, 1996.

_____*Pizzorno J. Encyclopedia of Natural Medicine 2nd Edition.* Rocklin, CA: Prima Health Division of Publishing, 1998.

Nez Heatherley, Ana. *Healing Plants, A Medicinal Guide to Native North American Plants and Herbs.* Toronto ON: Harper Collins Publishers Ltd., 1998.

O'Connor, D.J. *Understanding Osteoporosis and Clinical Strategies to Assess, Arrest and Restore Bone Loss.* Alternative Medicine Review 1997; 2(1): 36-47.

Ody, Penelope. *The Complete Medicinal Herbal.* Toronto, ON: Key Porter Books, 1993.

_____with A. Lyon and D. Vilinac. *The Chinese Herbal Cookbook. Healing Foods for Inner Balance.* Trumbull, CT: Weatherhill Inc., 2001.

Penny, M., Etherton, K. *Evidence that the antioxidant flavonoids in tea and cocoa are beneficial for cardiovascular health.* Current Opinion in Lipidology. Feb 2002; 13(1): 41-49.

Physicians Committee for Responsible Medicine, Melina V. *Healthy Eating for Life to Prevent and Treat Cancer.* New York, NY: John Wiley & Sons Inc., 2002.

Pitchford, Paul. *Healing with Whole Foods: Oriental Traditions and Modern Nutrition.* Berkeley CA: North Atlantic Books, 1993.

Prousky, J. *Anxiety Orthomolecular Diagnosis and Treatment.* Toronto, ON: CCNM Press, 2003.

Quercetin. Alternative Medicine Review 1998; 3(2): 140-143.

Robertson, Robin and Jon Robertson. *The Sacred Kitchen. Higher Consciousness Cooking for Health and Wholeness.* Novato, CA: New World Library, 1999.

Schroder, F.H., et al. *Randomized, double-blind, placebo-controlled crossover study in men with prostate cancer and rising PSA: effectiveness of a dietary supplement.* European Urology 2005 Dec; 48(6):922-30.

Sinclair, S. *Male Infertility: Nutritional and Environmental Considerations.* Alternative Medicine Review 2000; 5(1):28-38.

Vanderhaeghe, L.R. and K. Karst. *Healthy Fats for Life Preventing and Treating Common Health Problems with Essential Fatty Acids.* Kingston, ON: Quarry Health Books, 2003.

_____Bouic, P.J.D. *The Immune System Cure.* Toronto, ON: Prentice Hall Canada, 1999.

_____*Healthy Immunity Scientifically Proven Natural Treatments for conditions A-Z,* Toronto. ON: Macmillan, 2001.

Whitaker, J. *The Memory Solution.* Garden City Park, NY: Avery Publishing Group, 1999.

Zampieron, E., E. Kamhi and B. Goldman. *Alternative Medicine Guide to Arthritis.* Tiburon, CA: AlternativeMedicine.com Books, 1999.

Yogurt Sources

Probiotics

Dairy Council of California
www.dairycouncilofca.org/PDFs/probiotics.pdf
Probiotics information sheet

International Scientific Association for Probiotics and Prebiotics
www.isapp.net
A science-based site based on evaluating and dispersing reliable information on probiotic and prebiotic products.

Dairy

Canadian Dairy Information Centre
www.dairyinfo.gc.ca
Provides information on the Canadian dairy industry including milk ingredients, safety and quality.

National Dairy Council
www.nationaldairycouncil.org/Pages/Home.aspx
Represents U.S. dairy farmers to provide science-based nutrition information.

Yogurt

National Yogurt Association
www.aboutyogurt.com/index.asp
A U.S. based national trade organization representing manufacturers and marketers of live and active culture yogurt products and yogurt industry suppliers.

University of Georgia, National Center for Home Food Preservation
www.uga.edu/nchfp/publications/nchfp/factsheets/yogurt.html
Fact sheet on making yogurt at home

Yogurt Equipment

There are several yogurt makers available online and at kitchen or department stores. The following is a list of equipment that is available.

Cuisipro Donvier
www.cuisipro.com

Deni
www.deni.com

Euro Cuisine
www.eurocuisine.net

Waring Pro
www.waringproducts.com

Yogotherm
www.abiasa.com/siteYogotherm/en/yogotherm.html

Yogourmet
www.lyo-san.ca/english/yogourmet.html

Yolife
www.yolifeyogurt.com

Other Equipment

Cuisipro Donvier
Donvier Ice Cream Machine
www.cuisipro.com
Frozen yogurt maker

KitchenAid
www.kitchenaid.com
Ice cream maker for the stand mixer (a stand mixer attachment)

Library and Archives Canada Cataloguing in Publication

Crocker, Pat
    The yogurt bible / Pat Crocker.

Includes index.
ISBN 978-0-7788-0255-6

    1. Cookery (Yogurt). 2. Yogurt—Health aspects. I. Title.

TX759.5.Y63C76 2010   641.6'7146   C2010-903238-1

Index

Note: Page references in **bold type** indicate a major entry in the Whole Foods section. The notation (v) indicates a recipe variation.

A

açai berries, **109**
  Berry Yogurt Flip, 290
  Orange Slushie, 288
adrenal glands, 77, 79
After Dinner Cocktail, 285
air quality, 103–4
alfalfa, **143–44**
allergies, 83, 102
almonds, 91, 104, **138**
  Almond Pie Crust, 271
  Berry Yogurt Flip, 290
  Cherry Almond Topping, 57
  Crispy Baked Fish, 221
  Granola Topping, 58
  Peach Paradise Smoothie, 293
amaranth, **134**
anchovies
  Caesar Dressing, 207
  Creamy Salsa Verde, 258
antibiotics, 71
antioxidants, 63, 103
anxiety, 95–96
apple cider vinegar, 72
apple juice
  Black Currant Smoothie, 290
  Pear and Basil Lassi, 282
apples and applesauce, 65, 72, **109**
  Apple and Cheddar Cheese Flan, 271
  Apple-Cinnamon, 49
  Beet Soup, 193
  Breakfast Cocktail, 286
  Creamy White Sauce, 260
  Grated Carrots with Ginger-Spiked Citrus Sauce (v), 198
  Lamb Tagine with Plums and Apricots, 245
  Spiced Pear Salsa, 50

apricot nectar
  Minty Peach Smoothie, 292
  Tropi-Cocktail, 288
apricots, **109–10**
  Apricot and Oatmeal Breakfast Special, 289
  Apricot Explosion, 289
  Apricot Topping, 47
  Dried Fruit Nut Topping, 56
  Granola Topping, 58
  Lamb Tagine with Plums and Apricots, 245
  Orange Slushie, 288
  Pineapple Kiwi Smoothie, 293
  Raspberry Smoothie, 295
  Turkey Breasts in Tarragon Cream Sauce, 237
  Yellow Coconut Curry Sauce, 264
arame, **141**
arthritis, 13, 89
artichokes, **119**
  Artichoke and Leek Tart, 174
  Baked Chicken with Couscous and Pesto Yogurt, 230
  Mediterranean Bean Salad, 199
  Roasted Garlic and Artichoke Dip, 170
  Spinach and Artichoke Risone, 212
artichokes, Jerusalem, **124**
asparagus, 65, **119**
asthma, 102
astragalus, **144**
atherosclerosis, 62
avocado, 85, **119**
  Avocado Aïoli, 170
  Avocado Sauce, 261
  Guacamole, 167

B

Baba Ghanouj, 171
back pain, 89
bacteria
  in intestines, 70–71
  in yogurt, 15–16

Baked Chicken and Mushroom Risotto, 231
Baked Chicken with Couscous and Pesto Yogurt, 230
Baked Spinach, Beans and Feta Cheese, 217
Baked Vegetable Falafel, 177
bananas, **110**
  Banana Purée, 47
  Best Berry Smoothie, 285
  Black Currant Smoothie, 290
  CocoNog, 291
  Grapefruit Greetings, 291
  Pineapple Soy Smoothie, 294
  Tropi-Cocktail, 288
barley, 98–99, **134–35**
Basic Evaporated Milk Yogurt, 22
Basic Lower-Fat Milk Yogurt, 21
Basic Whole and High-Solid Milk Yogurt, 20
basil (fresh), **144**
  Creamy Basil Dressing, 205
  Pear and Basil Lassi, 282
Basque Chicken Sauté, 229
beans, 65, 73, **131–33**
  green, **120**
  Baked Spinach, Beans and Feta Cheese, 217
  Baked Vegetable Falafel, 177
  Black Bean Chili, 210
  Black Bean Quesadillas, 176
  Chipotle Corn and Black Bean Soup, 191
  Mediterranean Bean Salad, 199
  Potato and Onion Fritters, 180
  Summer Beans with Pappardelle, 203
  Turkey, Red Beans and Rice, 238
beef
  Boneless Beef Chuck Pot Roast, 239
  Ground Beef, Leek and Mushroom Pilaf, 242
  Gulyás, 241
beets, **120**
  Beet Soup, 193
bell peppers. *See* peppers, bell

More Great Books
from Robert Rose

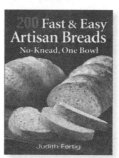

Appliance Cooking

- 200 Best Pressure
  Cooker Recipes
  by Cinda Chavich

- 200 Best Panini Recipes
  by Tiffany Collins

- The Mixer Bible,
  Second Edition
  *by Meredith Deeds and
  Carla Snyder*

- The 150 Best Slow
  Cooker Recipes
  by Judith Finlayson

- Delicious & Dependable
  Slow Cooker Recipes
  by Judith Finlayson

- Sensational Slow
  Cooker Gourmet
  by Judith Finlayson

- Slow Cooker
  Comfort Food
  by Judith Finlayson

- The Healthy Slow Cooker
  by Judith Finlayson

- The Vegetarian
  Slow Cooker
  by Judith Finlayson

- The Dehydrator Bible
  *by Jennifer MacKenzie,
  Jay Nutt & Don Mercer*

- 300 Slow Cooker
  Favorites
  by Donna-Marie Pye

- 300 Best Bread Machine
  Recipes
  *by Donna Washburn
  and Heather Butt*

- 300 Best Canadian Bread
  Machine Recipes
  *by Donna Washburn
  and Heather Butt*

Baking

- 1500 Best Bars, Cookie
  Muffins, Cakes & More
  by Esther Brody

- 200 Fast & Easy
  Artisan Breads
  by Judith Fertig

- The Complete
  Baking Cookbook
  by George Geary

- The Complete Book
  of Pies
  by Julie Hasson

- 125 Best Chocolate
  Recipes
  by Julie Hasson

- 125 Best Cupcake
  Recipes
  by Julie Hasson

- Bars & Squares
  by Jill Snider

- Cookies
  by Jill Snider

- Complete Cake
  Mix Magic
  by Jill Snider

Healthy Cooking

- 125 Best Vegetarian
  Recipes
  *by Byron Ayanoglu
  with contributions from
  Algis Kemezys*

- 125 Best Vegan
  Recipes
  *by Maxine Effenson Chu
  and Beth Gurney*

- 175 Natural Sugar
  Desserts
  *by Angelina and
  Ari Dayan*

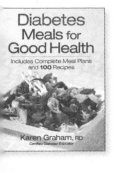

- Diabetes Meals for Good Health
  by Karen Graham, RD
- Canada's Diabetes Meals for Good Health
  by Karen Graham, RD
- 200 Best Lactose-Free Recipes
  by Jan Main
- 500 Best Healthy Recipes
  Edited by Lynn Roblin, RD
- Complete Gluten-Free Cookbook
  by Donna Washburn and Heather Butt
- 250 Gluten-Free Favorites
  by Donna Washburn and Heather Butt
- The Best Gluten-Free Family Cookbook
  by Donna Washburn and Heather Butt
- America's Complete Diabetes Cookbook
  Edited by Katherine E. Younker, MBA, RD
- Canada's Complete Diabetes Cookbook
  Edited by Katherine E. Younker, MBA, RD

Recent Bestsellers

- The Complete Book of Pickling
  by Jennifer MacKenzie
- 12,167 Kitchen and Cooking Secrets
  by Susan Sampson
- Baby Blender Food
  by Nicole Young

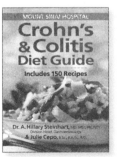

- 200 Easy Homemade Cheese Recipes
  by Debra Amrein-Boyes
- The Convenience Cook
  by Judith Finlayson
- Easy Indian Cooking
  by Suneeta Vaswani

Health

- 55 Most Common Medicinal Herbs Second Edition
  by Dr. Heather Boon, B.Sc.Phm., Ph.D. and Michael Smith, B.Pharm, M.R.Pharm.S., ND
- Canada's Baby Care Book
  by Dr. Jeremy Friedman MBChB, FRCP(C), FAAP, and Dr. Norman Saunders MD, FRCP(C)
- The Baby Care Book
  by Dr. Jeremy Friedman MBChB, FRCP(C), FAAP, and Dr. Norman Saunders MD, FRCP(C)
- Better Baby Food Second Edition
  by Daina Kalnins, MSc, RD, and Joanne Saab, RD
- Better Food for Pregnancy
  by Daina Kalnins, MSc, RD, and Joanne Saab, RD
- Crohn's & Colitis
  by Dr. A. Hillary Steinhart, MD, MSc, FRCP(C)
- Crohn's & Colitis Diet Guide
  by Dr. A. Hillary Steinhart, MD, MSc, FRCP(C), and Julie Cepo, BSc, BASc, RD

Also Available
by the same author

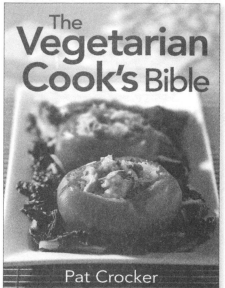

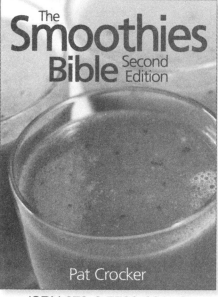